WINNER OF THE SAMUEL ELI[illegible] AWARD FOR NAVAL LITERATURE

PRAISE FOR *ACT OF WAR*

"Sweeping in its power and importance as a historical document and absolutely riveting in its personal stories of sacrifice and heroism, *Act of War* is the best kind of narrative nonfiction. From the halls of power in Washington to the heaving seas of the Pacific and to the cold, stark torture rooms of *Pyongyang*, this book leaves no stone unturned. This is a masterwork by Jack Cheevers."

—Michael Connelly, #1 *New York Times* bestselling author of *The Black Box*

"A riveting, superbly researched, and revealing account of a Cold War clash at sea between the United States and North Korea—and of the courageous captain of the *Pueblo*, who stood up both to his brutal captors and to the Navy brass who tried to make him a scapegoat to cover up their own failures."

—David Wise, author of *Tiger Trap: America's Secret Spy War with China*

"Cheevers skillfully brings to life one of the most dramatic events of the Cold War, a story of torture, imprisonment, secret negotiations, and White House deal making. Today, the *Pueblo* remains the only commissioned U.S. ship on display as a war trophy by a foreign government. *Act of War* sheds new light on how that happened, and at the same time, it shows how quickly espionage, and miscalculation, can lead to all-out war."

—James Bamford, author of *Body of Secrets*, *The Shadow Factory*, and *The Puzzle Palace*

"Jack Cheevers is not only a terrific researcher but a master storyteller. *Act of War* reads like a Cold War thriller—I couldn't put it down."

—James Scott, author of *The War Below*

"With vivid clarity, Cheevers tells the amazing story of the capture of the *Pueblo* and its crew—one of many dangerous showdowns between North Korea and the U.S. A fascinating, well-rendered account of a little known episode in the ongoing conflict on the Korean peninsula."

—Sheila Miyoshi Jager, author of *Brothers at War: The Unending Conflict in Korea*

continued . . .

"A fitting tribute to the *Pueblo* crew, a timely reminder of the nature of the North Korean regime (now developing nuclear weapons), and, not least, a great read."

—Jack F. Matlock Jr., U.S. ambassador to the Soviet Union, 1987–91, and author of *Reagan and Gorbachev*

"Using a trove of declassified CIA materials and interviews, Cheevers provides a valuable new addition to our understanding of what happened in January 1968 when the North Koreans attacked and captured the USS *Pueblo*."

—Larry Berman, author of *Zumwalt: The Life and Times of Admiral Elmo Russell "Bud" Zumwalt Jr.*

"Outstanding and necessary." —*Booklist* (starred review)

"A deep, gripping narrative of the *Pueblo* story . . . harrowing."

—Alastair Gale, *The Wall Street Journal* blog

"Readers who appreciate intense accounts of survival against difficult circumstances will find this book enthralling. . . . It deserves a wide audience."

—*Library Journal* (starred review)

"Jack Cheevers's true account of the USS *Pueblo* will not only glue you to your seat—you'll be stunned anyone survived at all."

—John Geoghegan, author of *Operation Storm*

"Comprehensive and compelling . . . a narrative as fascinating as any fictional spy story . . . *Act of War* is likely to be the definitive account of the Pueblo incident." —*The Virginian-Pilot*

"*Act of War* is international in scope, well written, and an enjoyable read . . . highly recommended . . . [a] gripping account of personal service, tragedy, sacrifice, and perseverance of the crew that played out within the heightened international tensions of the Cold War." —*Proceedings*

ACT OF WAR

★

LYNDON JOHNSON, NORTH KOREA, AND THE CAPTURE OF THE SPY SHIP *PUEBLO*

JACK CHEEVERS

NAL Caliber
Published by the Penguin Group
Penguin Group (USA) LLC, 375 Hudson Street,
New York, New York 10014

USA | Canada | UK | Ireland | Australia | New Zealand | India | South Africa | China
penguin.com
A Penguin Random House Company

Published by NAL Caliber, an imprint of New American Library, a division of Penguin Group (USA) LLC. Previously published in an NAL Caliber hardcover edition.

First NAL Caliber Trade Paperback Printing, December 2014

NAL Caliber Trade Paperback ISBN: 978-0-451-46620-4

THE LIBRARY OF CONGRESS HAS CATALOGED THE HARDCOVER EDITION OF THIS TITLE AS FOLLOWS:
Cheevers, Jack.
Act of war: Lyndon Johnson, North Korea, and the capture of the spy ship *Pueblo*/Jack Cheevers.
p. cm.
ISBN 978-0-451-46619-8 (hardback)
1. Pueblo Incident, 1968. 2. Johnson, Lyndon B. (Lyndon Baines), 1908–1973.
3. Korea (North)—Foreign relations—United States. 4. United States—
Foreign relations—Korea (North) I. Title.
VB230.C44 2013
359.3'4320973—dc23 2013021620

Printed in the United States of America
10 9 8 7 6 5 4 3 2 1

Set in Minion Pro • *Designed by Elke Sigal*

PUBLISHER'S NOTE
While the author has made every effort to provide accurate telephone numbers and Internet addresses at the time of publication, neither the publisher nor the author assumes any responsibility for errors, or for changes that occur after publication. Further, publisher does not have any control over and does not assume any responsibility for author or third-party Web sites or their content.

For my mother and father

Regina A. Cheevers	*John S. Cheevers*
1927–1957	*1918–2003*

and for my grandmother
Mary A. Cheevers
1893–1972

CONTENTS

You can't understand command till you've had it. It's the loneliest, most oppressive job in the whole world. It's a nightmare, unless you're an ox. You're forever teetering along a tiny path of correct decisions and good luck that meanders through an infinite gloom of possible mistakes. At any moment you can commit a hundred manslaughters.

—*The Caine Mutiny* by Herman Wouk

It requires more courage to suffer than to die.

—Napoleon Bonaparte

ACKNOWLEDGMENTS

I came across the *Pueblo* story one Saturday morning while scrounging for something to read at my neighborhood coffeehouse in Venice, California. The place sold used books along with the java, and for a dollar I bought a well-thumbed copy of a 1970 memoir by the *Pueblo*'s captain, Lloyd M. Bucher. I took it home, thinking I'd read a chapter or two before getting into my weekend routine. Instead, I spent the rest of that day and all of the next utterly engrossed in *Bucher: My Story*.

Later I called the long-retired skipper at his home in Poway, California, and asked whether I could interview him. He consented and over the next few years we met a half dozen times, talking for up to eight hours at a stretch. At the end of these sessions I often took Bucher and his wife out to dinner, where he continued to regale me with vivid anecdotes about his rough childhood, Navy career, and *Pueblo* experiences.

I conducted multiple in-depth interviews with six other former crewmen whom I wanted to highlight in this narrative. Some of the most enjoyable talks were with Charlie Law, the bass-voiced former quartermaster who'd lost all but his peripheral vision as a result of malnutrition in North Korean prisons. I met him several times for breakfast on a hotel patio overlooking

San Diego's sparkling Mission Bay. In spite of his badly damaged eyesight, Law never failed to spot a pretty woman passing by on her way to the beach.

In all, I interviewed more than 50 people, including onetime members of President Johnson's administration; the Air Force general who tried desperately to rescue the spy ship when it came under attack; and the lawyer who led the Navy's controversial public inquiry into the *Pueblo* disaster. With the help of the indispensable Freedom of Information Act, I obtained more than 11,000 pages of once-secret Central Intelligence Agency reports, military messages, transcripts of closed-door Navy hearings, and summaries of State Department negotiations with North Korea.

Through a little-known procedure called mandatory declassification review, I got hold of a CIA psychological profile of Bucher as well as National Security Agency studies of how severely the loss of the *Pueblo* and its large trove of classified materials compromised national security. (The NSA doesn't let such information out of its grasp easily; these secret "damage assessments" took more than seven years to acquire.) I also have drawn on archival material from the United States, South Korea, the former Soviet Union, and Eastern Europe.

One important question I haven't been able to answer is exactly what motivated North Korea to seize the *Pueblo.* Bucher believed that the communists mistook his vessel for a South Korean ship. But declassified transcripts of National Security Agency radio intercepts show that Pyongyang's gunboat commanders knew the spy craft was American before they opened fire on it. My speculation is that North Korean dictator Kim Il Sung simply couldn't resist the opportunity to harass and humiliate the United States, while simultaneously diverting its attention and military resources from the Vietnam War. Kim had long urged other socialist nations to do anything they could to injure his capitalist archenemy and, to back up his words, had sent a handful of his pilots to fly combat jets for North Vietnam. I wrote to Kim Il Sung's son, Kim Jong Il, requesting an interview, and North Korean officials at first showed some interest in granting it, but then apparently changed their minds.

Any book is, of course, the child of its author, but this one was born and raised with the help of many people. In particular I'd like to thank Doris M. Lama, a Freedom of Information officer for the Navy who steered me to a large batch of *Pueblo* records early in my research; Stuart Culy, who provided box upon box of key documents from the National Archives in College Park, Maryland; and William J. Bosanko, director of the Information Security Oversight Office in Washington, D.C., who worked diligently over several years to help declassify revealing documents from the CIA and the National Security Agency. My researcher in South Korea, Hyunjung Lee, dug up useful material from the South Korean foreign ministry archives and South Korean newspapers. Senior archivist Rebecca Greenwell and others at the Lyndon Baines Johnson Library in Austin, Texas, assisted me in declassifying scores of documents that had been locked in the library's files, unavailable to the public, for years.

Former *Pueblo* crewmen Jim Kell, Peter Langenberg, Tom Massie, and Skip Schumacher were unstintingly generous with their time and memories, as was Harry Iredale, a civilian oceanographer aboard the spy ship. E. Miles Harvey and Captain William R. Newsome, U.S. Navy, retired, gave me many details and much insight into the Navy court of inquiry that investigated the *Pueblo* fiasco. Lieutenant Commander Allen Hemphill, U.S. Navy, retired, helped me understand the risks and excitement of being a Navy submariner in the 1950s and 1960s. My editor at New American Library, Brent Howard, is nothing short of amazing. (My gratitude also to my previous editor, Stephen Power, who helped make the manuscript tighter and more focused when it was at John Wiley & Sons.) My agent, Mel Berger, of William Morris Endeavor, provided wise and timely counsel throughout long years of research and writing. And William D. Cohill, of Orrtanna, Pennsylvania, reminded me of the power and grace of an unexpected kindness.

I'm deeply indebted to the fine work of several journalists who preceded me on the *Pueblo* story, especially Trevor Armbrister, of the *Saturday Evening Post*; Bernard Weinraub, of *The New York Times*; George C. Wilson, of the *Washington Post*; and Ed Brandt, of the *Virginian-Pilot*. As my footnotes testify, I borrowed shamelessly from Armbrister's superb 1970 book, *A Matter of Accountability*, about the U.S. military's failure to rescue the *Pueblo*. Professor Mitchell Lerner of Ohio State University, author of the well-researched and insightful *The Pueblo Incident: A Spy Ship and the Failure of American Foreign Policy*, gladly and generously shared source material. My dear friends and former *Los Angeles Times* colleagues Rick Barrs and Leslie Berger read an early draft of the book and gave invaluable critiques. My old friend Bob McAuliffe, professor of economics at Babson College in Wellesley, Massachusetts, also reviewed the manuscript with a discerning eye. Miles Corwin, another ex-*Times* cohort and a writer whom I've long admired, offered something every would-be author craves: early encouragement.

And to my loving wife, Kathleen Hope Matz, I can only say, in the words of the old Waylon Jennings song, where would I be without you?

Jack Cheevers
Oakland, California
April 2013

ACT OF WAR

PROLOGUE

On an October day in 1952, a Soviet coast guard cutter eased its way toward a headless corpse floating off Yuri island, a small link in the Kuril archipelago that stretches from northern Japan to Siberia.

Clad in a black flight suit, the body was the earthly remains of a U.S. Air Force lieutenant named John R. Dunham. The 24-year-old officer had been navigating an RB-29 reconnaissance plane northeast of Japan's Hokkaido island when two Soviet fighters opened fire. The lumbering, propeller-driven American aircraft caught fire and crashed into the sea; Dunham and seven other airmen perished. The Russians buried Dunham a few days later on Yuri without bothering to hold a ceremony or notify his next of kin.

The incident was just one of many Cold War run-ins—some of them fatal—between U.S. intelligence collectors and communist defenders. Starting in 1945, American planes, surface ships, and submarines skirted the borders of the USSR, China, North Korea, and various Eastern European nations, probing and analyzing their defenses.

The Sea of Japan was a hot spot in this little-known drama. U.S. planes monitored hundreds of miles of coastline running from Wonsan, a major North Korean port protected by scores of MiG fighters, to Vladivostok, headquarters of the Soviet Pacific Fleet, and farther north to Petropavlovsk, another important Russian naval station near the tip of the Kamchatka Peninsula. Flying aboard lightly armed aircraft stuffed with eavesdropping equipment, specialists known as "ravens" tuned in on communist radio, Morse code, and radar emissions. Their planes usually stayed in international airspace, but occasionally they darted over the border, as if on a bombing run, to "spoof" communist air defenses. When alarmed ground commanders switched on antiaircraft radars, the ravens carefully noted their location and frequencies, crucial targeting data in the event of war. The American aircraft also recorded details of how Soviet jets were scrambled, and sniffed the atmosphere for telltale chemical traces of nuclear tests.

Soviet and North Korean fighters often were content simply to fly alongside, watching the watchers. But sometimes they reacted with lethal fury. Between 1950 and 1956, for instance, seven U.S. reconnaissance aircraft were shot down over the Sea of Japan, the Kurils, or near Siberia; at least 46 airmen were killed or listed as missing. (Another plane bearing 16 Americans disappeared in a typhoon.) Washington responded with sharply worded protests and more spy flights.

U.S. submarines, meanwhile, kept an eye on Soviet naval operations. Often prowling perilously close to shore, they taped distinctive propeller noises made by Russian subs, compiling an audio "library" that could identify any Soviet undersea boat anywhere in the world. American crews planted listening devices on the ocean floor to detect communist naval movements. They observed sea trials of the Russians' new missile subs and measured the telemetry of ballistic rockets as they arced from launch sites in the USSR to splash down in the Pacific.

Aircraft and submarines were an expensive way to spy, however. They had the additional disadvantage of being able to stay on target for only relatively short periods. The Navy sometimes used destroyers for surveillance, but such missions took fighting ships away from more pressing duties.

Faced with the same problems, the Soviets solved them by loading eavesdropping gear aboard fishing trawlers, inexpensive, harmless-looking vessels that could loiter in the same area for days or weeks on end. By 1965, almost three dozen trawlers were watching American nuclear subs coming and going from bases in South Carolina, Scotland, and Guam; studying the tactics of U.S. battle groups maneuvering on the high seas; and warning the North Vietnamese whenever Navy fighter-bombers lifted off from aircraft carriers in the Gulf of Tonkin.

The trawlers sometimes even tried to interfere with the carriers, cutting across their bows as they turned into the wind to launch planes. One Soviet boat, the *Gidrofon*, was involved in six "provocative incidents" in the South China Sea during a single month, December 1965. Another trawler nearly collided with an American destroyer off Long Island, New York, as the Russian captain rushed to recover a test missile fired from the atomic sub USS *George Washington*.

The United States soon began outfitting its own small, cheap spy ships under Operation Clickbeetle, a top secret Navy program to pack refurbished freighters with advanced electronics. Clickbeetle was the pet project of Dr. Eugene Fubini, an energetic, bushy-haired physicist who oversaw key Pentagon research initiatives in the early 1960s. Fubini believed the snooper boats could play an important role in keeping tabs on the Soviets' rapidly expanding blue-water fleet, which was challenging the U.S. Navy's supremacy in both the Pacific and the Mediterranean. He wanted up to 70 such vessels, although the Navy ultimately commissioned only three.

The most tragically famous of these was the USS *Pueblo*, which was attacked and captured by North Korean patrol boats in January 1968.

The loss of the *Pueblo*—which was jammed with sophisticated electronic surveillance gear, code machines, and top secret documents—turned out to be one of the worst intelligence debacles in American history. The ship's seizure pushed the United States closer to armed conflict on the Korean peninsula than at any time since the Korean War in the early 1950s. And subsequent investigations by Congress and the Navy revealed appalling complacency and shortsightedness in the planning and execution of the *Pueblo*'s mission.

Nations spy on one another for a variety of reasons, some quite sensible. The most common one is the fundamental imperative of self-preservation: National leaders have a keen, if not mortal interest in knowing whether a rival state is getting ready to attack them or their allies. The main purpose of the *Pueblo*'s ill-starred voyage was to give the United States a clearer picture of North Korea's ability to wage war. "Our knowledge about North Korean military capabilities is limited and may not be altogether reliable," Under Secretary of State Nicholas Katzenbach wrote in a secret memo to President Lyndon Johnson. "Our limited intelligence makes it difficult to estimate the precise nature of the threat to South Korea." That blind spot was particularly alarming, since 50,000 American troops were then stationed in South Korea as a bulwark against the aggressive north.

But intelligence gathering can be a double-edged sword. On one hand, acquiring reliable information about an enemy's intentions and capabilities may have a calming effect on international relations. If Country A verifies that Country B is not, as rumored, massing troops on their common border, Country A is less likely to mobilize its own forces, thereby reducing the chances of war. Paradoxically, good spy work can also create dangerous volatility between states. Such was the case in 1962, when a U-2 aircraft photographed Soviet technicians installing long-range missiles in Cuba, leading the United States to impose a naval quarantine on the island and raising the fearsome specter of nuclear war between the two superpowers.

In some instances, the very act of spying can catalyze international tension, as the *Pueblo* episode demonstrates.

Then as now, North Korea was one of America's most implacable enemies. In the late 1960s, it possessed one of the largest air forces in the communist world, along with a formidable army. Its Stalinist leaders were deeply committed to conquering South Korea. And with so many U.S. soldiers deployed in the south, Washington had ample reason to pursue additional information about what North Korea was up to.

Today, more than 45 years after the events described in this book, North Korea is still a dangerous threat to peace and stability in Northeast Asia. Its economy is a shambles and its citizens are impoverished and underfed. Its armed forces remain large and potent, and its new, 28-year-old leader, Kim Jong-un, seems bent on producing nuclear weapons and the long-range missiles needed to deliver them. The United States still conducts reconnaissance forays and North Korea still strives to fend them off. In 2003, four North Korean MiG jets tried to force down an unarmed RC-135 spy plane. Despite the risk of being attacked, the American aircrew resisted communist demands to land (one MiG pilot flew to within 50 feet of the RC-135 and gave hand signals for it to descend) and flew back to their base in Japan.

Why should the *Pueblo*'s sole mission, bungled so long ago, matter to us now? Without a doubt, unremitting surveillance by American ships, aircraft, satellites, and human agents around the globe has helped us better understand our foes' strengths and weaknesses. For diplomats trying to preserve the peace, or military strategists trying to win a war, the importance of accurate, timely intelligence cannot be overstated. But snooping on other countries is inherently provocative. (Indeed, North Korea regarded the *Pueblo*'s activities as an "act of war.") Since intelligence collection often carries the potential to set off an international crisis or even war, we as citizens must endeavor to restrain excessive risk taking and recklessness on the part of our professional watchers.

In order to be effective, clandestine reconnaissance missions must, of course, be clandestine. Risk-to-reward ratios can't exactly be debated in public before such operations are set in motion. In our democracy, we depend on Congress—especially members of the House and Senate intelligence committees—to provide close and continuous scrutiny of the nation's spy agencies. (The news media occasionally reveal details of intelligence operations, although usually after the fact.) Congressional oversight isn't always as robust as it should be, however. Members of Congress had little, if any, advance knowledge of how much risk was involved in the *Pueblo*'s doomed journey to the Sea of Japan. It was only later that investigators uncovered the false assumptions, negligent planning, and embarrassingly inadequate equipment that culminated in the vessel's capture and set the stage for a dangerous showdown between the United States and North Korea.

As we unleash spies and covert operations against a growing list of twenty-first-century adversaries, we'd do well to remember the painful lessons of the *Pueblo*.

CHAPTER 1

SPIES AHOY

The strange little ship lay at the far end of the pier, rolling gently in the morning chop. Ensign F. Carl Schumacher stared at it from the bucket seat of his Porsche, then got out and walked down the dock, brimming with anticipation.

Schumacher didn't know much about the diminutive boat that was to be his new home. It certainly stood out from the vast gray warships cruising majestically through San Diego Bay, many of them bound, in that autumn of 1967, for the Vietnam War. Just 176 feet long, the USS *Pueblo* was smaller than some Navy tugboats. With no deck guns and a poky top speed of 13 knots, it was unfit for serious combat at sea. Indeed, the canvas awning that shaded its afterdeck made the *Pueblo* look more like a tramp steamer than a naval vessel, with one curious difference: Its topsides bristled with tall antennae, swaying in the breeze like giant fishing rods.

Though Schumacher hadn't been told yet, the *Pueblo* was an electronic intelligence collector—a spy ship—newly outfitted to eavesdrop on military installations along communist coastlines in the Far East. Before its conversion to seagoing ferret, the *Pueblo* had been an Army cargo ship, hauling food and supplies to remote South Pacific island bases after World War II. Given its lowly pedigree, some of its crewmen jokingly compared it to the

USS *Reluctant*, the down-at-the-heels Navy freighter in the movie *Mister Roberts.*

"Skip" Schumacher was 24 years old, a bright, perceptive Missourian who relished arguing about philosophy and trading humorous barbs with relatives and friends. Slim and blond, he had a sly smile, an unexpectedly deep voice, and a young man's studiedly cynical facade. The son of an affluent St. Louis insurance broker, he'd had a privileged youth, attending a local prep school and a private college, Trinity, in Connecticut. After graduating, he signed on as a Navy officer candidate, mostly to make sure he didn't get drafted into the Army and shot up in some Indochinese rice paddy.

His first sea assignment had been aboard a refrigeration ship that delivered food and beer to the busy aircraft carrier crews at Yankee Station in the Gulf of Tonkin. It was safe, dull duty, and Schumacher wanted a bit more adventure. When his transfer orders to the *Pueblo* arrived, he immediately tried to find out what sort of boat it was. Nobody seemed to know, and, mysteriously, it wasn't listed in the Navy directory of ships. Several weeks later, Schumacher got a letter from the *Pueblo*'s executive officer, telling him only that the vessel was to conduct "oceanographic research" in the Sea of Japan. That was the spy ship's cover story. For its public commissioning ceremony in Bremerton, Washington, the Navy had gone so far as to bring in a local college professor to extol the *Pueblo*'s anticipated contributions to helping mankind extract more food from the sea.

Seeing it now for the first time, Schumacher wondered whether the *Pueblo* could even stay upright in a storm. He'd never seen a Navy ship so small that its gangplank led *down* from the dock rather than up. Nonetheless, he saluted its American flag, marched over the gangway, and presented his orders to a petty officer.

Schumacher was taken on a tour of the ship and then to lunch in the wardroom. As he sat down, conversation among the other officers fell off; that usually happened when a new face appeared in officer country.

The lull didn't last long.

The *Pueblo*'s captain burst into the compartment like a sudden clap of thunder over a calm sea. Tough, charismatic, and cheerfully profane, Commander Lloyd M. Bucher had just turned 40. His arms bulged with muscle and his eyes shone with intelligence and a touch of mischievousness. He had a handsome, square-jawed face, an easy grin, and a bullhorn of a voice that could stop a belowdecks fistfight cold. To Schumacher, the skipper's presence seemed to electrify the very air around him.

Even seated Bucher had a dynamic quality. While one big hand shoveled food into his mouth, the other switched on a tape player mounted in the bulkhead, filling the wardroom with the rollicking ballads of Johnny Cash. Schumacher was introduced and the captain's right hand shot out in greeting. "Glad to have you," he boomed. "Where'd you come from?" Badly intimidated by his new boss, the young ensign stammered a few words of personal history.

Bucher was an ex–submarine officer, a superb navigator and ship handler. In the late 1950s, he'd served aboard subs with the delicate and dangerous job of eavesdropping on Soviet naval activities in the North Pacific; in the early sixties, he'd planned such missions for a Japan-based sub squadron. A voracious reader, he kept a set of Shakespeare's works in his stateroom. He played chess with merciless speed and waded into barroom brawls with happy abandon; a friend aptly described him as an "intellectual barbarian."

A taskmaster at sea, Bucher was a major-league drinker and party animal onshore. With his loud singing and even louder off-duty outfits, he was often the center of attention at officers' clubs and wharfside dives alike. For all that, he was a surprisingly sensitive man, given to choking up in emotional moments. He preferred to be called by his boyhood nickname, Pete.

The captain loved the adventure and camaraderie of subs and longed to command one of his own. Instead, the Navy "surfaced" him—removed him from the submarine corps—and made him skipper of the *Pueblo* in 1966. Bucher was bitterly disappointed, but he resolved to do his best with the intelligence ship. Before long he realized how similar the *Pueblo*'s cruises would be to his old sub missions—a lone vessel patrolling a hostile coast for days or weeks at a time. The big difference was that now he'd travel on the surface.

Shortly after taking command of the *Pueblo*, Bucher flew to Washington, D.C., for ten days of classified briefings on his upcoming missions. Following a series of security checks, he was ushered into the Fort Meade, Maryland, headquarters of the National Security Agency, the secretive government organization that monitored radio transmissions, telephone traffic, and radar signals worldwide. The NSA also developed the complex code machines used by the American military to send encrypted messages. In conjunction with the Navy, the NSA would assign the *Pueblo* specific eavesdropping targets. Bucher also paid a visit to the Naval Security Group, which ran the Navy's own global network of electronic surveillance.

The *Pueblo* was to be home-ported in Japan, within cruising range of three potential wartime foes: the Soviet Union, China, and North Korea. Bucher wouldn't find out until later which nation he'd sail against first, though he suspected it was the USSR, which was doing its level best to discourage U.S. seaborne reconnaissance. When the first unarmed spy boat, the USS *Banner*, was sent out under Operation Clickbeetle, the Russians had tried to scare it away from their shores by playing hair-raising games of chicken. Soviet destroyers trained their guns on the *Banner* and raced directly at it, as if intending to ram, before veering away at the last moment. During night maneuvers at close quarters, they tried to blind the *Banner*'s skipper by aiming powerful searchlights at his bridge.

But Bucher's briefers told him there was little chance that he and his vessel would actually be harmed. His best protection, they said, was the centuries-old body of international law and custom that guaranteed free passage on the high seas to ships of all nations. The *Pueblo* had a legal right to patrol foreign coasts as long as it didn't violate territorial waters. While the United States enforced only a three-mile offshore limit, most communist nations claimed 12 miles. As a precaution, the *Pueblo* was ordered to stay at least 13 miles from land at all times. The captain also was advised that he could take comfort in a much older and far less civilized doctrine: an eye for an eye. Because if the Soviets were foolish enough to attack his vulnerable, solitary spy ship, the United States could just as easily go after one of theirs.

Bucher enjoyed his stay in Washington, but was unimpressed by the NSA bureaucrats, who struck him as "pipe-smoking characters" trying to act like Ivy League professors. As he wrote later, he couldn't help but wonder whether any of these men had ever "enjoyed a wild Saturday night drunk, got into a good fight over a poker game, abandoned themselves to a hot extramarital affair, or, for that matter, brazenly run a stop light before the eyes of a traffic cop."

His briefings finished, the captain departed for the Puget Sound Naval Shipyard in Bremerton, Washington, where he expected to oversee the finishing touches on the *Pueblo*'s metamorphosis from washed-up cargo hauler to cutting-edge intelligence platform.

The great yard was roaring with activity when he arrived in January 1967. Welders, pipe fitters, electricians, and other workers swarmed over sleek warships, readying them for action off Vietnam. But Bucher felt a stab of dismay when he spotted his new boat bobbing forlornly among much bigger and grander cruisers, missile frigates, and nuclear submarines. Dusted off from the Navy's mothball fleet near San Francisco and towed north to Bremerton, the dilapidated old freighter had been subjected to months of hammering and drilling, yet its conversion was far from complete. Rust streaked its hull. Scaffolding, shipping crates, tools, and random wires clogged its decks. Bucher thought it resembled nothing so much as an abandoned derelict.

A small group of officers and enlisted men already had reported aboard to help civilian contractors build out the ship's most important section, the Special Operations Department, or "SOD hut." The claustrophobic hut, also known innocuously as "the research spaces," housed the radar detectors, radio receivers, oscillators, spectrum analyzers, amplifiers, dosimeters, and four-channel demultiplexers that gave the *Pueblo* its purpose. Behind a triple-locked steel door, highly trained Navy communication technicians, or CTs, would operate the top secret eavesdropping hardware.

The amount of work still to be done stunned Bucher. Dozens of problems in the engine room, berthing areas, mess decks, and elsewhere needed to be fixed. With few sealable hatches between compartments, the ship's watertight integrity was questionable. Its windlass, which raised and lowered the anchor, was unreliable, meaning that the *Pueblo* might drift helplessly into communist waters in the event of engine failure. Instead of an intercom to transmit orders from bridge to engine room, the skipper had to rely on an antiquated system of bells installed by the Army. A subsequent inspection by Navy experts counted no fewer than 462 mechanical and design deficiencies.

The captain began haunting shipyard managers, vociferously demanding improvements to the *Pueblo*'s operating equipment and living areas. He clashed so often with the superintendent that he was criticized in a fitness report as "overzealous."

Part of the problem was that few people working on the spy ship had high enough security clearances to be told of its true function. They treated it according to its old designation as an auxiliary cargo ship, light, or AKL. An AKL carried a crew of 27, but the reconfigured surveillance vessel would bear 83 men, including 30 communication technicians. Bucher had to fight for more berths and better hygiene facilities for his unusually large crew. After long days of wrangling, he characteristically invited the shipyard boss to the officers' club for conciliatory cocktails.

By June 2, the *Pueblo* finally was ready for sea trials in Puget Sound.

The first exercise involved the basic task of dropping anchor, but the anchor chain jumped off the faulty windlass. Next were maneuverability tests. Cruising in reverse, Bucher ordered left full rudder. That caused the cable connecting the rudder to the steering engine to snap, freezing the rudder in its turned position. The *Pueblo* could only sail in circles until Bucher made a humiliating call for a tugboat to tow his new ship home.

Three days later, the cable parted again. Grunting and cursing, Bucher's men fitted a heavy cast-iron tiller to the rudder in order to manually turn it. The sight of men pulling mightily on ropes to swing the big tiller back and forth made one sailor wonder what it was like to be a galley slave in the fourth century B.C. But spare parts were no longer available for the steering engine, manufactured during World War II by a now-defunct Wisconsin elevator company, and the Navy decided the cost of replacing it was prohibitive. By the time the *Pueblo* completed its sea trials, the steering engine had failed 180 times.

Bucher knew his new ship was unlikely to ever be much more than a balky, patched-together tub. Yet he found himself developing a distinct affection for the *Pueblo*; it was his first command, after all. He also held many of his men in high regard, especially his taciturn chief engineer, Gene Lacy, a 36-year-old from Seattle who was fast becoming the captain's best friend aboard.

Besides the fragile steering engine, Bucher worried about the large load of classified materials on board, and whether he'd be able to destroy it in an emergency. The *Pueblo* carried not only electronic surveillance gear and code machines but also hundreds of pounds of top secret paper: military plans, intelligence reports, repair and operating manuals for the encryption devices, and other sensitive documents.

Submarines he'd served on had crude but effective quick-destruction systems: dynamite canisters that could blow a hole in their hulls and send their secret contents to the bottom in minutes. But the *Pueblo* crew had only sledgehammers and fire axes to break up electronic devices. Documents could be fed into two small, sluggish shredders, burned in a 50-gallon drum, or torn up by hand and heaved overboard in weighted canvas bags. Busting up well-built machines and disposing of mounds of paper took time, however. If the ship lost propulsion near an unfriendly shore or ran aground in a storm, it might not be possible to get rid of everything in time. What if the *Pueblo* got stranded on, say, the Siberian coast? An impressive cache of national secrets easily could wind up in Soviet hands.

Bucher fired off a letter to his superiors, requesting, "in the strongest possible language," a specially designed destruction system. The missive found its way to the office of the chief of naval operations, Admiral Thomas Moorer, the Navy's highest-ranking uniformed official. Moorer's office asked the Army whether putting explosives aboard its former freighter made sense. Many weeks later, Bucher was informed that such a system was too expensive.

Most of the captain's other requested upgrades were denied as well. Acutely aware of the rising costs of the Vietnam War, the Navy slashed $1 million from the *Pueblo*'s $5.5 million makeover budget. When the bean counters turned down his requisition for a fuel-fed incinerator, an irritated Bucher went out and bought a smaller commercial model, dipping into the crew's recreation fund for the $1,300 purchase price.

The need for rapid destruction was tragically underscored when Israeli jets and torpedo boats attacked a much larger intelligence ship, the USS *Liberty*, in the Mediterranean Sea during the Six-Day War of June 1967. A pair of Israeli fighters strafed the lightly armed *Liberty* with 30-millimeter cannon, shattering its bridge and badly wounding a number of officers. After the jets ran out of ammunition, two more swept in and dropped napalm. Crewmen screamed in pain, gaped at hemorrhaging wounds, and struggled to control spreading fires. In the research spaces, communication technicians worked feverishly to destroy secret equipment.

A trio of Israeli torpedo boats moved in to finish off the smoking, blood-smeared American vessel. One torpedo blew a forty-foot hole in the *Liberty*'s hull. The explosion killed a number of sailors outright; others, trapped in damaged compartments, drowned in terrifying darkness as seawater flooded in. A crewman later reported that an Israeli boat machine-gunned several of the *Liberty*'s life rafts in the water.

By the time the harrowing attack ended, 34 Americans lay dead or dying. Another 171 were wounded, many grievously. The *Liberty*'s skipper, William McGonagle, weakened by blood loss from a severe leg wound, calmly directed firefighting and damage-control efforts for the next 17 hours. With his compass ruined, McGonagle lay on his back on an open deck that night and navigated by the stars toward a dawn rendezvous with two U.S. destroyers racing to deliver medical aid; he subsequently was awarded the Medal of Honor. Israel's government claimed its forces had mistaken the *Liberty* for an Egyptian warship shelling Israeli troops in the Sinai Peninsula. Although many crewmen and some top Navy officers believed the attack was deliberate, President Lyndon Johnson accepted Israel's apology and indemnification.

Israeli gunfire had made it impossible for *Liberty* sailors to burn classified documents in a topside incinerator. Instead, they were forced to feed codes and other paper materials into fires lit in wastebaskets. Weighted ditch bags stuffed with thick manuals and other publications proved too heavy to throw overboard, and in any event the water was too shallow for jettisoning.

The destruction problem nagged at Bucher, but he couldn't do much more about it. Several months behind schedule due to construction delays, he and his crew finally set sail in early September 1967 from Bremerton to the massive San Diego naval base, where the *Pueblo* was to undergo readiness tests. From there it would head for Hawaii to refuel before continuing on to its new home port of Yokosuka, near Tokyo.

Bucher also was concerned about his young crew's lack of experience. About half of the men had never been to sea. The seamanship skills of his new executive officer, Lieutenant Edward R. Murphy Jr., didn't impress him. Schumacher, though smart and capable, had been in the Navy only two years. The ship's other ensign, 21-year-old Tim Harris, had been commissioned just four months before stepping aboard the *Pueblo*. Bucher viewed Lacy, the veteran chief engineer, as his only truly experienced, reliable officer.

By the time the *Pueblo* reached San Diego, the captain had made up his mind to teach his officers everything he could about ship handling.

A few days after pulling up to the pier in his Porsche, Schumacher was invited to demonstrate his stuff. He stood on the flying bridge as Bucher observed from a chair behind him. Calling commands to the helmsman in the pilothouse below, Schumacher managed to back away from the dock without incident and head for the busy San Diego ship channel. Then he tried to make what he thought was a slight course correction.

"Left five-degree rudder," he ordered, and the *Pueblo* began turning to port. Within seconds, however, the ship had swerved not five degrees but 30—and was barreling straight toward a sandbar. Bucher leaped up and shouted a new bearing, averting a mortifying gaffe in full view of numerous Navy officers on nearby vessels. Schumacher expected a high-decibel reaming, but the captain quietly gave him back the conn.

"I guess that was a little unfair of me," he told the chagrined ensign. "This ship's got a rudder as large as a damn barn door. All you ever need to use for this kind of maneuvering is two- or three-degree rudder."

Schumacher began to like his rambunctious boss more and more. Bucher enjoyed playing with ideas and seemed curious about almost everything. When the *Pueblo* paused on its way to San Diego for a weekend liberty in San Francisco, he took the fun-loving Tim Harris to the Haight-Ashbury neighborhood to check out the hippies and their Summer of Love. The skipper could talk knowledgeably about anything from the prospects of the San Diego Chargers to U.S. naval tactics in Vietnam to the novels of Lawrence Durrell. Schumacher subscribed to *Esquire* and *National Review*, which turned out to be two of Bucher's favorite magazines.

Schumacher also appreciated his new commander's directness and informal submariner's ways. If the captain had a question about radio communications, he went straight to the radio operator for an answer, bypassing—and sometimes angering—the man's immediate supervisor, usually a senior petty officer. Although he was a demon about enforcing spit-and-polish rules while his ship was in port, the skipper didn't much care what his men wore at sea. Bucher himself was a bit of a slob, showing up for work in shabby khakis and a tatty straw hat, or for lunch in the wardroom in a T-shirt and flip-flops.

Like many men who'd served beneath the waves, Bucher enjoyed being a little different. One manifestation of that trait was his adoption of a theme song for the *Pueblo*: "The Lonely Bull," by Herb Alpert and the Tijuana Brass. The melancholy, Spanish-accented tune blared from the ship's loudspeakers whenever it entered or left port, much to the amusement of onlookers. Many Navy ships had their own insignias and letterhead, but not their own song. The captain, however, considered "The Lonely Bull" a morale booster; it gave his men something special to take pride in. He also felt the song's title reflected the *Pueblo*'s unique charter as a solitary sentinel on the immense gray wilderness of the sea.

His casual clothes and eccentric flourishes aside, Bucher was a demanding leader. He set high standards and vocally enforced them. To Schumacher, he seemed to possess an amazingly detailed knowledge of his vessel's mechanical innards. He didn't view the *Pueblo* as just another career stepping-stone, as some officers might, but rather as a serious assignment to be executed well for its own sake.

Despite his devotion to running a tight ship, the captain had no problem with his men cutting loose now and then. Indeed, Bucher, himself a former enlisted man and connoisseur of good times, often led the pack. When he, Lacy, and Harris hit the beach for drinks after work, Schumacher could barely keep up.

At an officers' club or civilian bar, the gregarious captain was marvelous company, singing and telling jokes and attracting knots of revelers, male and female alike. "You'd get a couple of nice-looking babes walk into the place, and inside of three minutes he'd have 'em smoking and joking and laughing," Schumacher recalled in an interview 35 years later. "He'd start telling his corny jokes; he was really something."

Bucher particularly enjoyed the companionship of Lacy, who of all his officers most closely matched him in age and Navy tenure.

Schumacher was drinking with Bucher at the starchy Admiral Kidd Club in San Diego one day when the captain issued a typically unorthodox summons for Lacy to join them. Bucher lunged onto the terrace and, with no warning to the high-ranking brass tippling around him, unleashed an ear-piercing, double-fingered whistle in the direction of the *Pueblo*, tied up nearby. When he had the attention of the ship's watch, he began rapidly flapping and windmilling his arms, as if he were trying to take off and fly. Other officers stared at him, transfixed. Bucher was signaling in semaphore for Lacy to come ashore. The chief engineer showed up a few minutes later.

Reserved and self-assured, Lacy had enlisted out of high school and spent so much time amid pounding pistons and screeching drive shafts that he was partially deaf. He'd served on a variety of ships, including Navy icebreakers, and had seen action in the Korean War. With his chiseled face, brush-cut dark hair, and dignified bearing, he was often mistaken for a captain himself. Though he was a tough disciplinarian, his fairness earned him the respect of the men under him in the engine room.

Bucher bonded further with the engineering officer when they conspired to steal a large painting of a nude woman that adorned the submarine officers' club in San Diego.

The generously endowed beauty, enticingly supine, hung behind the bar at the Ballast Tank, a small, lively hangout that rang with the shouts and good-natured taunts of many of Bucher's old sub mates. One slow night, Bucher, Lacy, and Harris played pool at the club as they waited for the right moment. When the bartender went to collect empty glasses in the next room, Bucher followed and delayed him with small talk. As Lacy distracted other customers, Harris vaulted the bar, grabbed the nude, and scampered out a side door. He deposited the booty in his car trunk and sauntered back into the club as if nothing had happened. The bartender somehow failed to notice the glaringly empty spot above a row of bottles, and the grinning thieves slipped away undetected.

Bucher displayed the prize in the *Pueblo*'s wardroom and encouraged everyone from officers to mess cooks to come in and savor it. The Ballast

Tank, meanwhile, buzzed with theories about the identities of the malefactors who'd lifted the beloved nude; sitting at the bar again, Bucher gleefully speculated about various suspects. When he learned that Navy criminal investigators were on the case, the painting discreetly reappeared in the submariners' haunt.

The Great Naked Art Heist endeared the captain to many in his crew. But after witnessing his reaction when the shore patrol arrested three of his men, some sailors were ready to run him for Congress.

The three, all young communication technicians, had seen a movie in downtown San Diego and were looking for a bar to knock back a few beers in before calling it a night. A shore patrol truck pulled up and a policeman accused them of being drunk. Despite their denials, they were hauled to the SP station and booked for violating a Navy rule against wearing "inappropriate clothing" off duty—specifically, jeans and sport shirts.

Late that night, the trio returned to the *Pueblo*. Their sleeping captain was roused and informed of his men's misfortune. Bucher thought back to his enlisted days, when overly aggressive cops had often ruined a good night out. Furious, he gathered up the three CTs along with Ensign Harris and drove to the police station.

The duty officer, a lieutenant junior grade, was clearly displeased at being confronted by an angry superior in the middle of the night. When he pulled out a thick manual and quoted the regulation under which the sailors had been picked up, Bucher began loudly chewing him out. The captain noted that the regulation also prohibited wearing Bermuda shorts in public places. Yet he'd seen high-ranking officers in such attire at the post exchange; why weren't admirals getting busted along with swabbies? Bucher demanded that the lieutenant get his boss on the phone.

The hapless SP man eyed Bucher as if he were from another planet. "It's zero two ten, sir," he said, using the military time for 2:10 a.m. "The district shore patrol commander is at home, asleep."

"I know what goddamn time it is, mister!" Bucher exploded. "I took the trouble to leave my ship in the middle of the night and come down here to deal with the harassment of my crew. So get your CO on the line right now!"

The outranked lieutenant had no choice but to call. When the drowsy police commander answered, Bucher snatched the phone and gave him a tart summary of the evening's events. The SP chief replied that he resented being awakened at such a grim hour over a "trifling" matter; Bucher barked that the unjustified detention of his men was a serious issue to him and hung up.

Still fuming, the captain later banged out a letter of complaint to the admiral in charge of the Eleventh Naval District, which encompassed the San Diego base. Almost immediately, he was ordered to report to the admiral's chief of staff.

The staff chief, a grizzled senior captain, told Bucher he'd been put on report after the outraged SP commander raised a ruckus. Bucher emphatically restated his belief that his men had been hassled for no good reason. "If they'd gotten drunk and broken up some joint, I'd personally bust them," he said. "But for wearing Levi's and loud shirts?"

The senior officer regarded him carefully. The shore patrol duty officer, he said, had reported that Bucher was inebriated when he barged into police headquarters.

"Negative, sir!" snapped Bucher, although some of the sailors with him that night might have disagreed.

The senior captain drummed his fingers thoughtfully on his desk. "Well, all right," he said finally. "I can sympathize with your grievance. But on the other hand, we can't compromise discipline by ignoring a dress regulation that does not suit us." He promised to relate their discussion to the admiral, and he hoped the matter would end there. He closed by urging Bucher to "show a little more discretion in the future."

Bucher told no one on the *Pueblo* about being called on the carpet. His sailors had their own sources, however, and found out. They were astonished that he'd stuck his neck out so far for enlisted men. Most officers would never risk such a potentially career-damaging clash with higher-ups. "When he stood up for us like that," said one of the arrestees, "we figured we had the captain of all captains." The episode convinced Schumacher of something else: that on some deep psychological level Bucher, who'd grown up as an orphan, viewed his men as the brothers he never had.

The sailors, meanwhile, threw themselves into preparing for the readiness tests.

Navy crews had to pass tests that applied to all ships as well as those designed for their particular type. But again there was a complication with the *Pueblo*: nothing in the voluminous training books covered drills for this new kind of spy ship. As a result, training officers treated the vessel like the freighter it once was. They wanted the crew to demonstrate proficiency in taking aboard stores and transferring them to other ships while under way.

For the same reason, the sailors received no training in maneuvers with particular relevance to the *Pueblo*, like coping with Soviet harassment. Bucher approached the admiral in charge of training with his dilemma, but even he had never been informed of the *Pueblo*'s actual purpose and offered little help in tailoring special exercises.

Nor were there any tests designed specifically for communication technicians working in the all-important SOD hut, a 20-foot-long, ten-foot-wide metal bread box that sat on the main deck forward of the bridge.

Flooded with cold fluorescent light, the hut was manned 24 hours a day. The CTs sat back-to-back along a narrow aisle, working on floor-to-ceiling racks of gadgets. Most of the men were in their twenties, and much brighter than the average enlistee. Twenty-two-year-old Peter Langenberg, for example, had dropped out of Princeton because he was bored. Like Schumacher, the polite, slightly built Langenberg hailed from St. Louis and had joined the Navy to avoid getting drafted into the Army. Schooled as a Russian translator, he previously was attached to the top secret Kamiseya communication station in Japan, where his job was to monitor Soviet navy radio traffic.

There was a certain amount of tension between the regular sailors and the CTs, sealed inside their special chamber like some secretive priesthood. The whiz kids wore their own arm patch—a quill crossed with a lightning bolt—and refused to let ordinary seamen through their triple-locked door or to discuss anything that went on behind it. That bugged Bucher, who, though cleared to know the lock combinations, preferred to pound on the door with his fist until someone inside opened it.

The officer in charge of the CTs was Lieutenant Stephen R. Harris, a Harvard graduate and fluent Russian linguist. Harris had been given responsibility for the SOD hut despite his relatively youthful age of 29. With his beaklike nose, incipient double chin, and self-effacing manner, the lieutenant seemed more like a shy academic than a naval officer. The only child of two Boston-area schoolteachers, he loved the romantic concertos of Rachmaninoff and belonged to a club devoted to preserving electric streetcars. He seemed to write a letter every night to his new wife, a lovely blond secretary named Esther. A devout Presbyterian and born-again Christian, Harris had met her through her brother, a fellow member of the Officers' Christian Union.

Bucher instinctively liked Steve Harris, even though the CT commander was unlike any Navy officer he'd ever met.

The crewmen passed their readiness exams and, on the misty morning of November 6, 1967, the spy ship cast off for Hawaii, its loudspeakers streaming "The Lonely Bull."

Going back to sea thrilled Bucher. He was enjoying his two young ensigns, especially Schumacher, who, with his natural competence and irreverence, was proving to be an excellent shipmate. Despite its mechanical problems, the *Pueblo* handled well at sea, although it had a small ship's tendency to roll and buck. But good weather prevailed, and Bucher relished all the sensations of an ocean passage: the satisfying whump of the bow plowing into gray rollers, the reassuring throb of Lacy's two diesel main engines, the mouthwatering smell of pork chops frying in the galley.

Not everyone found the trip as pleasurable.

Some CTs got so seasick they wondered whether they'd live to see the sunrise. Even veterans remarked how roughly the ship sailed, shuddering from bow to transom as it bashed into wave after wave. In the forward berthing compartment, enlisted men tried to get some sleep on bunks stacked three and four high amid the fusty odor of never-quite-clean bodies and clothes. About two feet of headroom separated each bunk. Gulping Dramamine but unable to keep his food down, Langenberg wedged himself into his rack and just tried to endure. "I was seasick the whole time," he recalled. "To get horizontal was wonderful. You just kind of lie there and moan and wish you were dead."

The crew also had to deal with the dysfunctional steering engine, which was now dying an average of two times per four-hour watch. Most Navy ships had hydraulic steering; the *Pueblo*'s was electromechanical. An entry in the ship's deck log for November 12 demonstrated the persistence of the problem:

> 0825 [8:25 a.m.]: Lost electrical steering, all engines stop. 0826: Regained electrical steering, all ahead full. 0829: Lost electrical steering. 0830: All stop. 0833: Shifted to manual steering. 0834: All ahead standard, shifted to electrical steering. 0839: All ahead full. 0909: Lost electrical steering, all stop. 0910: Shifted to manual steering. 0910: Regained electrical steering. 0911: All ahead standard. 0913: All ahead full. 0914: Lost electrical steering, all stop.

In spite of its fitful steering, the ship reached Pearl Harbor eight days after leaving San Diego. Bucher tied up at the submarine base; old sub buddies, he figured, were probably lurking at the local officers' club. He spent several hours making sure the *Pueblo* and its intractable steering engine received priority at the repair yard. Later he paid a visit to the headquarters of the commander in chief of the Pacific Fleet—CINCPACFLT, in Navy acronym-ese.

Bucher still hadn't been told the target of the *Pueblo*'s first mission, so he paid a call on an old friend, Lieutenant Commander Erv Easton, now serving on the CINCPACFLT intelligence staff. Bucher was headed for North Korea, not the USSR, said Easton, and the voyage was rated low-risk. The *Pueblo*'s sister ferret, the USS *Banner*, had transited the North Korean coast a couple of times without incident, and Easton promised to give the captain copies of its mission reports. Bucher, he said, should consider his maiden trip a shakedown cruise, a chance to make sure his surveillance gear worked and give his crew a taste of what to expect on more serious outings in the future.

Bucher knew little about North Korea other than that it'd started the Korean War 17 years earlier and possessed only a bathtub navy of patrol boats, sub chasers, and a handful of aging Soviet-built subs. The idea of such a fourth-rate country attacking a commissioned ship of the mighty United States Navy, he believed, was absurdly far-fetched. Yet he wanted to know what the Navy planned to do if the impossible somehow happened. Easton didn't know, so he passed Bucher on to Captain George Cassell, CINCPACFLT's assistant chief of staff for operations. Bucher asked Cassell how the Navy would react if the North Koreans went beyond Soviet-style harassment and started shooting. What if they tried to capture his ship on the high seas?

The odds of that happening were extremely long, Cassell replied. The *Banner* had had no trouble off North Korea and neither would the *Pueblo*. But in the highly unlikely event that he did come under attack, Bucher was on his own. The Navy simply didn't have enough combat ships to give him immediate relief, although help would be sent as soon as possible. And if the Navy didn't get to the *Pueblo* in time, Cassell promised, a retaliatory hammer would come down hard on North Korea within 24 hours.

"Contingency plans for such an occurrence," he said, "are written and approved." In other words, the *Pueblo* was expendable, but the Navy would swiftly avenge it.

Festooned with antennae, the *Pueblo* attracted plenty of attention at Pearl Harbor, and Bucher invited aboard any and all officers with a role in its mission. To preserve its cover story, the Navy called it an "auxiliary general environmental research" ship, or AGER, a designation few Navy officers recognized. Between briefings and tours of the vessel, though, Bucher wanted to make sure his officers and men got time off to enjoy the delights of Hawaii. In fact, he was eager to hit the beachfront bars and nightclubs of Waikiki himself.

On their first evening in port, the officers all went to a club that featured the entertainer Don Ho and luscious Tahitian dancers. The men tossed 20 bucks apiece into a food-and-drinks kitty. But the money ran out by the end of the first show, and Lieutenant Murphy was perturbed at having to kick in more. Bucher ignored him, and the wardroom had a fine time. Tim Harris lost his shoes after a bout of hula dancing, and Bucher and Lacy didn't get back to the *Pueblo* until five a.m. Despite his pique, Murphy covered for his captain later that morning when some CINCPACFLT bigwigs showed up to inspect the *Pueblo* and Bucher couldn't seem to rouse himself from bed.

The tireless skipper hit the beach again that night with Lacy, Tim Harris, and about 25 enlistees and petty officers. Unlike many commissioned officers, Bucher made no effort to maintain an attitude of authoritarian aloofness toward the lower ranks. He didn't think downing a few brews with his men in some dive undermined good shipboard order and discipline; on the contrary, such comradely elbow-bending just might foster loyalty and make the ship run better. Whatever respect the swabbies had for him, he believed, depended on his abilities as a wise leader and problem solver—not on how often he struck heroic solo poses on the bridge. If big-ship officers subscribed to the notion that familiarity bred contempt, Bucher thought familiarity aboard smaller vessels—such as subs and crowded little spy boats—was unavoidable.

After three days, the Honolulu yard workers emerged from the *Pueblo*'s bowels, weary and defeated, saying they could do no more to patch up the steering engine. Bucher would have to hope for the best on the next leg of his trip and make permanent repairs in Yokosuka. On the afternoon of November 18, the ship pulled away from its dock at Pearl and headed north and west.

The steering engine failed yet again on the second day out. Sailors were still losing their lunches over the side, and the ship's limited hygiene facilities compounded their misery. For a crew of 83 there were only four shower stalls and six washbasins. The head in the first-class petty officers' compartment continually backed up, spitting feces and urine on the deck. (The men nicknamed it "the shooter.") The air belowdecks was rank; by the end of the tropical days, the broiling bunk areas reeked.

Bucher stopped midocean for a "swim call," a tradition popular with sub crews on lengthy patrols. His sailors loved it. They pulled on trunks and jumped off the low-slung well deck into the water. Then some horseplay began, with bigger men throwing in smaller ones. Someone shoved Langenberg off the deck. He landed on top of radioman John Mullin, who shrieked in pain.

The ship's veteran corpsman, Herman "Doc" Baldridge, thought Mullin's back might be broken. But the *Pueblo* had no doctor or proper sick bay, and Baldridge couldn't do much beyond giving the injured man painkillers. Bucher radioed Pearl Harbor for advice and was told to rendezvous with a destroyer tender, the USS *Samuel Gompers*, which was on the same course to Japan and rapidly catching up with him. The *Gompers* carried doctors, X-ray equipment, and other trappings of a small hospital.

The sunshine and smooth seas gradually disappeared as the *Pueblo* plodded on in the volatile North Pacific. A gray curtain of rainsqualls on the horizon drew closer and thickened into a steady downpour. The skies darkened and the wind accelerated, heralding a storm. Visibility dropped to a few miles. The *Pueblo* jerked and heaved even more violently than usual; Mullin, strapped to his bunk, groaned in distress. Finally, the *Gompers* appeared on the *Pueblo*'s radar screen. Thirty minutes later, the big tender broke into view through the driving rain, its signal lights flashing:

STAND BY

IN MY LEE

TO RECEIVE OUR DOCTOR.

Bucher took the conn, silently praying that the steering engine wouldn't quit again. Just in case, he stationed a team on the fantail, the men ready to spring into action with ropes and iron tiller. As rain and flying spume pelted him on the open bridge, the skipper edged closer to the *Gompers*'s downwind flank, watching intently as the bigger ship swayed ponderously alongside him.

The destroyer tender launched its whaleboat, which puttered close enough for an agile physician to leap across the last few feet of churning sea onto the *Pueblo*'s rain-slick well deck. He hurried below, examined Mullin, and confirmed Baldridge's diagnosis. Although it was risky to transfer the radioman in the storm, he had to be taken to the *Gompers* for treatment.

There was no way to safely deposit Mullin in the *Gompers*'s bucking whaleboat. Instead, he was lashed to a stretcher and placed in the *Pueblo*'s motor launch. Bucher had only a handful of men who were even halfway qualified to lower the boat into the water and maneuver it over to the *Gompers* in such rough conditions. But he had no choice. He gave Ensign Harris command of the launch, and then spurred the *Pueblo* a little nearer to the protective bulk of the *Gompers*. Harris and his crew managed to plop into the sea without capsizing. They beelined for the *Gompers*, which quickly and expertly winched up their boat and its patient.

The drama wasn't over: Harris still had to get back to the *Pueblo*. As he and his men approached the ship, a sudden squall engulfed them. They could barely see in the heavy rain. They banged into the hull and had to back off. They tried again, only to be waved away by sailors on deck. On the third try

Harris and his men made it. They were hoisted back on board, soaked to the bone and freezing, but proud of their deliverance of an ailing shipmate.

The *Gompers* sped off into the squall line and disappeared.

Bucher treated every man who'd been in the launch or out on deck to a two-ounce bottle of brandy. The grog, according to one sailor, "boosted morale about 600 percent."

After two weeks at sea, Bucher was generally satisfied with the way his crew was shaping up, with one notable exception: Ed Murphy, his executive officer.

Tall and owlish behind horn-rimmed glasses, Murphy came across as a strictly-by-the-book type. His black shoes gleamed, a gold clip firmly secured his tie, and his shirtsleeves were rolled all the way down. A devout Christian Scientist, the 30-year-old lieutenant was a teetotaler who also didn't smoke or drink coffee. His job as the *Pueblo*'s number two officer was to ensure that the captain's orders were carried out quickly and efficiently. But after working with him only a few months, Bucher regarded his deputy as a bungler and a stuffed shirt.

The son of a general-store proprietor, Murphy had grown up in the lumber town of Arcata in Northern California's redwood country. After college, he enrolled in officer candidate school in Newport, Rhode Island. Posted to a fleet oiler, he later served on a destroyer as assistant navigator, earning good fitness reports.

Murphy liked the Navy and wanted to make it his career. In 1964, he was assigned, as a full-fledged navigator, to a guided missile destroyer in the Tonkin Gulf. By then his father had died and his mother was trying to run the family store herself. That became more and more difficult as her health deteriorated. In 1965, Murphy made a difficult decision to put his shipboard career on hold and got a humanitarian transfer to a small Navy shore facility near Arcata. During off hours, he helped his mother get the store ready to sell.

Murphy might be straitlaced, but he had mettle. Walking along the beach near the base one winter morning, he and another lieutenant spotted a foundering crab boat getting knocked to pieces in heavy surf. At first the officers thought the vessel was abandoned. Coming closer, they saw three men aboard. Murphy and his colleague plunged into the frigid ocean, swam to the boat, and hauled the crabbers to shore. For risking their lives, both officers were awarded the Navy and Marine Corps Medal.

From his first moments aboard the *Pueblo*, however, Murphy rubbed Bucher the wrong way. The lieutenant prissily turned down a cup of coffee, saying, "I never use it, thank you," as if he'd been offered a bowl of opium. When the wardroom retired that afternoon to the Bremerton officers' club to toast the new executive officer with martinis, Murphy sipped a ginger ale and left early.

Bucher believed that compatibility was as important as competence among officers on a small ship. Murphy certainly wasn't very compatible with the captain's style of hard work and boozy hard play. To Bucher, the XO seemed unable to cope with his paperwork or carry out shipboard policies. Nor did he join the other officers in their frequent beer-and-bull sessions after work. He seemed preoccupied with his family, especially his mother's ongoing difficulties with the store.

More and more, the exec found himself cut out of the wardroom loop. In port, Bucher often made decisions about ship's business while out on the town with his more convivial officers. Murphy didn't find out until he tried to give someone an order later, only to be told, "The captain said we weren't going to do that."

Bucher also regularly embarrassed Murphy by dressing him down—"chewing ass," the captain called it—within earshot of others. Murphy felt his boss was obsessed with his refusal to consume alcohol, seeing it as a sign that the executive officer regarded himself as morally superior. Murphy considered that ridiculous; he was simply living the tenets of his faith, not turning up his nose at anyone else.

How to run the ship was another source of friction between the two men. Murphy disliked the skipper's tendency to act as if the *Pueblo* were a submarine instead of a surface vessel. He referred to the flying bridge as the "conning tower" and the crew's mess area as the "after battery." Murphy approved of some of Bucher's sub-style practices, such as the midafternoon "soup down," which let the men put something hot in their stomachs before going on the four-to-eight-p.m. watch. But the captain, a confirmed night owl, also canceled reveille, routinely held on surface ships but not on subs, whose crews can't usually be lined up on deck for head counts. Murphy thought eliminating reveille made it more difficult to get the *Pueblo*'s men up for morning work details.

Bucher's vexation with his second in command peaked just before Thanksgiving, as the ship snorted and churned its way toward Japan.

Murphy had been aware for some time that the cooks were using bourbon and wine to prepare some meals. Thinking Bucher was trying to bait him, the exec said nothing. Before setting sail, the skipper had tripled the *Pueblo*'s alcohol allowance. Murphy didn't question that; nor did he complain of the frequency with which liquor was broken out for nonmedicinal purposes. What Bucher and the others drank was their business.

Shortly before the holiday, the officers were chatting in the wardroom when Tim Harris suggested that the mincemeat pies be laced with brandy. Suspecting a trap, Murphy didn't object. Then Schumacher piped up, asking what the lieutenant thought should be done. Murphy, a big fan of mincemeat, peered through his glasses and said perhaps a compromise was in order. All the holiday pies could be spiked save one, for those who might want a nonalcoholic dessert.

"Hell, no!" Bucher roared. "We'll put brandy in all the pies, and that's that!"

On Thanksgiving, Murphy took a pass on the mincemeat.

In the final week of its voyage, the *Pueblo* ran into gale-force winds and mountainous seas. It rolled as much as 50 degrees, so far over that Bucher feared a fatal capsize. Pots, pans, and plates flew every which way in the galley; green-gilled CTs pressed themselves tighter into their bunks. In spite of all the trouble with the steering engine, the main engines functioned flawlessly. The ship crawled up and over row after row of towering graybeards.

Finally, on December 1, the main Japanese island of Honshu appeared. The *Pueblo* rounded Cape Nojima and cruised past the long headland that protects the entrance to Tokyo Bay. Darkness had fallen by the time the storm-lashed ferret entered the Yokosuka channel, bound for its new home. Every man not on duty came out on deck, gazing eagerly at the bright lights of shore.

Bucher felt a flush of satisfaction at having finished his first sea journey as a commander. He had many sub buddies in Yokosuka and he was determined to impress them by gliding to a perfect stop at his designated dock. But he blew it, chugging right past the berth. Realizing his error, he threw the twin diesels into reverse. The steering engine chose that moment to quit completely. Since he didn't dare approach the dock with only rope-and-tiller steering, the skipper had to call for a tug.

As the spy ship was nursed into its slot, Bucher saw some familiar faces gathered under the pier lights.

They were laughing at him.

CHAPTER 2

DON'T START A WAR OUT THERE, CAPTAIN

Five days before Christmas, the USS *Banner*—the first spy ship sent out under Operation Clickbeetle—returned to Yokosuka from its latest patrol and tied up next to the *Pueblo*. After several weeks at sea the *Banner*'s unshaven crew looked like tired pirates. Bucher and his men soon would replace them in the wintry Sea of Japan.

Like its sister a onetime freighter, the *Banner* had ferried coconuts, pigs, and pregnant women around the Mariana Islands for years. In 1965, workmen at Bremerton converted it into a spy platform in just seven weeks—so fast that one Navy officer observed that it had been "literally put together like a plate of hash."

The *Banner*'s first commander was Lieutenant Bob Bishop, a South Carolinian who seemed to possess a sixth sense for extricating himself from white-knuckle situations. His inaugural mission was intended to gauge the Soviets' reaction to the presence of a lone unarmed intelligence vessel near their shores. And the communists weren't shy about demonstrating their displeasure.

Their destroyers and patrol boats tried to drive off Bishop by speeding straight at the *Banner* and swerving away moments before a collision. The harassment didn't faze the American skipper, but the horrendous weather did. After 20 hours of plowing into a Siberian storm, he realized the *Banner* had been pushed two miles *backward*. The storm left so much ice on the ship's topsides that Bishop worried it might turn turtle.

The Navy wanted Operation Clickbeetle focused on the USSR, its biggest maritime rival. But when it became clear, after half a dozen voyages, that the *Banner* was acquiring high-quality intelligence, the National Security Agency began lobbying for the ship's itinerary to be broadened to include China and North Korea. Navy officials objected, saying that doing so would negate Clickbeetle's central premise: that American ferrets would be protected by the gentlemen's agreement between the United States and the Soviet Union that neither would harm the other's boats for fear of reciprocal action. China and North Korea were bound by no such constraints. They possessed only coast-hugging navies incapable of ranging far enough from shore to eavesdrop on foreign adversaries. Thus they had less to lose by going after American snoopers. But the NSA prevailed in the debate.

Bishop faced his most alarming harassment in December 1966, when six Chinese gunboats surrounded the *Banner* off Shanghai. Each of the 60-foot patrol boats had a machine gun on its forward deck, manned and pointed at the American ship. The Chinese vessels apparently doubled as fishing boats, since all had lines running from their masts with fish drying on them. Their pilothouses bore the same painted slogan: "Chairman Mao is the envy of our hearts." Bishop turned and headed back to sea at full speed; the communists trailed along for a while but made no move to stop him.

Lieutenant Commander Charles Clark, another surfaced submariner, succeeded Bishop in 1967. Clark had been friends with Bucher at sub school in the mid-1950s and promised to keep him informed about his experiences on the *Banner*.

In a series of vivid letters to Bucher while he was in Bremerton, Clark told of furious storms, dangerous icing on his superstructure, and Russian patrol boats coming at him with guns manned and signal flags warning: HEAVE TO OR I WILL FIRE. On Clark's first trip, to Vladivostok, a Soviet destroyer tailgated him at night, beaming a searchlight into the *Banner*'s pilothouse and making Clark feel like he was "on a freeway in a go-cart with a Greyhound bus roaring up" from behind. For several nights in a row, a second destroyer steaming at 30 knots slashed past him with just 50 yards to spare. But, like Bishop, the pipe-smoking Clark had a finely calibrated sense of danger, always wriggling out of bad situations before they spun out of control.

A favorite trick of Clark's was to act as if he didn't understand a communist captain's signal flags. During the summer of 1967, the *Banner* encountered several Chinese patrol boats in the East China Sea. Though they weren't communicating with standard international shapes, the Chinese obviously wanted Clark to stop.

"They were flying all kinds of signals that we had reason to believe meant it was going to be serious," remembered his former executive officer, Dick Fredlund. "They kept signaling us and we kept signaling back, 'We don't know what you're saying'; 'Would you please repeat that?'; 'Isn't it a nice day?' That kind of stuff." Clark kept it up until he was safely away from the Chinese.

After the *Banner*'s pre-Christmas arrival in Yokosuka, Bucher pumped Clark for more details of his experiences. Clark had tape-recorded some of the confrontations, and Bucher listened to the tension-filled audio in the *Banner* skipper's stateroom. Bucher was particularly impressed by one episode in which both of the *Banner*'s main engines suddenly quit, leaving the ferret drifting helplessly as Chinese boats circled. A Navy destroyer 400 miles away started toward the *Banner*, and U.S. jets were alerted in case Clark came under attack. But his engineers managed to get the diesels going again, and the spy ship slipped away.

Interestingly, while the Chinese and Russians always sent out combat ships in an effort to intimidate Clark, the North Koreans hadn't reacted on the two occasions when the *Banner* transited their coast.

Clark's briefings made Bucher think harassment was just part of the game. It'd be nerve-racking but no worse than that. The *Pueblo* captain was more concerned by Clark's accounts of erratic radio contact with his home base. Communication nulls caused by atmospheric disturbances were all too common in the Sea of Japan. It had once taken the *Banner* more than 24 hours to lock on an open circuit—a delay that could spell disaster in an emergency.

Bucher's preoccupation with his upcoming mission, however, soon gave way to Yuletide merrymaking.

On Christmas Day he and his crew threw a party for some Japanese orphans, complete with cake, ice cream, and Donald Duck cartoons. Quartermaster Charles Law, a burly 26-year-old who'd emerged as a leader among the enlisted men, played Santa Claus to perfection.

A few days later, Bucher organized a spirited "wetting down" party at the Yokosuka officers' club to celebrate his promotion to full commander, which had come through several months earlier. He invited his men, their wives or girlfriends, officers from every sub in port, and a host of others to join him at the club, gaily decorated for the season in red, green, and gold. With typical flair, Bucher seeded the floor with 300 balloons, forcing guests to weave and trip hilariously among them. The grinning skipper wore yellow trousers, a candy-striped sport coat over a red vest, a bow tie, and a straw boater. A button on his lapel read, "POETS," which stood for "Piss on Everything, Tomorrow's Saturday."

Expertly holding a martini glass and a cigarette in one hand, Bucher lined up his five officers by the piano and led them in vigorous song:

"Here's to the *Pueblo*, she sure is a swell ship,

Here's to the *Pueblo*, she sure is a peach.

Boom-yakle-yakle; boom-yakle-yakle; boom-yakle-yakle . . ."

Lieutenant Steve Harris did a crazy dance amid the balloons, popping several with a cigar. Even Murphy seemed to enjoy himself. Watching the whole scene, Schumacher, himself recently promoted to lieutenant junior grade, marveled at his boss's bottomless appetite for life.

As he got to know him better, Schumacher began to think the skipper's hunger for human contact was rooted in his childhood, a period of his life so bleak it could have been conjured by Charles Dickens.

Born in 1927 in Pocatello, Idaho, he was adopted as an infant by Austin and Mary Bucher, who ran a local restaurant. Two years later, Mary died of uterine cancer and Austin, a Great War veteran and heavy drinker, went to prison for bootlegging. The toddler lived for a time with his grandparents on a small farm outside town, but they lost their land in the Depression. In 1933, they packed young Lloyd (he hadn't yet acquired his nickname), two other relatives, and their suitcases into a creaky sedan and headed for the promised land of California.

The clan settled in Long Beach, where the boy caught his first sight of what would become his life's passion, the Pacific Ocean. Bucher's grandparents got jobs managing motor-court apartments; his grandfather tried to supplement their meager income by selling vacuum cleaners door-to-door. The old couple had brought a supply of wheat from their farm, and they and the boy often boiled it for breakfast and dinner. Eventually Bucher's grandfather fell ill and quit his sales job, and his grandmother decided they could no longer afford to raise Lloyd. At age seven, he was put aboard a train by himself and sent back to his adoptive father in Idaho.

By then paroled, Austin Bucher had lost his restaurant and moved into a shack by the Snake River with half a dozen other hard-drinking vagrants. The men played endless card games, brought in women for sex, and rustled sheep from nearby farms. They taught Lloyd card tricks, but weren't at all happy about having a kid in their midst. At night, the boy often slept in a firewood bin outside the shack without benefit of blankets. He wasn't enrolled in school and spent much of his time running around with a gang of other vagabond children.

After several months, his dad was again imprisoned and the shack's remaining denizens evicted Lloyd. At a time when he should've been attending second grade, he had neither parents nor a home. To survive, he fished in the Snake and foraged in restaurant garbage cans. On cold nights he'd find a back alley and crawl into a flimsy shelter made of cardboard boxes. Sympathetic cops sometimes bought him a meal or took him to the town jail so he at least had a warm bed.

Soon he was arrested for trying to steal fishhooks from a five-and-dime store. He wound up in a Mormon orphanage in Boise, where other kids teased him mercilessly for being a "cat licker"—a Catholic. Yearning for his grandmother and the smell of salt water in Long Beach, he ran away but was quickly nabbed. At the behest of a well-to-do Catholic woman on the orphanage's board, he was sent in 1938 to a Catholic children's home in northern Idaho.

Bucher felt safer and happier there than he ever had in his life. For three years he thrived at the wilderness mission school run by the Sisters of St. Joseph. He helped milk the mission's cows and shuck its corn. He devoured the adventure novels of Robert Louis Stevenson and Rafael Sabatini, author of such stirring maritime classics as *Captain Blood* and *The Sea Hawk*.

One day Bucher read an article about the movie *Boys Town*, starring Spencer Tracy and Mickey Rooney. It told of the famous Omaha, Nebraska, home for abandoned and abused boys founded by a lanky Irish priest, Edward J. Flanagan. Besides being a bookworm, Bucher also was an aspiring athlete, and Boys Town boasted an excellent football team. The boy wrote to Father Flanagan, pleading for admittance. By the summer of 1941 he was on a train for Omaha.

Then 14, Bucher dove into the "City of Little Men" with the gusto and ebullience that were becoming his trademarks. He sang in the Boys Town choir and served as captain of the school's cadet corps, organized after the Japanese attack on Pearl Harbor. He did well in subjects he liked—math, science, and geography—and not so well in those he didn't, such as grammar and Latin. He made friends easily, as he was to do throughout his life. He read everything he got his hands on and began to envision a career in the Navy.

His favorite extracurricular activity was the football team. Though he stood only five-ten and weighed less than 160 pounds, he played tackle regularly from his sophomore year on, impressing his coach with his intelligence and hard work. Bucher and his teammates traveled by train from one end of the country to the other, going up against powerhouse squads from public as well as parochial high schools, often before huge crowds. It was during this time that the boy shed his given first name and adopted the nickname "Pete" in honor of his idol, All-America end Pete Pihos of Indiana University.

At the start of Bucher's senior year, in 1945, his peers elected the popular footballer mayor of Boys Town, a top school honor. But someone spotted him kissing an usherette at a local movie theater and informed Father Flanagan, who criticized Bucher for "irresponsibility" and stripped him of his title. Angry and embarrassed, Bucher asked the priest to sign papers so he could enlist in the Navy as a minor. Flanagan obliged and, just eight months short of graduation, Bucher dropped out, hitchhiked to San Diego, and entered boot camp.

The product of rigidly controlled institutions for much of his young life,

Bucher did well in the service. He trained as a quartermaster, honing his navigation and signaling skills aboard a supply ship in the Pacific. But the war had ended and the humdrum routine of enlisted life eventually began to bore him; he realized he'd made a mistake by not staying at Boys Town until he graduated. He wrote to a former teacher, asking for another chance. In 1946, he was granted a diploma after completing his remaining coursework by mail.

The Navy discharged him the following year and, after working as a bartender in Idaho and a farmhand in Oregon, he enrolled at the University of Nebraska in 1948. He joined a fraternity and lettered in freshman football.

On a blind date in the spring of 1949 he met Rose Rohling, a shy, pretty Missouri farm girl with silky brown hair and a brilliant smile. A devout Catholic, the 20-year-old Rose was a telephone switchboard operator in Omaha. After a summer of picnics, hand-holding, and long drives past fields fragrant with ripening wheat, Bucher had fallen hopelessly in love.

The couple married 15 days before the Korean War broke out in June 1950. The Navy recalled Bucher, but let him stay in college on the condition that he join the Naval Reserve Officers Training Corps and serve two years of active duty after graduation. In 1953, he finished his studies with a bachelor's degree in secondary education, an associate degree in geology, and some credits toward a master's in micropaleontology.

Commissioned that year as a reserve ensign, he was assigned to the USS *Mount McKinley*, a communications ship. He found Navy life much more agreeable as an officer and, about a year after reentering the service, applied for submarine school. A sub assignment, he knew, would be accompanied by hazardous-duty pay. And with a wife and, by then, two young sons in tow, he needed the money.

In 1955, Bucher moved to New London, Connecticut, for training. His neighbor and fellow classmate turned out to be Chuck Clark, future commander of the *Banner*. The two young officers became friends, sometimes getting together with their wives for an evening of charades.

But there was little time for such diversions, given the intensity of the classes. Students were expected to know how to operate every piece of equipment on a sub, how to troubleshoot electrical problems, and how to outwit and kill Russian captains. After graduating in the middle of his class, Bucher was detailed to the USS *Besugo*, a World War II–era diesel sub home-ported in San Diego.

Elevated to lieutenant, he enjoyed the challenge of navigating huge expanses of ocean. He also savored the adrenaline rush of spy missions. In the late 1950s and early 1960s, he served on three subs that engaged in surveillance of communist naval operations.

Bucher's boats sat silently outside Vladivostok harbor, watching for Soviet warships putting to sea in telltale formations that would signal the start of World War III. He and his comrades monitored Soviet torpedo tests and antisubmarine warfare exercises. When a Russian sub fired a test missile, Bucher's vessel radioed a one-letter code to another American submarine waiting near the splashdown site. The latter would then measure the telemetry and photograph the rocket as it zoomed downrange and plunged into the Pacific. In one particularly tense operation, Bucher's boat landed an agent on an empty North Korean beach.

His submarine career took him all over the Western Pacific. He visited Japan, Hong Kong, Singapore, Australia, and Tasmania. His crewmen generally ranged in age from 18 to mid-30s, and after weeks or months at sea, they were more than ready for a good time ashore in some of the Far East's most exotic ports. Among their favorite stops were the notorious red-light districts in Olongapo, near the big U.S. naval base at Subic Bay in the Philippines, and Kaohsiung, a Taiwanese port known for its government-inspected brothels.

Officers gravitated to the nearest officers' club, drinking and laughing long into the night. "Some of those parties were real down and outers," Bucher remembered. "If you didn't limit yourself to two or three drinks, you'd be there till four in the morning, singing songs. We'd be chasing women around. And the nurses! The nurses were round-heels, those Navy nurses. It wasn't that you didn't love your wife, 'cause you did. It was just that your hormones were raging. Some of the guys out there were real straight arrows. I admired them."

In 1964, Bucher was posted to Submarine Flotilla Seven, composed of half a dozen spy subs based in Yokosuka, the hub of Navy underwater surveillance operations in the Far East. As the squadron's assistant operations officer, he helped plan sub missions in conjunction with the National Security Agency and the Naval Security Group.

Bucher's boisterousness was on full display in Japan. At one party he downed 13 martinis and dumped a pitcher of water over his boss's head. "I'd jump on top of a table and start leading everyone in song," he recalled. "And I knew damn near every song that had ever been written."

Bucher's zest for life, superb navigation skills, and strong work ethic won him many friends and admirers. He knew as much if not more about Western Pacific sub operations than anyone in the Navy. In his two and a half years on the SUBFLOTSEVEN staff, his fitness reports were consistently excellent. But not everyone thought he was ready to command a sub.

"Pete Bucher was—I'm trying to choose my words carefully here—a good guy, a life-of-the-party sort of fellow," said one former superior who, even decades later, didn't want to be named. "In the wardroom he was always quick with jokes and things like that. But he wasn't a submarine commander.

"I never had the confidence with him that I had with some of the other officers. I just wasn't sure about his professional abilities—naval, technical, leave it at that. Just running a submarine. A submarine is the only vessel where one man can cause the loss of the boat. On a carrier, a cruiser, a battleship, whatever, it takes a lot of men screwing up to cause a loss. . . . It's probably a defect in my character, but Pete Bucher was a little too free and easy and all that—devil-may-care—for my taste as a submarine captain. I wanted officers that had their head screwed on right."

By 1966, Bucher was in line to get his own sub. But there were 35 other qualified officers and only 17 available boats. Bucher ranked 20th on the list of candidates, and the Bureau of Naval Personnel informed him that he wouldn't get his dream job.

The Navy captain in Washington, D.C., who'd made the ruling, Lando Zech, soon began to hear from some of Bucher's former bosses, including two captains and an admiral. All thought Zech had made a bad call. Zech couldn't reverse his decision, but he strongly recommended that Bucher be given command of the next available surface ship.

That turned out to be the *Pueblo*. And now, back in Yokosuka, Bucher made ready for his first mission, although most of his men still didn't know where they were headed.

The captain was determined to get the steering engine fixed once and for all. Navy mechanics examined it and agreed it was outmoded. But they noted its similarity to the *Banner*'s, and the other ferret hadn't had much trouble while under way. Again, Bucher would have to make do.

In some ways, however, the Navy bent over backward to help him. The *Pueblo*'s main engines were completely overhauled. To Murphy's chagrin, Bucher got a Lucite windscreen installed on the flying bridge to protect deck officers from the elements. Murphy thought the barrier was another ridiculous attempt to run the *Pueblo* like a submarine, by giving it a faux conning tower. But the skipper felt the uppermost deck gave the best visibility, and Schumacher and Tim Harris were grateful for the added comfort while on watch.

The man behind the Navy's solicitude was the *Pueblo*'s new operational commander, Rear Admiral Frank L. Johnson. The genial, white-haired Johnson was an ex–destroyer captain and holder of numerous medals, including several for bravery in World War II. Not long after the *Pueblo* arrived in Yokosuka, Bucher paid a call on Johnson, whose title was Commander, Naval Forces, Japan, or COMNAVFORJAPAN. The admiral was responsible for ensuring that the *Pueblo* was ready for sea. He also was tasked with protecting the spy boat during its voyage—even though he had no dedicated air or sea forces with which to do that, as Bucher was to discover. His grand-sounding title aside, Johnson was in charge mostly of Navy shore stations and small craft scattered throughout Japan and Okinawa. The only oceangoing ships under his direct command were the *Pueblo* and the *Banner*.

After the Israeli assault on the *Liberty*, the Navy decreed that all ships, including AGERs, be armed. When Bucher discovered that a three-inch deck gun was to be mounted on the *Pueblo*, he "almost threw a fit." Such a heavy piece of ordnance, he believed, could capsize his little vessel the first time it fired. Navy officials relented and decided to arm the *Pueblo* with three

.50-caliber machine guns instead. But Admiral Johnson didn't approve of even the lighter weapons. Their presence, he felt, destroyed the logic that the spy boats' best protection was their very lack of armament. And in a real fight, the machine guns weren't powerful enough to hold off anything larger than an armed junk. An enemy equipped with a single deck cannon could pound the *Pueblo* to pieces from thousands of yards away with no fear of ever being hit by .50-caliber slugs.

Bucher agreed with Johnson's analysis. Originally, the *Pueblo* carried only a handful of small arms: Thompson submachine guns, rifles, .45-caliber pistols, and some fragmentation grenades for use against enemy swimmers. Its lone gunner's mate had no experience with heavy machine guns.

The Navy eventually delivered only two machine guns, and neither had an armored shield to protect gunners from enemy fire. Bucher mounted one weapon on a railing on the starboard side of the bow and the other near the stern.

While it foisted unwanted weapons on Bucher, the Navy also kept adding to his pile of classified documents, with more paper accumulating each time the ship reported to a new command. CINCPACFLT had contributed to the stash, and so did COMNAVFORJAPAN. Someone forgot the *Pueblo* was no longer a cargo ship and sent it an AKL's allotment of intelligence publications. Somebody else screwed up and delivered documents intended for a converted escort carrier.

Now the *Pueblo* groaned under the weight of a small mountain of secret papers. They overflowed the storage lockers, forcing the communication technicians to stack the excess in passageways. Some of the documents—such as instructions on routing mail—probably didn't merit a "secret" stamp. But others were highly sensitive, including a report on the Pacific Fleet's intelligence collection program and a memo outlining the fleet's electronic warfare policy. Also on board was a copy of the North Korean "electronic order of battle," indicating the location and frequencies of all known radar and radio stations. If war broke out, that document would guide U.S. jets and warships as they tried to knock out or jam critical enemy defenses.

In addition to all the classified paper, the *Pueblo* carried several types of top secret code machines. One was the KW-7, a compact device that transmitted encrypted messages between Navy ships and shore stations at a rate of more than 50 words per minute. The KW-7 was the workhorse of U.S. military communications, widely used by Army, Navy, Air Force, and Marine units from Vietnam to Germany. Another machine, the KWR-37, deciphered "fleet broadcast" messages sent to all U.S. warships around the clock. Each mechanism came with a special set of codes to operate it.

Bucher requested permission to offload part of this extraordinary cache, to make sure it never fell into enemy hands. Admiral Johnson consented, but the *Pueblo* still was left with a large quantity of classified documents and at least a dozen code machines—and no fast, reliable means of getting rid of them in an emergency.

Bucher began scouring Yokosuka for submarine-style dynamite canisters. The Naval Ordnance Facility on Azuma Island had none, so he contacted old friends at SUBFLOTSEVEN to see if he could take some TNT from a sub rotating back to the States. No luck. He talked to Chuck Clark, who opposed bringing explosives on the *Banner.* Bucher finally gave up, lest Admiral Johnson conclude he was more interested in blowing up his ship than in executing his mission.

Even as the captain grappled with these and other problems, his relationship with the man he should've been relying on most for help—Murphy—continued to deteriorate.

The executive officer's pregnant wife and toddler son had arrived in Japan in mid-December, and Bucher thought he was attending to his duties even less diligently than usual. For one thing, the ship's office, which Murphy oversaw, was a mess, with paperwork backing up despite the best efforts of the *Pueblo*'s affable yeoman, Armando "Army" Canales.

Bucher was tired of having to hunt down Murphy whenever he needed him, and had concluded that his deputy simply wasn't up to the job. The captain thought about relieving Murphy of duty but procrastinated, knowing such a drastic move would destroy the younger man's career. He felt he owed Murphy at least one trip to the Sea of Japan to prove himself. Nevertheless, Bucher drafted a letter requesting Murphy's replacement. He showed it to the exec and told him to shape up, or else.

The tension between the two officers subsided somewhat in early January

1968, as the *Pueblo*'s departure date neared. Several new CTs came aboard at the last minute, as did two civilian oceanographers; they and their water-sampling equipment substantiated the cover story that the *Pueblo* was merely engaged in scientific surveys.

Among the late arrivals was Robert Hammond, a wiry 22-year-old Marine sergeant with piercing eyes who was supposed to serve as a Korean translator on the voyage.

He reported aboard along with another Marine sergeant trained in Korean, Bob Chicca. The two noncoms were to listen in on North Korean voice communications around the clock and tell Bucher if any aggressive moves were made against his ship. But both men had told superiors at the Kamiseya communication facility, their normal duty station, that they hadn't used their Korean since 1965, had forgotten much of it, and would be of little use to Bucher. Chicca still understood a little of the language, but only when it was spoken slowly. The sergeants' protests were to no avail, however. With the *Pueblo* scheduled to sail only a few days later, there was no time to replace them.

Scuttlebutt about the ostensible linguists spread quickly, with more and more crewmen figuring out their true destination.

On the morning of January 4, Bucher, Murphy, Steve Harris, and Schumacher caught a ride to Admiral Johnson's headquarters for a presail briefing. The admiral's intelligence staff provided a long-range weather report and pointed out North Korean coastal defenses on a map. They discussed recent clashes between communist and allied troops in the demilitarized zone separating the two Koreas, as well as North Korea's aggressive harassment of South Korean fishing boats north of the seaward extension of the DMZ. North Korean patrol craft probably would pester the *Pueblo*, they said, but nothing more.

As he had in Hawaii, Bucher asked what kind of help he could expect if he was attacked. The briefers confirmed that no Navy warships would be close enough to bail him out. Should he use his new machine guns against a boarding party? Definitely, said Captain Thomas Dwyer, Johnson's assistant chief of staff for intelligence. If the communists kept coming, should he destroy his classified materials? Yes again.

Admiral Johnson appeared toward the end of the briefing. He reiterated his opposition to arming the AGERs, telling Bucher such action "could lead to trouble for you for which you are not prepared." He urged the skipper to "keep your guns covered and pointed down, or, better yet, stow them belowdecks."

Bucher had invited Chuck Clark to the briefing, and the *Banner* skipper said he intended to keep his guns belowdecks. After the meeting, Bucher argued with Clark about hiding his weapons. If the Navy's top leaders wanted spy boats armed, then so be it. Bucher said his guns would stay on their mounts, visible to the North Koreans and ready for action.

"If those bastards come out after me," he pledged fiercely, "they're not going to get me."

The next morning, Johnson personally inspected the *Pueblo.* He cast a wary eye on Bucher's .50-calibers, draped with heavy canvas tarpaulins.

"Remember, you're not going out there to start a war, Captain," he said. "Make sure you keep them covered and don't use them in any provocative way at all. It doesn't take much to set those damned communists off and start an international incident. That's the last thing we want!"

CHAPTER 3

ALONG A DREAD COAST

The *Pueblo* began backing out of its berth shortly after nine a.m. on January 5, 1968.

Bucher perched proudly on the flying bridge; directly below him in the pilothouse, Schumacher called orders to the helmsman. Some of the skipper's sub buddies had gathered in the wardroom earlier that morning to toast his departure with eggnog, and now they were waving good-bye from the dock. Bucher serenaded them with "The Lonely Bull."

The captain had decided against taking the northern route, over the top of Hokkaido island, because of winter storms. Instead, the *Pueblo* would head southwest, sailing around Kyushu at the bottom of the Japanese archipelago. Bucher then would turn north, top off his tanks at the port of Sasebo, and continue through the Tsushima Strait toward North Korea.

Within hours of leaving Yokosuka, the *Pueblo*'s officers noticed the rapidly alternating swells and troughs of a "young sea," the harbinger of a newborn storm. The weather deteriorated abruptly. The sun fled behind menacing dark clouds and the air temperature plummeted. Freezing salt spray whipped the faces of sailors mopping the open decks. The winds rose; the sea began to heave.

The *Pueblo* pitched and rolled madly as the storm overtook it. Over and over, the little ship staggered up the face of an oncoming wave, toppled over its crest, and slewed crazily down its back. Steering became so difficult that a second helmsman had to be summoned to help the first control the wheel. High winds and steep waves pushed the boat so far over that the railings on its main deck disappeared in the foaming water. The inclinometer recorded rolls of up to 57 degrees.

The wild seesawing created chaos belowdecks, flinging men, chairs, desks, and electronic gear around like toys. Thrown off balance by one sharp tilt, a young radioman hurtled down a passageway and crashed into Bucher, knocking him to the floor.

"Jesus Christ, sir, I'm sorry!" the sailor said with a gasp. "Are you hurt?"

The two men clung to each other as the ship careened over in another wide roll. Bucher said he was okay, that he was counting on the radioman to keep his equipment up and running in the storm.

The sailor gave a wan smile and adjusted his water-spattered glasses.

"Yes, sir, I'll be ready. But right now—excuse me, sir, but I've got to puke." He ran off along the lurching passageway.

Bucher saw fear in his men's faces as they wondered whether their frail cockleshell of a boat could survive all this twisting and pounding. Almost everybody was throwing up, even experienced hands. One of the few exceptions was Quartermaster Charlie Law, who seemed steadied by some internal gyroscope as he calmly marked the ship's slow progress on a chart.

The storm appeared to be moving in the same direction as the *Pueblo*. Bucher hoped to escape the worst of it when he swung north toward Sasebo. But the tempest, perversely, pivoted with him, tearing at his ship as it fought its way past the threatening shoals of Kyushu's west coast. Waves surged higher as contrary currents in the area collided. Hail, rain, and snow pelted the ship, and the wind accelerated to 50 knots—a force-ten gale. A big antenna snapped off in the rising howl.

So loud was the storm that the men in the engine room had to communicate by hand signals. In the forward berthing compartment, fetid with vomit and anxiety, shoes and other personal items floated on several inches of sloshing water. Men's heads, elbows, and knees slammed into hard metal objects, inducing shrieks of pain.

Communication technicians skittered across the SOD hut deck in unsecured chairs, banging into steel consoles and gauges. Someone on the bridge tried to warn the men below by yelling, "Roll!" over the public address system each time the ship started to shift. But the CTs got bashed anyway, since their chamber lacked a loudspeaker. Two generators supplying electricity to the hut went dead.

In the dizzily swaying pilothouse, Bucher struggled to keep the ship from skidding sideways in a trough and getting flipped over by the next wave. He applied power alternately to the port and starboard propellers, trying to keep moving in a relatively straight line. The steering engine was holding so far. But after another round of vertiginous rolls, the skipper ran for shelter in the lee of a coastal island.

A few hours later, as the big blow subsided and the crew recovered somewhat, Bucher ordered the *Pueblo* to get under way again for Sasebo, still 100 miles away. Weary from his exertions on the bridge, the captain turned the conn over to Tim Harris and descended to his stateroom for a brief rest. He'd dozed for no more than an hour when the buzzing telephone next to his bunk woke him. He picked it up and heard a heart-stopping report from his inexperienced ensign:

"Captain, we are on course, but I think I see breakers about a half mile dead ahead."

It was one of a ship commander's worst fears. The *Pueblo* was headed directly toward a large rock.

"Back down emergency full!" Bucher shouted into the phone, ordering the twin diesels thrown into reverse. "And come dead in the water! I'll be right up there."

He raced to the bridge. Sure enough, there was the deadly black mass, ringed by white breakers and looming out of the slanting rain 1,000 yards away. Bucher sweated blood for several minutes while he maneuvered away from the reef and took soundings to make certain the *Pueblo* had enough water under its keel to proceed safely.

Harris had been following a course plotted by Ed Murphy. If not for the ensign's timely call to his captain, the ship might be getting battered and gouged to death right now. Bucher could barely contain his anger. He remained on the bridge just long enough to chart a new course for the shaken Harris. Then he returned to his quarters and summoned Murphy.

The captain demanded an explanation of what he viewed as a stupid and potentially fatal navigation error. The exec replied that it wasn't his fault; his course had been accurate, but young Harris hadn't followed it correctly. Bucher felt himself losing it.

"Jesus Christ, mister!" he yelled. "Don't you think maybe you should get the hell out of this business? . . . Shit, man! After all the time and chances you've had, do you really expect me to take this kind of crap from you?"

Murphy stared in distress at his superior.

"I laid out the course as carefully as I could in these conditions, Captain," he replied, a defiant note in his voice.

"You are my executive and navigation officer!" Bucher bellowed. "If I can't rely on you in those duties, what the hell use are you?"

Murphy's Adam's apple bobbed up and down. "Yes, sir, Captain, I'm trying my best, but . . ."

"It's not good enough!"

A pained silence followed, broken only by the moan of the wind and the crash of green seas on the decks above. Murphy made a stab at a formal exit, trying to come to attention in the rolling cabin and almost missing the door as he walked out. Bucher was convinced the time had finally come to get rid of his XO. But still he couldn't bring himself to take such drastic action during this inaugural mission.

At least Bucher now knew exactly what the mission was. Admiral Johnson's headquarters had radioed him the last details after the *Pueblo* left Yokosuka. The main objective was to collect fresh information on North Korean shore defenses. The hermetic communist state was believed to have both antiaircraft and antiship missile batteries along its mountainous east coast. Bucher's crew was to sail to a point near North Korea's border with the Soviet Union and then turn around and move slowly south, sampling the electronic environment and making visual observations. The Navy and the National Security Agency were particularly interested in coastal radar.

The *Pueblo* also was to observe North Korean naval activity, including any movements of the four Soviet-made submarines the North Koreans were suspected of operating out of the port of Mayang-do. After about two weeks, Bucher and his men would head back to Japan, photographing and listening to Soviet warships along the way.

Throughout the voyage the *Pueblo* was to maintain strict emission control, meaning its radar and radios were to be kept off unless Bucher was certain his ship had been identified. Only then was he to transmit situation reports to COMNAVFORJAPAN. At no time should the ferret creep closer than 13 nautical miles to the North Korean mainland or offshore islands; the Navy wanted to make sure it stayed outside the communists' claimed 12-mile territorial limit.

Admiral Johnson also reiterated his verbal instruction that the machine guns be covered or stowed. The captain was to use them, in the terse language of his sailing order, "only in cases where threat to survival is obvious." But since the ship would operate entirely in international waters, the order continued, the mission's risk was rated "minimal." Once again, Bucher was led to believe that a high-seas assault was unlikely.

The *Pueblo* arrived in Sasebo on January 9, already behind schedule due to the storm. For the first few hours most of the seamen simply rested, recovering from the stomach-inverting first leg of their journey. Then they began getting ready for the next segment. The boat had to be cleaned up and tossed-about gear put back in place. A hairline crack had appeared in the hull; Japanese divers went down to repair it.

Lieutenant Steve Harris offloaded more excess classified documents—15 sealed containers in all. But to his dismay he discovered that enough new paper was being delivered to the ship in Sasebo to more than offset what he'd gotten rid of. Why was it that seemingly every Navy command in the Pacific wanted to give him this stuff? So large was the volume of material, he realized, that it couldn't possibly fit into the canvas bags in which it was supposed to be dumped overboard in an emergency.

Although Bucher had expected only a 12-hour layover in Sasebo, repairs and refitting took nearly two days.

The ship was to depart at six a.m. on January 11. At five a.m., a courier arrived with even more classified publications for Steve Harris's heap. At 5:45 a.m., Bucher rushed aboard after a long night of drinking and playing cards ashore.

Less than half an hour later, the *Pueblo* edged out of Sasebo harbor. Despite his lack of sleep, Bucher had the conn. Nearby was Charlie Law, navigating in the chilly predawn darkness.

The captain had given Law more navigation watches after the near-miss with the reef, and that delighted the quartermaster. He loved the Navy and was proud to the point of cockiness of his talents as a course plotter. He also was grateful to Bucher for qualifying him as an officer of the deck, meaning Law could steer the ship on his own, a rare and exalted station for an enlisted man.

A tenth-grade dropout, the barrel-chested quartermaster had spent his adolescence in Tacoma, Washington, a blue-collar city permeated by the stench from surrounding mills that sawed and pulped the rich forests of the Olympic Peninsula into wood and paper products. His parents split up when he was four, and his no-nonsense mother raised him with money she made running a tiny greasy spoon. Law tried to enlist at 15, lying about his age and telling the recruiter the timeworn fable that his birth certificate had been destroyed in a fire at the county hospital. But his mother refused to sign the papers. The day he turned 17, he enlisted on his own.

He worked mostly as a deck ape, chipping paint and mopping decks aboard a Navy tug, an oil tanker, and a supply ship based in Japan. He was a brash kid, a smart-ass, but he learned fast. Somewhere along the line, a senior quartermaster took Law under his wing and taught him the fine points of shooting stars and fixing a ship's position.

Law's prowess with the sextant and pelorus made him someone aboard ship. He had exceptional vision, 20/13 in one eye, 20/14 in the other. He often competed with Bucher, himself an excellent navigator, to spot the first evening star, and Law usually won. He liked that officers depended on him, made important decisions based on his calculations. They simply took his word for where they were. "And I always knew where we were at," he said in an interview many years later, his pride still evident. "It was the only thing I was really that good at in my life."

In the eyes of many younger sailors, Law, at 26, was a respected old salt. He didn't need chevrons on his sleeves to establish his authority; he was one of those men whose presence is more imposing than his rank. "He was a sailor first and foremost and made no bones about it," said a shipmate. "I don't recall anyone ever telling him a lifer joke."

Law helped guide the *Pueblo* into the Tsushima Strait, where the imperial Japanese navy had crushed the Russian tsar's fleet in a historic 1905 duel. Bucher intended to hug the Kyushu coast as long as possible, hiding among Japanese fishing boats and hoping Soviet naval units didn't spot him. Then he'd angle north-by-northwest for the six-hundred-mile run across the Sea of Japan.

At first, the *Pueblo* encountered only moderate swells. But by nightfall, with land no longer in sight, the freezing Siberian wind grew stronger and snow flecked the air. It was so cold in the forward berths that one sailor crawled into bed wearing two shirts, two pairs of socks, pants, a work jacket, and a wool cap. Another rough winter storm was at hand.

The seas butting the bow head-on became so heavy that Bucher had to tack back and forth, as if he were beating upwind in a nineteenth-century schooner. Even on this zigzag course, the *Pueblo* rolled as badly as it had on the way to Sasebo. Seasickness again erupted among the crew, especially the greener CTs. A particularly steep pitch sent one of them clattering in his chair right out the door of the SOD hut.

Gradually the energy went out of the storm. The captain held drills on the machine guns, checking how long it took to uncover, load, and fire them. The shortest time was ten minutes, the longest more than an hour. The guns were difficult to aim and jammed frequently. Sailors heaved 50-gallon drums over the side and tried to hole them. Even at less than fifty yards, they often missed.

By January 13, the ship lay opposite Wonsan, the biggest and most heavily defended port on North Korea's east coast. Bucher still was maintaining strict electronic silence. The *Pueblo* had dropped out of the Navy's movement reporting system, so no one on Admiral Johnson's staff knew exactly where it was. Bucher kept sailing north, paralleling the coast thirty to forty miles out to sea. At night, the spy boat cruised with its running lights doused.

So far the North Koreans hadn't reacted, and the sailors settled into a daily rhythm. Breakfast was served at six a.m., lunch at eleven, and supper at five p.m. The food was plentiful but nothing to write home about. The chief cook, Harry Lewis, was pretty good, but the minuscule galley cramped his style. Movies were shown twice a day in the wardroom or crew's mess. Among the available titles were *Twelve Angry Men*, *The Desperate Hours*, *In Like Flint*, and several romantic comedies.

A poker game went on day and night in the forward berth area, new players taking the place of those who had to go on watch. Unable to shake his seasickness, Tim Harris stayed in his bunk most of the time. Before dawn one morning, a sailor delivering a weather report found Bucher in the wardroom wearing a T-shirt, khaki pants, sneakers, and sunglasses. The old man never seemed to sleep.

The sharpest break in the routine came one day when Schumacher accidentally threw the ship into a 40-degree roll.

Bucher had decided that the *Pueblo* was too close to shore and told Schumacher to change course and get some sea room. It was lunchtime and belowdecks the cooks were serving spaghetti from big tubs.

Schumacher ordered left full rudder and immediately realized the ocean was rougher than he'd thought. "Stand by for heavy rolls!" he yelled into the voice tube. Halfway through the turn the ship stopped. It wouldn't go any farther. Heavy seas struck it broadside, pushing it far over.

Spaghetti flew everywhere. In the wardroom, Ensign Harris toppled over in his chair and slid on his side right out the door. The captain's books and *Playboy* magazines shot out of his stateroom into a passageway.

"What the hell's going on up there, Skip?" Bucher shouted over the intercom.

"Trying to come around, Captain," the stricken lieutenant replied. "It's a little worse up here than I thought."

"You realize you just cost us our lunch?"

"Yes, sir."

Ten minutes later, Bucher joined Schumacher on the bridge and calmly explained how such turns should be executed. The crew wound up eating cold cuts and broken potato chips. Unwilling to face their wrath, Schumacher retreated to his cabin with a bag of peanuts.

On January 16, the *Pueblo* reached its first objective: the port of Chongjin, just south of the Soviet border. Bucher stopped about 15 miles offshore. The world seemed drained of color: The sky was a gray smear, the sea a vast sheet of hammered lead. In the distance rose black mountains, summits daubed white. Peering through the "big eyes," twenty-two-inch binoculars mounted on the flying bridge, the captain and Schumacher could see smoke curling out of factory chimneys. They also saw North Korean torpedo boats patrolling the mouth of the nearby Tumen River.

In the SOD hut, the CTs straightened up and got to work. After weeks and in some cases months of idleness and menial tasks, they were excited about finally performing the top secret specialties they'd trained for. But their equipment picked up little military traffic. Only a few freighters and fishing boats ventured out of Chongjin in the frigid winter weather.

Its topsides coated with snow and ice, the *Pueblo* began to resemble a ghost ship. The growing weight made the captain uneasy. He calculated that his vessel could flip upside down with as little as four inches of ice on its superstructure and exposed decks. He ordered a work detail onto the main deck with steam hoses, but the melted ice refroze before it spilled over the sides. The men then attacked with scrapers, wooden mallets, and shovels.

Freezing air stung their lungs, but they made progress. Bucher joined in the chipping and, when the job was finished, goaded his men into a snowball fight. That evening, he made sure each member of the deicing party had a small bottle of brandy to warm up with.

After two days of surveillance, the intelligence take from Chongjin was negligible. Disappointed, Bucher headed south for his next stop, the port of Songjin. He kept the ship 13 to 16 miles from shore during daylight, and withdrew at night to 25 to 30 miles. The captain instructed Law to crosshatch the navigation charts with a red pencil to the west of the 13-mile barrier, and to draw a thick blue line at 14 miles from shore. Navigators were under orders to call Bucher to the bridge if they even approached the blue mark.

On the morning of January 19, the spy boat was 15 miles east of Songjin. Frustrated CTs were acquiring precious little data. They'd pick up an electronic signal and, after the ship traveled a bit farther, pick it up again. In theory, recording the same signal from two different angles pinpointed the sending station. On a chart, two lines were drawn toward the signal from the two points at which it was detected; the lines' intersection indicated the signal's point of origin. But the SOD hut receivers weren't accurate and most of the lines didn't cross. In cases where they did, the sending station was invariably marked on the charts already. Boredom again blossomed among the CTs.

The *Pueblo* drifted farther south. Steve Harris confided to Murphy that North Korean fire-control radar had locked on the ship. The XO knew that didn't necessarily mean the *Pueblo* was in danger. But it was a little disconcerting that the communists were tracking them.

Bucher still hoped to photograph a North Korean submarine in the vicinity of Mayang-do. Such a coup would make the whole mission worthwhile. But no subs appeared, heightening the commander's sense that he was wasting his time. He wrote in a report that the voyage to date had been "unproductive." Schumacher wryly concluded that he'd learned an important lesson about the North Koreans: Unlike the half-frozen crew of the *Pueblo*, they knew better than to wander about the Sea of Japan in the dead of winter.

While the CTs' annoyance grew, the two civilian oceanographers were quite pleased with the way their work was going.

Dunnie Tuck and Harry Iredale were a study in contrasts. Tuck, who'd served on the *Banner* the previous summer during trips to the USSR and China, was an almost maniacally gregarious Virginia native. Balding at 30, he was a funny, storytelling charmer who boasted of many romantic conquests. His nickname was, of course, Friar. His 24-year-old sidekick, Iredale, a bright, bespectacled former Penn State math major, was shy and fidgety, painfully aware of his short stature, and luckless at bedding women. He, too, had served briefly aboard the *Banner*.

Twice a day, the two men walked to the well deck and dropped over the side a dozen yellow Nansen bottles attached at intervals to a long wire. Later they winched the heavy brass canisters back up and tested the water samples from different depths for salinity, sound conductivity, and temperature. The measurements provided the veneer of peaceful research, but they had important military applications as well, particularly in submarine operations.

The *Pueblo* arrived off Wonsan early on the morning of January 22.

Besides having a busy harbor, the city served as a major railroad hub that American warships had shelled repeatedly during the Korean War. It was well defended by antiaircraft batteries and dozens of MiG fighters. In the SOD hut, the CTs finally began to get some interesting signals.

Shortly after lunch Gene Lacy called from the bridge to report two North Korean trawlers approaching. The captain hurried up for a look. He ordered Schumacher to join him and the CTs to tune in on the trawlers' communications. The rest of the crew picked up on the ripple of activity; seamen rushed up to the main deck to watch the action.

Both boats carried nets and other fishing gear and appeared to be unarmed. Their smokestacks were emblazoned with a red star inside a white circle.

The trawlers began slowly circling the *Pueblo* from about five hundred yards away. Their crewmen all seemed to be on deck, pointing and talking excitedly. Suddenly one of the vessels changed course and charged toward the spy ship, veering off when it was just one hundred yards away.

Some *Pueblo* sailors raised their middle fingers at the passing North Koreans. Bucher ordered everyone below, hoping the communists wouldn't wonder why so many men were on such a small boat. The two trawler captains then withdrew several miles and pulled close together, as if conferring. At about two p.m., they headed back toward the *Pueblo*. Fearing a ramming, Bucher fired up his engines. The trawlers steamed to within twenty-five yards and began circling again, their crews taking photographs. The communists' faces were clearly visible and, as one *Pueblo* sailor noted, "They looked like they wanted to eat our livers."

Bucher called one of the Marine translators, Bob Chicca, to the bridge to decipher the trawlers' names. Armed with a Korean dictionary, Chicca gazed intently at the vessels.

"One of them is *Rice Paddy* and the other is *Rice Paddy One*, Captain," he said.

Bucher still was observing emission control, but he figured the *Pueblo*—with "GER-2" painted on its hull in large white letters—had definitely been identified this time. At three p.m. both trawlers withdrew to the northeast. The captain began to prepare a situation report, or SITREP in Navy jargon, to inform COMNAVFORJAPAN of what had happened.

By about five p.m., the narrative was ready and a radioman opened a circuit to Kamiseya.

The North Korean commando stared through his field glasses at the big city spread out below him. He hadn't expected Seoul to look so beautiful and prosperous.

The morning mist had lifted on Pibong Hill, north of the South Korean capital, where Second Lieutenant Kim Shin-jo and his thirty fellow guerrillas lay hidden. From the hillside they could see their target: the South Korean presidential mansion, known as the Blue House. Come nightfall, the infiltrators planned to shoot their way into the building and cut off the head of South Korea's iron-fisted president, Park Chung Hee. Then they'd kill his family and staff, steal vehicles from the presidential motor pool, and escape.

It was Sunday, January 21.

Kim and his comrades were officers in North Korea's highly trained 124th Army Unit, which specialized in unconventional warfare and political subversion. For two years they'd practiced behind-the-lines fighting as part of North Korean dictator Kim Il Sung's ruthless scheme to foment revolution in South Korea and reunify the peninsula by force. The communists hoped President Park's assassination would create political chaos in the south, giving North Korean troops a pretext to march in and "stabilize" the country.

The members of Lieutenant Kim's platoon were in superb physical condition and armed to the teeth. Their ages ranged from 24 to 28. With leg muscles hardened by running with several pounds of sand sewn into their trouser cuffs, the men could cover a herculean six miles of rugged terrain an hour with sixty pounds of equipment on their backs. Each officer carried a Russian-made submachine gun, a semiautomatic pistol, three hundred rounds of ammunition, eight antipersonnel grenades, and an antitank grenade. If their guns jammed, they'd fight with their bare hands and feet, every man having mastered judo and karate.

To prepare for the attack, the commandos had studied Blue House floor plans and staged mock assaults on a two-story North Korean army barracks. On the night of January 17, their unit was bused to a checkpoint in the demilitarized zone. From there guides led them to a chain-link fence recently erected to keep out North Korean intruders. The guerrillas cut through the barrier and slipped past soldiers from the U.S. 2nd Infantry Division who were supposed to guard that sector.

The North Koreans slept during the day and moved fast over snowy hills at night. On the afternoon of January 19, four South Korean brothers cutting firewood stumbled across them. Some squad members wanted to kill the brothers, but their leader, a 24-year-old captain, said no. Instead, the North Koreans harangued the woodcutters for several hours about the glories of socialism under Kim Il Sung. The brothers were released with a warning not to inform South Korean authorities, or the communists would return to kill their families and burn down their village.

The woodcutters, however, immediately alerted local police, who in turn informed the South Korean army. Security was tightened in Seoul, and South Korean and American troops began scouring the countryside north of the capital. Soon more than 6,000 soldiers and policemen were in the hunt. But the raiders were traveling faster than expected and eluded their pursuers.

On the night of January 21, wearing brown coats over South Korean army fatigues, the commandos slipped into Seoul. They'd tuned in on busy police and army radio frequencies and formulated a bold strategy for dodging the search operation. By ten p.m., they'd shed their overcoats and were brazenly marching through the streets in column formation.

Less than half a mile from the Blue House, a suspicious Seoul policeman challenged them. The North Koreans claimed they were southern troops, returning from an antiguerrilla patrol in the mountains, and kept marching. Unsatisfied, the cop called his superiors, and the district police chief hurried to the scene in a jeep.

When the chief asked for more identification, the commandos' nerves snapped. They shot him and hurled grenades at nearby transit buses as a diversion, killing a driver, a conductor, and a 16-year-old boy on his way home from the library. Someone fired a flare into the night sky; its glare threw the cityscape into eerie relief. The communists fled in all directions.

Gunfire and grenade explosions punctuated the rest of that night and the next day as the infiltrators tried to claw their way out of Seoul. One of them hopped from rooftop to rooftop until he crashed through the tiles into the home of a 32-year-old man who worked for the South Korean information ministry. The man grappled with the guerrilla while his sister flailed at him with a rubber sandal. The struggle went on until the intruder finally shot and killed the South Korean man.

By the end of the first full day of the manhunt, five commandos had been killed. A sixth evidently committed suicide with a hidden grenade while under interrogation at National Police headquarters. Lieutenant Kim was captured.

Although it failed, the plot to murder President Park badly rattled South Koreans. Seoul was reported to be in a state of "extreme tension." Hoarding by citizens afraid of more attacks or even war drove the price of rice sharply higher. The black-market value of the dollar jumped against the South Korean won as affluent southerners converted their assets into more stable U.S. currency.

South Korean authorities interrogated Lieutenant Kim and made him the star of a sensational press conference. He claimed he and his comrades originally had several targets in Seoul. Besides killing Park, they planned to murder the American ambassador and his wife, attack South Korean army headquarters, and blow open the gates of a prison that held communist agents. But shortly before leaving North Korea, the hit team decided to concentrate on the Blue House. Kim also revealed that 2,400 other North Korean soldiers were in training to carry out guerrilla attacks and instigate revolution in the south.

In the snow-blanketed countryside north of Seoul, meanwhile, the remorseless search for the remaining commandos went on. Allied soldiers pursued them with helicopters, armored personnel carriers, and dogs. They waited in ambush holes dug in the frozen earth and broke up ice covering the Imjin River near the DMZ, so no one could cross on foot.

One by one, the exhausted North Koreans still at large were cornered and killed. Troops shot one to death at a farmhouse where he'd stopped to beg for food. The young captain who'd led the assassination squad met his end on a rocky hilltop after refusing to surrender. Another infiltrator was slain just five miles south of the DMZ. Only two were believed to have made it home.

The attempted assault on the Blue House was an astonishing act of international savagery that might well have touched off a new Korean War had it succeeded. The South Korean army was placed on maximum alert; North Korea braced for possible retaliatory attacks by Park's forces.

Bucher and his men arrived off Wonsan the morning after the Blue House raid was broken up. It was an extraordinarily tense moment. North Korea easily could have interpreted an intelligence ship lurking near a key port as a scout for a counterattack, a dire threat that must quickly be neutralized.

Yet no one bothered to inform Bucher of the incendiary events in Seoul, or of how the North Koreans might now be expected to react to his ship.

CHAPTER 4

SOS SOS SOS

Bucher rolled out of bed just before seven a.m. on January 23. He hadn't slept much. It had taken nearly 14 hours for his SITREP of the previous afternoon to reach Kamiseya, in part because of heavy traffic on frequencies the *Pueblo* used. The captain had anxiously checked with his radiomen during the night; any communications delay was worrisome, but one this long was dangerous. Now, feeling tired and stiff, he shuffled into the wardroom for a cup of coffee. The ship smelled sour; Bucher resolved to tell the men to air out their bedding.

Fortified with caffeine, the skipper pulled himself up the ladder to the flying bridge and joined Gene Lacy, that morning's officer of the deck. The weather was improving. The temperature had risen to a tolerable 20 degrees, and a four-knot wind was blowing out of the northwest. The sea undulated with gentle swells; high, thin clouds reflected the first pale fingers of dawn.

Bucher checked the ship's position: 25 miles out. He told Lacy to close to 15 miles, making it easier for the CTs to detect radio or radar emanations from Wonsan. Then he went back down to the wardroom for breakfast, convinced this was to be another routine day in the Sea of Japan.

By ten a.m., the captain could clearly see the islands of Ung-do and Yo-do, lying at the mouth of the large bay that leads to Wonsan. As he had done ever since the near-shipwreck on the way to Sasebo, Bucher double-checked Murphy's navigation. Then he rang up all-stop on the annunciator. The *Pueblo* went dead in the water exactly 15.5 miles from the nearest landfall. He saw no activity outside Wonsan—not a single patrol boat, freighter, or fishing vessel. Aside from yesterday's excitement with the trawlers, the communists seemed to be ignoring the American ship. Bucher felt a bit disappointed.

Friar Tuck and Harry Iredale ambled out on deck for their daily plumb of the depths. A work party came topside to clear snow and ice that had accumulated during the night. With the temperature edging higher, there was little buildup. Bucher heard the rhythmic sloshing of the ship's superannuated washing machine as it cranked to life in the fo'c'sle with the first laundry of the day.

Steve Harris called from the SOD hut to report that the CTs were picking up signals from two search radars conducting normal sweeps. There was also something new: voices on North Korean radio channels.

"Anything indicating an interest in us?" Bucher asked.

"Not that we can read, Captain. Probably routine traffic, but we're recording and will go back over the tapes."

Bucher had no use for that process. Taping and translating the communist chatter would take hours, as the two Marine sergeants went over the recordings inch by inch with Korean dictionaries in hand. They were supposed to be Bucher's early-warning system, but their inability to translate in real time meant he had to guess at what the communists were up to. To reassure himself, he again scanned the coast with his binoculars: still no movement.

It seemed as if the *Pueblo* were the only ship in the world.

At noon the captain was back in the wardroom for lunch. The mess was into its second seating, 25 men digging into generous portions of meat loaf, mashed potatoes, gravy, and succotash. Lacy, who'd turned over the conn to Charlie Law, squeezed in with the rest of the officers.

"Everything okay on your watch, Gene?" Bucher asked.

"Yes, sir," the chief engineer answered, smiling. "And we're catching up with some housekeeping in this nice weather."

"Yeah, almost like the balmy winters on Newfoundland's Grand Banks," cracked Schumacher.

A call from the bridge interrupted the conversation. Law reported an unidentified vessel approaching from about eight miles away. Bucher told him to call again if it got within five miles. The officers continued talking and eating; there was no cause for alarm. The captain had tucked into his second helping of meat loaf when the phone buzzed again. The alien craft was now five miles out and closing rapidly.

Maybe this wasn't such an ordinary day after all.

Bucher dropped his fork and hurried to the bridge. The air was noticeably colder; the sun glowed weakly through wintry overcast. He focused the big eyes on the incoming vessel and made a tentative identification: a submarine chaser, flying a North Korean ensign and bearing down on the *Pueblo* at flank speed.

The sight irritated the captain; leave it to these godless bastards to interrupt his midday meal. He called for Schumacher and Steve Harris to join him on the bridge. To reinforce the *Pueblo*'s facade as a research vessel, Bucher told Tuck and Iredale to lower their Nansen bottles. Then he ordered his signalman to hoist flags indicating oceanographic activity.

The sub chaser kept coming. Bucher clambered down to the pilothouse to recheck the *Pueblo*'s position. It had drifted farther out, floating 15.9 miles from Ung-do. The captain returned to the flying bridge with Harris, who studied the communist boat and flipped through his identification book.

"She's a Russian-built, modified SO-1-class submarine chaser," the lieutenant concluded, confirming Bucher's ID. Modern versions of such craft, 138 feet in length, were armed with two 25-millimeter antiaircraft guns and four 16-inch torpedo tubes. This one also had a 57-millimeter deck cannon.

On its bow the gunboat displayed the number 35.

"Get below," Bucher told Harris, "and find out if your CTs can eavesdrop on any talk with her base."

Unbeknown to the captain, a U.S. reconnaissance aircraft at that moment was flying about 50 nautical miles east of his position, listening to North Korean military channels. The crew of the Air Force C-130 heard the North Koreans dispatch several warships to intercept the *Pueblo*.

"We have approached the target here," sub chaser No. 35 radioed as it sped toward Bucher's boat. *"It is U.S. Did you get it? It looks like it's armed now. . . . I think it's a radar ship. It also has radio antennae. It has a lot of antennae, and, looking at the wavelength, I think it's a ship used for detecting something."*

Bucher, clad only in a khaki shirt, trousers, and shower slippers, sent below for his leather flight jacket and boots. He pulled a white ski cap with a red tassel over his head and began to dictate a running account of No. 35's approach into a portable tape recorder, as Chuck Clark had done when the *Banner* was harassed.

The sub chaser closed to 1,000 yards. Through his field glasses Bucher saw helmeted men manning its guns. The captain ordered Lacy to replace Law as officer of the deck. So far, the incident was nothing out of the ordinary, but Bucher wanted his most experienced officer at his side if things got dicey.

He told Schumacher to work up a situation report to keep Admiral Johnson in the loop. The captain also ordered his enginemen to light off the twin diesels, in case he decided to bail out.

No. 35 came closer and began circling the *Pueblo*. On the second circuit, it ran up a signal flag: WHAT NATIONALITY? Bucher ordered the American colors hoisted.

Ensign Harris, excited and apprehensive, joined the others on the upper bridge. Bucher put him to work writing a narrative of communist actions in the log. Harris climbed back down to the pilothouse, plopped into the padded captain's chair, and started scribbling.

Lacy sang out that three torpedo boats also were racing toward the *Pueblo* at better than 40 knots, their rooster tails visible several miles away.

This was beginning to look like full-blown harassment. Part of the *Pueblo*'s mission was to test the North Koreans' reaction to a ferret's prolonged presence, and they certainly were reacting. The captain told Murphy to check the *Pueblo*'s position yet again; it was still nearly three miles outside the no-go zone.

Closing to 500 yards, the sub chaser ran up an attention-getting set of flags: HEAVE TO OR I WILL FIRE.

The message baffled Bucher. His ship already was stopped. What were these idiots talking about? He told Murphy to look up the precise meaning of "heave to" in a nautical dictionary, to make sure there were no nuances he didn't know about. There weren't.

As the captain struggled to divine their intentions, the North Koreans settled on their course of action:

"We will close down the radio, tie up the personnel, tow it, and enter port at Wonsan," one communist gunboat radioed. *"We are on the way to boarding."*

Hearing this, the Americans aboard the C-130 tried to alert Bucher. They had no direct way to contact him so they radioed Kamiseya, urging that he be informed immediately of the trap that was about to snap shut on him. But no warning came from Japan.

Bucher dropped down the ladder again to the pilothouse. He wanted to check his coordinates once more, to make absolutely sure of where he was. Radar didn't lie: The *Pueblo* was now 15.8 miles from the nearest shore. Murphy had plotted their position a half dozen times; it was impossible that both he and the captain had been wrong over and over again. Bucher hauled himself back up to the flying bridge and told his signalman to raise another string of flags: I AM IN INTERNATIONAL WATERS.

Schumacher hurried below to have the SITREP sent out. He entered the crypto room, just off the SOD hut's main compartment, and watched as CT Don Bailey pounded out the message on the keyboard of an encoding machine. Steve Harris suggested the report's priority be upgraded to CRITIC, a designation that would propel it ahead of other Navy traffic to the Pentagon, the National Security Agency—and the White House.

"We have a CRITIC tape already cut, Skip, if the captain wants to wake up the president," advised Harris.

Schumacher returned to the bridge to find the situation worsening. No. 35 was still circling, its guns aimed squarely at the American vessel. The three PT boats continued to close at high speed, their torpedo tubes loaded and their machine guns trained on the intelligence ship as they skimmed across the cold gray sea.

Bucher was taken aback by how fast things were happening. Just 20 minutes had elapsed since the sub chaser was first spotted. A pang of uneasiness shot through him. He still didn't think things were out of hand, but how far would the communists go? Would he need to destroy his classified material? How long would that take?

He turned to Lacy. "Could we scuttle the ship quickly if we had to?" he asked.

Lacy gave his commander a searching look. "Not quickly, sir," he replied. "About two hours to flood the main engine room, after unbolting and disconnecting the saltwater cooling intakes." Then more time until inrushing seawater breached the bulkhead of the auxiliary engine room and its accumulating weight began to pull the ship under.

With its engines crippled and its hull filling with water, however, the *Pueblo* would wallow helplessly. If American jets or warships showed up and attempted a rescue, Bucher couldn't maneuver. And what if his men had to abandon ship? Their vessel carried a 26-foot whaleboat and more than enough life rafts for everyone. But some sailors might spill overboard. The water temperature was 35 degrees, cold enough to kill a man in minutes. Would the North Koreans pick up survivors or simply leave them adrift on the high seas in the dead of winter?

Bucher called down to the pilothouse for a depth sounding. "Thirty fathoms!" someone shouted back—180 feet. The relatively shallow water increased the chances that North Korean divers could recover classified material if the ship were deliberately sunk.

The captain noticed some nervousness among his men. Though he rarely smoked, Tim Harris lit a cigarette. Bucher knew it was important for him as their leader to act with supreme confidence, to display not a trace of worry. But that was getting harder to do with each passing minute. The torpedo boats arrived, zooming to within 150 feet of the *Pueblo.* The sleek craft had a top speed of 50 knots, nearly four times faster than the spy ship.

From point-blank range No. 35 leveled its guns at the *Pueblo.* Bucher sent up a defiant flag set: INTEND TO REMAIN IN THE AREA. He noticed his signalman trembling as he tied in the pennants; whether from fear or the icy air, the captain couldn't tell. To buck up his men on the bridge, Bucher loudly declared: "We're not going to let these sons of bitches bullshit us!"

At that moment, two MiG fighters roared overhead at about 1,500 feet. In the distance Bucher saw a second sub chaser as well as a fourth PT boat sprinting toward him.

"Should we think about going to general quarters, Captain?" Lacy asked.

A call to general quarters would bring helmeted and battle-jacketed sailors running on deck to man the machine guns. Bucher's instructions were to avoid provoking the communists, to deny them any pretext for inciting an international incident. So far, they'd only tried to spook him. Bucher told Lacy he didn't want to go to general quarters just yet, and watched as consternation spread across the engineering officer's face. He also ordered Schumacher to draft a second SITREP.

No. 35 halted about 300 yards off the *Pueblo*'s starboard bow. One of the torpedo boats motored over to the larger craft to discuss matters. The two communist crews communicated by megaphone, their excited voices clearly audible across the slow swells. Then, to the alarm of the *Pueblo* officers, soldiers with AK-47 rifles began jumping from the sub chaser to the PT. The torpedo boat reversed its engines and began backing toward the American vessel. There was no mistaking the North Koreans' intent to board the *Pueblo*.

It was about one p.m.

"I'll be goddamned if they're going to get away with that!" Bucher burst out.

He shouted at Schumacher to include the boarding attempt in his next SITREP.

The North Koreans obviously were prepared to go far beyond any harassment encountered by the *Banner*. Bucher yelled into the voice tube, "All ahead one-third!"

He called for Murphy to give him the best course for the open sea. "Zero-eight-zero, sir!" came the reply—away from the coast at an almost perpendicular angle.

"Build up speed to two-thirds, then full," the captain ordered. The *Pueblo* would withdraw in a calm, dignified manner, not in panic.

Black smoke and a series of guttural coughs erupted from the stack. The *Pueblo* began to move. As it did so, an anguished cry arose from the bow.

"For God's sake, stop!" shrieked Tuck. His Nansen bottles were still in the water. As the ship plowed forward, the containers came boiling to the surface in its wake.

"Friar," Bucher yelled back, "get that damn gear up here, because I'm leavin'—now!"

The backing PT boat was nearly close enough for its soldiers to leap onto the *Pueblo*. But the intelligence ship, gathering speed, churned past the communist vessel, leaving the would-be boarding party behind. Two other torpedo boats began cutting back and forth directly in front of the *Pueblo*, trying to impede its escape.

For a few minutes it looked like Bucher might break free. No. 35 lowered its HEAVE TO flags and chugged along indecisively behind the *Pueblo*, gradually dropping back more than 2,000 yards. But Bucher wasn't convinced he'd get away. He passed word to prepare for emergency destruction. Then he raised a new array of flags: THANK YOU FOR YOUR CONSIDERATION—I AM LEAVING THE AREA. The message struck Schumacher as a bit flippant.

The torpedo boats kept playing porpoise just ten yards ahead. Schumacher jotted down his new situation report, describing the boarding attempt. Bucher pounded the lieutenant's back, shouting, "Get it going, get it going! Hurry up, goddamn it!"

Astern, the lagging sub chaser again ran up HEAVE TO OR I WILL FIRE. The gunboat sped up, rapidly regaining ground it had lost. Filled with dread, Schumacher departed again for the SOD hut to transmit his report.

"They saw us and they keep running away," No. 35 radioed its base. *"Shall I shoot them?"*

Instinctively trying to present the smallest possible target, Bucher ordered his helmsman to come right ten degrees. The sub chaser easily countered that move, pouring on more speed and turning outside the *Pueblo* to give its gunners a broadside shot. Bucher called for another ten-degree turn to the right. No. 35 accelerated and angled farther outside. The MiGs made another pass, thundering low over the *Pueblo*.

Suddenly, all four PT boats veered away.

Bucher realized that if he kept turning right, he'd soon be heading back toward North Korea. As he contemplated what to do next, a blood-chilling sound rolled across the water:

Ba—ROOOM! Ba—ROOOM! Ba—ROOOM!

Cannon shells whistled over the *Pueblo* and cut harmlessly into the sea. But one round cracked into a radar mast, spraying Bucher and two sailors on the open flying bridge with shrapnel.

The skipper fell to the deck. A metal splinter had drilled into his rectum; white-hot pain stabbed his bowels. He almost fainted, but a surge of adrenaline mixed with rage revived him. Moments later, he heard the angry hammering of machine-gun bullets on the superstructure as the torpedo boats opened up.

"Commence emergency destruction!" Bucher shouted. Shrapnel had hit his signalman and his phone talker, too, but neither was seriously hurt. Law popped up on the bridge, checking for injuries. Assured that everyone was okay, he turned and unleashed a furious barrage of profanities at the communist boats.

Bucher resisted a powerful urge to shoot back. He figured that would be futile: The *Pueblo*'s paltry armaments were no match for six combat ships and two jets. Even one sub chaser, sitting beyond the range of the *Pueblo*'s weapons, could chop the spy boat into scrap metal with its deck cannon. In a firefight at closer quarters, American gunners would have to run across exposed decks, pry off frozen tarpaulins, and wrench open ammo boxes before they could bring the two .50-calibers into action. With no protective shields, the gun mounts were vulnerable to enemy fire from several directions. Ordering men to the machine guns in such circumstances, the captain believed, was tantamount to ordering them to their deaths.

"Set a modified general quarters!" Bucher yelled into the voice tube. "Nobody to expose themselves topside!" With any luck, his men would stay off the outside decks and no one would get killed needlessly.

In the crypto room, Steve Harris and CT Bailey searched frantically for the precut CRITIC tape. Another CT, Jim Layton, shoved Bailey out of his chair and banged out a message by hand:

SOS. SOS. SOS. SOS. SOS. SOS. SOS. SOS. SOS. SOS. SOS. SOS. SOS.
SHIP POSITION 39-34N, 127-54E. SOS. SOS. SOS. SOS. SOS. SOS. SOS.
SOS. SOS. SOS. SOS. SOS. SOS. SOS. SOS. SOS. SOS. OUR POSITION

39-34N, 127-54E. WE ARE HOLDING EMERGENCY DESTRUCTION. WE NEED HELP. WE ARE HOLDING EMERGENCY DESTRUCTION. WE NEED SUPPORT. SOS. SOS. SOS. PLEASE SEND ASSISTANCE PLEASE SEND ASSISTANCE PLEASE SEND ASSISTANCE PLEASE SEND ASSISTANCE SOS SOS SOS WE ARE BEING BOARDED.

In his haste Layton had gotten ahead of events; no one had boarded, at least not yet. The MiGs made another screaming pass. Whether as a warning or by accident, the lead pilot fired a missile that zipped into the sea several miles away. But it was clear the fighters were armed and ready to back up their comrades on the water.

No. 35 fired a second, more accurate cannon salvo. Shells ripped into the *Pueblo*'s masts and rigging, making peculiar popping sounds and producing another dangerous shower of shrapnel. Other projectiles slammed into the smokestack and superstructure. At the same time, the PT boats blasted away with machine guns, stitching the pilothouse and flying bridge from both sides.

"Clear the bridge!" Bucher shouted. Law, the signalman, and the phone talker jumped off the deck, landing in a heap outside the pilothouse. The captain attempted a more dignified descent on the ladder, but dropped down quickly when bullets spattered the steel walls just inches away. He noticed that the PT boat firing at him had uncovered one of its torpedo tubes and trained it out for a close-in shot.

The pilothouse was a shambles. Its portside windows were blown out; glass shards littered the floor. With the exception of Lacy, who was still standing, Bucher found the entire watch hugging the deck for protection against the deadly hail of shells and bullets. When the communist machine guns paused, the captain yelled, "Everybody on your feet!"

Ten or 12 men stood up. Helmsman Ron Berens, who'd been steering the ship from a crouch, was the first to his feet, muttering angrily. Tim Harris, who'd thrown himself out of the captain's chair, got up and resumed writing his narrative. Bucher noticed that the only one who didn't rise was Murphy. The executive officer stayed on his hands and knees, glasses askew. It looked like he'd been trying to stick his head under a radiator.

"But, sir, they're still shooting at us!" he pleaded.

"No kidding, Ed!" Bucher rejoined angrily. "So get off your ass and start acting like my XO!"

When Murphy failed to move fast enough, the captain gave him a sharp kick in the rear end. (The executive officer later denied getting booted, saying that while he and others were crouched or prone for protection, they kept doing their jobs.)

With a ragged semblance of order restored in the pilothouse, Bucher decided to call Steve Harris to make sure emergency destruction was under way. The captain grabbed the secure phone to the SOD hut and vigorously cranked the growler. No one answered. Bucher cranked again—no response. "Goddamn it, answer the fucking phones!" he spat. Then he realized he'd picked up the wrong handset. The mistake rattled him. Was he cracking under pressure? He switched phones and Harris's voice came on.

"Emergency destruct is in progress, Captain, and our communications are open with Kamiseya," the lieutenant said. Despite his confident report, Harris sounded shaken.

That wasn't surprising in view of the situation in the hut. Eight to ten CTs were desperately trying to annihilate classified electronics with sledgehammers and fire axes; the cramped compartment rang with the clang and crunch of metal striking metal. Just outside the security door, other sailors were hurriedly trying to burn secret papers in wastebaskets. But with the ship's portholes dogged shut and its ventilation system turned off, smoke from the fires swirled into the hut. CTs coughed and gagged and dropped to the deck, gasping for air.

The electronic instruments were sensitive but solidly built; sledgehammers bounced off their steel cases. A sledge handle broke in one CT's hands; another man nearly brained himself when his hammer ricocheted back from an unyielding metal box.

In the crypto room, Don Bailey asked another CT to relieve him so he could burn his code lists. Turning around, he found Lieutenant Harris on his knees, praying.

"I'm going to have to get busy and destroy this gear, sir," Bailey said as evenly as he could. "You're going to have to get out of the way." Harris got to his feet and departed.

In the pilothouse, Bucher peered through blown-out windows. The *Pueblo* was still lumbering toward the open sea at top speed. But the gunboats matched its 13 knots effortlessly, almost mockingly. Schumacher and others were doing their best to torch classified documents in the small, pitifully inadequate incinerator behind the smokestack. Bucher told them to take cover under the nearby whaleboat if enemy gunners got too close. "But," he added urgently, "keep that stuff burning, burning, burning!"

Lacy reappeared after conferring with damage-control parties below. His face was ashen, but he reported the ship intact except for some minor hits to the hull above the waterline.

"Okay, Gene," Bucher said. "We're still afloat and under way. We'll keep trying to bull our way through."

The sub chaser's cannon boomed again. A shell flew through one empty window frame and out another, missing Lacy and Tim Harris by inches. Bucher and the others hit the deck. More shells burst around them. What happened next was to become the subject of bitter dispute between the captain and Lacy.

In Bucher's telling, he struggled to his feet after the barrage ended and was met with "a wild-eyed look" from Lacy.

"Are you going to stop this son of a bitch or not?" the chief engineer yelled, according to Bucher.

The captain claimed that with no specific command from him, Lacy then racked the annunciator to all-stop. Lacy would later insist Bucher told him to do so.

In any event, enginemen below immediately rang answering bells. The diesel engines abruptly halted; the ship decelerated rapidly.

Bucher turned his back on Lacy and walked to the starboard wing of the pilothouse. What the hell was he supposed to do now? If he kept running, the North Koreans could blast the *Pueblo* to splinters and kill any number of good men. Then, despite the bloody sacrifice, the communists would commandeer his ship and its classified treasures anyway.

The firing ceased as the ferret coasted to a stop. Bucher stood on the wing, temporarily paralyzed. A PT boat bobbed 40 yards off his starboard quarter, its gunners staring impassively at him through their sights.

Bucher felt utterly alone. His first mission as a commander had turned into a disaster. The comforting mantra that international law would shield him on the high seas, so often repeated by Navy brass, had been exposed as a foolish illusion. The *Pueblo*'s inability to defend itself, its lack of a rapid destruction system, the absence of air or sea forces to protect it—all the faulty assumptions and half measures and corner-cutting had caught up with the captain and his men with a vengeance.

Smoke from burning secrets billowed from the *Pueblo*'s flanks and topside incinerator. Bucher wondered whether the North Koreans had quit shooting because they thought they'd disabled his ship. Four of his five officers were with him in the pilothouse, but no one offered any advice about what to do.

The skipper looked at each man in turn. Lacy stood by the annunciator, staring out a window and rubbing his hands as if they'd been burned when he rang all-stop. Schumacher and Tim Harris seemed to be pleading silently for something more important to do than burn paper or write log entries. Murphy swayed unsteadily next to a dead radiotelephone.

Bucher was trapped. The communists were in a position to board the *Pueblo* at any moment. The only thing that mattered now was keeping classified documents and equipment out of their hands. The captain decided to play for time.

"Everybody not needed to work the ship will bear a hand at burning—everybody!" he told his officers. "What can't be burned goes over the side. Never mind the shallow water. Now move!"

More signal flags rose on the lead sub chaser: FOLLOW ME—I HAVE A PILOT ABOARD. Bucher ignored the demand. He headed for the SOD hut to inspect the destruction efforts.

The scene there appalled him. Smoke filled the passageway outside the hut. Men coughed, cursed, and stumbled around in the choking gloom. The deck just inside the security door was covered with publications and files that had been dumped there to be fed into the wastebasket fires. Steve Harris and his CTs had flattened themselves on the floor during the last salvo and hadn't budged even though the shelling was over. Bucher spotted the lieutenant wedged behind a rack of radio receivers.

The skipper yelled at Harris and his CTs to stand up. "The shooting has stopped, so get off your asses and get on with the destruction down here!"

Harris pulled himself out from the radio rack. His face was gray, and he coughed and wheezed as he spoke.

"Yes, sir, Captain—we're getting it done!" he exclaimed. He started yanking open file drawers and dumping their contents on the deck. To Bucher he seemed dazed, on the brink of panic.

The CTs scrambled to their feet and resumed the frenzied destruction. One of them delivered a staggering blow to an electronic instrument with a sledgehammer, but couldn't stave it in. Other men tore apart heavy bindings and stuffed chunks of paper into ditch bags to be heaved over the side.

Bucher hurried over to the two Marine translators, who were listening in on radio transmissions from the North Korean boats.

"Well, what about it?" he demanded. "Haven't you guys been able to make out anything they're saying out there?"

The Marines shook their heads in dismay.

Bucher shouldered his way into the crypto room. He was about to dictate another communiqué to Japan when Lacy called. The North Koreans were insisting that the *Pueblo* follow them, the engineer reported. The captain lurched out of the hut, trusting Harris to finish wrecking everything in it.

Back in the pilothouse, Bucher saw North Korean sailors angrily pointing at No. 35's FOLLOW ME flags. He wanted to keep stalling without getting hit with a prodding barrage of cannon shells, so he rang up all ahead one-third. Inching along at four knots might give his men enough time to polish off the classified material before they entered communist waters. Also, there still was a chance that the cavalry—Navy destroyers or Air Force fighters—would show up. But if anyone was coming, they'd better get there soon. The North Koreans clearly meant to capture Bucher's ship, not merely board it, and force it into Wonsan.

The *Pueblo* swung around in a wide arc and fell in behind the sub chaser.

Bucher told Murphy to get rid of all navigation records: charts, logs, loran fixes. The bridge was a blur of activity as sailors unearthed an astounding amount of paper that had to be done away with. The skipper joined in, shuttling publications to the incinerator outside. Smoke poured from the little furnace, but it could handle only three pounds of paper at a time, and only loose sheets at that. Thick manuals had to be torn into separate pages, one by one. Paper piled up far faster than it could be consumed. The ship had two shredders, but they were capable of chewing up only an eight-inch stack of documents every 15 minutes. And if the men in the pilothouse were having this much trouble, what was happening in the SOD hut, which held 50 times as much of this stuff? Bucher decided to stop the ship if necessary to buy more time—even if it meant getting shot up again.

"Captain, they are signaling us to put on more speed," Lacy called out.

"To hell with 'em!" Bucher shouted back. He went to the starboard wing, where he saw North Koreans on the nearest PT boat gesturing at him to hurry up. The commander shrugged his shoulders, feigning incomprehension. The communists held their fire.

Bucher suddenly remembered he had classified materials in his stateroom and went below to destroy them.

Through the eye-stinging haze he saw dark figures setting fire to stacks of paper that kept arriving from the seemingly inexhaustible supply in the SOD hut. More than half of the crew seemed to be crammed into the mess deck and adjoining passageways. Some men were actively getting rid of classified materials, but others stood around, unsure what to do.

The captain buttonholed a sailor to come with him to his quarters. He threw open the door and his small cabin immediately filled with smoke. He groped for some confidential publications, his Navy records, and letters and photographs from his wife. He ripped up everything and passed out the pieces to be burned. Then he told the crewman to toss his personal sidearms, a Ruger .22-caliber pistol and a .38-caliber pistol, into the sea. He'd be damned if he'd let the commies get their hands on his cherished guns.

Bucher made his way back toward the pilothouse. He noted with grim satisfaction that two safes near his stateroom that had contained codes were open and empty. Secret papers still were being thrown into fires or packed into ditch bags; the sound of sledgehammers bashing electronics was audible throughout the *Pueblo*. With more time, the captain thought with faint optimism, maybe, just maybe they could get rid of everything. He rang up all-stop.

No. 35 reacted swiftly, sending a long salvo of shells crashing into the American vessel. At the same time, the torpedo boats opened up again with machine guns. Chunks of metal ricocheted all over the spy ship. The sub chaser's gunners rammed in another clip and five more shells thudded into the *Pueblo*'s thin steel walls.

"All ahead one-third!" Bucher yelled. It was senseless to sit dead in the water while the North Koreans cut him to pieces. The shooting stopped as soon as the ship started moving again. Muffled shouts rose from below. A sailor with a headset turned to the captain: "Sir, there are casualties reported from Damage Control Two! One . . . two men hit!"

Bucher descended once again into the smoke-shrouded interior. Exploding shells had badly damaged the mess deck and stateroom areas. The captain headed for a passageway leading to the SOD hut. As he opened a hatch, something with the heft and moistness of a small steak plopped onto his shoulder: a slab of human flesh.

A shell had sliced through the steel outer wall into a corridor where several men were burning papers. The result was carnage. Blood and pieces of flesh were splattered on the walls and deck; crumpled, half-burned papers were everywhere. Amid the mess lay a 20-year-old fireman, Duane Hodges, his eyes glazed and his head lolling. The projectile had struck him in the groin, all but shearing off his right leg. Intestines oozed from his blown-apart abdomen; his penis and testicles were gone. Doc Baldridge was trying unsuccessfully to stanch the gush of blood.

The sight of the dying sailor shocked Bucher. "You'd better amputate that leg!" he urged Baldridge.

"Then he'll only bleed to death faster, sir," the corpsman answered.

Other men had been hit, too. Another fireman, 19-year-old Steve Woelk, leaned against a wall, a dazed look on his face as bloodstains spread across the front of his pants. Sergeant Chicca was bleeding copiously from a thigh wound.

The captain picked his way to the SOD hut. CTs were still bashing and burning at a frenetic pace, but a large amount of paper remained. Two mattress covers stuffed with documents that Bucher had seen earlier had never been jettisoned. Steve Harris was ripping apart publications with spasmodic bursts of energy, his face flushed and grim. The skipper again ordered everything dumped overboard. Then he hurried into the crypto room, where he found CT Bailey bent anxiously over the Teletype as it spit out a message from Kamiseya:

> LAST WE GOT FROM YOU WAS "ARE YOU SENDING ASSIT." PLEASE ADVISE WHAT KEY LISTS YOU HAVE LEFT AND IF IT APPEARS THAT YOUR COMM SPACES WILL BE ENTERED.

"Key lists" was Navy jargon for monthly lists of codes; Kamiseya wanted to know whether the North Koreans were likely to get hold of the *Pueblo*'s. The captain told Bailey to be ready to send a reply. But Bailey was too nervous and another CT, Don McClarren, had to sit in for him. McClarren typed furiously as Bucher dictated:

> HAVE O KEY LISTS LEFT AND THIS ONLY ONE HAVE, HAVE BEEN REQUESTED FOLLOW INTO WONSAN, HAVE THREE WOUNDED AND ONE MAN WITH LEG BLOWN OFF, HAVE NOT USED ANY WEAPONS NOR UNCOVERED 50 CAL. MAC . . . DESTROYING ALL KEY LISTS AND AS MUCH ELEC EQUIPT AS POSSIBLE. HOW ABOUT SOME HELP, THESE GUYS MEAN BUSINESS. HAVE SUSTAINED SMALL WOUND IN RECTUM, DO NOT INTEND TO OFFER ANY RESISTANCE.

No high-ranking officer came on the circuit to overrule Bucher's plan or give him fresh orders. The only reply was from the Kamiseya Teletype operator:

> ROGER, ROGER. WE DOING ALL WE CAN. CAPT HERE AND CNFJ [COMNAVFORJAPAN] ON HOTLINE. LAST I GOT WAS AIR FORCE GOING HELP YOU WITH SOME AIRCRAFT BUT CAN'T REALLY SAY AS CNFJ COORDINATING WITH I PRESUME KOREA FOR SOME F-105. THIS UNOFFICIAL BUT I THINK THAT WHAT WILL HAPPEN.

The anonymous operator was trying to encourage him, suggesting that F-105 fighter-bombers might be headed his way, but Bucher figured the odds of rescue were getting longer by the minute. He hurried out of the crypto room.

On his way back to the pilothouse, the captain kicked several fittings in frustration and swore at the torpedo boats shadowing the *Pueblo*. The air had turned bitingly cold; Bucher estimated the temperature at zero.

In the pilothouse, a radioman was smashing electronic gear with a hammer. Tim Harris noted the captain's return in his narrative and then looked up imploringly. Bucher gave him a wry smile.

"Okay, Tim," he said. "Now put down there that the captain orders the narrative log destroyed—and destroy it!"

Harris did so with relish, shredding his report and tossing the pieces out a window like confetti. Bucher noticed a long stream of paper fragments floating in the *Pueblo*'s wake—and a PT boat churning heedlessly through the top secret debris.

Steve Harris called from the hut, asking permission to inform Kamiseya that he was unable to destroy all classified publications. Bucher angrily demanded to know what would be compromised. "Mostly technical pubs and such," said Harris, his voice trailing off. The captain said to send the message if he had to, but to keep destroying at full tilt.

Minutes later, No. 35 signaled the *Pueblo* to stop. A torpedo boat powered in alongside, a squad of armed boarders ready on deck. The other communist ships trained their guns on the *Pueblo*. Bucher reluctantly told Lacy to ring all-stop.

Below, Schumacher was trying to burn the papers Duane Hodges had been holding when he was wounded, but they were soggy with blood. The lieutenant was nauseated and angered by the sight of his comrades' flesh and blood smearing the passageway. Where were those goddamn American jets? Wasn't any help coming? Would the Navy just stand by and let these commie pricks shoot them to pieces and steal their ship in broad daylight?

Schumacher watched admiringly as CT Peter Langenberg, the Princeton dropout, came down the corridor with a bag of papers over his shoulder. Blood streamed from behind his right ear; the same shell that struck Hodges had wounded Langenberg. Undaunted, the CT calmly walked to the exposed outer railing and heaved the bag over the side, then went back for another one.

A moment later Bucher hustled past Schumacher into his cabin. The lieutenant followed and found him sitting on his bunk, jaws grinding in frustration. The captain pulled on his arctic boots and stood up. He adjusted his new commander's hat on his head. Schumacher realized he was dressing to surrender. The two officers said nothing; Schumacher was afraid he'd burst into tears if he tried to speak. He looked on sadly as Bucher left to meet the boarding party.

At about that time Lacy's voice crackled over the loudspeaker: "Now hear this! All hands are reminded of our Code of Conduct. Say nothing to the enemy besides your name, rank, and serial number!"

The North Koreans on the PT boat tried to throw a rope onto the *Pueblo*'s stern but missed. They succeeded on the second try, and a swabbie mechanically tied the line to a bitt. A deathly silence descended over both craft. About ten soldiers hefting automatic rifles with fixed bayonets swarmed over the side, followed by two officers in green uniforms with red-and-gold epaulets.

One of the officers strode toward Bucher, his pistol pointed at the captain's head.

The *Pueblo*'s first situation report reached the Navy's mightiest warship at 2:30 p.m. By coincidence, the USS *Enterprise* had departed Sasebo that same day and was about 500 miles south of Wonsan in the East China Sea. But no one aboard the nuclear-powered aircraft carrier had ever heard of the spy boat. Nor did they know what it was doing so close to North Korea.

The *Enterprise* was the flagship of Admiral Horace Epes, who called for a ship identification manual to look up the *Pueblo*. The admiral plotted its position and how far away it was. He asked his meteorologist what time darkness would fall on Wonsan and what the weather was like there. Then he called for a status report on his strike aircraft and how long they needed to get airborne.

On the crowded flight deck, crewmen began clearing takeoff lanes.

Escorted by a guided-missile frigate, the huge carrier—nearly as long as four football fields—was bound for the Gulf of Tonkin, from which its 59 fighter-bombers would resume pounding North Vietnam. Normally, most of the jets would be on the hangar deck while the carrier was in transit. But today they were packed together on the flight deck; the hangar deck below had been emptied so the crew could play basketball and watch movies while docked in Sasebo.

Epes controlled the air wing, but the carrier itself was commanded by Captain Kent Lee, a forceful South Carolinian who'd flown carrier planes in World War II and the Korean War. With a master's degree in nuclear physics, Lee had leapfrogged a number of more senior officers to become, at 44, boss of the *Enterprise*, the Navy's most prestigious sea command.

Despite their close working relationship and similar career arcs, Lee didn't like Epes. Lee viewed his superior as a poor air commander and a "creature-comfort admiral"—too attached to perks like fresh tablecloths, polished silverware, and new drapes in his flag quarters. Nor did Lee think much of the admiral's habit of leaving strict instructions that he not be disturbed while he watched a movie in his stateroom every night.

When Lee wasn't needed on the bridge, he enjoyed drinking coffee and swapping sea stories with a fellow captain, Frank Ault, who formerly commanded the carrier USS *Coral Sea* off Vietnam. Ault was now Epes's chief of staff, but he was no more a fan of the admiral than Lee. Epes didn't seem to know a lot about the carrier's nuclear dynamics, which Ault and Lee frequently had to explain to him. Ault also regarded his boss as indecisive.

Now Epes was faced with a very tough decision. Another message came in from the *Pueblo*. With North Koreans firing at and trying to board it, the surveillance vessel clearly needed help.

On its way to Japan, the carrier had been enveloped by a typhoon that damaged a number of jets. Mechanics were working on them, but only 35 aircraft were now flyable. About three hours would be needed to fuel and arm them, brief their pilots, and get them over the Wonsan area. In the carrier's war room, Epes and Ault gathered all available intelligence on the port city's air defenses, which appeared to be strong. Any attacking planes would have to run a gauntlet of 14 antiaircraft batteries, two surface-to-air missile sites, and as many as 75 MiG fighters.

Epes considered his options. By the time any sizable group of his jets reached the *Pueblo*, it would be dark—sunset was at 5:41 p.m.—and the spy ship probably would be in Wonsan harbor. Epes stood to lose a significant number of aircraft, maybe even enough to render the carrier and its 5,500 crewmen vulnerable to counterattack by North Korean planes.

If many American pilots were killed, or the carrier was damaged or even sunk, the pressure on the United States to retaliate would be tremendous. If it did so, the communists might then execute the *Pueblo* crew. Where would the escalation end? And all this over a rinky-dink surveillance ship that hadn't directly asked the *Enterprise* for assistance.

Epes didn't want to jeopardize his flagship. He didn't want to do something that might entangle his country in another Far East war. At 3:06 p.m., his cautious approach was confirmed by a higher authority. A message from Admiral William F. Bringle, commander of the Seventh Fleet, told him to take "no overt action until further informed." The decision was final: No rescue attempt would be mounted from the carrier.

At Fuchu Air Station, north of Tokyo, the man who controlled all land-based American combat jets in Northeast Asia was furiously working the phones.

Air Force Lieutenant General Seth McKee was determined to help the *Pueblo*. He sat at a phone-strewn table in a glass-walled war room, flanked by a dozen members of his battle staff, all of them making call after call. McKee commanded the Fifth Air Force, comprising all U.S. military planes in Japan, South Korea, and Okinawa.

He knew he didn't have much time. Minutes earlier, an aide had handed him a copy of the *Pueblo*'s rescue plea. Like the officers of the *Enterprise*, the general had never heard of the spy ship, although he knew his fighters had been alerted that they might have to protect the *Banner* on a couple of its 16 missions.

McKee fired question after question at his staff. On the other side of the glass was a command center, where airmen posted markers on wall maps showing the positions of American and hostile aircraft in the region. It was like a scene from an old movie about RAF Bomber Command.

The 51-year-old general spoke very rapidly, in clipped but precisely worded sentences accented with the rich drawl of his native Arkansas. After nearly 30 years in the Air Force, he was accustomed to crises. During World War II, he'd flown 69 combat missions over Europe in a P-38 Lightning, downing two enemy aircraft. He flew cover for the Normandy landings during the bloody Armageddon of D-day. During the Battle of the Bulge, he commanded an air base in Belgium that lay directly in the path of advancing German tanks.

So far, he was having little luck scrounging up combat-ready planes for the *Pueblo*. McKee had jurisdiction over two Marine fighter squadrons at Iwakuni Air Base in Japan, just 375 miles—less than an hour's flight—from Wonsan. But only four planes were available there, and their ground crews needed three hours just to load ammunition. Two other American bases in Japan were switching to modern F-4 Phantoms from older fighters, and none of the new aircraft could be ready to fly in less than several hours.

McKee also was in charge of American air units in South Korea. But with the Vietnam War sucking up planes from bases everywhere, the only ones in South Korea were six Phantoms, configured for nuclear bombs, which were part of the Pentagon's global standby network of aircraft, submarines, and intercontinental missiles that would rain atomic destruction on the USSR in the event of war. McKee ordered the Phantoms reloaded with conventional 3,000-pound bombs. But that would take several hours, and the jets still had no air-to-air guns or missiles to fight MiGs. Even properly armed, a handful of Phantoms wouldn't stand much chance against dozens of MiGs, many of which, McKee knew from intelligence, already were in the air.

There was another possibility. The South Korean Air Force consisted of more than 200 combat aircraft, some located at Osan Air Base near Seoul, only 25 minutes by air from Wonsan. McKee told a subordinate to check on their availability through U.S. Army General Charles Bonesteel, an eye patch–wearing former Rhodes scholar who commanded all United Nations forces in South Korea, including that country's air force.

But Bonesteel had no intention of further inflaming a South Korean public already angry and frightened over the Blue House raid. To many southerners, the outrageous attempt to kill their president represented a dramatic escalation of their long-running blood feud with the north that could be answered only with massive retaliation, even invasion. The *Pueblo* hijacking, Bonesteel believed, would only intensify that sentiment. And if multiple southern pilots died while trying to rescue the ship, the resulting public rage might be just enough to tip South Korea into war. Since many South Korean jets were aging U.S.-built F-86s, no match for North Korea's advanced MiGs, southern casualties indeed could be heavy. Bonesteel passed word that South Korean planes were off-limits in any attempt to save the *Pueblo*.

McKee moved down his list of prospects. He knew the *Enterprise* and its fighters might be close enough to help. So he placed a call to Honolulu, trying to reach a good friend, Admiral Ulysses S. Grant Sharp, commander in chief of all U.S. forces in the Pacific. McKee had a novel proposition for Sharp: that he, an Air Force general, be given operational control of the *Enterprise*, the Navy's most prized asset. Then McKee himself could order carrier planes into the air. But Sharp was in Vietnam conferring with Army commanders there. A deputy took McKee's call and flatly refused his request.

That left McKee only one card to play: his F-105 fighter-bombers at Kadena Air Base on Okinawa, more than 1,100 miles from Wonsan.

Air Force Major John Wright was in his wing commander's office at Kadena when the call came in.

The wing boss picked up the phone and sat bolt upright. "Yes, sir," he said. "No, sir. Yes, sir." A pause. "Yes, sir, I know where it is. Yes, sir, we can get planes over there right away." A couple more "yes, sirs" and he hung up, cursing vehemently.

"Do you know that someone stole a Navy ship?" he asked Wright.

"What kind of ship?"

"I don't know, but the goddamn Navy just got one of their ships stolen."

The caller had been McKee, who wanted as many fighters as possible sent aloft as soon as possible. They were to fly to Osan Air Base, refuel, and immediately take off to attack the North Korean gunboats herding the *Pueblo*. The wing commander put Wright in charge of the operation.

The 38-year-old Texan quickly assembled several other officers from the 18th Tactical Fighter Wing to go over their available aircraft. A maintenance officer made a few hasty calls and said he could pull together a dozen F-105s. Half of them were airborne in training exercises. Several more were being repaired. Wright decided to launch the planes in pairs, as fast as they could be readied. The major and his wingman would bring up the rear.

The first two F-105s blasted off from Okinawa at 4:11 p.m., afterburners punching them into the sky with a deafening roar.

In his war room outside Tokyo, McKee received the liftoff news with mixed emotions. Time was running out for the *Pueblo.* The Okinawa jets needed roughly two and a half hours to get to where the ship was believed to be. But with a refueling stop at Osan, McKee's pilots had little, if any, chance of reaching Bucher and his men before nightfall, when a rescue attack was no longer feasible.

"Those poor bastards," the general muttered to no one in particular. "What's happening to them?"

CHAPTER 5

WE WILL NOW BEGIN TO SHOOT YOUR CREW

"I protest this outrage!" Bucher yelled at the North Korean aiming the gun at his head. "We are a United States ship operating in international waters and you have no damned right to attack us like this. As captain, I order you to get off my ship at once."

The communist officer gave no sign of comprehension. His soldiers moved quickly to take control of the *Pueblo*. They forced some sailors back to the fantail and made them sit, shivering, on the cold steel deck. Others were ordered to the well deck near the bow. The boarders tied the Americans' hands and blindfolded them with torn bedsheets. Anyone who resisted was instantly bludgeoned with the butt of an AK-47 or kicked with a heavy boot.

The two North Korean officers shoved Bucher up to the pilothouse. One pointed at sub chaser No. 35, still flying FOLLOW ME pennants, and indicated with vigorous hand motions for the captain to get his boat moving. Bucher ordered all ahead one-third, telling his helmsman to steer in the gunboat's wake. The other communist officer pantomimed for Bucher to turn off the sole radio transmitter that was still intact and crackling. When he refused, the North Korean promptly clouted him in the head with his pistol and ripped out the power cord himself.

The skipper then was prodded at gunpoint toward the aft machine-gun mount and told to remove the frozen tarp draping the weapon. He again shook his head no and again was pistol-whipped.

Blindfolded on the fantail, Schumacher heard the sickening smack of steel against bone. Along with about 15 other crewmen, he squatted on the icy deck, hands tightly bound. A soldier had fired a terrifying burst from his automatic rifle over their heads, making sure they got down and stayed down. In minutes the Americans had been snatched from the snug, seemingly predictable world of the *Pueblo* and thrust into a dark parallel universe of fear and uncertainty. No one spoke. On the well deck, where about half of the crew sat in rows, the stench of a fresh bowel movement filled the air.

Schumacher kept telling himself it was all a bad dream. How could a bunch of goons from some tin-pot country take over with such impunity a ship belonging to the world's most powerful navy? He wondered whether the communists planned to machine-gun the entire crew. Or maybe they'd just let the Americans freeze to death on this windswept deck and toss the rigid corpses overboard like so much old furniture.

The North Koreans ordered sailors from both ends of the ship to the forward berthing compartment, where at least it wasn't as cold. Schumacher's supercharged thoughts and emotions crashed into one another like bumper cars at some crazy amusement park: Anger collided with fear; frustration piled into bewilderment. He couldn't figure out what the North Koreans hoped to gain by seizing the *Pueblo*. Were they trying to incite a new war with the United States? Did they think they could exchange the crew for a lucrative ransom? The U.S. government would never cave in to such extortion. So what was their game?

The spy ship crawled toward Wonsan. From the pilothouse Bucher could see the jagged silhouettes of mountains turning reddish purple in the twilight. He figured his ship was barely inside the 12-mile territorial limit and a good 20 miles from the port of Wonsan, at the far end of its deep bay. He remembered Kamiseya's hopeful words—AIR FORCE GOING HELP YOU WITH SOME AIRCRAFT—and ransacked his brain for more ways to stall. His eyes swept the darkening horizon, straining for the electrifying sight of F-105s with cannon ablaze. If the jets did come, he'd grab the loudspeaker mike and shout for his men to attack their captors. A bloodbath would ensue, but he thought his guys could win.

About nine miles from shore, a communist officer jerked the annunciator to all-stop. A torpedo boat pulled up to the *Pueblo*'s stern and deposited a second boarding party, led by a North Korean colonel with scars on his face and neck that marked him as a veteran soldier. A translator who resembled the actor Maximilian Schell accompanied him. The Americans later nicknamed the pair Colonel Scar and Max.

Max's English was a little stiff but his meaning was clear: "You will conduct us through a complete inspection of this ship at once and without any tricks of concealment," he told Bucher. "At once! Go now!"

"Tell your colonel I demand that all his people leave my ship immediately," the captain shot back.

The interpreter related the message to Colonel Scar, who ignored it. "Go now!" Max repeated. A soldier kicked Bucher in the lower back for emphasis. The North Koreans had brought a civilian pilot, and he pushed Bucher's helmsman out of the way and rang up all-ahead-flank.

The captain led the North Koreans to the passageway where Duane Hodges lay on a stretcher, unconscious.

"I need medical attention for this man and several others whom you wounded," Bucher told Scar. The colonel didn't reply and barely glanced at the mortally injured sailor. The soldier kicked and shoved Bucher on toward the mess.

A forlorn-looking pile of ashes and brown-edged scraps of paper bore witness to the convulsive activity in the compartment just 30 minutes earlier. Scar quickly surmised what had happened.

"What were you doing here?" he asked through his translator. "Burning your secret orders?"

"Making ice cream," Bucher answered.

A trooper kicked the captain backward into a bulkhead so hard he saw stars. His knees buckled but the North Korean jerked him to his feet to continue the inspection.

After brief tours of the engine room and galley, Bucher and his escorts arrived at the SOD hut. The skipper's heart sank. Heaps of unburned documents lay near the open security door. Just beyond was a mattress cover stuffed with more paper. Bucher didn't know what the materials were, but he was shocked that Steve Harris and his men hadn't gotten rid of them.

Scar's eyes widened as he took in the racks of banged-up listening equipment. Bucher stepped into the crypto center, noting with relief that the code machines appeared to be thoroughly smashed. One KW-7 remained online, humming faintly. Max ordered Bucher to shut it off, but he refused. A soldier decked him with a savage hand chop to the back of the neck, and the interpreter cut the power.

Lying on the floor, Bucher saw a couple of other soldiers clearing papers away from the heavy steel door. He felt in his pants pocket for his cigarette lighter, thinking he might be able to start a fire and slam shut the door. But before he could make his move, a trooper dragged him to his feet and held a bayonet to his chest. Then, amazingly, the North Koreans forced him out of the hut and closed the door behind them, inadvertently locking it. The captain silently rejoiced. Now there was no way to get in without a blowtorch.

Bucher was marched to the forward berth area. Almost all of his crew sat before him blindfolded and bound. Soldiers were thumping them with rifle butts while confiscating their personal property. "One of those thieving bastards just stole my watch," growled an angry sailor. "Share the wealth—that's communism," said another. A sharp command from Scar halted the plunder.

Bucher wanted to stay with his men, but the North Koreans took him back to the passageway where Hodges lay. The young fireman made no sound or movement. Baldridge, the corpsman, was tending to the other wounded fireman, Steve Woelk, who was bleeding from his groin, hip, and buttocks.

"What about Hodges?" the captain hissed.

"He's dead, sir," replied the medic. "Died about ten minutes ago." Woelk, he said, needed a surgeon.

A soldier responded to their hushed conversation by kicking Bucher in the back, while another karate-chopped Baldridge's neck. The captain's back throbbed with pain from the multiple assaults. Two troopers started to work him over, kicking and clubbing with their rifles. Bucher curled into a ball next to Hodges's corpse to protect himself. His ribs felt like they were about to cave in.

The captain was deposited in the wardroom for the rest of the trip to Wonsan. About three hours after the *Pueblo* was seized, he saw the glow of dock lights through a porthole. He felt the engines slow and then a hard bump as the ship thudded against a wharf. Shouts broke out and the deck overhead vibrated with the clomping of military boots.

Colonel Scar and Max reappeared with what Bucher thought were a North Korean admiral and general in tow. The skipper was pushed into his stateroom, frisked, and, in spite of his loud protests, relieved of his ring, watch, and wallet.

"Why are you spying on Korea?" Max demanded. "You are a CIA agent bringing spies to provoke another war!"

"Absolutely not!" Bucher rejoined. "We were conducting oceanographic research in international waters. This is a research ship that has nothing to do with the CIA or armed aggression."

Jabs to his jaw and neck cut him off. "You will all be removed from the ship, tried, and shot," Max said angrily. Bucher's hands were tied and a blindfold pulled over his eyes.

The captain and his men were forced across a narrow gangplank onto a floodlit pier. The night air was intensely cold. As soon as the sailors appeared, angry shouts erupted from what sounded like a large crowd. Bucher's eye covering slipped just enough for him to see soldiers straining to hold back hundreds of furious civilians. The mob surged toward the sightless crewmen, shrieking and spitting and, despite the soldiers' exertions, landing some punches and kicks. Policarpo Garcia, a ship's storekeeper from the Philippines, got booted in the rump with such force that "the toe almost go inside my rectum."

Bucher knew these enraged, lunging people would tear him and his men to shreds if the soldiers didn't keep knocking them down and pushing them back. Years of relentless anti-U.S. propaganda by Kim Il Sung's regime had made Americans as popular in North Korea as smallpox. Someone in the crowd screamed in English, "Death to the American bastards!"

The sailors were hustled past the apoplectic civilians onto waiting buses. Moments after sitting down, Bucher was taken off and returned to the ship. His blindfold was ripped away, and he saw several North Koreans struggling with the SOD hut door.

"Open it!" Max commanded. The captain shrugged as if the massive door with its combination lock were a mystery to him.

Someone stuck a pistol in his ear. "Open it or be shot right now!" Stubbornly, courageously, Bucher refused. At least he'd die fast, without having to endure torture. Instead of blowing his head off, a trooper kicked him hard in the belly. Then Steve Harris was brought back and told to open the door. He, too, bravely refused.

Bucher was blindfolded again and frog-marched past the screeching crowd at the pier. Gobs of spit landed on him.

On the bus, soldiers had resumed looting the Americans. Over the commotion Bucher thought he heard his Filipino and Mexican-American sailors being singled out for especially harsh treatment. He realized why when Max loudly proclaimed, "You have been trying to make infiltration of North Korea with South Korean spies! You are criminals who will be tried in our People's Court and shot!"

"Bullshit!" Bucher yelled. "There is nobody but Americans in this crew!"

He was dragged off the bus and placed in what seemed to be a staff car; guards on both sides pummeled him. Max got in, and the captain demanded that his men be kept together and treated in accordance with the Geneva convention.

"You capitalist dogs and Korea are not at war, so no Geneva convention applies," the interpreter said contemptuously. "You have no military rights at all. You will be treated as civilian espionage agents of the CIA."

After a bumpy ride that lasted about 15 minutes, the car stopped. Bucher was taken into what might have been a police station. His men already were there and being beaten, as their cries and groans attested.

"Stop this brutality!" the skipper hollered. The North Koreans shoved him into a small room and slammed the door.

In the sudden quiet, Bucher realized his hands had gone numb from the bindings. His gut ached from the soldier's boot, as did much of the rest of his exhausted body.

Soon he was in the staff car again. After another brief ride he arrived at what sounded like a railroad station, with an old steam locomotive hissing as it awaited passengers. He was guided up some steps, down an aisle, and into an ice-cold, coach-style seat. The skipper sensed the presence of his men. No one breathed a word, hoping that the short lull in the beatings would be extended. A whistle blew and the locomotive pitched forward.

God only knew where it was headed.

John Wright sat strapped in the cockpit of his F-105, feeling the powerful Pratt & Whitney engine idling behind him. On the tarmac his crew chief drew himself to attention and snapped off a salute.

Wright lived to fly fighters, and the F-105 Thunderchief was his favorite. It was the Cadillac of combat jets—big, comfortable, easy to fly, and damn near indestructible. He returned the salute and taxied to the flight line.

The major had flown 100 combat missions during the Korean War and 140 more during Vietnam. He commanded one squadron that suffered such heavy losses over North Vietnam that it had to be disbanded. Still, he couldn't get enough of aerial combat. Though married and the father of four, he was prepared to die for his country at any time.

The tower cleared him for takeoff at about ten p.m. His wingman was nearby; they'd fly the last two F-105s to Osan. Wright pushed his throttle forward and his jet began to roll. He ignited the afterburner and the plane rocketed into the night sky, a cone of fiery red streaming from its exhaust nozzle.

Wright got to the South Korean air base around midnight. Snow skittered across dark runways. Ground crews were hastily uploading bombs to 105s that had arrived earlier. It was much too late to prevent the capture of the *Pueblo*, and General McKee had called off that operation. Now Wright's squadron was about to be handed a new, more dangerous mission.

The major strode into the run-down flight operations building and got on the scrambler phone to Fifth Air Force. He knew virtually nothing about the *Pueblo*, but a high-ranking officer in Japan told him about its importance. If the communists were permitted to dismantle and study the ferret's contents, the officer said, U.S. military secrets would be "compromised for ten years." The Navy didn't know for sure how much classified material Bucher had gotten rid of, or indeed whether he'd disposed of any.

Wright asked what his orders were.

"I want you to sink that ship at all costs," his superior replied.

"All costs?" Wright asked, the implications hitting him. "Does that mean all of my twelve airplanes?"

"That's right. I want that ship sunk. The Navy lost it, and we're gonna sink it."

Wright's small band of pilots was likely to be met over Wonsan by a wall of antiaircraft fire and a horde of MiGs; the Americans' chances of survival were virtually nil. Nonetheless, the major swung into action. He told the Osan maintenance officer to remove his jets' drop tanks and attach more bomb racks. That meant his men wouldn't have enough fuel to get home in the unlikely event they got away from Wonsan in one piece. But they'd have extra bombs to do the job.

Another complication was that no one knew whether the *Pueblo*'s crew was still aboard or not. Wright wasn't thrilled about the possibility of bombing Americans, but orders were orders.

He and his operations officer began planning the mission route and tactics. As the two men worked, excited pilots kept barging into the room, offering to help. Wright finally had to shoo them to another part of the building, saying he'd brief them in a couple of hours and they should get some sleep. But there were no blankets and only a frigid concrete floor to lie down on, and the men were too keyed up to sleep anyway.

The pilots filed into a shabby briefing room at about five a.m. on January 24. They still didn't know what the *Pueblo* looked like or where it was in Wonsan's capacious harbor. The Navy had sent over two officers to tell them as much as they could. Wright knew his men would be taken aback when they learned of the mission's one-way nature, and he tried to think of a way to lighten the mood. One of the Navy briefers inadvertently provided it.

"Gentlemen," the naval officer began, "your target is to sink the *Pueblo*."

Wright couldn't resist a joke. "'Scuse me," he drawled. "I know what a pueblo is in Arizona; it's where the Indians live. I don't think any Indians are livin' over here."

The Navy man acted as if he'd been insulted. The *Pueblo* was a *ship*, he said, an intelligence ship, and it had to be destroyed. Unfazed, Wright asked whether the briefer had any pictures of the *Pueblo*. He didn't. Well, Wright asked, how were his people supposed to find it? How were they to know which ship, out of perhaps dozens in Wonsan harbor, to bomb? The Navy officer paused for a few seconds, thinking.

"Did you see the movie *Mister Roberts*?" he finally asked.

Wright had.

"That's exactly what the *Pueblo* looks like."

Wright turned to his pilots. "We're gonna sink Mr. Roberts's ship," he said, his broad smile triggering raucous laughter. Then he got up to explain how they'd do it.

The F-105s would fly northeast out of Osan as low and fast as possible. At 600 miles per hour, flight time to Wonsan was 25 minutes. As they neared the harbor, the pilots would hit their afterburners and hurtle up to 17,000 feet. On the way up, Wright and his ops officer each planned to pick out a ship they believed was the *Pueblo*. If they agreed, the entire squadron would dive-bomb that target. If they disagreed, the planes would divide into two groups and attack both ships. The big jets dove like winged anvils, plunging nearly two and a half miles in 30 seconds. The pilots would have ten seconds to aim.

The final phase of the attack posed a delicate problem for Wright. His orders were to take out the *Pueblo* at all costs, and he intended to do that. His pilots needed to know that no one was to leave Wonsan as long as the *Pueblo* remained afloat. But he couldn't simply order them to crash into the ship; military law and custom, not to mention basic morality, prevented commanders from telling subordinates to commit suicide.

The major chose his words carefully.

"Here's the rules: If that ship is still floating and you're the last one alive, go back around and sink it." He had a family on Okinawa, he said, but he wasn't leaving Wonsan until the spy boat went under.

Wright didn't directly order a kamikaze assault. After all, the last surviving pilot theoretically could send the *Pueblo* to the bottom with a well-aimed bomb or by riddling it with cannon fire. But that wasn't what the squadron leader meant.

"Does everybody understand what I'm telling you?" he asked.

One pilot pulled back the corners of his eyes until they became slits. "*Ah so*, Major," he said, mimicking a Japanese accent.

The pilots climbed into their jets in the predawn darkness. They'd had no time to pack winter clothes before leaving Okinawa, so they wore only thin green flight suits. A red flare was to signal takeoff.

Wright and each of his men sat alone in a freezing cockpit, waiting for what probably would be the last flight of their lives.

The train bearing the *Pueblo* crew wheezed and clanked to a halt. A voice announced that they'd reached their destination and would leave the coach in order of rank with their hands up, in the abject manner of criminals. The Americans were untied and their blindfolds removed.

They were supposed to keep their heads contritely down, but Schumacher let his eyes slide up the body of the man sitting opposite him. It was Bucher. The captain's big eyes shone with anger and he was kneading his deadened hands in frustration. Max walked up to him.

"Now we will take you off the train," he said. "Captain, you first, then the others."

Bucher didn't move. For several long moments, he glared coldly at Max. Finally he rose and led Schumacher, Lacy, and Tim Harris down the aisle and out the door.

Small suns exploded in the captain's face as North Korean news photographers took flash pictures of him stepping onto the passenger platform. Adding to the blinding brightness were the klieg lights of TV cameramen, eagerly recording the humiliation of the American spy chief and his lackeys. Bucher brought his hands down to shield his eyes; a soldier batted them back in the air with his rifle.

Schumacher felt like an animal in a ferociously illuminated zoo. He stole a quick look at his watch: six a.m., January 24. He wasn't sure where they were but figured it was Pyongyang, the capital. Looming over the train station was a tower adorned with a huge portrait of Kim Il Sung, set in a gold frame against a red background.

Schumacher glanced at his shipmates, their breath visible in the chilly air as they stamped their feet to stay warm. They looked disheveled and smelled bad after their long night of captivity. The men were trying to seem composed, but their faces registered shock, doubt, fear.

Soldiers herded them on two buses that then headed down a broad boulevard. Mercury-vapor lights cast eerie pools of green on the streets. Workers were beginning to line up at bus stops, and blue fluorescent lights were already on in some shops. But mostly the place looked as sterile and lonely as a vacant parking lot.

The buses drove through the city and crossed a bridge over the wide Taedong River. Schumacher's sense of disorientation was so strong that he thought he was losing touch with reality. He fought a powerful desire to sleep. He tried to think about what he'd be doing at this hour on a normal day. Aboard the *Pueblo*, he'd be on morning watch. Dawn at sea was his favorite time. Watching the sun climb slowly out of the water and into the sky, he felt, was like seeing God write poetry.

The lieutenant raised his eyes long enough to glimpse ugly buildings and littered door stoops flash by. Everything seemed so dead. Maybe this was what the far side of the River Styx looked like. A hard whack to the top of his head interrupted his musings; Schumacher obediently dropped his chin to his chest.

The buses turned off the boulevard onto a dirt road. They jounced along until they pulled into a large courtyard behind a four-story concrete building that stood black against the early-morning gray, icicles dripping from its eaves. It looked like a barracks. Schumacher saw 200 to 300 soldiers massed in the courtyard, jeering and chanting with an almost hypnotic rhythm. They made him think of a lynch mob working itself into a frenzy.

The soldiers on the bus got out and waded into their brethren in the courtyard, shoving them back to make way for the captives but in the process creating a gauntlet. The crewmen headed into it. A soldier stepped into Steve Harris's path and punched him in the mouth, drawing blood. Bucher got down stiffly from the bus and caught a karate kick in the back. That did it. He whipped around and went after the small, moon-faced soldier who'd kicked him, fists flying. Four other North Koreans dove on top of Bucher and all of them collapsed in a flailing, swearing pile.

Soldiers manhandled the captain into the building, up three flights of stairs, and into a small room. They slammed him down on a crude bed, where he lay gasping for breath and scanning his new surroundings. The entire building smelled of hay and horse manure; the sailors later nicknamed it the Barn.

Bucher's cell measured about 12 by 17 feet. It was furnished with a wooden chair, a small table, and a steam radiator that made little headway against the cold. The sole window was covered with brown paper on the inside and canvas on the outside. From the ceiling a bare lightbulb emitted wan yellow light. The heavy wooden door had multiple cracks, through which an eye sometimes peered.

Suddenly the door flew open. In strode a communist junior officer shrieking, "Imperialist aggressor! You'd better make sincere confession, or we shoot spying imperialist liar!" He stomped his feet and slapped his holstered pistol to drive home his point. By his side was a guard who looked no older than 15, nervously clutching a bayonet-tipped carbine. The boy eyed Bucher with a mixture of fear and revulsion. The officer railed on angrily for several minutes before earnestly asking the captain, "How you feel? Perhaps need to go to toilet, yes?"

Bucher was led down the corridor to a foul-smelling lavatory. He limped to a urinal and voided mostly blood. The filthy basin already was streaked with other men's blood—probably his crew's, Bucher thought. He wheeled on the junior officer. "Where are my men?" he bellowed. "I demand to speak to them right now!" The North Korean told him to shut up.

The officer and his jumpy adolescent sidekick escorted Bucher back down the hall. The skipper saw a dozen or more rooms, their doors closed. "Good luck, Captain!" called a distinctly American voice from behind one. Bucher couldn't tell who it was, but his spirits soared; at least some of his guys were alive and confined on the same floor with him.

Not long after he returned to his cell, another guard appeared with a plate of boiled turnips and a soggy piece of buttered bread. Bucher refused to eat, partly because of his determination not to cooperate with his captors in any way, partly because of nausea from the pain of his beatings and untreated wounds. The captain hadn't told the North Koreans of his injuries out of fear he'd be sent to a hospital and separated from his men. The food-bearing guard withdrew, looking insulted.

He soon came back to prod Bucher at bayonet point to another room for what turned out to be his first interrogation. In the room were more guards and a narrow-eyed North Korean major who was sitting at a table with some folders on it. Among them was the skipper's personnel file, which he'd ordered destroyed during the attack. The captain knew his jacket contained only routine material—date of commissioning, various duty stations, service schools he'd attended. But if the communists had captured this, what else did they have?

The major began asking questions obviously based on what he'd read in Bucher's file, and the captain saw no reason to stonewall. The North Korean seemed uninterested in his years aboard submarines, but paid sharp attention to his attendance at the Navy's Combat Information Center School, in Glenview, Illinois.

"That proves you are a trained spy!" the major blurted triumphantly. "Counterintelligence school—part of infamous CIA!"

Bucher didn't bother to explain the difference between the CIA and a CIC, or combat information center, an area on a Navy ship where gunnery targets were plotted. He merely repeated his cover story about engaging only in peaceful research and again demanded the release of his men. The guards responded with a hail of kicks, punches, and karate chops that left him curled in the fetal position on the floor.

The skipper was dumped back in his cell. His rectum and right leg burned from shrapnel wounds; his mind reeled with worry. Could he and his men hold up under beatings that probably would escalate to systematic torture? What if the North Koreans turned up the heat on quiet, unassuming Steve Harris and his CTs, their heads crammed with secrets? And what of Bucher himself? The captain had endured 16 hours of sporadic beatings that left him mottled with bruises. He hadn't slept in 27 hours. How much more could he take? Already he felt himself disintegrating physically and mentally.

Bucher was ordered out of his room again at about midmorning. Lined up single file in the corridor were his five officers, heads bent submissively. The Americans were marched down the hall to a large room where some desks had been arranged in the shape of a horseshoe. At the center desk sat a fat communist general, wearing an elegant olive uniform and chain-smoking. Several more field-grade officers sat at desks on either side of him. Facing the communist officers was a row of six empty wooden chairs. Sheets covered the windows, and dim ceiling lights gave the room a menacing aspect. It looked like the stage for a Stalinist show trial in the 1930s, with Bucher and his officers in the role of the doomed defendants.

The Americans shuffled to their chairs and sat down. The general said nothing, letting the tension in the room build until it became almost unbearable. He rocked back and forth in his chair, glaring at his prisoners one by one. The tang of garlic wafted through the air.

Finally, the general launched into an angry harangue in Korean, with Max translating as fast as he could.

"You are guilty of heinous crimes against the Democratic People's Republic of Korea," he shouted, using the communists' preferred name for their country. "You are spies; you shall be treated as spies!"

The tirade went on for at least 15 minutes. At the end of it the general fixed his eyes on Bucher.

"What is your name and what is your job on the ship?"

The captain started to answer, but Max cut him off.

"Don't you know to stand up when addressing a senior officer?"

Bucher gave him a tired look and slowly got to his feet. He stated his name and rank.

"What was your ship doing?" the general demanded.

"My ship," the skipper answered in a strong, clear voice, "was conducting oceanographic research in international waters. I demand that my ship and my crew . . ." Max motioned for him to stop. The general snorted contemptuously. The rest of the *Pueblo* officers were asked the same question in turn, and each repeated the cover story. The general muttered gutturally and signaled the men to sit down.

"You were spying!" he exploded. "Spying against the peace-loving Democratic People's Republic of Korea. Captain, will you admit to that? Will you admit you were spying, that you violated our coastal waters?"

So that was their game, to justify their piracy by falsely claiming an intrusion into their territorial waters. Bucher leaped to his feet, shouting that the *Pueblo* had never come closer than 15 miles.

The general then demanded to know why the imperialist, warmongering United States had 50,000 troops in South Korea.

"Because the government of South Korea found it necessary to ask our help in defending their country," Bucher replied calmly.

A communist colonel seated a few feet from the captain reacted to this heresy by lunging at him and throwing a wild punch that barely missed his head. The general told his livid subordinate to calm down and turned again to the Americans.

"You have no rights under any Geneva convention rules as criminal spies and agents making provocations in time of peace against us! Do you not admit this is why you are here? Answer now!"

One by one, the *Pueblo* officers denied they were spies.

The general then leaned forward and spread his hands, palms up, as if events were now beyond his control.

"You are espionage agents," he said matter-of-factly. "How do you want to be shot? One at a time or all together at sundown?"

Bucher again jumped to his feet and did something astonishingly, almost insanely brave.

"Shoot me!" he yelled. "But let my officers and crew return to their ship and take it home."

"No, Captain! Because we caught you spying, ship now belongs to us."

"You seized us in international waters, where we had every right to be, dammit!" Bucher argued. "You've committed an act of war against the United States!"

"It is you who commit act of war by spying!" the general shouted back. "You will be shot this afternoon!"

The Americans were lined up in the hall again, heads bowed, and taken back to their cells. They had no chance to talk among themselves about the surreal, kangaroo court sentence that had just been imposed on them.

Schumacher tried tidying up to keep his mind occupied but wound up staring dumbly at his ceiling light. Murphy was sharing a room with three enlisted sailors, and they wanted to know what was going to happen to them. He told them about the general's interrogation but decided not to mention the promised executions, since he didn't want to scare them any more than they already were.

Steve Harris also was billeted with three seamen but took the opposite tack, telling them their officers were to be shot within hours. The men stared at him in shock, pinpoints of sweat emerging on their foreheads.

A guard pushed his way into Bucher's room bearing, of all things, a tray of milk and cookies. This time when the skipper refused to eat he was slugged. Shortly afterward, he was taken from his cell for what he thought might be an appointment with a firing squad. But it was another interrogation, conducted this time by the colonel who'd tried to punch him earlier.

The North Korean promptly flew into a screaming diatribe, with a translator frantically trying to match his decibel level and manic pace. The effect might have been comical had the colonel's anger not been so ferocious. Bucher's first impulse was to cower, but he checked his fear by forcing himself to study the North Korean. For all its venom and wild energy, the colonel's outburst had a choreographed feel to it. Bucher sensed he'd given this kind of performance before.

The captain watched, riveted, as the communist officer pounded the table with his fist and stamped his boots. Finally, he shoved a typewritten statement at Bucher.

"You will sign confession now!"

The skipper's refusal led to his worst beating yet. Guards took him back to his cell and slammed him into the walls over and over until he lay semiconscious on the floor. When he was later offered more food, the captain began to doubt that the communists intended to kill him, at least right away. And if they didn't, was he in for even more nightmarish treatment at the hands of well-practiced torturers?

Sometime between noon and one p.m., Bucher was again taken down the hall to the dimly lit interrogation room. Again he faced the narrow-eyed major, sitting at a table that now was piled with classified documents from the

Pueblo. Stunned by the profusion, Bucher could only hope most of them were relatively routine operating manuals. He tried to conceal his alarm as he slid into his seat.

The captain couldn't read the titles on most of the papers from where he sat. But he did spot the *Banner* cruise reports he'd picked up in Honolulu. Those could be highly compromising. The *Banner* and the *Pueblo* were nearly identical vessels. Since the captured reports detailed the *Banner*'s surveillance of the Soviet Union and China, it was reasonable to assume its sister ship was doing the same thing off North Korea.

"Do these belong to your ship?" the interrogator asked.

"Yes, obviously. So what?"

"Are they official American Navy documents?"

"Yes, obviously. We are an official U.S. Navy ship operating on the high seas."

"Do you deny they prove you were spying?"

Bucher answered that the documents demonstrated only that his ship had collected some incidental intelligence while carrying out scientific research.

"Ah, then you will sign this confession!" the major exclaimed, producing the typewritten document that the angry colonel had earlier pressured Bucher to sign.

The skipper scanned the statement. He was struck by its stilted phrasing and mangled grammar. Among other things, it claimed the CIA was in charge of the *Pueblo*'s mission and had promised Bucher that if he succeeded, "a lot of dollars would be offered to the whole crew members of my ship and particularly I myself would be honored." The captain realized later he should've signed right then and there; the "confession" obviously hadn't been written by a native English speaker. If the North Koreans tried to claim that a U.S. naval commander had signed it without coercion, they'd look ridiculous in the eyes of the world. But Bucher, determined not to yield to his captors, still refused to put his name on it.

He steeled himself for another pounding. The major, however, only asked a few more questions and banished him to his room. More food was brought in, but the captain didn't eat. The hall outside echoed with the sounds of doors being opened and slammed shut, followed by violent scuffling and screams. The other Americans evidently were being worked over, one by one. The skipper paced back and forth, his helplessness gnawing at him.

"Stop beating my men, you bastards!" he shrieked at his closed door. "Stop beating my men and let us out of here!"

Jesus God, Bucher, he thought, *get hold of yourself.* He couldn't let the communists think he was cracking; that's just what they wanted. He made himself step back from the door.

The faint glow of daylight on his covered window gradually faded to black. The deadline for executing the American officers came and went. It had all been a bluff. But the North Koreans weren't finished with Bucher.

His next interrogation came at about eight p.m., in a small, dingy room on the second floor. For the second time he faced the angry colonel, now accompanied by several guards and interpreters. One interpreter held a semiautomatic handgun.

Sitting behind a plain wooden desk, the colonel wore a well-made military greatcoat and a fur hat against the penetrating cold. He was tall, thin, and well-groomed. His jet-black hair was combed straight back, without a part, and his eyes glittered behind green-tinted glasses. Bucher began to think he was the real power in the prison. The crewmen later nicknamed him "Super C." Although they didn't know it at the time, the communist officer had been implicated in the deaths of 200 American POWs during the Korean War.

Super C seemed calm at first, almost amiable. He told Bucher that North Korea wanted only peace, and for peace to be preserved, the captain must admit his spying forthwith. He again presented Bucher with the typed confession he'd already spurned twice that day.

"Sign it and you will all shortly be returned home without more unpleasantness between us," the colonel cajoled through an interpreter.

Bucher was strongly tempted but still refused. Super C's affability vanished. He pounded the desk with his fist and screeched insults.

"You have exactly two minutes to decide to sign, sonabitchi," he yelled, "or be shot!"

Two guards pushed Bucher to his knees facing a wall. The interpreter with the pistol cocked it close to the captain's ear.

Bucher figured he'd soon be lying in a puddle of his own blood. He was determined not to show the terror that gripped him. His mind raced with thoughts of what it felt like to be shot in the head. Would there be horrible pain as the bullet pierced his brain, or just a split-second explosion as the world went black? He desperately sought a way to distract himself from what was about to happen.

"I love you, Rose," he said quietly. Then again: "I love you, Rose." He murmured his devotion to his wife over and over as the seconds ticked away.

Super C again asked whether he was ready to sign. The skipper shook his head and whispered for the last time, "I love you, Rose."

"Kill the sonabitchi!"

The metallic snap of the hammer made Bucher's body jerk. But the gun didn't go off.

Super C acted surprised. "That was a misfire," the interpreter said. "Very lucky! So then take another two minutes—a last chance to confess without trusting to luck again."

But when the triggerman jacked back the slide to reload, no ejected dud hit the floor. Through his fear and exhaustion Bucher realized the gun wasn't loaded. He'd been played, subjected to the old interrogation trick of mock execution. That knowledge helped him get through the next two minutes. When the time ran out, he still wouldn't put his name on the confession.

"You are not worth a good bullet," snarled Super C. "Beat him to death!"

Every Korean in the room except the colonel set to viciously kicking, punching, and karate-chopping Bucher. They concentrated on his stomach, testicles, and the small of his back. When the captain tried to protect his middle, they went for his head and neck. When he tried to cover his upper body, they pummeled his crotch and kidneys. As he later wrote of the ordeal: "They drowned out my screams with furious curses and kept beating, beating, beating until I was a retching, winded wreck being whipped back and forth between them like a rag doll in the hands of a gang of frenzied psychotic children." Mercifully, he blacked out.

The battered commander came to on the bed in his cell. His eyesight seemed tinged with blood; his kidneys and testicles felt swollen and raw. The slightest movement sent pain flaring through his body. He sensed some bones had been broken, but when he swung out of his rack he realized none were. The only part of his body not throbbing was his face.

Bucher staggered to his feet and called out, "*Benjo!*"—the Japanese word for toilet. A guard appeared and escorted him at rifle-point to the malodorous latrine. When he tried to urinate, more blood came out. On the way back to his room, the guard yelled at him to assume the penitential head-down position. Bucher still had enough moxie to holler back, "Fuck you, bud—leave me alone!"

He sat down heavily on the chair in his cell. His muscles and internal organs felt as if they were seizing up from all the blows they'd absorbed. About 30 minutes later a stocky communist lieutenant banged through the door and shouted, "Get up! Out now! Move quick!"

A pair of guards had to help the skipper down the stairs to the ground floor. At the bottom stood Super C, wrapped in his luxurious greatcoat, smoking a cigarette.

"Now we must show you how we treat spies in our country," his interpreter said.

Ice-cold night air washed over Bucher, chilling his sweaty body. He was bundled into the back of a car between the two guards. The rear windows were covered and an opaque screen separated the backseats from the front.

Ten minutes later the car stopped outside a large concrete building similar to the one where the crew was being held. Bucher was ushered out of the vehicle and down a staircase into a barren basement.

Before him was a horrifying sight. The limp body of a man hung from a wall, held up by a leather strap around his chest. The man had been brutally tortured and looked barely alive. A welter of dark bruises covered his shirtless torso. One of his arms was broken and a jagged bone had sliced through the skin. His face was a bloody mush. An eyeball had been knocked almost out of his head; it dangled from its socket amid an ooze of dark fluid. In his agony the man had chewed his bottom lip to shreds. To maximize the shock value of the scene, the North Koreans had trained two spotlights on the unconscious man, who frothed at the mouth and occasionally twitched.

Revulsion coursed through Bucher. He thought the victim was one of his men until the interpreter announced he was a South Korean spy. "Look at his just punishment!" the interpreter trilled. The captain couldn't take his eyes off the mangled creature. He felt trapped in a waking nightmare that just kept getting worse. His shock intensified until he lapsed into some sort of blackout.

The skipper had no memory of leaving the torture chamber. When he came to, he found himself back in the room where he'd first met Super C, staring into the communist's unforgiving eyes.

"So now you have seen for yourself how we treat spies," his interpreter said. "Perhaps you will reconsider your refusal to confess."

Numbly, reflexively, stubbornly, Bucher replied that he would not.

Guards promptly bashed him out of his chair, kicked him across the floor, and rammed him into a wall. Super C ordered them to drop the reeling American back in the chair.

"You must be sincere," he warned. "You must sign this confession as proof that you wish your crew to be treated leniently and humanely. The evidence is complete. Why do you not sign?"

"Because of all the lies it contains about my country," the panting captain replied.

"The world must know about the United States' imperialistic warmongering," Super C declared. He sounded genuinely upset. Bucher figured he was desperate for a signature. Yet in spite of the universe of suffering that still could be inflicted on him, the skipper said no.

"We will see," Super C snapped. His tone suggested that a sharp escalation of brutality was about to commence. "We will now begin to shoot your crew. We will shoot them one at a time, right here in front of your eyes so that you can see them die. We will shoot them all, starting with the youngest one first and so on, sonabitchi, until you sign confession.

"And if you have not signed when they are all dead, then we still have ways of making you do it, and all your crew will be dead for nothing. You are not sincere. We now bring in the crew member Bland to be shot."

A guard departed, presumably to get Howard Bland, a ship's fireman from Arizona who'd recently turned 20. Was Super C bluffing or would he actually kill the young sailor before Bucher's eyes? The confession, the captain knew, was filled with clumsy English and blatant propaganda. No one in America would believe he'd voluntarily written it. Was it worth gambling Bland's life to withhold his signature from a collection of obvious lies?

The skipper turned around. Bland stood just outside the door. Bucher couldn't bring himself to roll the dice.

"All right," he said resignedly. "I will sign."

CHAPTER 6

A MINEFIELD OF UNKNOWNS

President Lyndon Baines Johnson sat in a high-backed chair of gleaming dark leather, his forehead creased with apprehension. Arrayed around him at a long conference table in the White House Cabinet Room were a dozen of his brightest, most experienced advisers. With the *Pueblo* crisis less than 24 hours old in Washington, Johnson and his men were struggling to find a way to address it without making it worse.

Several of these men were holdovers from the Kennedy administration, whom Johnson had persuaded to stay on after he ascended to the Oval Office following his youthful predecessor's assassination. They'd been at LBJ's side through the euphoria of his landslide 1964 victory over Barry Goldwater, the devastating inner-city riots of 1967, and the long, bloody frustration of Vietnam. There was Dean Rusk, the Georgia farmer's son who rose to become president of the Rockefeller Foundation and John F. Kennedy's surprise pick for secretary of state, and who now served Johnson in the same role. There was Walt Rostow, the diminutive former MIT history professor turned Vietnam hawk who advised Johnson on national security. And there was Robert McNamara, the iron-disciplined, data-crunching defense secretary who Johnson feared might be headed for a nervous breakdown—even suicide—under the murderous stresses of running the American military effort in Vietnam. A key architect of the war, McNamara had come to believe it was futile and immoral.

The president's counselors fell silent as he read aloud from a wire-service account of a purported confession by the *Pueblo*'s commander, Lloyd Bucher.

North Korean radio had broadcast the statement earlier that day, January 24. A voice the communists identified as Bucher's claimed the *Pueblo* had "intruded deep" into North Korean waters while engaged in espionage. The captain condemned his own actions as "criminal" and "a sheer act of aggression," adding that he and his men hoped they'd be "forgiven leniently" by the government of North Korea. He said the CIA had promised that if the mission went well, he and his men would pocket "a lot of dollars."

The "confession" was clearly a propaganda sham, reminiscent of forced declarations by U.S. servicemen captured during the Korean War. Besides his fractured grammar, Bucher also had misstated some key facts. He gave his age as 38, not 40, and claimed that the CIA, not the Navy, had sent his ship into the Sea of Japan. But the captain otherwise described his mission accurately and in remarkable detail, noting that the *Pueblo* had tried to disguise itself as an oceanographic vessel and had eavesdropped on communist military activities near Wonsan, Chongjin, and other ports. Coerced or not, his statement gave the North Koreans a convenient, after-the-fact rationale for seizing his ship: It had violated their territorial waters in order to spy. And they'd wasted no time in broadcasting Bucher's admission to the world.

Johnson and his men were taken aback by the captain's damaging words. Had the communists drugged him? Had they threatened to kill him or his crew? LBJ and his advisers knew from the *Pueblo*'s radio messages that it hadn't fired a shot. Was it possible that its skipper was a traitor who gave up his ship for money or ideological reasons?

"I frankly do not see how they could get a U.S. Navy commander to make statements like that," said Rusk.

"Look very closely at his record," the president ordered. McNamara assured him that an intensive background investigation of Bucher was under way.

As serious as it was, the *Pueblo* incident was just one of the burdens on Johnson's shoulders. A few days earlier, a Strategic Air Command B-52 bomber had crash-landed on an ice-covered bay in Greenland, setting off an explosion that blew chunks of four hydrogen bombs around the crash site; U.S. specialists on dogsleds were hunting for radioactive fragments. Thousands of North Vietnamese troops were slowly encircling the isolated Marine firebase at Khe Sanh, in the mountainous northwest corner of South Vietnam. Topping it all off, U.S. intelligence had reports that the Vietcong planned major attacks throughout South Vietnam during the celebration of the lunar new year. The holidays—known as Tet—were just a few days away.

By 1968, the Vietnam War had become a conundrum that not even LBJ, with his legendary skills of political suasion, was able to solve. By turns compassionate and cruel, brilliant and boorish, painfully honest and infinitely devious, Johnson strode the American political landscape like a colossus in the wake of his overwhelming victory over Goldwater. With his volcanic energy and relentless drive, he rammed a head-spinning array of social programs through Congress: Medicare and Medicaid for the elderly and the poor; civil rights and voting rights for African-Americans; protections against air and water pollution; food stamps for the needy; measures to preserve land and expand housing; and numerous consumer protection laws. He created the National Endowment for the Arts, the Corporation for Public Broadcasting, and the John F. Kennedy Center for the Performing Arts. He drove his White House aides and an army of federal bureaucrats day and night to eradicate poverty and rebuild the nation's slums. But, like a fast-growing weed siphoning nutrients away from an orchid, the Vietnam War was draining more and more money from Johnson's cherished Great Society programs.

Now, the *Pueblo*, too, demanded the president's attention. The sheer outrageousness of the seizure made it politically impossible to do nothing. On the other hand, carrying out a retaliatory strike against North Korea—bombing an air base or port, for example—was freighted with risk. Even a single blow could touch off a sharp reaction by Kim Il Sung, up to and including a communist invasion of the south. If that happened, the United States—with thousands of troops encamped along the demilitarized zone—would be quickly embroiled in a new Korean War. With Vietnam straining his military resources to the breaking point and creating combustible divisions in American society, the last thing LBJ needed was another war in Asia. His strong preference was to settle the *Pueblo* standoff by peaceful means. But he was well aware that, depending on how the situation unfolded, he might have to resort to force.

Shortly after the spy ship was taken, Navy commanders in the Pacific had ordered the *Enterprise* and the missile frigate escorting it to reverse course and head for Wonsan. Four destroyers scattered around Northeast Asia were told to join the carrier as soon as possible. This task force was to prepare for air strikes and other actions.

Informed of the capture during a dinner party at his Honolulu home, Admiral John J. Hyland Jr., commander in chief of the Pacific Fleet, had been caught completely off guard. No one in the Navy had anticipated that the North Koreans would have the nerve to attack an American naval vessel—even one so alone and lightly armed—on the high seas. But Hyland and his staff soon cooked up a high-risk rescue plan that seemed like a throwback to the days of Commodore Stephen Decatur and the Barbary pirates.

The concept was simple: When the *Enterprise* battle group reached Wonsan, one destroyer was to dart into the harbor and lash the *Pueblo* to its side as carrier jets and naval guns pounded communist shore defenses. A raiding party of Marines and sailors would go ashore and try to free Bucher and his men, assuming they could be located nearby. If by some miracle the destroyer survived saturation attacks by North Korean MiGs and missile- and torpedo-firing patrol boats, it would literally rip the intelligence ship from its moorings and drag it back out to sea. The scheme, Hyland said years later, was "the only thing I could think to do."

In Washington—14 hours behind Korean time—Walt Rostow woke the president at 2:20 a.m. on January 23 and told him what had happened in the Sea of Japan. LBJ needed time to think. If some overeager field commander made a precipitous move, the possibility of ending the crisis peacefully might evaporate. New orders went out to the Pacific; the *Enterprise* and its accompanying warships were halted in their tracks. Reconnaissance flights against North Korea were scrubbed. All U.S. forces were directed to stay well clear of Wonsan. The *Enterprise* began steaming in circles as Johnson and his advisers tried to figure out what to do.

Many war-weary Americans applauded the president's restraint. But others, infuriated by the spectacle of a small communist country attacking and capturing a commissioned ship of the United States Navy, called for vengeance. Declaring the seizure "an act of rank piracy and an insult to the American flag," Republican Senator Strom Thurmond of South Carolina urged a military response if the ship and crew weren't returned by a specified deadline. A columnist for the *New York Daily News* said the situation amounted to "a test of national honor and prestige" not matched since the Cuban Missile Crisis in 1962.

Telegrams recommending swift—in some cases extreme—action against North Korea piled up at the White House. "Drop the atomic bomb like Harry Truman did," demanded a Skokie, Illinois, man. GOP Representative Bill Brock of Tennessee cabled that the president should "employ any and all means that may be necessary to secure the immediate release of the USS *Pueblo*."

Some citizens seemed more angered by the White House's reluctance to use force than by the capture itself. "Our government handling of the *Pueblo* seizure is the most gutless unpatriotic act this government has ever perpetrated," a Madison, Wisconsin, man wrote to Johnson. The *Milwaukee Sentinel* sarcastically suggested that a chicken replace the eagle as America's national emblem.

So upset was a Montclair, New Jersey, man that he could only spit out a one-word telegram to the president: "Coward."

Gathered now in the Cabinet Room, LBJ and his men tried to fathom the meaning of the seizure and devise a suitable response. They faced a minefield of dangerous unknowns. Why had North Korea grabbed the spy ship in the first place? Were the Russians involved in planning or executing the operation? And now that the North Koreans had the vessel and its crew, what were they likely to do?

CIA Director Richard Helms saw Moscow's fingerprints on the hijacking. He believed the Soviets had colluded with North Korea to divert Washington's attention from Vietnam. Kim Il Sung had publicly proclaimed that all socialist nations had a duty to help Ho Chi Minh in his struggle against American imperialism, and Helms noted that Kim had backed up his rhetoric by sending some MiG jets and pilots to North Vietnam. More ominously, a

Romanian source had told the CIA that the North Koreans wanted to open a "second front" on the Korean peninsula to tie up U.S. forces that otherwise could be deployed in Vietnam.

"This is a very serious matter," Helms told the president.

A related North Korean goal, the CIA chief speculated, was to scare the South Koreans into withdrawing their troops from Vietnam. One of America's staunchest allies, South Korea had nearly 50,000 soldiers in Vietnam, and LBJ was leaning on Seoul to send more. But the Blue House raid had left South Korea trembling, and the *Pueblo* episode only heightened the national sense of dread. Some South Korean politicians and journalists were calling for their troops to be brought home in case they were needed to repel another, larger North Korean attack, maybe even a full-fledged invasion.

For the men in the Cabinet Room, the possibility of Soviet involvement sharply raised the stakes. Helms and McNamara believed the Russians at a minimum had known in advance of the seizure; Rostow suggested they wanted to get their hands on the *Pueblo*'s advanced electronics. He later informed LBJ that a North Korean plane had taken off for Moscow laden with "792 pounds of cargo"—possibly surveillance hardware stripped from the ship.

But firm evidence of the USSR's culpability was sparse. Asked by Johnson to back up his theory of Soviet foreknowledge, McNamara could only cite the Russians' reaction when the U.S. ambassador to the Kremlin, Llewellyn Thompson, solicited their help, just nine hours after the seizure, in persuading the North Koreans to disgorge the *Pueblo*. An official of the Soviet foreign ministry told Thompson his nation couldn't act as intermediary and brusquely turned him away. McNamara argued that the Russians couldn't have prepared such a quick rejection unless they'd known of the capture beforehand. But a plausible alternative explanation—that Moscow didn't want to be seen publicly lending a hand to its capitalist archrival—wasn't considered.

While the president hoped to avoid using military force against North Korea, he wasn't pleased by the Pentagon's anemic initial reaction to the seizure. Apart from General McKee's audacious launch of his F-105s from Okinawa, no Pacific commander had lifted a finger to help the besieged spy ship. LBJ wasn't overly impressed even by McKee's actions; he wanted to know why the general's fighter-bombers had been held on the ground in South Korea. McNamara replied that the Air Force commander hadn't wanted his pilots to have to face an unbeatable number of MiGs over Wonsan. Johnson nevertheless demanded a report giving the "full story in detail," as well as a copy of McKee's order halting his aircraft at Osan.

With many Americans clamoring for revenge, the president knew he eventually might have to strike back at North Korea. But McNamara believed the moral and political basis for doing so was weakened by uncertainty over the *Pueblo*'s precise track during its voyage. Its position reports, coupled with intercepted radio calls from the North Korean gunboats, clearly showed it was in international waters when taken. But for 12 days before that Bucher and his men had observed radio silence. Could they have penetrated communist waters—accidentally or deliberately—during that time? Without being able to interview them, the U.S. government couldn't prove their ship *hadn't* entered a forbidden area at some point.

Under international law, however, the *Pueblo*'s whereabouts were irrelevant. Leonard Meeker, the State Department's general counsel, noted in a memo that even if a naval vessel intruded into another nation's waters, the offended state had the right only to escort the trespasser back to the high seas. Warships had the same status as sovereign territory: No country could legitimately shanghai another's military vessels under any circumstances short of war.

But LBJ and his advisers never made use of that powerful legal argument. They seemed more concerned about reactions in the court of public opinion—both at home and abroad—if they hit North Korea without convincing evidence that no intrusion had occurred. McNamara insisted that the White House would "need the fullest justification" to retaliate, including "proof of the exact location of the *Pueblo* when it was attacked."

The president rejoined his counselors in the Cabinet Room at 7:50 p.m. on January 24 for another brainstorming session that ended with him making a series of sweeping decisions.

Johnson began by reading a summary of TV evening news reports on his administration's handling of the crisis. The stories emphasized the president's desire for a peaceful solution. NBC and ABC also used footage of Rusk talking to reporters on Capitol Hill. Asked whether the bloody seizure constituted an act of war against the United States, the secretary of state said it did.

"I would not object to characterizing it as an act of war," he said, "in terms of categories in which such acts can be construed."

From the White House's point of view, Rusk's comment was a dangerously inflammatory misstep. An act of war—one nation bombing or invading another, for example—made the use of reciprocal violence justifiable under international legal doctrine. Shooting up and commandeering an American naval vessel on the high seas in peacetime certainly qualified as an act of war. But for a high-ranking government official to openly describe the incident that way ratcheted up the political pressure on the president to respond in kind. No administration official uttered such sentiments in public again.

LBJ wanted his advisers to give him a clear set of choices, both diplomatic and military. McNamara outlined plans for a massive movement of American arms and men to reinforce South Korea. He proposed sending a fleet of 250 jet fighters, bombers, and reconnaissance aircraft to the Far East from bases in the United States and elsewhere. To backfill the resulting defense gaps, McNamara urged that nearly 15,000 Air Force and Navy reservists be summoned to active duty—the biggest call-up since the Cuban crisis.

Like his boss, the defense secretary often saw events in different parts of the world through the dark and sometimes distorting lens of Vietnam. McNamara believed the United States should "respond promptly and in a firm manner" to the *Pueblo* capture lest Washington appear weak and irresolute not only to the North Koreans but to the North Vietnamese. American underreaction in Korea, he feared, might encourage Hanoi and thus "prolong the Vietnam War substantially."

McNamara also wanted to shift 26 B-52 bombers to Okinawa from airfields in California and Scotland. Taking off from the island, the all-weather heavy bombers could be over North Korea in only two and a half hours, decimating communist troops and armor if they crossed into the south. Finally, the defense chief recommended a secret, high-altitude reconnaissance flight over North Korea, both to check whether Kim Il Sung's forces were massing for an invasion and to pinpoint the stolen spy ship in Wonsan harbor.

After being assured that no airpower would be diverted from the coming struggle at Khe Sanh, the president approved all of McNamara's recommendations. In addition, two aircraft carrier battle groups were to join the *Enterprise*. Counting land- and carrier-based aircraft, a total of 361 U.S. warplanes would be available if fighting broke out.

But Johnson had no intention of using these forces if he didn't have to. He turned to Rusk, his top diplomat, who urged that Washington bring its case before the United Nations as soon as possible.

The world peacekeeping body had had a special interest in Korean affairs ever since the Korean War, in which troops from the United States and 15 other nations fought under the blue-and-white U.N. flag against North Korea and China. The U.N. Charter required member states to attempt to resolve their differences peacefully before resorting to military action, and for LBJ this obligation was a godsend. Bringing the issue before the U.N. Security Council would buy time for the American public to cool off, thereby easing pressure on the White House to uphold national honor with violence.

"It is one way of putting prestige factors in the refrigerator for a few days," Rusk had noted at a previous meeting that day.

Given more time, LBJ could pursue diplomacy even as he positioned combat forces in and around the Sea of Japan. There was a potential downside to the U.N. strategy, however. The Security Council could end its deliberations with a call for further restraint by Washington, thus undercutting the legitimacy of any American use of force, at least under present circumstances.

Johnson decided to take his chances.

Rusk also proposed a second appeal to the Soviets. They had a mutual defense treaty with Pyongyang, and any large-scale outbreak of fighting on the Korean peninsula could suck them in as well. It was in Moscow's interest to help defuse the situation by leaning on its North Korean allies to back off.

Rostow suggested calling the Soviets on the White House hotline to underscore the urgency of the matter, but Johnson demurred. He wanted to do nothing that might suggest an already dire situation was deteriorating. He instructed Rusk to draft a communiqué and transmit it to the Kremlin through ordinary channels the next day.

"Make it strong," the president emphasized.

At a closely guarded airstrip on Okinawa, CIA pilot Jack Weeks climbed into an extraordinary aircraft to go see whether Kim Il Sung was preparing for war.

With its needle nose, knife-edged delta wings, and jet-black titanium skin, the top secret A-12 looked like some huge, ethereal bird of prey. Built by Lockheed and flight-tested under tight security over the Nevada desert, the reconnaissance jet shot through the sky at a breathtaking 2,100 miles per hour—three times the speed of sound and more than four times faster than the craft it replaced, the famous U-2.

A squadron of A-12s at Kadena Air Base on Okinawa had been flying surveillance over North Vietnam in recent months. Now Washington wanted fast answers about what North Korea was up to.

Weeks's plane raced down the runway, bright-orange fireballs flaring from its two big engines. It lifted off and headed north. Weeks zoomed over the Yellow Sea and switched on his high-resolution cameras before flying west to east over North Korea's midsection. He made two more passes, spending just 17 minutes over communist territory. Soaring more than 80,000 feet above Wonsan, the pilot spotted the *Pueblo*, anchored in a small inlet at the north end of the icy bay, through his view scope. A single torpedo boat guarded the spy ship, although more patrol boats were nearby.

Upon Weeks's return to Kadena, his film was rushed into the hands of CIA photo analysts. Besides the *Pueblo*'s location, the pictures revealed 54 MiG fighters at Wonsan airfield and three Komar-class guided missile patrol boats that had never been photographed before. But, to the relief of those who saw them, the images showed no concentrations of troops and tanks near the demilitarized zone.

On January 25, at a somber breakfast meeting and then again over lunch, LBJ peppered his advisers with Socratic questions about the wisdom of the impending U.S. buildup. He seemed to be having doubts.

Wouldn't a huge infusion of American weaponry antagonize the Soviets, leading them to beef up their own forces in the Sea of Japan? How would the

Chinese react? And once all of the U.S. aircraft and warships were in place, what then?

The president's guests included Clark Clifford, a veteran Washington lawyer and Democratic Party power broker scheduled to replace McNamara as defense secretary in a few weeks. Clifford believed the military expansion would sharply escalate tensions in the Far East and was too risky; Johnson couldn't raise such a big sword over Kim Il Sung's head and then do nothing with it. Rather than send American ships and planes abroad, Clifford said, the president should assemble them at home and wait to see what the communists did next. Public anger over the *Pueblo* would die down; in the meantime the United States must proceed with great caution.

"I am deeply sorry about the ship and the eighty-three men," he said, "but I do not think it is worth a resumption of the Korean War."

Other advisers, however, argued that the United States needed much more military muscle in the region. Although the North Koreans weren't gearing up to invade now, they could decide to do so at any moment. South Korea had a bigger army than the north, but Pyongyang possessed a stronger air force, including many newer MiG fighters. The United States had only a handful of aircraft in South Korea, and the two American army divisions stationed there were significantly understrength. If war came, a lack of readiness could spell disaster.

An increase in American combat power also would serve as psychic balm for the many South Koreans who were deeply upset by the double shock of the Blue House raid and the *Pueblo* attack. Some even wanted to invade the north as payback. The Johnson administration had sternly warned against such action, and South Korea's President Park had pledged not to do so, at least for the time being. But Park believed counterattacks on North Korean "terrorist training camps" were necessary, and it seemed likely that he'd strike back hard if the north engaged in more aggression. Indeed, Washington learned that South Korean military leaders were secretly preparing "retaliatory raids." Tellingly, they refused to show their plans to General Bonesteel, the U.N. commander who ostensibly controlled South Korea's armed forces.

Johnson ultimately concluded that the buildup, though risky, was unavoidable. "We must move up our forces to awaken the people to the danger," he told his advisers. "We have to get our hands out and our guard up." But he also kept pressing them for a solution to his most immediate problem: how to get back the *Pueblo* and its crew. Rusk reiterated his recommendation to buy time at the United Nations. McNamara suggested giving South Korea another $100 million in military aid.

But no one knew how to save the 82 surviving sailors being held somewhere in North Korea.

The fog was so dense when Captain John Denham's destroyer caught up with the *Enterprise* that he heard the giant carrier before he saw it.

On the flight deck loudspeakers blared and jet engines revved. But it wasn't until Denham was just 100 yards away that the *Enterprise*'s gray enormity finally materialized out of the mist. He pulled his vessel, the USS *Ozbourn*, alongside the carrier's starboard beam. Admiral Epes, the air commander, waved to him.

Denham and his crew had been at Okinawa, taking on fuel and water while en route to Vietnam from Japan, when they received orders to join the *Enterprise*. The *Ozbourn* dashed out of port just past midnight on January 24, kicking up a six-foot-high rooster tail as it sped north. Denham rendezvoused with the carrier 14 hours later. When he heard of the dangerous plan to lasso the *Pueblo* and drag it out of Wonsan, he volunteered for the job.

The scheme might have seemed harebrained to some, but Denham thought it could work. The only question was how many of his sailors would die making that happen.

Many of them were battle-toughened veterans of Vietnam, where the *Ozbourn* had operated since the summer of 1966. Recently the destroyer had been active in Operation Sea Dragon, streaking in from the open ocean to shell bridges and highways along North Vietnam's coast before scooting away in a hail of enemy fire.

A 43-year-old San Francisco native, Denham believed he and his men were uniquely qualified to go after the *Pueblo*. After lying his way into the merchant marine at age 16 during World War II, he'd worked on a variety of ships. As a tugboat hand, he learned how to tow other vessels. Later in his career he commanded a military cargo ship almost identical to the original *Pueblo.* As a destroyer navigator during the Korean War, he participated in naval bombardments of Wonsan, familiarizing himself with local waters. He was a top-notch ship handler and his men knew how to fight at close quarters, having used small arms to battle Vietcong guerrillas on the banks of the Mekong River, sometimes only 100 feet away.

As the *Enterprise* battle group steamed around and around, awaiting a green light for action, Denham's men practiced taking back the *Pueblo.*

The *Ozbourn* was to rush into Wonsan harbor after other warships had laid down a punishing shore barrage. Clad in bulletproof vests, up to ten sailors and Marines would leap aboard the *Pueblo* as their shipmates raked surrounding areas with machine-gun, rifle, and mortar fire. When the boarding party had secured the ferret to the *Ozbourn* with polypropylene lines, Denham would reverse his engines, tearing the *Pueblo* from its moorings. While a second destroyer moved in to provide covering fire, the *Ozbourn* would hustle the spy vessel back to the high seas. Denham gave command of the boarding party to his executive officer, who, the destroyer skipper said, was "just crazy enough" to think the recovery plan was a good idea.

The snatch could unravel in a number of ways, however. For one thing, Denham had no information on the harbor's winds and currents, which could push his destroyer off course as he slowed down and tried to stop next to the *Pueblo.* No one knew whether North Korean soldiers were aboard the spy boat or if it was booby-trapped. Its anchor chain might be wrapped around a concrete piling, making it harder to yank free than if it were moored only with ropes. And any delays could prove fatal to the boarders.

"I didn't know what this would cost us, but I couldn't see us getting out of there free," recalled Denham.

He nevertheless forwarded his final plan to the *Enterprise*, and Epes approved it. *Ozbourn*'s sailors rehearsed every day, laying out where their lines would go and how they'd fight off enemy troops.

From his bridge Denham intently watched the dry runs and waited for the order to go.

On January 26, the White House received a reassuring message from an unexpected back-channel source: a Soviet KGB agent in India.

The Russians already had rejected LBJ's second public entreaty for help in settling the *Pueblo* mess. In a letter hand-delivered to the Kremlin on January 25, the president warned Soviet premier Aleksey Kosygin that the hijacking had "created a deep sense of outrage among the American people." But Kosygin replied that the United States was on its own in dealing with Pyongyang. The spy boat, he declared, had violated North Korean waters and thus "responsibility for the incident falls entirely on the American military command."

Prudently, the Soviets withdrew their own surveillance ships from American coasts.

By openly beseeching them, however, Washington had committed a tactical blunder. The Russians had much to lose by helping Johnson, at least overtly. Kim Il Sung was likely to resent any such intercession, and his pique could drive a new wedge between his country and the USSR, allies whose relationship often waxed and waned. China, Moscow's longtime rival in courting Pyongyang, undoubtedly would try to widen the rift by loudly denouncing the Soviets for giving aid and comfort to the imperialists.

But even as they publicly rebuffed Johnson, the Russians quietly tried to signal that they'd had nothing to do with the capture, declaring their innocence to Westerners at diplomatic receptions and in other settings.

Some lower-echelon U.S. intelligence officials, despite their superiors' suspicions, tended to believe the Soviets. Moscow, these analysts noted, had no interest in being drawn into a potentially explosive conflict with the United States over something as insignificant as a spy ship. "The USSR appears to have been caught unawares by the *Pueblo* incident," reported the State Department's Bureau of Intelligence and Research, adding that there was "no indication that Moscow instigated" the seizure or even knew about it beforehand.

When Kosygin made a state visit to India, the Soviets saw another opportunity to get across their message. Boris Batrayev, a KGB officer attached to the Russian embassy in New Delhi, approached some American journalists covering Kosygin's tour. Batrayev told the newsmen that contrary to its rejection of LBJ's requests for help, Moscow privately was trying to end the *Pueblo* impasse. The Soviet Union's public brush-off of the White House, he said, was a piece of political theater necessary to preserve its influence with Pyongyang.

One of the reporters the KGB man spoke to was Adam Clymer, the *Baltimore Sun*'s correspondent in New Delhi, who cabled a story home. The *Sun*'s Washington bureau chief passed a prepublication copy of the article to Walt Rostow, who related its hopeful contents to Johnson.

The president, meanwhile, decided it was time to speak directly to the American people about the crisis.

Just before four p.m. on January 26, the three television networks cut to Johnson as he stood at a White House podium and called the *Pueblo* capture a "wanton and aggressive act" that "cannot be accepted." He said he was doing everything possible to resolve the situation peacefully, but that "certain precautionary measures" were being taken to strengthen South Korea's defenses. LBJ also announced he was taking the matter before the U.N. Security Council.

That same afternoon, in New York City, the American ambassador to the United Nations, Arthur Goldberg, presented the case against North Korea in an emergency session of the Security Council that was reminiscent of the tense days of the Cuban Missile Crisis.

A bit of international intrigue preceded Goldberg's speech. American officials suspected that communist U.N. members were plotting to stymie him, and FBI men in Washington and New York hurriedly contacted sources in embassies and diplomatic missions of nations on friendly terms with North Korea. The agents discovered that the communist bloc was indeed planning to draw attention away from Goldberg's address by challenging Taiwan's right to a U.N. seat.

But that skirmish never materialized, and the white-haired Goldberg rose to declare that North Korea had created a "grave threat to peace." The United States, he said pointedly, "is exercising great restraint in this matter." Using a large map to show the *Pueblo*'s movements, Goldberg vividly recounted the assault on the ship. Intercepted position reports from sub chaser No. 35 proved that the spy boat hadn't violated North Korean waters on the day of its capture, he asserted. In fact, only minutes after the American vessel was boarded, communist seamen radioed their location as more than 21 miles from shore.

The ambassador also decried North Korea's "systematic campaign of infiltration, sabotage, and terrorism" against South Korea. Northern commandos had expanded their attacks far beyond the demilitarized zone, striking throughout South Korea and killing 153 soldiers and civilians in 1967—a more than fivefold increase over the previous year. The communist campaign had reached "a new level of outrage," Goldberg said, with the attempt to assassinate President Park. When the Soviet representative retorted that Bucher's recent admission demonstrated that the *Pueblo* had entered North Korean waters, Goldberg, a tough-minded former labor lawyer and U.S. Supreme Court justice, shot back that he was well acquainted with "the Soviet experience in coerced and fabricated confessions."

Goldberg finished by warning the Security Council that to ignore the *Pueblo* incident and communist depredations in South Korea was to invite catastrophe. But he was careful not to demand any specific action, such as a resolution demanding that North Korea return the ship and its men. The Soviets could veto that, abruptly cutting off debate in the U.N. and intensifying domestic political pressure on Johnson to mount a military attack. With no motion from Goldberg, the Security Council's members scheduled more talks over the weekend.

"What are they gonna do?" the president asked Goldberg in a phone call following the envoy's speech.

"Not a damn thing, just between us," Goldberg replied. "They'll fiddle around."

LBJ knew he'd bought himself some time, but not much.

When the United Nations eventually did conclude its deliberations, he told Goldberg, "We going to have to do something."

At 7:29 p.m. that evening, Johnson greeted two journalists in the Oval Office for an off-the-record "backgrounder" on the *Pueblo*.

Hugh Sidey was a prominent columnist for *Time* magazine. Garnett "Jack" Horner was the White House correspondent for the *Washington Star*, a scrappy afternoon newspaper read by many on Capitol Hill. The president laid down strict ground rules for the interview.

"There should be no attribution to anybody on this," he said. "I do not want any stories attributed to the president or to the White House. Is that clearly understood?"

"Yes, sir," both newsmen answered.

The background session gave LBJ the opportunity, with minimal political exposure, to address uncomfortable questions being raised in Congress, such as why the spy ship lacked protection during its mission. He told Sidey and Horner that neither the United States nor the Russians provided armed cover for surveillance ships, since doing so would require "navies and air forces enormously greater than their present forces."

Bucher probably waited before calling for help, said the president, because the harassment at first seemed routine. When he finally did request a rescue, it was too late. "Darkness was close at hand," said Johnson, explaining why General McKee grounded his F-105s at Osan. "The [seizure] operation was evidently preplanned, with MiGs on station which might have endangered the aircraft we might have sent in." The president said he could "find no fault" with field commanders who decided against engaging the hornet's nest of enemy jets in the Wonsan area.

Although McNamara had told him there was no proof that the *Pueblo* hadn't strayed into North Korean waters while observing radio silence, Johnson asserted to the journalists that the ship had been in international waters "at all times."

The president said he was making diplomatic overtures, but also pledged gravely that the United States would "defend our allies from aggression." To that end, American planes were being flown to South Korea starting that day. Horner posed the question that most bedeviled LBJ: What would he do if diplomacy failed?

"I hope it will not be necessary to use military force," Johnson said. "I am neither optimistic or pessimistic about this. It may be that we will lose the ship and the men, although I do not want to even think about that."

Acting on the president's demand for an in-depth background probe of Bucher, Navy detectives knocked on the doors of his friends and acquaintances in Bremerton, San Diego, and Japan.

Agents of the Naval Investigative Service examined the captain's financial records and made a "discreet inquiry" into rumors that he drank to excess. One informant said he thought Bucher had been drunk one afternoon at the Bremerton shipyard; the captain had red eyes and smelled of alcohol. But the yard superintendent, who'd clashed so often with Bucher, came to his defense, denying he was ever intoxicated during duty hours.

The NIS gumshoes also contacted several officers who'd served with Bucher in Submarine Flotilla Seven. Captain Henry Sweitzer, Bucher's commanding officer at the sub base, praised him as "a very fine officer" who put in 12- and 13-hour days and usually spent Saturdays and Sundays at the office as well. Sweitzer said he had "nothing but good things to say" about Bucher's professional performance, adding that he was a loyal Navy officer and dedicated family man.

Bucher's immediate supervisor at SUBFLOTSEVEN, Captain Maurice Horn, didn't hold him in such high esteem. While Bucher generally was hardworking and dependable, Horn said, he fell short on occasion. For instance, he might forget an important detail when drafting an operational order for one of the squadron's subs, or abruptly leave the office "when he felt he had worked long enough." Horn rated him as merely "a good sailor." Off duty, added Horn, Bucher was "a hard-charger party type" who "knew virtually every bar-girl in Yokosuka."

Investigators found a large kernel of truth in Horn's exaggeration. They delved deeply into Bucher's nocturnal rambles through Yokosuka, a garish bluejacket's paradise that featured some 250 nightclubs and bars teeming with receptive Japanese "hostesses." The women earned a percentage of the money customers spent on drinks for them. Their paychecks averaged $110 a month, and many supplemented that meager income with prostitution. Some hostesses took drugs or dealt in black-market goods, while others worked in the bars in hopes of finding an American to marry. Those with criminal records often supplied information to Navy and Japanese police; some were reputed members of the Japanese Communist Party.

The NIS men grilled hostesses, bartenders, and old Navy buddies, asking bluntly about Bucher's "morals." One ex-shipmate, Lieutenant Phil Stryker, grew so incensed at the questions that he threw a punch at his interviewer. Nonetheless, the agents soon discovered Bucher had done his share of philandering in his SUBFLOTSEVEN days. Two bar girls confided having had sex with the captain, one on "several occasions." A third implied that she'd had a serious affair with him in 1964, when his wife, Rose, was still in the States.

The detectives also interviewed an "attractive" 42-year-old bar owner who often accompanied Bucher to officers' clubs. Their relationship apparently was purely social; indeed, the bar owner also became friendly with Rose after she moved to Japan, describing her as a "very personable woman who appeared devoted to [Bucher] and their children." The bar owner and virtually everyone else the NIS bloodhounds spoke to characterized the captain as an intelligent, engaging man who drank steadily but never lost control or blabbed military secrets to whoever happened to be sitting on the next bar stool.

Bucher had, however, invited several Japanese civilians aboard the *Pueblo*, according to the NIS dossier. That may have been his way of thumbing his nose at Steve Harris and his spook superiors, but it was still a potential security breach. In addition, the captain had escorted an inebriated bar girl to the wardroom late one night for coffee. She stayed overnight but claimed she didn't have intercourse with Bucher. On another occasion he assigned Gene Lacy to give three Japanese university students a tour of the *Pueblo*, again creating a security problem.

As Navy investigators made their rounds, the CIA was delivering a secret psychological assessment of Bucher to the White House.

The Agency profilers apparently limited their research to reading the skipper's fitness reports and medical records and interviewing one former commanding officer. His early performance in the Navy, they said, was only average; Bucher seemed to need "somewhat more supervision" than others of his rank. He drew his lowest ratings in the categories of "military bearing, cooperativeness and personal conduct of his affairs." The psychologists were especially interested in why he'd signed the North Korean confession. They didn't believe a seasoned naval officer like Bucher would crack "even under intense psychological coercion." It evidently didn't occur to them, sitting in their comfortable stateside offices, that much of the coercion might have been brutally physical. The only possible explanation, they felt, was that Bucher had signed the statement "without realizing its significance"—a deduction that defied credibility in view of the captain's intelligence.

The CIA analysts concluded that there was no reason to think Bucher was anything but a loyal American. However, they couldn't resist pointing out what they seemed to regard as a significant character flaw: the captain's "strong inclination to become too involved with his men."

By the end of January, the American buildup in South Korea was in full swing. So many fighters, bombers, and reconnaissance aircraft poured into Osan, Kunsan, and other air bases that an overcrowding problem arose. Ground crews worked around the clock to accommodate the new arrivals; airmen slept on cold hangar floors for lack of barracks space.

Two more aircraft carriers—the USS *Yorktown* and the USS *Ranger*—joined the *Enterprise* in the Sea of Japan. The flattops and their accompanying cruisers, destroyers, and supply vessels formed a powerful battle group: about 25 warships in all. On the *Enterprise* flight deck, two jets bearing nuclear bombs sat ready for instant takeoff, pilots in their cockpits at all times. In addition, nine submarines kept an eye on both North Korean coasts.

Concerned by the presence of this American armada relatively close to their shores, the Soviets made their own show of force. By February 7, more than a dozen Russian warships—including two cruisers and three guided missile destroyers—had taken up station near the U.S. carriers. One or two Russian submarines were believed to be in the vicinity, and more ships were steaming down from Vladivostok.

A Soviet destroyer shadowed the *Ranger*, and a surveillance trawler, the *Gidrolog*, trailed the *Enterprise*. The crowded waters soon produced a collision. A Russian merchant ship, the *Kapitan Vislobokov*, ran into an American destroyer screening the *Ranger*. The USS *Rowan* suffered a three-foot gash in its hull above the waterline, but no one aboard either vessel was hurt.

Early one morning, a squadron of Soviet jet bombers, flying just 100 feet above the sea to avoid radar detection, roared over the *Yorktown* before it had a chance to scramble its own fighters. Russian bombers flew over the *Enterprise* and other U.S. warships as well, closely tailed by American jets. With so many hostile planes and ships jockeying for position, the odds of a miscalculation multiplied.

Intercepted radio traffic indicated that North Korea had fully mobilized its armed forces. American troops in South Korea were brought to full alert and their ammunition stocks replenished. General Bonesteel, the U.N. commander, worried about possible commando attacks on isolated Nike-Hercules missile sites, where tactical nuclear warheads were stored. His men hastily built bunkers to protect the missiles and threw up chain-link fences capable of stopping rocket-propelled grenades. Extra military police were brought in to guard the sites.

The Pentagon didn't advertise the buildup, although it transmitted relevant radio messages in the clear to make sure Pyongyang got the point. But the massive influx of weapons and men generated its own fearful momentum: The greater the preparations for war, the greater the chances war would break out, perhaps by mistake.

At the same time, LBJ was trying to get a handle on the extent to which the loss of the *Pueblo* had jeopardized national security. Bucher's final broadcast said he was destroying secret codes and as much surveillance equipment as possible. But how much had he actually gotten rid of? Even if he'd burned all the code material, the ship carried many other classified documents. Had the communists gotten their hands on them?

McNamara informed the president that "some equipment had been compromised," but that American units worldwide had switched to new codes immediately after the capture, so the intelligence loss probably wasn't too bad. A few days later, however, General Maxwell Taylor, a top White House military adviser, told congressional leaders that "we have sustained a rather serious loss in the equipment, which has gone into the hands of the enemy."

That wasn't the only issue Congress wanted addressed, however. The

Pueblo affair marked the first time since 1807 that an American naval commander had surrendered his ship without a fight, and it raised a host of nettlesome questions. The prior episode involved the capture of the unprepared frigate USS *Chesapeake* off Cape Henry, Virginia, by the British man-of-war *Leopard* amid the Napoleonic Wars. But at least the *Chesapeake* had been taken by what was then the world's preeminent sea power. A small communist country with a bathtub navy had picked off the *Pueblo*. How had this national mortification come to pass? Why hadn't the ship been rescued? Did the potential gains of seaborne surveillance justify the risks?

Indeed, at a closed-door hearing of the Senate Foreign Relations Committee on January 26, Secretary Rusk had been raked over the coals for excessive risk taking by Senator Karl Mundt of South Dakota. Though a Republican, Mundt was a strong supporter of President Johnson's Vietnam policies. Rusk tried to explain that a recent sharp rise in armed clashes along the demilitarized zone made it imperative for the United States to acquire fresh intelligence about North Korean military capabilities and intentions. But Mundt rejected that rationale, saying the risk of igniting another Asian war far outweighed the "very small amount of information" the *Pueblo* might collect.

"This is a very serious blunder on the part of the government in these times when we have got this [Vietnam] war on our hands," said the senator. "I just don't see any value at all of sending a ship close enough to provoke the enemy to do what it did."

Johnson, himself a veteran of Congress, knew what to expect next on Capitol Hill: a high-visibility hunt for those responsible for the fiasco, complete with public hearings and embarrassing questions in the glare of TV lights. "All of the committees will begin investigations of this incident once it cools down," he warned aides.

In an attempt to forestall such probes, LBJ repeatedly called ranking members of key congressional committees to the White House for detailed private briefings by McNamara; Army General Earle Wheeler, chairman of the Joint Chiefs of Staff; and others. The president's experts explained that no U.S. warships had been close enough to help the *Pueblo*, no planes could have arrived in time to make a difference, and the costs of combat ships escorting spy ships were prohibitive.

But some Republican congressmen were deeply angry over the hijacking, which they saw as prima facie evidence of colossal bungling by the administration. "All of you seem to have a good reason for not doing something," House Minority Leader Gerald Ford of Michigan snapped at LBJ and his top men during one briefing.

Johnson also promised to appoint international lawyer George Ball to get to the bottom of the *Pueblo* incident and report his findings to Congress. Ball, who'd once served as LBJ's under secretary of state, was widely respected in Washington for his persistent internal criticism of the administration's Vietnam policies. But the president, speaking to congressional leaders on January 31, pointed out an unpleasant truth underlying all covert intelligence operations: The men who carried them out were expendable.

"When you send out a spy," said LBJ, "he sometimes does not come back."

With American reinforcements almost completely in place in South Korea, the president faced his most important decision: What should be done with them?

Since the start of the crisis, an interagency team of government specialists dubbed the Korean Task Force had worked furiously to give him some feasible options. The group was headed by Sam Berger, a hard-driving former ambassador to South Korea known for his candor and strong distaste for traditional diplomatic bowing and scraping.

Berger and his people labored in the State Department's locked-door operations center, where Teletypes clattered nonstop with the latest cables from American embassies around the world. Berger often put in ten-hour days, six or seven days a week, racking his brains for ways to deal with the *Pueblo*.

"With Sam, you could almost feel the tension bouncing off the walls," recollected one task force member. "His mind was always churning over, over, over."

The pressure on Berger and his staff was enormous. His chief deputy soon developed heart-attack symptoms and had to be replaced. On January

29, the task force presented LBJ with ten possible courses of action. The trouble was that each one risked escalating the crisis—and none offered much hope of getting back the ship and its crew.

One possibility was to capture a North Korean naval vessel and swap it for the *Pueblo*. But most of Kim Il Sung's combat ships were high-speed patrol boats, equipped with radar and difficult to surprise at sea. Most also were based near Wonsan, meaning that even if the U.S. Navy did manage to grab one in that area, it would have to be sailed to the nearest port in South Korea, Mukho, 129 miles away. North Korean MiGs could be expected to pounce on U.S. forces every step of the way, inflicting significant losses. Nearby Russian men-of-war might try to interfere, directly involving the Soviet Union in the conflict. Moreover, such a "reciprocal" abduction amounted to a reprisal, a violation of the U.N. Charter that would make the United States appear as ruthless and piratical as North Korea. And in any event, Pyongyang was unlikely to trade its great propaganda prize, the *Pueblo*, for a mere patrol boat.

A far more aggressive option was an air strike against the big MiG base and the Munpyong Ni naval station near Wonsan. Ninety-two American and South Korean jets would hit the two installations, with the aim of punishing Kim Il Sung for both the *Pueblo* and guerrilla raids on South Korea. But the Joint Chiefs of Staff argued that in order to minimize U.S. losses, the entire North Korean air force had to be wiped out at the same time.

The consequences of such a colossal attack could only be guessed at. If all or most of Pyongyang's airpower—about 400 jet fighters and 80 light bombers—were knocked out, could President Park resist the impulse to invade the suddenly vulnerable north? Might the Soviets and Chinese feel compelled to move in to defend a prostrate ally? World reaction would be severe, the Korean Task Force warned, with a majority of U.N. member states condemning the massive retaliation as "a dangerously excessive measure, disproportionate to the provocation and too risky in terms of resumed hostilities in Korea."

Berger's group also suggested a naval blockade of Wonsan or a tank assault across the demilitarized zone aimed at destroying the headquarters of a North Korean infantry division. But a blockade would leave American ships open to attack by MiGs or deadly Styx missiles fired from patrol boats, while causing only minor inconvenience to communist naval vessels, which tended to hug the shore anyway. A punitive armor thrust through the DMZ would produce high casualties and, as Berger's team noted, might also "result in major ground action which would be difficult to stop."

The president's impulse was to commandeer a North Korean ship. But doing that wasn't likely to get the *Pueblo* crew home; nor was any other military action. On the contrary, any serious retaliation might prompt the communists to execute Bucher and his men.

And that was a horror that no one in the White House could abide.

For three days, Major Wright and his pilots sat in their cockpits, waiting for the signal to take off in their F-105s and sink the *Pueblo.* But the order never came and they finally were told to stand down.

Steaming with the *Enterprise* task force, Captain Denham was informed that his men needn't practice lassoing the spy ship anymore; higher-ups had canceled the daring scheme to snatch it back from the North Koreans.

CHAPTER 7

SUICIDE IN A BUCKET

In the early hours of his second day in prison, Bucher decided to kill himself.

He was a physical and emotional wreck. Repeated beatings had left him pissing blood. Sleep was nearly impossible; his arms, legs, back, sides, and chest bore so many painful bruises that it was difficult even to lie down. Lingering nausea erased any desire for food.

A profound sense of shame tormented him. He berated himself for caving in so quickly to Super C. He should've held out longer, absorbed more kicks and punches and karate blows. Why hadn't he called the communists' bluff when they brought Howard Bland to the interrogation room? Maybe they wouldn't have shot the young seaman after all.

It had all happened so fast, still was happening fast. Shortly after confessing, the captain was forced to appear at a staged press conference during which North Korean "journalists" hissed at him and angrily demanded details of how he'd spied on their country. Exhausted, deeply depressed, and reading from a prepared script, Bucher robotically confirmed every allegation.

There was no telling what the North Koreans would try to extract next. So far they'd been content merely to use him as a mouthpiece for obvious propaganda. What if they wanted more? His mind was a treasure chest of military secrets: details of U.S. naval war plans, submarine operations, undersea surveillance techniques, and agent landings. Could the communists pry open that mental lockbox with the diabolical levers of pain and fear? The truth was that they probably could.

Snow flurries thrummed against the window of his threadbare room. The ceiling light burned around the clock. Despair and loneliness plagued him. By now, he figured, the communists probably had pumped all the classified information they could out of Steve Harris and shot him. Other crewmen might be dead from wounds suffered during the attack or beatings in prison.

Suicide was contrary to Bucher's life-loving nature and staunch Catholicism, but he felt he had no choice. He sensed he already was close to a breaking point from all of the beatings and intimidation; more concentrated forms of pain probably would cause him to fall apart completely. He feared torture much more than death, and killing himself quickly seemed a lot better than letting Super C's thugs do it slowly. The last thing he wanted was to be reduced to a shattered wretch babbling his country's secrets in exchange for even a brief respite from the torturer's dreadful tools.

But if he were to take his own life, how exactly to do it? Bucher had no gun to blow out his brains with, and he lacked the physical strength and demonic willpower to bash them out against a wall. He might be able to fashion a noose from a blanket, but there was nothing to hang it from. He thought of breaking his window and using a glass shard to slit his wrists, but the noise would attract the guards who patrolled continuously just outside his door. If he jumped out the third-story window, he'd probably end up with no more than a broken leg.

The only other possibility was a metal pail in his cell. It had been filled with water so he could wash his face. In his desperation the skipper began to think he could drown himself in it. He'd heard that drowning wasn't too unpleasant once you stopped struggling. To anyone in a normal frame of mind, the notion of drowning yourself in a bucket would be absurd. But the bereft captain thought it might work.

It had to work.

His cell was so cold that a thin layer of ice had formed over the water in the pail. Bucher speared his head through the ice. Most of the water slopped out and the shock of the freezing liquid brought him to his senses. To end his life this way, he realized, was impossible. Drenched and defeated, he pulled his head out.

By January 26, his third day in prison, Bucher was so weak he could barely walk. Interrogations and beatings went on day and night; the skipper heard shouts, scuffling, and muffled cries as his men were slugged and pistol-whipped. He tried to get a few minutes of sleep whenever he was left alone in his room. But almost as soon as he closed his eyes, horrific images filled his head: explosions ripping through his ship, bloody bodies carried off on stretchers, a man dangling from a meat hook.

Bucher developed a fever, his body racked by chills. Slumped in his chair, he sank into torpor and confusion. At times he thought he was delirious. He couldn't distinguish between the moan of the wind outside the winter-bound prison and the cries of his men within. When the Koreans unexpectedly gave back his watch, he stared at it obsessively, trying to restore his sense of time. He began to hallucinate, seeing the dial replaced by the angry face of an interrogator shrieking threats at him. A nurse entered his cell and injected him with something; he wasn't sure what.

When he finally had to move his bowels, he nearly fainted from the pain of the shrapnel lodged in his rectum. His body stank from stale sweat and suppurating leg wounds. Concerned by his shivering and lack of appetite, his captors moved him across the hall to a cell where the radiator actually emitted some warmth.

In his lucid moments the skipper yearned to see a mushroom cloud billowing above Pyongyang. An American nuclear strike meant his own immolation, of course, but Bucher wanted these piratical animals punished regardless. His Navy briefers had promised swift and forceful retaliation if anything happened to him and his men, but thus far there'd been no visible action. The North Koreans seemed nervous about the possibility of an air strike or commando raid, and kept the prison blacked out at night. They threatened to kill Bucher if his countrymen tried to rescue him or avenge the *Pueblo*'s capture.

He didn't particularly care. Unable to sleep, he shuffled back and forth in his cell, his mind buzzing with unanswerable questions.

What classified materials had the North Koreans salvaged besides the documents he'd been shown? How many sailors had signed phony confessions? Had the U.S. government seen through the ludicrous propaganda sham that was Bucher's own statement? He reproached himself for not radioing Japan while the ship was under attack and specifically stating that it had never trespassed in North Korean waters. Was the Pentagon's uncertainty over the ship's whereabouts the reason for the absence of retaliation?

He struggled to understand why the communists grabbed the *Pueblo* in the first place. The only explanations that made any sense were that they wanted to start another war with South Korea or to distract the United States from Vietnam. Why didn't they seem interested in using him for anything other than propaganda? When they'd pounded enough "confessions" out of him and his crew, would the seamen be freed or left to rot for years in this miserable sty? Or simply taken to an empty field and shot?

The more he thought about it, the angrier he got at the Navy for ordering him into the Sea of Japan with such poor preparation and equipment. His request for a specially designed destruction system for the SOD hut had been rejected. He'd been saddled with too many secret papers and given peashooters to defend against 57-millimeter cannon. Worst of all, he'd been lulled into a false sense of security.

In the final analysis, though, the disaster had happened on his watch. And according to the age-old custom of the sea, a captain was solely responsible for everything that took place on his ship. At least one of his men was dead and the rest reduced to quivering hostages. His ship had been stolen, his country's security compromised, and he had to shoulder the blame. He should've off-loaded more classified material in Japan, he told himself, no matter how much higher-ups complained. He should never have put to sea until he had enough dynamite to blow the SOD hut sky-high. Why hadn't he ridden Steve Harris harder during the attack to get rid of his electronic gear? Why hadn't he ordered secret documents stacked in a compartment, doused with diesel fuel, and set on fire, even if the blaze spread uncontrollably and burned the ship to the waterline?

The skipper had only limited time for such self-flagellation, however. At any hour of the day or night he might be pulled from his room and brought before Super C, invariably chain-smoking and looking immaculate, for another arduous round of questions and threats. Bucher had to admire the colonel's endurance. He'd grilled the skipper again and again in the past few days—often for hours on end, in the dead of night—yet his alertness and ramrod bearing never faltered.

Super C always greeted his quarry the same way, asking through his translator: "How is your life these days?"

Filthy, bone-tired, and in constant pain, Bucher studied his antagonist to see whether he was mocking him. He decided to concede nothing.

"I am only interested in the condition of my men, especially the wounded ones," he replied during one session.

Super C ignored his request for news and launched into a long speech.

"You must be aware of the tortures which the Korean people suffered during the Fatherland Liberation War with the United States," he began, using the communist name for the Korean War. "Every Korean lost relatives in the war. CIA tortured them, killed them. Koreans hate the lackeys of imperialism, not the American people." He went on to blame the United States for keeping the people of North and South Korea divided for so many years. He characterized President Johnson as a CIA puppet and "murdering enemy of Koreans."

Super C's translator was proficient in English but hardly fluent. Bucher nicknamed him Wheezy, for his habit of coughing and wheezing to cover up his frequent stumbles. As long as Super C spoke in a calm, measured fashion, Wheezy did reasonably well. But he fell behind as the colonel's harangues gathered speed.

The American people, Super C charged, were "in the clutches of the Johnson murder clique and the Rockefeller gluttons and bloody-handed Wall Street warmongers—and kept oppressed with vicious murder by paid running dogs of CIA! We know that American workers are whipped slaves of Morgan Steel! We know that Americans will be our friends when they overthrow the CIA."

The colonel paused to let Wheezy catch up, and then went on in a more personal vein.

"You must show your gratitude and sincerity to the Korean people by honest confession of your crimes. Then you may go home to your loved ones. You will soon see what I mean. You see, I have a message for you from your wife, Madame Rose."

The mention of his beloved spouse hit Bucher like an emotional right hook. Was it possible that she'd gotten a message to North Korea so fast? He doubted it; this had to be another attempt to manipulate him.

Wheezy began reading from what sounded like an American news interview with Rose. She spoke of the agonizing ordeal of not knowing what had become of her husband, and her hopes for his rapid release and safe return home. The translator mentioned that a friend named "Hemmel" had appeared with her at a press conference in San Diego. The captain knew no one by that name and stared suspiciously at Wheezy, who tried another pronunciation: "Hemple." Bucher brightened. It had to be Lieutenant Commander Allen Hemphill, who'd served under him on the submarine USS *Ronquil*. Since there was nothing aboard the *Pueblo* to indicate they were friends, the news story had to be true. The skipper's heart filled with immense yearning for Rose, along with gratitude toward his old buddy for standing by her.

Super C didn't miss Bucher's reaction. "Very nice message from Mrs. Rose and your friend," he said. "Now we will help you every way to be sincere and make forgiveness from peace-loving Korean people so you can go home."

The captain, feeling he was being played again, angrily shouted, "How about my man Hodges whom your people murdered? What have you done with his body? We did nothing to provoke your ships into firing on us—nothing!"

As Wheezy's translation sank in, Super C's face turned a dark, furious red. He ordered Bucher to stand at attention. For the next three or four hours the North Korean ranted, raved, and emoted over the full catalog of American imperialistic sins: the CIA, the Vietnam War, the craven U.S. puppets running the Seoul government. Though he felt a grudging admiration for the colonel's staying power, Bucher was never quite sure what to make of these endless declamations. Sometimes Super C struck him as little more than a buffoon in uniform. Amid one extended tirade, the colonel nearly tied himself in a knot trying to haul a foot over his head to simulate how GIs supposedly strung up North Korean civilians by their heels during the Korean War.

But there was no denying Super C's intelligence: He'd read Shakespeare, was familiar with Greek and Roman mythology, and spoke of attending a Moscow military academy. His one vanity seemed to be a fondness for luxurious, Western-style leather shoes, possibly purchased in Shanghai. He was relatively well-informed about U.S. history and current events, although his knowledge was filtered through, and distorted by, his Marxist ideology. After several sessions with him, Bucher realized that an interesting dynamic was at work during these verbal marathons. No matter how long he bellowed and blustered, the colonel always paced himself, carefully gauging the impact of his performance on his captive. And while the skipper had no illusions about Super C's capacity for violence, he never seemed to apply more than necessary to achieve his ends.

Bucher also found that he needed to stay alert for the North Korean's rhetorical gear shifts, when he'd abruptly switch from an assault on the U.S. government to a personal attack on the captain.

"Why you use insincere, unusual English language in your confession?" he suddenly asked one day. "Do you not think we are aware of such tricks?"

The question was an odd one, especially coming from Super C, who had, after all, dictated Bucher's confession and pressured him relentlessly to sign it. What lay behind the query? Maybe it meant that the U.S. media and public had reacted skeptically to the forced statement, as the skipper hoped they would, and that the North Koreans now understood their mistake. On the other hand, maybe it signified that communist language experts had blocked release of the confession because it sounded inauthentic. There was no way of telling.

The colonel threw so many curveballs, in fact, that Bucher often lay awake at night trying to suss out what they all meant. He replayed the tedious interrogations over and over in his head, trying to interpret every twist and nuance. What were all the questions Super C asked, and how had the skipper answered each one? Had he given away some important secret without knowing it? It was the kind of compulsive mental wheel-spinning that can drive an imprisoned man to madness. But the captain couldn't stop it.

One thing was clear: It was Super C who ran this place. Guards jumped at his every command; prisoners were subject to his every whim. And having broken Bucher, he could turn his attention to crushing other Americans.

Like Schumacher.

The lieutenant had been beaten on January 26 and again, much more severely, the next day. Taken to the big interrogation room where the *Pueblo* officers had been threatened with a firing squad, Schumacher was ordered to kneel down and raise his arms over his head. Two guards cocked their AK-47s and pointed them at his temples, bayonets jabbing within inches of his face.

"What oceanographic measurements did you take?" an interpreter with fierce black eyes demanded in precise English.

The American officer responded with a defiant question of his own: "Why did you shoot at our ship?"

Like Bucher's, Schumacher's head was crowded with military secrets. He'd written the daily narrative of the *Pueblo*'s voyage, noting the positions of intercepted radar and radio stations. As the ship's communications officer, he knew a fair amount about the code machines. And, perhaps most dangerously, he knew which communication technicians specialized in which electronic instruments.

Schumacher felt a strong obligation to protect the secrets entrusted to him—with his life if need be. Sitting alone in his ice-cold cell, he'd decided to adhere rigidly to the Code of Conduct for Members of the Armed Forces of the United States—the famous injunction that captured servicemen should reveal nothing to the enemy beyond name, rank, and serial number.

Yet as much as he wanted to obey the code, Schumacher knew his pain threshold wasn't particularly high and it was only a matter of time before he cracked. Now, kneeling in the interrogation room with his upraised arms beginning to ache, he tried to keep from trembling. While the fierce-eyed interrogator and guards worked on him, five other North Koreans watched with detachment, like medical students observing an interesting new surgical procedure.

When Schumacher refused to talk about oceanographic activities, one guard began karate-kicking his elbow while the other kicked him in the chest. Pain shot down his arm like high voltage; he thought he'd suffocate from the boot strikes to his rib cage. The beating went on for at least 15 minutes, until his upper body felt as if it were on fire and his thoughts began to blur and break up like images on a badly tuned TV.

Schumacher couldn't hold out much longer. It seemed silly to get kicked to pieces over such innocuous information. To cough it up was to violate the Code of Conduct, but did the code even apply in this nightmare situation? The United States and North Korea weren't at war, so how could he be a POW? And what if the communists beat him into some grayed-out state of derangement in which he lost all control of his words and actions? Who knew what he might blurt then? He had to put an end to this insidious pounding.

"All right," he said, breathing heavily. "Stop kicking me and I'll tell you."

He described how the *Pueblo* measured ocean temperatures and salinity. The North Koreans had begun to jimmy their way into his mind, and that terrified Schumacher. On January 28, he tried to commit suicide the same way Bucher had, using the water pail in his cell. But, like the skipper, Schumacher soon discovered he couldn't drown himself in such a small amount of water.

The communists didn't confine themselves to breaking only officers. The day after he tried to kill himself, Schumacher walked down the corridor and saw Harry Iredale, the junior oceanographer, kneeling in a room with his arms in the air.

At five feet, six inches tall, Iredale was one of the shortest members of the crew and quite self-conscious about it. What he called his "vertical deficiency" had made him the target of gibes for much of his life. The son of a pipe fitter, he was raised in a loving but, he felt, overprotective blue-collar family near Philadelphia. He channeled much of his energy into academics, racking up nearly straight As in high school (he got a single B). He also loved sports, particularly basketball, football, and volleyball. Teammates nicknamed him "Half Pint," but Iredale could be a tigerish competitor.

Like some other crewmen, he tried to survive his first days in prison by drawing as little attention to himself as possible. On the third night, however, Iredale was rousted from bed at three a.m. and taken to a room with four or five guards gripping AK-47s. He refused to confess to violating North Korean waters and was ordered to his knees. An interpreter told him to pick up a wooden chair by its front legs and hold it over his head. After a few minutes his arms and shoulders began to throb with pain, then burn. When his arms sagged, guards kicked him in the sides and upper body. He struggled to maintain his balance but finally keeled over onto the sooty floor. The North Koreans began kicking his entire body except for his head.

Several times he picked up the chair, held it aloft as long as he could, dropped it, and curled into a ball as boots thudded into him. Even a much bigger and stronger man couldn't have performed this cruel stunt very long. Iredale knew some details of the *Pueblo*'s mission, but he wasn't familiar with eavesdropping equipment or most Navy intelligence operations. What could he reveal that was so bad? Absorbing this much pain and abuse for nothing, he told himself, was stupid and dangerous. He didn't want to wind up dead or in a coma on the floor of this dirty, freezing room. After about 25 minutes of kicking, he agreed to confess.

An interpreter looked at him with contempt. "You're a weakling," he said. "You gave up too early."

Since their arrival at the Barn, the sailors had subsisted on watery turnip soup, rice, stale bread, and sometimes a small hunk of foul-smelling fish they dubbed "sewer trout." This miserable fare was served for breakfast, lunch, and dinner each day. Guards dropped off the rice outside the sailors' doors in buckets that looked like they ordinarily were used to wash the floors.

At lunchtime on the day he signed his confession, Iredale got the same slop as his cellmates, but a much larger portion. The extra food deeply embarrassed him. "It looked like I was being rewarded," he recalled. "It made me look bad." Too hungry to reject the meal, he ate his usual amount and gave the rest to the other Americans. The whole experience left the bantam oceanographer twitching with anger.

By far the most harrowing punishment was inflicted on one of the Marine sergeants, Bob Hammond.

About a week after his arrival at the Barn, Hammond was taken for interrogation. The North Koreans demanded to know whether he spoke their tongue. The Marine figured they'd seen the notation in his service jacket for Korean language training, but he decided not to take the easy way out. Rather than confirm something the communists almost certainly knew, Hammond refused to say anything except his name, rank, and service number.

He, too, was forced to hold up a chair and then kicked in the hands, arms, and sides as it inevitably sank. The blows only made Hammond mad. "I was determined not to tell them anything at all, for as long as I could last," he said. For the next six *hours* he was punched, kicked, and karate-chopped from head to toe by up to four soldiers at a time.

His hands and an arm soon went numb. When he couldn't hold up the chair any longer, his tormentors slammed a two-by-four board behind his knees and made him squat down on it. Then they used him as a punching bag while an interpreter asked, over and over, whether he spoke Korean.

The Marine kept blacking out and toppling over. Usually the guards yanked him back into a squatting position. Sometimes they just kicked him while he sprawled semiconscious on the floor. Several times they picked him up by the shirt and dropped him, his head bouncing off the concrete. Once, a guard stepped on his throat and Hammond thought he'd suffocate. At another point, he was taken to a different room and beaten some more as a group of about ten Koreans—including some women—watched wordlessly.

Angered by his resistance, the guards dialed up the violence. They propped him against a wall in a sitting position and stomped several times on his groin. When he screamed, a rag was stuffed in his mouth. He was placed in a chair and guards hand-chopped his neck and head, closing his right eye and paralyzing his neck. Two soldiers held him upright as the interpreter clubbed the backs of his legs with the two-by-four. To make the whacks hurt more they made him take off his pants. Finally, he mumbled through swollen lips, "Okay, okay." Then he was interrogated for 13 hours, during which he "wrote a brief confession and answered a lot of questions."

Hammond's condition shocked his cellmates when he returned. Fearless and obstinate, he'd absorbed an almost superhuman amount of punishment. "His face was beaten so that it was distorted," remembered another enlisted man. "His body was swollen and his stomach was so black and blue it looked as though his intestines were spilling out." For days Hammond vomited blood. He couldn't eat. For almost a week he couldn't get out of bed.

His only regret was not holding out longer.

After nine days at the Barn, Bucher still was wearing the same bloodstained, dirt-caked clothes he'd been captured in. The stink of his own unwashed body nearly made him retch. It was a miracle, he thought, that his wounds hadn't become infected in this filthy pen. He often saw rats scurrying through the latrine. Whenever he lay down, tiny gray bugs swarmed out of his rice-husk mattress and bit him all over.

He thought endlessly about how to signal the U.S. government that the *Pueblo* had never entered North Korean waters, and that any statements to the contrary by him or his men were lies extracted under heavy duress. He also tried to find a way to reach out to his sailors, kept apart and isolated in their cells.

While a few men had been badly beaten, it was becoming apparent that the communists weren't trying to kill them. In fact, the physical abuse seemed to be tapering off in frequency as well as severity. Whenever a guard worked over one of the Americans a bit too enthusiastically, an officer restrained him.

But the North Koreans never stopped stoking the climate of fear. One day, for example, an officer Bucher had never seen before burst into his room and shrieked, "Speak Korean? You speak Korean?" The question was a dangerous one, the captain figured, because the communists probably considered such fluency prima facie evidence of espionage.

Bucher denied that he or his men spoke anything but English. The next night, the sounds of a violent struggle erupted in the corridor outside his door. Alarmed, the captain wondered whether the North Koreans had zeroed in on Hammond and Chicca. Later Bucher glimpsed a badly beaten American being hustled past his cell door on a stretcher. Who it was, he couldn't tell.

On a different night the skipper was brought before a North Korean in a blue naval uniform. Scowling grimly to emphasize his serious purpose, the man said through an interpreter that he was announcing "rules of life" that the prisoners must obey at all times. Violators would be severely punished. Bucher listened carefully as the communist went down the list:

1. The daily schedule will be strictly observed.
2. You will always display courtesy to the duty personnel when they enter your room.
3. You must not talk loudly or sing in your room.
4. You must not sit or lie on the floor or bed except during prescribed hours; otherwise you should sit on the chair.
5. You must wear your clothes at all times except when washing your face and in bed.
6. You must take care of your room, furniture, and all expendables issued to you.
7. You will keep your room and corridors clean at all times.
8. You will entertain yourself only with the culture provided.
9. If you have something to do, ask permission from the guards, who will escort you to the appropriate place.

Trudging back to his cell he mulled the implications of the new edicts. They suggested the North Koreans intended to keep their captives around for a while and wanted them to behave in an orderly, disciplined manner. In fact, the communist rules weren't much different from those governing life in a U.S. military stockade.

The prospect of death receded even further in Bucher's mind until one night when a North Korean lieutenant and two soldiers charged into his room at about 10:30 p.m. The officer trained a pistol on the captain, who'd taken off his clothes in preparation for bed.

"You must dress," the officer snapped. "Must hurry!"

So this is it, Bucher thought, terrified. He'd be hooded, shoved against a wall, and shot.

"You will go now for bath," the lieutenant explained, his stern expression not changing.

A bath? At this time of night? Now Bucher knew he was doomed. All he wanted was a quick end. If torture seemed imminent, he'd attack a guard or try to run away—anything to get himself killed fast. A feeling of calm resignation settled over him as he slowly put on his grimy clothes. The communist officer again urged him to move faster. He also handed him a sliver of soap and a ratty towel.

The guards hustled him down the stairs and out the front door into a crisp, clear winter's night. The captain looked up appreciatively at the stardusted black sky as he crunched through the snow toward a waiting bus. Two more guards got in behind him and the bus lurched off down the road.

Bucher guessed they were going to the dungeon where he'd seen the mutilated South Korean, but the bus stopped before traveling that far. Outlined against the darkness were three gloomy cement buildings. Several officers and soldiers stood outside, stamping their feet in the biting cold. The skipper was led into one of the buildings and told to take off his shoes—an odd way to get ready for execution, he thought.

Entering a white-tiled room, Bucher was met not by a row of riflemen but by soothing clouds of steam. Jesus, they really were taking him for a bath! A feeling of relief hit him so hard his legs nearly buckled. Stripping off his reeking clothes, he wanted to laugh out loud.

The scene became even more unreal when a platoon of cameramen barged in, grinning like madmen. They switched on klieg lights and recorded the naked captain, also beaming, as he stepped into a sunken tub filled with deliciously clean hot water. Knowing he was once more being used as a propaganda patsy, Bucher, still smiling, made a fist at the photographers and extended his index and little fingers. The gesture, easily recognized by American enlisted men and college students, meant "bullshit," and the skipper hoped that anyone in the United States who saw a picture of him would understand his message. After the camera crew departed, he was allowed to spend a blissful hour in the tub.

At six o'clock the next morning he was taken from his cell at the Barn to another room on the same floor. There he was told to strip and put on a prisoner's uniform consisting of a jacket and pants of blue padded material, a white cotton shirt, coarse underpants lacking a fly, and socks. He was not given shoes, perhaps to discourage any thought of trying to escape through the snow-covered countryside. The new clothes hung on his undernourished frame like a potato sack on a scarecrow. At least they were clean. Being forced to wear his grungy Navy togs for so long had been a low-grade form of torture.

On the evening of February 7, Super C summoned the captain for another round of theatrics. He opened with his usual greeting—"How is your life these days?"—and then began a shrill denunciation of alleged U.S. atrocities during the Korean War.

With Wheezy coughing and sputtering his translation, the colonel argued that he was shielding Bucher and his men from the righteous wrath of the Korean people, who would instantly dismember the Americans if they ever got their hands on them. Bucher believed him. He'd already begun thinking of ways to escape, but it seemed impossible that his mostly Caucasian crew, even if they succeeded in breaking out of the Barn, could make their way on foot through an Asian police state whose inhabitants were universally hostile to them. One or two of his Filipino or Mexican-American sailors might be able to pass for Korean and reach the demilitarized zone or the coast, where they could perhaps steal a boat and sail south. But an escape by a large number of white sailors almost certainly would fail.

Bucher was imagining various breakout scenarios when Super C suddenly ended his philippic and proclaimed, "Tomorrow you will be given a special treat! Tomorrow is the great Korean holiday—the anniversary of the beginning of the Korean People's Army!" The celebration, Super C promised, would include apples, candies, cakes, and other "special food" for the captives. Bucher's mouth watered at the thought of such delicacies, but he merely shrugged and was dismissed.

The next day a pair of women in drab army dresses came into his room, spread a cloth over the little table, and positioned a bowl of apples as a centerpiece. Then they brought in platters of boiled fish, steamed rice, and bread and butter. An officer told Bucher not to touch anything yet, and the captain steeled himself for the possibility that the feast would be snatched away the moment the requisite propaganda pictures were taken.

The same gang of cameramen who filmed his late-night bath rushed into his cell. An anxious major accompanied them, fussily rearranging Bucher's sparse furnishings. The skipper nicknamed him Jack Warner and his subordinates the Warner Brothers. The two army "maids" reappeared, wearing colorful native costumes and bearing still more food: rich pork and potato soup and sparkling beer. As Bucher gaped in disbelief at the feast, Jack Warner signaled for filming to begin.

The captain knew the North Koreans wanted to convey the image of a well-fed and cared-for "guest" of their government. Warner's footage probably would be broadcast throughout North Korea and in other countries as well. But Bucher couldn't resist the bait. He decided to eat his fill while sabotaging the propaganda by acting as if he hadn't had a meal in days. Picking up the bowl of soup in both hands, he slurped it with piggish abandon. He drained the beer like a construction worker after a day in 100-degree heat. If nothing else, the skipper wanted to wolf down as much food and drink as possible before it was taken away. To his surprise it wasn't, even after the filming stopped. Bucher ate until he was stuffed. When he was finished, a communist officer arrived with a small glass and a bottle of ginseng liquor. The officer filled the glass again and again—five times in all—until the captain felt the room spin. He was gloriously, sumptuously drunk. He staggered to his bed for a nap. And no one woke him up.

In spite of the unexpected rest and nourishment, Bucher's psychological state remained fragile. The day after the army anniversary, an alert young seaman, Stu Russell, was assigned to scrub the captain's floor. When a guard caught them whispering, both Americans were beaten. Nevertheless, Russell showed up for the same duty the next day. A new guard looked away for a moment and Russell murmured, "What are our chances, Captain?" Embittered by the previous day's clobbering, Bucher replied, "They'll get what they can, then get rid of us."

A few days later, the captain passed a note to Schumacher saying he didn't think he'd survive prison and that he felt responsible for Duane Hodges's death. He asked the lieutenant to visit Rose if he ever got out. Suspecting the skipper was contemplating suicide, Schumacher sent back a note urging him to stay alive.

As Bucher struggled to keep his mental balance, the North Koreans stepped up their efforts to exploit him and his men for propaganda.

One day in early February, the captain was escorted to the big interrogation room for another press conference. Through the blinding TV lights he saw a crowd of people that included, to his amazement, the *Pueblo*'s five other officers. They were all alive and together for the first time since they'd been threatened with a firing squad. Bucher was so elated that he had to stifle the impulse to shout happily and throw himself into his men's arms.

The other Americans had lost weight and looked haggard; their eyes were bloodshot and they seemed jumpy. Bucher noticed a bad cut on one of Ed Murphy's ears. The captain knew he, too, looked like hell, but he felt a surge of confidence at finding his wardroom intact.

About 20 North Koreans in civilian clothes were jammed into the room, which had the look of a U.S. Senate committee chamber at the start of an important hearing: curls of cigarette smoke, TV cables everywhere, cameramen rushing back and forth, heat, anticipation. Schumacher recognized most of the North Koreans as army officers in mufti. But several others were representatives of the Korean Central News Agency and other communist media outlets.

The journalists laughed boisterously and called out to one another. They sat at a large, U-shaped table facing the Americans, who were at a rectangular table laden with apples, cigarettes, candies, and cookies. After the chill of his cell, the hot lights made Murphy a little sleepy.

Earlier, the Americans had been ordered to memorize answers to a series of questions they'd be asked at this conference. They also were told to always refer to North Korea as the Democratic People's Republic of Korea. Colonel Scar opened the proceedings, and Bucher fielded the first couple of questions, describing the health of his men as good and the North Koreans as "gentlemanly and understanding."

As the communists had instructed him, Murphy falsely stated that the *Pueblo* penetrated North Korean waters at six different points. Steve Harris explained the CTs' jobs, revealing so many accurate details that Schumacher winced.

The charade lasted five nerve-racking hours, as the Americans regurgitated predetermined answers to prearranged questions. Toward the middle of the conference, a glimmer of Bucher's old impishness broke through. He'd been groping for ways to subvert the show, and an opportunity eventually presented itself. A North Korean correspondent mentioned that two top Japanese government officials had publicly asserted that the spy ship was boarded on the high seas, not in North Korean waters. What did the captain think of their statement?

"That's nonsense. I am sure Japanese Prime Minister Sato and Foreign Minister Miki were not on board our ship," he replied earnestly. "If they were on board, they would have been captured together with us and detained in the Democratic People's Republic of Korea, wouldn't they?" The absurdity of Bucher's denial that a pair of internationally known Japanese politicians had been his passengers underlined the inanity of the entire press confab—especially the notion that the Americans were speaking of their own free will.

Unperturbed, Super C pronounced the event a great success. A few days later, he again summoned the *Pueblo* officers and demanded that they now write a letter of apology to the North Korean people. The apology, the colonel said, must be completely sincere if the Americans ever hoped to win the people's forgiveness. Otherwise, he threatened, the crew would face the full fury of socialist justice.

Super C turned over the letter project to Colonel Scar, who laid down the general line he wanted followed. The Americans were ordered to sit at a table, issued pencils and paper, and told to start writing. Again Bucher saw an opening. If he and his men could twist the letter's phrasing the right way, they could signal those in the United States who read it that their "apology" was just another bucket of bilge.

Armed guards stood outside the room. The Americans were told not to talk about anything not directly related to the letter. A new translator, quickly dubbed Silver Lips because of his relative fluency in English, accompanied Scar. Silver Lips listened to everything the *Pueblo* officers said and scrutinized everything they wrote.

Bucher and his men tried to stall the writing process as long as possible. They debated the exact meaning of various words. They argued about the best synonyms for those words. They consulted a dictionary, and consulted it again. They deliberately misspelled words so it took longer to find them in the dictionary. The exercise turned into something akin to an unending game of Scrabble played by patients in a lunatic asylum. Bucher's group wrote a draft apology, then rewrote it, then rewrote the rewrite. Days passed. The Americans enjoyed one another's company, and they especially liked jerking around Colonel Scar and his minions.

Finally Scar began to lose patience. Hoping to streamline the writing committee, he sent all of the Americans back to their cells except the captain and Schumacher. That was a mistake. No one in the wardroom was more adept at word games than Schumacher, who'd majored in religion in college. With his brains and command of Old Testament language, Schumacher uncorked long, baroquely tangled sentences that sounded grand but on closer examination were meaningless.

After nearly a week of this literary burlesque, the communists had had enough. They drafted the apology themselves and handed it to Bucher. Though riddled with the usual leaden propaganda slogans, it was reasonably well written and made good use of American idiom. The captain argued for changes but was overruled.

At two a.m. on February 15, guards rousted all of the Americans from their beds for a mass signing of the apology. Bucher and his officers were taken to the third-floor interrogation room, and then the enlisted men were brought in, about 20 at a time.

They looked gaunt and fearful. Many exhibited signs of abuse: black eyes, lumpy jaws, and stiff, painful gaits. They made no attempt to communicate with their officers. Hammond seemed in the worst shape: pale, his face badly swollen, his body quivering with pain.

The sight of his bedraggled men made Bucher's throat constrict with pride and affection. Many sailors in turn seemed surprised and relieved to see him alive. The captain wanted to assure them that in spite of his devastated appearance, he was all right and ready to resume his role as their leader. But no talking was allowed and the North Koreans kept the officers and men apart.

Cynically, Super C had handed Bucher the task of persuading his crew to sign the apology—and thus violate the Code of Conduct. Article V of the code specifically called on POWs to "make no oral or written statements disloyal to [their] country . . . or harmful to [its] cause." The skipper figured some of his people would refuse and suffer awful punishment as a result; a few, including the steel-willed Hammond, might die while resisting. Bucher couldn't bear the thought of that. Surely his country didn't expect men to perish over a piece of paper. And ultimately, the captain knew, the communists could and would force every member of the crew to sign.

He decided to let them all off the hook.

Jack Warner switched on his lights and started filming. Bucher broke into a sweat as he faced his men to speak. The last thing he wanted them to think was that he was pressuring them to collaborate. Super C watched him closely.

"Men, I'm delighted to see all of you looking so well," he said, using a flat tone to disguise his sarcasm. He wanted to underscore his point with a wink, but the communists would pick up on that. He let his body sag slightly instead.

"As you can see, I'm still with you, and have been given the same humane treatment by the marvelous peace-loving Korean people, regular chow to keep me fit, and a room all to myself—which is why we haven't seen each other for a while."

A collective apology, the captain said, could help expedite their release from prison. He also insisted that he was the only man on the *Pueblo* who knew for sure whether the ship had actually violated North Korean waters.

He wasn't asking them to sign, he said grimly. "I'm telling you to sign."

It occurred to Bucher that by ordering subordinates to ignore the Code of Conduct, he might be exposing himself to Navy discipline if he ever got home. He wasn't going to worry about that now, though. Getting the crew's signatures on the apology was the only way he could think of to shield them from beatings or worse.

But in trying to keep his men's heads off one chopping block, the captain was potentially placing them on another. The apology made the entire crew culpable for entering North Korean waters for the purpose of spying, giving the communists a handy pretext to shoot them all. It also contained additional "admissions" shrewdly calculated to tie Washington's hands in dealing with the crisis. For example, the letter said the *Pueblo* intrusions weren't due to technical problems, making it more difficult for the Johnson administration to claim that navigational error was behind any inadvertent violations.

The signing exercise made clear that Pyongyang's goal was to squeeze a mea culpa not just from the sailors but from the U.S. government—and that the communists had no compunction about using the crew as hostages to get what they wanted. "Our fate," the crew's letter said, "depends largely on whether or not the government of the United States, which has forced us into espionage, makes public the facts of crimes to the fair world opinion and apologizes to the government of the Democratic People's Republic of Korea."

One by one, the sailors approached the table where the document lay. Some gazed intently at their commander; others wouldn't meet his eyes. Some signed hesitantly, others with indifference. Still others tried to obscure their signatures with wild flourishes or by slanting the letters too much. When the first group finished, the next 20 were prodded in. Bucher repeated his speech and they signed, too.

And so, in only a few weeks, the North Koreans had broken a large group of American fighting men. They'd done so with a combination of physical pain; food, sleep, and heat deprivation; and, most of all, fear. No one had been killed or maimed in prison. No one had his fingernails pulled out, his legs broken, or his brain washed. Yet all had succumbed, becoming fresh proof of the barbarous old adage that, if subjected to enough pressure, a man can be made to do anything.

CHAPTER 8

AT THE MAD HATTER'S TEA PARTY

North Korea went on red alert after taking the *Pueblo*, girding for a possible revenge attack. On the first night Pyongyang was blacked out. People in the capital heard artillery bellowing in the distance, but it wasn't clear whether the guns were firing at U.S. jets and warships or just practicing.

A government radio announcer hailed the capture as a great victory over the imperialist spy dogs. North Korean waters had been encroached upon from time to time, the communist media said, but the *Pueblo* had gone too far. The ship was said to have fired first on North Korean patrol boats, which then shot back, killing an American gunner. The brave socialist sailors were praised and the arrogant Yankees ridiculed for surrendering in spite of their superior armaments, including "tens of anti-aircraft machineguns" and "tens of thousands of hand grenades."

North Korean forces shifted to a war footing. Sixteen reserve army divisions were mobilized, and military jets crisscrossed the skies over Pyongyang. Troop-laden trucks rushed to and fro in the city; factory workers performed martial drills. Industrial plants were evacuated and schoolchildren sent to live in the countryside. All citizens over the age of five were instructed to carry food and other necessities in backpacks wherever they went.

Yet many North Koreans didn't seem particularly afraid of what the

United States might do. An East German diplomat in Pyongyang reported to superiors that many civilians believed their superpower ally, the Soviet Union, would fight on their side if war broke out.

The people's defiant confidence also had roots in their boundless hatred of Americans, a sentiment carefully cultivated by their absolute ruler, Kim Il Sung. Kim had long accused his depraved archenemies of committing all manner of atrocities during the Korean War and now of plotting a new war on the peninsula. Kim told his subjects over and over that their discipline and martial spirit would prevail in any clash with the world's most vicious capitalist power, notwithstanding its arsenal of nuclear weapons.

Kim perfected over many years his methods of controlling and manipulating public opinion. The son of an herbal pharmacist and a teacher, he'd been kicked out of school at 17 for taking part in communist activities. In the early 1930s he joined Chinese guerrillas fighting the Japanese army in Manchuria, eventually becoming a commander. By 1941, however, the Japanese had crushed the partisans in Manchuria. Kim fled to the Soviet Union, where he underwent additional training in the armed forces of his hero, Joseph Stalin.

After World War II ended, Kim, wearing the uniform of a Red Army major, returned to Korea in the wake of Soviet occupation troops. The Russians touted Kim to his countrymen as a great wartime paladin and installed him as head of the communist regime that ruled north of the 38th parallel. Kim rapidly built up an army, a government apparatus, and an authoritarian political party modeled along Soviet lines. In 1950, with Moscow's encouragement and matériel, Kim's forces invaded South Korea in a brutal gamble to reunite north and south under communist leadership.

By the time the war ended in stalemate in 1953, much of North Korea lay in ruins. When high-ranking members of Kim's party attempted a coup against him, he easily deflected the thrust and, after a series of show trials, executed ten conspirators. In later years he purged numerous opponents, real and imagined, arrogating all state power to himself and creating a cult of personality second only to that of Mao Zedong. Kim billed himself as North Korea's "peerless patriot, national hero, and ever-victorious, iron-willed commander." He was the *saryong*, the supreme leader, "without precedent in West or East in all ages."

Kim proved a temperamental ally of the two communist giants with whom he shared a border, China and the USSR. Playing one against the other, he often managed to extract more economic and military aid from both. From 1953 until the early 1960s he gravitated toward China, which had saved him during the war by sending hundreds of thousands of bugle-blowing "volunteers" to battle United Nations forces after they pushed Kim's troops nearly to the Yalu River. After Chinese Red Guards assailed him as an aristocrat and "fat revisionist pig" during the tumultuous Cultural Revolution of the mid-1960s, Kim edged back toward the Soviet camp.

The Russians rewarded him by opening wide the spigots of economic and military assistance, allowing Kim to modernize and enlarge his armed forces. By the late sixties, he'd built one of the most formidable air forces in the communist world—nearly 500 aircraft, more than half of which were Soviet-built MiG fighters and IL-28 bombers. Kim's army, consisting of about 350,000 men, also relied heavily on Soviet equipment, including medium tanks.

In spite of the Soviets' munificence, Kim went to some lengths to demonstrate that he wasn't their puppet. He criticized Moscow for not taking a more aggressive stance against the United States in Vietnam, even though Russian freighters were delivering a steady stream of military supplies to Haiphong harbor. When the Soviets passed along one of Lyndon Johnson's beseeching letters, plus their own request for a detailed explanation of the *Pueblo* seizure, Kim didn't bother to reply.

The North Korean leader never wavered in his efforts to reunite the sundered peninsula under his rule. For several years after the Korean War, his method was peaceful subversion. His agents merely spread propaganda in the south, particularly the idea of a loose north-south confederation. By 1961, he was convinced a revolutionary party must be organized in South Korea. Communist operatives became more militant, calling on southerners to engage in strikes and industrial sabotage, resist conscription, and expel American troops.

By 1965, however, it was clear this strategy had failed. Many South

Koreans, who had vivid memories of the savagery of Kim's soldiers and political cadres during the Korean War, despised the North Korean autocrat and wanted no part of a communist government.

Kim's campaign turned violent. He infiltrated more and more armed agents into the south in what General Bonesteel, the U.N. commander, aptly called a "porous war." North Korean marauders crossed the demilitarized zone to shoot up U.N. military outposts and pick off patrolling soldiers. U.S. intelligence believed Kim didn't want outright war, but was trying to nurture a revolutionary movement in the south that one day would morph into an armed insurgency, as Ho Chi Minh had done in South Vietnam. To that end, well-trained commando teams, dropped by high-speed boats on southern beaches, set up remote inland camps and sallied forth to attack police stations and attempt to indoctrinate villagers in the gospel of Kim Il Sung. But the communists found little popular support in South Korea.

With two hostile armies facing each other at almost spit-in-the-eye range, the demilitarized zone was a tense, dangerous place. It ran the width of the Korean peninsula—151 miles—through terrain that was hilly, dense with trees, underbrush, and tall grass, and, in autumn, often shrouded in fog—an infiltrator's dream. The DMZ's westernmost 18 miles, directly north of Seoul, were guarded by the U.S. 2nd Division; South Korean troops patrolled the rest.

The Americans bulldozed and defoliated their sector of the 4,000-yard-wide zone into a barren no-man's-land. Bonesteel erected a ten-foot-high chain-link fence topped with triple rolls of concertina wire. Just south of that barrier was a strip of carefully raked sand to record commando footprints. But the North Koreans kept coming and the number of violent clashes soared. While 50 "significant incidents" involving communist guerrillas in the south were reported in 1966, the following year saw 566 such episodes.

In August 1967, for example, infiltrators machine-gunned U.S. army engineers standing in a chow line, killing three and wounding 25. Raiders that year also blew up a 2nd Division barracks, leaving two soldiers dead, and derailed two South Korean trains, one carrying U.S. military supplies.

Meanwhile, South Korean intelligence reported that Kim Il Sung was digging in for war—literally. Communist airfield facilities, factories, ammunition dumps, and fuel depots were moved underground. High-ranking government officials underwent combat training several days a week, and many civilian industries were converted to production of artillery, machine guns, and other arms. Fifteen thousand soldiers were trained in unconventional warfare in preparation for attacks on southern targets, including storage facilities for U.S. nuclear munitions.

Kim's audacious capture of the *Pueblo* gave him a propaganda bonanza at home and abroad. The spy ship's presence off the North Korean coast was all he needed to validate his thesis that the hated Americans were planning a new war against the north. The dictator could therefore exhort his subjects to work harder and sacrifice more to build up the country's defenses. And on a purely personal level, the supremely egotistical North Korean leader must have rejoiced at his startling success in humbling the capitalist devils.

For several days after the seizure, North Korean state media mixed shrill demands for an apology with dire predictions of how badly the United States would suffer if it were foolish enough to retaliate. But behind the scenes, a delicate diplomatic minuet began at Panmunjom, a village in the DMZ where the Korean War armistice had been signed. Ever since the war ended, the allies and communists had been meeting at Panmunjom to haggle over alleged breaches of the cease-fire agreement.

American officials had secretly contacted members of the Neutral Nations Supervisory Commission, a multinational body that investigated charges of armistice violations. The NNSC was composed of representatives of four nations that hadn't taken part in the war: communist Poland and Czechoslovakia, and noncommunist Sweden and Switzerland. The U.S. government wanted the Swiss and Swedish commissioners to help with the *Pueblo*, but they were unwilling to intercede directly with the North Koreans.

However, the Swiss and Swedish members were "seriously disturbed" by Pyongyang's growing belligerence, and voiced their concerns to their communist counterparts. The Czech commissioner in turn approached Major General Pak Chung Kuk, an acerbic, chain-smoking veteran propagandist and negotiator for North Korea.

Shortly after midnight on January 28, the Swiss representative telephoned

American officials with the gratifying news that Pak had put out an apparent feeler.

Pak had given the communist commissioners a confidential message for the United States. It began with a harsh warning: If President Johnson used force in an effort to retrieve the *Pueblo* or its crew, he'd "get only bodies." But the North Korean general also said he was willing to discuss possible repatriation of the seamen if the negotiations were conducted "in a normal way"—an apparent reference to U.S.–North Korean talks at Panmunjom that had led to the release of two captured U.S. Army helicopter pilots in 1964.

At the White House, Pak's overture produced a swell of guarded optimism. "Sir, this is the break," national security adviser Walt Rostow wrote in a memo to the president. "The problem is how to do it with maximum dignity."

However, the American ambassador to South Korea, William Porter, a clear-thinking career diplomat with a reputation for tackling tough assignments, wasn't as sanguine. Porter had been in Korea for less than a year following a tour as deputy ambassador in South Vietnam. He was intimately familiar with communist-style guerrilla warfare and once spent a week traveling, by bus and on foot, through remote parts of South Korea to check on the inhabitants' readiness to fight off North Korean commandos.

Porter warned his State Department superiors in a secret cable that the "results could be explosive" if South Korea learned of Washington's covert contact with the communists. President Park Chung Hee and his top aides already believed, the ambassador wrote, that the United States was more concerned about getting back its sailors than stopping North Korean terrorism against the south. Alarmed by the Blue House raid, South Korean military leaders were quietly discussing the possibility of pulling their crack troops out of Vietnam to reinforce the home front. They also were talking about withdrawing from General Bonesteel's U.N. command in order to have a freer hand to retaliate against communist incursions. Porter didn't think they were serious, but who knew what might happen if they found out Washington was reaching out to North Korea without their knowledge or consent?

And sooner or later, he believed, the South Koreans would find out.

Porter's concerns drew a dry response from Sam Berger, head of the

Korean Task Force. Washington fully understood the political situation in Seoul, he cabled back, but wanted to make it as "easy as possible for [the North Koreans] to get off the hook." Raising the infiltration issue with the recalcitrant communists, he wrote, would only "complicate and delay" a solution to the *Pueblo* imbroglio.

Berger predicted that just one private parley between Washington and Pyongyang would be needed to get back the sailors, if President Park could be persuaded not to interfere. Berger noted that Park was "wise and a realist," and instructed Porter to promise him a wealth of new military assistance if he agreed to go along with the American game plan.

Porter did as he was told. He assured Park the multitude of American warplanes and ships that had arrived would be kept in the region for the time being. Washington also planned to provide millions of dollars in extra military aid, including two aging Navy destroyers whose delivery previously had been contingent on Park's sending more soldiers to Vietnam. The United States further pledged to give South Korea more counterguerrilla equipment, airlifting it with the same priority as supplies earmarked for American troops in Vietnam.

Porter's visit came not a moment too soon. Enraged by the Blue House plot, Park already had alerted his generals to be prepared to slash back at the north. But with all the additional military aid dangled before him, he agreed to stand down his forces and acquiesce in the U.S. negotiating strategy—at least for now. American officials then swiftly transmitted a letter to General Pak, saying they'd received his message via the Neutral Nations Supervisory Commission and wanted a closed-door meeting at Panmunjom.

But, in an early display of how mulish they could be in negotiations, the North Koreans promptly backpedaled.

Pak insisted he'd sent no prior communication and couldn't meet with the Americans if they continued to utter such "fabrications." If Washington wanted a get-together, he said, it must submit a new letter deleting all references to Pak's initial feeler.

Porter figured the communists were up to their usual Orwellian trick of trying to rewrite history for their own purposes. They wanted to establish a paper trail indicating that the United States came groveling to them first, and to erase the NNSC's role in brokering what Pyongyang evidently regarded as prestigious face-to-face negotiations with Washington.

Porter wanted the record kept straight. He decided to give Pak a letter that dropped the offending facts, but to supplement it with a cover letter accurately recounting the genesis of the talks. Of course, the North Koreans could simply throw away the cover letter and use the underlying document as propaganda grist. But Porter's approach ensured that the truth didn't get completely buried.

Pak accepted the ploy, and preparations began for the first clandestine rendezvous at Panmunjom. Washington's point man was Rear Admiral John Victor Smith, senior U.N. representative to the Military Armistice Commission, another post–Korean War agency set up to settle cease-fire breaches through negotiation.

A well-read Annapolis graduate with a lively sense of humor, Smith was the son of Marine Major General Holland M. "Howlin' Mad" Smith, who'd led amphibious invasions in the Pacific during World War II. Detailed to the MAC less than four months before the *Pueblo* seizure, the admiral had little enthusiasm for the job. He loathed the communists and the exhausting, hours-long rhetorical wrestling matches with his opposite number, General Pak, who made nonstop claims that U.N. troops were guilty of various outrages against the peace. "What we were doing was simply arguing for the world press, exchanging insults, and getting nowhere," Smith later lamented.

During an armistice commission meeting the day after the *Pueblo* hijack, for instance, Pak called Smith a "hooligan," referred to President Kennedy as a "putrid corpse," and labeled LBJ a "war maniac" fated to meet the same demise as Hitler. He characterized the United States as a "wolf [that] has gone mad and started biting anything that his fangs can reach." When Smith demanded the immediate return of the spy ship and its crew, Pak laughed in his face.

Such impudence infuriated the admiral, who reciprocated by contemptuously blowing cigar smoke at the North Korean general across the narrow negotiating table. When Pak was looking at him, Smith circumspectly sent the gray stream past his ear. But when the communist officer dropped his eyes to read something, Smith aimed his puffs directly at Pak's head.

Smith regarded the North Koreans as barbarians, and the endless, inconclusive squabbling at Panmunjom as a farce. Staring at Pak and his stone-faced aides in the MAC building, which sat directly athwart the cease-fire line dividing North and South Korea, the admiral felt physically vulnerable. Outside, U.N. and communist sentries spit, shouted epithets, and sometimes threw punches at one another. Gunfire often could be heard in the surrounding DMZ. Smith felt as if he were trapped in a big goldfish bowl, constantly exposed to possible kidnapping or assassination.

Then there was the pure tedium of commission meetings, which lasted as long as nine hours, partly because of the cumbersome translation process. Smith's statements had to be converted first into Korean and then Chinese, for the benefit of observers from the People's Republic of China, Pyongyang's rescuer in the Korean War. When Pak spoke, his words were translated into Chinese and English.

If anyone on the American side got up for a bathroom break, the communists accused them of not being sincere about preserving peace in Korea. Rather than risk an international incident over a full bladder, Smith made a habit of going without liquids for 24 hours preceding a session with Pak.

Despite Washington's hopes for an early breakthrough, the first secret meeting at Panmunjom, on February 2, went nowhere. Smith asked for names of the dead and wounded seamen, but Pak ignored his request, saying only that the survivors were in good health and were being detained "without any inconvenience in their life." He called the sailors "aggressors and criminals," and criticized Smith for trying to cover up the spy ship's provocative activities.

Smith repeatedly pressed the communist negotiator to state when the crewmen would be released. But Pak, a four-year veteran of the Panmunjom follies, dodged the question, instead asking Smith whether he had anything more to say. Seeming flustered, the admiral kept reiterating his demands until Pak coldly told him to "change your stand and attitude in addressing the subject." At the end of the session, Smith reported that he'd achieved "essentially nothing."

LBJ was disappointed at the failure of the inaugural meeting. The president had pushed hard for negotiations, which, if they succeeded, would obviate the need for military action. But the United States was no closer to getting Bucher and his men back after the second closed meeting, or the third, or the fourth. Smith kept denouncing the illegality of the *Pueblo* seizure, while Pak persistently accused Washington of trying to camouflage the ship's hostile actions.

After the second conference fizzled, Secretary of State Dean Rusk began to doubt that the smoke-blowing admiral was the right man for the job.

"This is no reflection on his abilities as [a] military man," wrote Rusk in an eyes-only cable to Ambassador Porter. "Pak has been in his job for years and has probably had [the] benefit of strenuous training in Communist polemics."

Porter and his embassy staff agreed. "We feel [Smith] is not psychologically suited nor does he have [the] temperament and mental agility for the job that has to be done at this time," the ambassador cabled back. "I regret that I must recommend in the national interest that he be relieved but this should be without prejudice to his naval career."

But Smith was not removed, perhaps because Rusk concluded that replacing him would take too long. The admiral stayed on until May, when his regular tour of duty with the armistice commission was up. Meantime, the State Department tightly scripted every word he said to Pak, cabling lengthy statements for Smith to read verbatim during the secret meetings.

Evidently unaware of the machinations to shunt him aside, Smith kept shuttling between Seoul and Panmunjom, often by helicopter. Security was a constant concern. At night soldiers guarded the drafty cottage he shared with his wife, Marion, at U.S. Eighth Army headquarters outside Seoul. Under his pillow the admiral kept a handgun.

The Smiths had a pretty Korean maid, Suzy, whom they suspected of working for South Korean intelligence. Suzy paid close attention to the admiral's lunch habits; if he didn't come home for his midday meal, he might be headed to Panmunjom. Marion kept the maid guessing by telling her to set the table for two every day, whether or not her husband was actually coming.

"Sometimes he couldn't return until late at night and I was horribly worried," she said in an interview more than 30 years later. "I'd sit up watching for the lights of the little helicopter to come over the mountains. It was a very tense period."

As Porter feared, the South Koreans soon found out about Smith's activities and a national uproar ensued.

Washington's restrained response to the *Pueblo* incident already had angered many South Koreans. America's failure to retaliate quickly and firmly, they believed, only encouraged Kim Il Sung to send more commandos to attack and kill southerners. But South Korean anxiety reached a crescendo with rumors that the United States might forge a separate peace with Kim. The most distasteful scenario involved an American apology to Pyongyang—an unthinkable humiliation, in the eyes of South Koreans, for their closest and strongest ally. As far as they were concerned, America's disgrace would be their own. Moreover, once its sailors were free, how much would Washington care about stopping communist intruders in the DMZ?

As the Panmunjom talks dragged on in February, South Koreans poured into the streets in protest. Students marched outside the U.S. embassy in Seoul, shouting over bullhorns for vengeance against Kim Il Sung. More than 100,000 people filled a Seoul stadium in 20-degree weather to demand more American and U.N. aid to stave off further Blue House–style raids. During the rally, South Korean veterans of Vietnam ceremonially nicked their foreheads and wrote anticommunist slogans in blood. Inside the American embassy, someone opened a letter from a man protesting North Korea's "barbarous acts" and found a severed finger.

At a bridge leading to Panmunjom, U.S. soldiers fired warning shots to stop a march by 500 students demanding an end to the covert negotiations. American spokesmen said none of the marchers, most of them teenage girls, were injured; Korean police reported nine seriously hurt. It was the first time American troops had clashed with South Koreans, an ugly and foreboding precedent.

South Korean politicians and editorial writers were as incensed as the country's youth. The National Assembly passed a unanimous resolution expressing "national indignation" at the talks; one legislator urged his colleagues to march on the American embassy and "make them come to their senses." Newspapers stressed the need for "resolute action" against the north and denounced U.S. diplomatic efforts as "appeasement, indecisive, disappointing, wishful thinking, and nonsensical." When Defense Secretary Robert McNamara acknowledged in a February 4 television interview that he couldn't say for certain the *Pueblo* hadn't crossed into North Korean waters at some point, many South Koreans interpreted the remark as a prelude to a craven American mea culpa.

Rather than parley with the North Koreans, many southerners advocated attacking them. "We have got to do something to teach them a lesson even if it starts a world war," fumed the chairman of the unicameral National Assembly's Foreign Relations Committee. South Koreans in and out of government demanded an immediate halt to the Panmunjom talks. Prime Minister Chung Il Kwon tried to explain to Porter the depth of his countrymen's anger by posing a hypothetical: If Cuban commandos attempted to storm the White House and murder President Johnson, and South Korea subsequently entered into closed-door negotiations with Fidel Castro, how would Americans feel?

Like his constituents, President Park, a former army general, was getting more upset over the talks. Since 1961, when he seized power in a coup, Park had presided with authoritarian boldness over his frontline state, the Berlin of the Far East, mortally threatened not only by its bellicose cousins to the north but by the twin colossi of the communist world, China and the USSR, right behind them. No one understood the precariousness of South Korea's position better than its austere, chain-smoking president.

At 50, Park was physically unimpressive, thin and short. He delivered dull speeches in a high-pitched monotone and lacked any semblance of personal magnetism. But he had a laserlike gaze that, as one observer noted, was intense enough to split rocks, and he excelled at dividing and neutralizing political enemies. The son of an impoverished farmer, Park lived modestly despite his high office, wearing inexpensive suits and stretching his rice dishes by adding barley. After seven years in power, the proud, nationalistic president was steadily leading his country toward its remarkable future as an industrial powerhouse, and he was acutely conscious of his growing stature as one of South Korea's greatest statesmen.

Park had grown up in the 1920s and 1930s, when Korea was under the harsh colonial thumb of an aggressively expansionist Japan. After training to be a schoolteacher, he joined the Japanese occupation army in Manchuria—which Kim Il Sung was fighting—in 1940, and later attended the prestigious Japanese Imperial Military Academy. After the war he returned home and became an officer in the fledgling South Korean armed forces.

Park fought against the north during the Korean War, rising to the rank of brigadier general. By the late 1950s, however, he, like many military officers, had become disgusted by the ineffectiveness and endemic corruption of the civilian government. In 1961, he led 4,000 paratroopers and marines into Seoul, taking control of the capital in a virtually bloodless coup.

Park moved quickly to "disinfect" South Korean politics. He imposed martial law, dissolved the National Assembly, arrested former cabinet members, and shut down newspapers. Suspected communists were tossed in jail; thousands of petty criminals were arrested and paraded through the streets in public humiliation. In a burst of puritanical zeal, Park's junta broke up prostitution rings and closed bars, dance halls, even coffee shops. "I resolved to uproot all the existent germs by cleaning the entire contaminated area as if digging with a shovel," he later explained.

But stories made the rounds that Park himself had a communist past. Shortly after the coup, *The New York Times* reported that he'd once been "under sentence of death as the ringleader of a Communist cell in the South Korean constabulary." The newspaper said Park had saved himself by giving South Korean intelligence a list of communist sympathizers in the army, setting off a "massive purge." The elimination of communist elements helped the army fight better when the North Koreans invaded in 1950, according to the *Times*.

Whatever his earlier political beliefs may have been, Park became one of the world's most staunchly anticommunist rulers. South Korea's salvation, he felt, lay in strong centralized government and rigid public discipline. At the time of the coup, his nation was a basket case, its people fearful and fatalistic, its anemic economy kept alive by huge infusions of American aid. Per capita income was a miserable $82 annually; 35 percent of the workforce was jobless or underemployed. Though ambitious, creative, and hardworking, South Koreans were burdened by a national inferiority complex born of generations of dominance by China, Japan, and, most recently, the United States.

American officials considered South Korea a vital bulwark against communist expansion in Northeast Asia and, between 1953 and 1963, reinforced it with more than $5 billion in aid, much of it military. Pledging to guarantee South Korean security, Washington stationed thousands of U.S. troops backed by nuclear weapons in the south. By the early sixties, American aid accounted for half of South Korea's budget and 70 percent of its military expenditures. So reliant on American largesse was their country that South Koreans had, in the words of one State Department analyst, "an almost psychopathic fear" of what would happen if the subsidies were reduced or canceled.

Not long after seizing power, Park began to revitalize South Korean society, enacting long-overdue reforms in banking, agriculture, foreign trade, and education. He initiated public works projects to employ more people, and confiscated billions of won from "illicit fortune makers." To the relief of American diplomats, the junta leader also promised an eventual return to civilian rule.

Park was suspicious of Western-style democracy, believing it had been grafted onto South Korea too abruptly, after centuries of feudalism, by U.S. troops at the end of World War II. In spite of that view, as well as initial suspicions that he might be a communist sleeper agent, American officials embraced Park as a "forceful, fair and intelligent leader who can be trusted with power."

By early 1963, however, popular support for Park's regime was crumbling. With inflation, corruption, and infighting among junta members on the rise, Park announced that elections scheduled for the spring were to be postponed and military rule extended another four years. Dismayed U.S. diplomats worried that the delay would lead to "upheaval, division, and probably bloodshed." After the Kennedy administration threatened to withhold economic aid, Park backed down, reinstating the elections. And following a bitterly fought but essentially aboveboard campaign that fall, he was elected president by a slim margin.

Park exchanged his army uniform for civilian garb and resumed his intrepid reforms. He normalized diplomatic and economic relations with Japan, Korea's ancient enemy, in the face of strong public opposition, including student riots so fierce that he briefly reimposed martial law. At the request of President Johnson, with whom he developed a close friendship, Park in the mid-1960s dispatched 46,000 of South Korea's best troops to fight alongside GIs in Vietnam—an act of considerable political courage in light of South Korea's internal security problems.

With U.S. advice and encouragement, Park raised interest rates to encourage savings, and balanced the national budget. Such policies ushered in several years of rapid growth and laid the foundation for South Korea's later emergence as an economic "tiger."

Park was reelected in 1967, yet he remained on unsteady political ground. Many older conservatives still considered him a usurper despite his two electoral victories. There was little emotional connection between the South Korean people and their dour president. Official corruption and graft were still pervasive problems. The roaring economy buoyed Park's government, lending it more legitimacy than it otherwise would have had. But the newfound prosperity was far from bulletproof.

One of the biggest threats to economic expansion was stepped-up aggression from the north. Park knew determined terrorist attacks against vulnerable South Korean utilities and factories could disrupt the economy and undermine popular support for him. Following the Blue House raid, he tightened security at such installations.

But the nearly successful attempt to kill him and his family shook Park badly. By exposing his inability to protect his capital from Kim Il Sung's commandos, it cost him a major loss of face. And the thought that his beloved son might have died horrified him. By February 1968, the South Korean leader was drinking heavily and sleeping with a loaded rifle next to his bed.

Captain Kent Lee was on the *Enterprise*'s navigation bridge when the call from Washington came through. He picked up the phone and, to his surprise, heard the distinctive Texas drawl of his commander in chief.

"Are those people from up north botherin' you?" LBJ wanted to know.

"Not at all, sir," Lee replied. "There's lots of ocean out here and we're doing very well."

A few days before, Soviet premier Aleksey Kosygin had complained to Johnson about the growing concentration of U.S. forces in South Korea and the Sea of Japan. The arrival of so many aircraft and warships, Kosygin warned, would only cause Pyongyang to dig in its heels over the *Pueblo*. In a secret reply, Johnson promised to halt the buildup, which was substantially complete anyway, and move the *Enterprise* away from Wonsan. Now the president personally ordered Captain Lee to steam the giant carrier south, stopping when he was about 12 hours from North Korea.

Even as the White House pulled back some forces, the Pentagon moved ahead with plans for a large-scale attack on North Korea, in case LBJ ultimately chose that route. On February 3, Admiral Ulysses S. Grant Sharp, commander in chief of all American forces in the Pacific, cabled the Joint Chiefs of Staff that contingency planning "continues on an urgent basis at all command levels."

One ambitious plan, code-named "Fresh Storm," was designed "to eliminate without delay the North Korean air order of battle"—the entire communist air force—"by striking all North Korean airfields." U.S. tactical fighters and B-52 bombers, possibly assisted by South Korean warplanes, would pound communist air bases and support facilities in around-the-clock attacks. In addition, General Bonesteel recommended that U.S. soldiers join the South Koreans in "black operations"—secret hit-and-run attacks—against the north. But higher authorities poured cold water on that idea.

As the days wore on, however, it became clear that no Pentagon scheme was any more likely to achieve the president's main goal—getting the crew back alive—than any of Sam Berger's options. At the same time, Johnson began to despair of the value of diplomatic efforts. Asked at a White House press conference whether he was confident of being able to bring home both sailors and ship, he replied flatly, "No, I am not."

Some of the president's men, meanwhile, were privately concluding that the *Pueblo* mission had been badly botched.

In a phone conversation with LBJ, McNamara characterized the eavesdropping foray as "poorly conceived." Anticipating a barrage of barbed questions at an upcoming hearing of the Senate Armed Services Committee, the defense secretary worried that administration officials were "flat on our ass" because of the feeble first reaction to the hijacking. And in a private letter to a State Department colleague, Ambassador Porter complained of the Navy's foolhardiness in not withdrawing the spy ship from the North Korean coast after the attempted attack on the Blue House.

The sharpest critique came from George Ball, the former under secretary of state whom the president asked to investigate the circumstances surrounding the capture. Ball had formed a small committee whose distinguished members included General Mark Clark, commander of all U.N. troops in the Korean War, and Admiral George Anderson, who'd been in charge of the U.S. Navy blockade of Cuba during the missile crisis. Johnson hoped the Ball Committee's findings could be used to head off any embarrassing congressional hearings, and he'd pledged to make them available on Capitol Hill. But the committee's candid conclusions evidently never were presented to Congress.

Ball's group criticized the "planning, organization, and direction" of the mission. A draft of the committee's report said spy ships should be equipped with reliable means of destruction and shouldn't be ordered into hostile waters without protection from a nearby combat vessel.

Since small states like North Korea regarded offshore eavesdropping as "a hostile act vaguely threatening their security," Ball and his colleagues added, Washington should carefully consider the likely reaction before sending barely armed surveillance boats into harm's way. The committee also criticized the Navy's orders to Bucher—to stand his ground yet not provoke the communists—as "ambiguous and self-contradictory."

Ball went over the report line by line with his committee members until they reached unanimous agreement. Then he delivered their conclusions in a face-to-face meeting with the president. At Clark Clifford's request, Ball destroyed all hard copies of the report, including his own. Its findings were scandalous and no one wanted them leaked to the press.

While the White House digested Ball's critique, more trouble was percolating in South Korea.

Porter cabled that many South Korean military men seemed to believe now might be the best chance in their lifetimes to conquer the north. With more American combat power in their country than at any time since 1953, the South Koreans thought the moment was ripe to pull the United States into a war to annihilate Kim Il Sung. Porter warned of the military's "hungering desire, which [President] Park shares, to close with the North Koreans."

In an effort to calm Park, Johnson sent him a private letter, detailing the cornucopia of U.S. military aid he'd soon receive. LBJ also acknowledged the "political and public relations problem" the Panmunjom talks had created for Park's government, and promised that the United States "will not . . . humiliate itself" in order to secure the sailors' release—a pledge that in coming months he wouldn't be able to fully honor.

The president advised Park to focus on the long-term problem of stopping communist intrusions and sabotage rather than on short-term difficulties arising from the *Pueblo* and Blue House outrages. LBJ had previously asked Congress to boost military aid to South Korea by $100 million for that fiscal year. In his letter to Park he threw in another $32 million for counterinfiltration equipment, including a dozen Huey helicopters, a self-propelled howitzer battalion, 900 rolls of barbed wire, 12,000 metal fence posts, 3,600 trip flares, starlight scopes, xenon searchlights, radio sets, and field telephones.

Johnson's words, however, didn't have the desired effect. When Porter delivered LBJ's message at the Blue House, the still-rattled South Korean president vented at him for two and a half hours. The *Enterprise*, he snapped, should have sailed north, not south, in order to blockade Wonsan. Park denounced Kim Il Sung as "a pirate and a thief" and warned that he'd have no choice but to retaliate if the communists struck his country again. That, he said bluntly, would mean war.

After Porter had departed, a Blue House aide telephoned him to say Park had changed his mind and now formally opposed the bilateral talks at Panmunjom. In addition, the CIA reported that Park was asking the National Assembly for emergency powers to withdraw his troops both from Vietnam and from General Bonesteel's U.N. command. The ambassador hastily cabled

Washington that the United States and South Korea "may be approaching [the] showdown stage."

The situation was lurching out of control. LBJ needed to do something, and fast.

On the night of February 9, an Air Force transport jet landed at John F. Kennedy International Airport in New York to pick up a lone passenger: a tall, patrician-looking man named Cyrus R. Vance.

Vance was a successful Wall Street lawyer and veteran Washington insider to whom President Johnson often turned in times of turmoil. The publicity-averse former deputy secretary of defense had been dispatched as the president's personal envoy to defuse crises in Panama and the Dominican Republic. In 1967, he'd helped to avert war between Greece and Turkey. During the Detroit riots that same year, he urged LBJ to deploy thousands of federal troops to restore order in the city's roiling streets; Johnson immediately did so.

Unflappable and relentlessly polite, the 50-year-old Vance had a low-key but forceful negotiating style and a lawyerly mind that rapidly analyzed complex political problems. Hobbled by chronic back pain, he often had to lie on the floor of his Pentagon office in order to work. Partly as a result, Vance returned to his law practice in 1967. (In later years he'd serve as President Jimmy Carter's secretary of state.)

Now Vance was flying to Seoul at Johnson's behest in an effort to talk President Park down from the roof. Vance's marching orders were to extract two solemn promises from the South Korean leader: that he wouldn't disrupt the talks between Washington and Pyongyang, and that he'd launch no military attacks without first consulting the United States. Vance's briefing book contained a memo, drafted by Sam Berger, intended to give him some insight into Park's personality and its quirks. The memo said the South Korean president was prone to fits of "anger and violent temper," but was too disciplined to let outsiders witness them. He was "usually forthright" rather than "Machiavellian or devious" in his dealings with others, and he didn't like flattery. His thinking was methodical; he was direct and terse in conversation. He had a disconcerting habit of snapping his fingers as he spoke, but probably wasn't conscious of it and Vance shouldn't let it bother him.

After picking up two trusted aides in Washington, Vance touched down in Seoul on February 11. The city was palpably on edge.

The jumpiness was particularly noticeable at the Blue House, where the atmosphere, General Bonesteel reported, resembled that of "the Mad Hatter's tea party." Park seemed "almost irrationally obsessed" with striking back at Kim Il Sung. The normally controlled South Korean, Vance was told, was in a volatile emotional state, drinking and throwing ashtrays at his wife and staff in anger and frustration. The troubleshooter made a mental note to be ready to duck. Despite the gravity of the situation, he expected to be in South Korea only a few hours.

Park coldly rejected Vance's request for an audience immediately upon his arrival. Instead, the president spent the afternoon target shooting in the Blue House basement. Vance walked into the lion's den the next day, meeting with Park and several of his key ministers.

Park wasted no time in stating his thesis that his archnemesis in Pyongyang was gearing up for war. While in the past the North Korean dictator had contented himself with blowing up barracks and railroad tracks, the Blue House and *Pueblo* incidents marked a dramatic escalation of his aggressiveness.

Gesturing excitedly, Park predicted that Kim would hurl thousands of specially trained guerrillas at South Korea come spring. Through sabotage and assassination, those fighters would disrupt the south's economy and destabilize its government. When his country was sufficiently weakened, Park warned, North Korea's regular forces would sweep in to finish it off.

Park said he didn't object in principle to the U.S. negotiations at Panmunjom; he just didn't think they'd work. He certainly sympathized with LBJ's desire to get his sailors out alive. But inertia in the face of increasing communist violence, he said, would lead South Korea to national extinction. Kim's guerrillas had sneaked to within 1,000 yards of the Blue House in an "open act of war" intended to overthrow the South Korean government. Future provocations, Park insisted, must automatically be met with heavy counterblows.

As dependent as South Korea was on the United States, Vance couldn't simply order Park not to march north; he had to persuade him. And so the lawyer began building his case against a reckless lunge across the DMZ with the same calm logic he might use to counsel a wound-up Wall Street mogul against an ill-conceived corporate takeover.

Vance asked Park to consider a basic question: What was Kim trying to achieve? Did he hope to provoke retribution that could become a pretext for all-out war? Widespread conflict, Vance noted, would wreck the south's economy, destroying the notable progress made under Park. On the other hand, left unscathed for a few more years, South Korea's economic locomotive was certain to pull far ahead of North Korea's in the race for dominance on the peninsula.

Yes, the attempted assault on the Blue House was appalling, acknowledged the American. But Park's troops and combat police had easily contained infiltrators in the past. Even if Pyongyang intensified its subversion campaign, couldn't that too be blunted, especially with millions of dollars of new counterinsurgency hardware from the United States?

Park was unconvinced. The communists understood only force, he insisted, and halfhearted responses to repeated aggression would simply embolden them. If the attacks continued, Park declared again, "We must counterattack." National survival demanded vengeance.

In fact, Park already was conducting covert counterattacks. Apparently without Washington's knowledge, his special forces made 11 eye-for-an-eye raids across the DMZ in late 1967. One assault was large enough to have knocked out the headquarters of a North Korean army division. The elite teams were directed by Park's hotheaded defense minister, whom Vance regarded as "an absolute menace." Park also had secretly assembled his own assassination squad to go after Kim Il Sung.

The South Korean president didn't tell Vance any of this. Instead, he asked how serious North Korean encroachments had to get before the United States took firm action. What if the communists tried to hit the Blue House again? What if they attacked a South Korean air base? Or a factory, hydroelectric dam, or other important economic target?

"We are not helpless," Park noted pointedly. "We have an army of six hundred thousand men."

The U.S. policy of passivity wouldn't work, he said. If Washington insisted on pursuing a deal at Panmunjom, he could keep his nervous countrymen under control—but only for so long. In the meantime, allied forces should blast North Korean warships and the army unit that fielded the Blue House commandos. If the Soviets reacted by threatening war, he added, Washington should "accept the challenge."

Vance said nothing in response to that incredibly irresponsible remark. He heard the agitated South Korean out, and then bore in again with a coolly reasoned rejoinder.

He appreciated Park's comments about Panmunjom, he said, and shared his desire for a rapid denouement to the talks. He added that he now had a clearer understanding of Seoul's views on retaliation. However, U.S. experts had carefully considered plans to hit North Korea and believed doing so could touch off a major counterstrike—and possibly war. He also pledged that America—which had sacrificed the lives of 33,000 soldiers to keep Kim Il Sung from swallowing the south in the early 1950s—wouldn't let him do so now.

On February 13, Vance offered similar assurances to Park's jittery ministers and got an earful in response.

The sharpest words came from the short-fused defense minister, Kim Song-eun. Washington's slow and inadequate response to guerrilla infiltrations, he charged, was responsible for the present threats to both South Vietnam and South Korea. Both nations had warned of the danger of armed subversion, only to be brushed off by American officials convinced they were being shaken down for more military aid.

Although Seoul had asked for counterinsurgency equipment two years ago, he said, only now—after the Blue House and *Pueblo* insults—was it being supplied. The defense minister said his government didn't question America's willingness to fight for South Korea in a full-scale war; lower-level aggression, however, was another matter. Washington was willing to passively spend money to strengthen South Korea's defenses, but when would it take real action against limited but escalating northern attacks?

President Johnson, the defense chief went on, hadn't started bombing North Vietnam until four-fifths of South Vietnam lay in Ho Chi Minh's hands. South Korea couldn't sit idly by as Kim Il Sung attempted the same thing. Prime Minister Chung then added his own warning that domestic political pressures might force President Park to withdraw South Korean troops from Vietnam.

Vance had heard enough. If South Korean soldiers pulled out of Vietnam, he declared, U.S. troops would pack up and leave South Korea—a nightmare scenario for Park's government. Hearing this frank threat, Chung "gasped, sputtered, and went out" of the room.

The American envoy knew that journalists from his country as well as South Korea expected a statement on what, if anything, his urgent mission had accomplished. He and his aides drafted a brief communiqué and gave it to the ministers for review. The South Koreans didn't like it, saying it contained almost nothing of substance. Hours of bickering failed to produce a consensus on what the public should be told.

That night Vance and his two assistants met a group of South Korean negotiators at the elegant Tower Hotel to work out the final wording. The discussions began at nine p.m. and spilled over into the next morning. The South Koreans contested every point, every nuance, fortifying themselves with whisky as the night wore on.

Vance's aides were John P. Walsh, the State Department's deputy executive secretary, and Abbott Greenleaf, an Air Force colonel. All three men were tired when they arrived at the hotel, and exhaustion tugged at them as the hours ticked by. His bad back throbbing, Vance eventually called for a break. The South Koreans, he told Walsh and Greenleaf, obviously were trying to wear them down. But he vowed to outlast them.

The Americans, Vance decided, would negotiate in shifts. While one man faced off with the South Koreans, the others would catnap in their hotel rooms. The Koreans offered drinks, but Vance and his men, determined to keep clear heads, declined.

The main point of contention was President Park's insistence on automatic retaliation. If his country was hit again, he wanted to lash back reflexively, no matter what the circumstances. Vance categorically opposed such a policy. He believed that reprisals should never be decided in advance of a provocation; they had to be weighed on a case-by-case basis, especially when they carried the risk of war. An attack on a car factory wasn't the same as an attack on an air base, and had to be handled differently.

At about five a.m. on February 14, Vance finally succumbed to his back pain, leaving the conference table to go lie down in his room. Walsh and Greenleaf stayed on, hammering out the last details of the communiqué at seven a.m. The strongest passage said only that Washington and Seoul would hold "immediate consultations" whenever South Korea's security was threatened.

Vance went to the Blue House the next day for a final colloquy with Park. The president's secretary general and closest adviser, Yi Hu-rak, intercepted him outside Park's office. Strongly pro-American, Yi said Park had decided to reject the communiqué as "not strong enough." Yi considered that a serious mistake. He implored the U.S. emissary to do everything in his power to change his president's mind.

Vance met Park and appealed for him to understand the domestic political pressures LBJ faced. Nineteen sixty-eight was an election year, Vance explained, and the antiwar movement was gaining influence. A major outbreak of fighting in Korea wouldn't play well with an American public already disenchanted with the Vietnam War. No one wanted the Panmunjom talks to go on indefinitely, Vance said. But Johnson felt he had to make every effort to settle the *Pueblo* mess peacefully before resorting to military means.

The envoy said he and his colleagues had worked through the night on the communiqué and, though it completely satisfied neither side, the document should be released to the press. To say nothing would unsettle the South Korean people and allow Kim Il Sung to crow that the allies were farther apart than ever. Vance also asked the South Korean leader for his word that he'd refrain from unilateral military action.

Park replied that he had no desire to add to President Johnson's burdens. Both he and LBJ understood how easily war might flare if North Korean aggression went unchecked. Their quarrel was over what tactics were most likely to stop it. He knew America didn't want to be fighting on two fronts in Asia. But, Park declared, the certainty of reprisal was the only realistic prophylaxis against future communist violence. Even if the allies decided to forgo payback for the Blue House and the *Pueblo*, they must issue an unmistakable warning that swift and devastating retaliation would inevitably follow any more such acts. So wishy-washy was the proposed communiqué, he said, that not only would it cause public trepidation if released, but it might actually encourage the North Koreans to believe they could attack again without consequences.

Park then abruptly reversed himself, saying he "did not care" whether the joint statement was issued or not. But if the Panmunjom talks became stalemated, he demanded, what did Washington intend to do?

A range of options was under study, Vance responded. They included a naval blockade, air strikes, seizing a North Korean ship, and trade sanctions. LBJ hadn't yet decided what course to take, and his choice would depend on future events.

That seemed to agitate Park. What if the attacks on his country didn't stop? Ambassador Porter would show up in his office pleading for patience yet again. Did the United States intend to do anything except exercise restraint?

Vance said he couldn't predict the future. But, he added, as close allies, South Korea and the United States had to consult when the actions of one so profoundly affected the other. President Johnson could have punished the communists severely after the *Pueblo* was taken, Vance noted. But that might well have exposed South Korea to serious collateral damage, including invasion.

Park promised not to strike back at Pyongyang "at this time." But, he added with chilling bluntness, further provocations would leave him no choice but to attack on his own. If the United States joined him, that would be fine, he said, "But unilateral action would have to be taken whether or not the U.S. joins." Park insisted his country "can overcome North Korea." He understood that "human casualties would be great," but he was willing to pay that price "in order to permit [his] people to survive." South Koreans had a right to defend themselves, and Washington shouldn't demand "endless patience in the face of endless aggressive acts by the other side."

Vance didn't fail to grasp the dark implications of Park's remarks. The battle-hardened ex-general was willing to thrust his country—and American troops defending it—into war regardless of U.S. wishes. Vance carefully explained that although Park's position "would create very grave problems" in Washington and might damage the two allies' close relationship, he'd convey his comments to LBJ.

Listening to this exchange, Park's adviser, Yi, grew "profoundly disturbed." He interrupted the discussion and, in rapid Korean, pleaded for Park to consider what he was saying. Heeding his trusted aide, Park tried to assure Vance that he didn't want to divide their nations. But when it came to protecting South Korea, he had no alternative.

The quick-witted Vance saw his chance, a last opportunity to change the mind of this strong but heavily burdened man. He asked whether Park already had decided to get even if Kim Il Sung hit him again. Park replied that he had to do that if another serious incident occurred.

Vance then asked whether South Korea would seek retribution for an attack on one of its airfields. Park said he'd make that call based on the situation at the time.

Yi jumped in, saying his boss had just made Vance's point. Park thought for a moment and burst into laughter. His assistant was right. Future retaliations couldn't be dreamed up without reference to future circumstances. The tough little president stood up, warmly put his arm around Vance, and thanked him for coming.

A Marine helicopter whisked Vance to the White House after his jet rolled to a stop at Andrews Air Force Base outside Washington. LBJ met him on the South Grounds and ushered him into the Cabinet Room, where the president's top defense and foreign-policy experts were waiting.

Vance didn't sugarcoat what he'd heard in Seoul. Although he'd succeeded in reducing the levels of anxiety and suspicion there, he reported that the situation remained "very dangerous." Fueled by a copious intake of alcohol, President Park was moody and erratic, Vance told the assemblage. He related the ashtray-throwing episodes and characterized the South Korean leader as "rather unsafe." With the exception of Yi, no one in his government had the nerve to tell him anything he didn't want to hear. If Kim Il Sung kept goading him, Vance warned, sooner or later Park would explode.

"Is [Park's] drinking irrationally something new?" Johnson asked.

"No, this has been going on for some time," his emissary responded.

Vance said he'd nonetheless nailed down some important commitments from Park. The South Korean had agreed not to stand in the way of the Panmunjom talks, provided they didn't take too long. He also promised no retaliation without first consulting Washington.

But Park had his price. His ministers had handed Vance a laundry list of additional defense goods they wanted, including six squadrons of F-4 Phantoms and four new airfields. Not only was that equipment expensive—Vance estimated a $1.5 billion price tag—but it also would strengthen Park's hand if he tried to strike a preemptive blow against the north.

Yet Vance thought Park deserved at least part of what he wanted. "We have to give them some F-4s," he told LBJ. Clark Clifford turned the discussion back to Park's mental state, saying he was disturbed by the South Korean's apparent instability. Did he have the power to unilaterally launch a sizable attack on Kim Il Sung?

"The generals would let us know and would drag their feet," said Vance, referring to the South Korean military. "But if he said 'go,' they would have to go."

That was a sobering thought for the men in the Cabinet Room. Clifford urged that Park be watched closely, and that Washington find a way to disengage from him if his armies suddenly headed north.

"This," Clifford warned, "is a weak reed we are leaning on."

The Soviets' weak reed was Kim Il Sung. Kremlin leaders were as wary as Lyndon Johnson of getting drawn into a war they didn't want by a belligerent client state.

Moscow had publicly condemned the U.S. military buildup as "fierce, rude, and aggressive." Privately, the Russians were upset at Pyongyang for taking the "unusually harsh" measure of violently seizing the American spy boat rather than simply shooing it away. They'd urged the North Koreans to now act with restraint and not give Washington any excuse to escalate the standoff.

But Kim had sent a chill through the Soviet leadership with a January 31 letter to Premier Kosygin in which he "expressed confidence" that their two nations "will fight together" if the United States attacked North Korea. Moscow's alarm grew when Kim mobilized his forces, informed his countrymen that "a war could begin any day," and began evacuating factories, government offices, and people from Pyongyang.

The Soviets decided it was high time they made their views known directly to Kim, and invited him to Moscow amid the gala celebration of the fiftieth anniversary of the Red Army. But the North Korean leader declined, saying he couldn't get away, and in his stead dispatched Minister of Defense Kim Ch'ang Bong.

On February 26, the defense chief met with Leonid Brezhnev, secretary general of the Soviet communist party. Brezhnev told him flatly that Moscow wanted no war in Korea and didn't understand the meaning of the evacuation that was under way in Pyongyang. Brezhnev also declared that the mutual assistance treaty between the two countries was of "a defensive character"—in other words, the Soviets felt no obligation to back up North Korea if it started a war against the south. The Russian complained that Pyongyang had provided no information about the progress of the Panmunjom talks, and strongly advised that the impasse with the Americans be resolved peacefully and without delay.

Brezhnev's lecture got Kim Il Sung's attention. On March 1, Kim received the Soviet ambassador to Pyongyang, assuring him that evacuation activities in the capital "did not have an emergency character." Kim also said he had no intention of "raising military hysteria" in his country and promised to squelch "panicky rumors" among his people.

CHAPTER 9

THE ENDURANCE OF MEN

Two guards shoved their way into Bucher's room on the afternoon of March 5. They ordered him to gather his belongings and line up with his men in the hall.

None of the Americans knew what was going on, but some of them whispered excitedly about maybe being headed for freedom. The seamen marched downstairs and out into the snow. Two buses, surrounded by armed soldiers, sat idling. Bucher demanded to know their destination; he was told to shut his mouth and get in.

The windows again were blacked out. Sitting next to the skipper, Murphy felt their vehicle roll across two bridges and stop at two checkpoints. After about half an hour, the buses pulled into another compound. The crewmen found themselves outside a three-story building, its entrance framed by two large columns. Steve Harris jumped to the nervous conclusion that it was a courthouse and, rather than being on the verge of release, the sailors were about to be put on trial.

Whatever its function, the place was a triumph of socialist grandiosity. Once inside, the Americans were taken aback by its sumptuousness. The entryway floor was made of polished marble. Beyond that was a wide staircase, also of marble, flanked by two columns emblazoned with red stars. The crewmen later dubbed it the "Country Club."

Super C arrived, wrapped in a gray overcoat and an air of importance. He was smiling, clearly enjoying the Americans' mystified reaction.

"Welcome to your new home," he said, speaking through Silver Lips. "I hope you will be comfortable here. Your commanding officer has requested better and more comfortable surroundings, and we have chosen this place for you. We hope that you will be able to exercise outdoors and take sunbaths."

The sailors were led to their new cells on the second and third floors. Each officer got his own quarters, while enlisted men had to bunk eight to a room, instead of four as at the Barn. But the Country Club was still an improvement over its predecessor. The lights could be turned off, and the windows weren't covered. For the Americans, even staring at the winter-bleak Korean countryside was preferable to the mind-warping claustrophobia of the Barn's sealed rooms.

At dawn the next morning, Bucher's face was pressed to his frosty window as he studied his new surroundings. The view stretched for miles, across snowy fields and into tall hills. An earthen berm about 15 feet high enclosed the compound. Atop it, half a dozen soldiers patrolled with automatic rifles. The grounds included a separate barracks for the guards, a jogging track, even a basketball court. The facility seemed designed to house troops rather than prisoners.

Indeed, the area around it was alive with military activity. In the distance Bucher saw a drop tower for parachute practice. Trucks loaded with soldiers rattled back and forth on nearby roads. Aircraft ranging from old biplanes to modern jets flew overhead; the captain figured a military airfield must be in the vicinity.

While the setting was different, the daily routine was much the same. Turnips and rice topped the menu at almost every meal, though now the sailors were required to wash their hands with a nauseating disinfectant that made the food even less palatable. The men ate together but no talking was allowed, either in the third-floor mess hall or anywhere else. Alone in his cell, Bucher sank into long hours of despondency, pondering various ways to try to kill himself if, as he dreaded, sophisticated Soviet interrogators arrived at the new prison.

After six weeks of a diet with few vitamins and virtually no protein, the crewmen were showing symptoms of severe malnutrition. The ship's cook, Harry Lewis, estimated they were consuming only 500 calories a day—the energy equivalent of three unbuttered English muffins. Most men were losing weight precipitously—Bucher had dropped 40 pounds—and many suffered from diarrhea. Episodes of flu blew up into pneumonia. Minor scratches became infected and the infections spread. Dale Rigby, a ship's storekeeper, got a rash over 90 percent of his body, an early sign of starvation. The skin above his waist peeled off, and ugly sores formed on his legs. A communist doctor prescribed a mud pack that only seemed to aggravate Rigby's condition. Another sailor's feet began to swell—also an indicator of starvation—and the physician tried to treat him with acupuncture, which had no apparent effect. Some men developed scurvy, a vitamin C deficiency that causes spongy gums, bleeding under the skin, and extreme weakness.

In mid-March a blizzard buried the prison. The communists decided to squeeze their captives for more propaganda fodder. Besides their collective apology to North Korea, Bucher and his men had been forced to send a letter to President Johnson, asking him to apologize on their behalf. But now the communists ordered their prisoners to write letters to relatives, politicians, and "influential people" in the United States. The letters conveyed a sinister threat: If the U.S. government didn't officially apologize, the seamen would face trial and possible execution. Steve Harris's letter to his wife and mother was typical:

"The penalty for espionage in this country is death," he wrote. "The only condition that we will be returned home on is for the U.S. Government to admit its crime, apologize and give assurance that it will not happen again. If these conditions are not met, then we will be executed. . . . I love you both so much that even as a grown man I have broken into tears many times."

Bucher wrote to LBJ and the director of Boys Town, warning that "Our situation is grave." Murphy wrote to Secretary of State Dean Rusk. Others petitioned governors and U.S. senators from their home states. Bob

Hammond, the hardheaded Marine who'd endured so much brutality at the Barn, began a letter to his wife with a chatty inquiry about their new baby, but concluded that "time is running out" for him and his shipmates. By the middle of April, more than 200 such letters had hit U.S. mailboxes, leaving the men's families more frightened than ever.

When the communists weren't forcing Bucher and his men to regurgitate propaganda, they were trying to make them swallow it. Every Friday night the sailors were taken to a large room on the third floor to watch a movie about the joys of life in North Korea. Translating the films was a short, intellectual-looking officer the Americans nicknamed Fee-ture Feel-um, for the way he pronounced the words in his ragged English. Fee-ture Feel-um energetically shouted out lines of dialogue and even sang song lyrics.

The plots often celebrated the unwavering dedication of heroic peasants and factory workers, inspired by the wisdom and courage of Kim Il Sung, to the success of the revolution. One such entertainment was titled *The Tractor Driver.* Its protagonist, a city dweller, was a committed proletarian who selflessly gave up his one day off work each week to help rice farmers boost production. Frustrated by the difficulty of getting his tractor through the deep mud of the rice paddies, he fashioned a novel solution: He put a rowboat under the tractor's front wheels. Naturally, the machine still bogged down in the muck. But the point seemed to be that good revolutionaries never stop trying to come up with imaginative approaches to building the socialist economy.

Another popular theme was the unrelieved wickedness of the American imperialist aggressors during the Fatherland Liberation War. This genre showed U.S. troops always in headlong retreat, committing unspeakable atrocities against North Korean women and children along the way. To Bucher and his men it was like watching one Western after another in which the cavalry always lost. Guards roamed around during the screenings, making sure no one talked or fell asleep. But the sailors usually spent most of movie night snickering and stifling laughter at the poor quality and droning heavy-handedness of the films.

The Americans' spirits rose considerably when Steve Woelk, the young fireman injured by the same shell that killed Duane Hodges, was reunited with them on March 17. Woelk had spent most of his time since the capture in a North Korean hospital; despite repeated inquiries, Bucher had been told little about him or his condition. An upbeat Kansan who enjoyed singing country-western songs, Woelk was well liked by his shipmates, and Bucher and the other officers greeted him happily as he hobbled through the Country Club's front door.

Woelk's description of his medical treatment sounded like something out of a horror novel. Blown backward by the shell's detonation, he'd dragged himself to the relative safety of the wardroom. A metal fragment had sliced into his upper right thigh, ripped through his abdomen, and exited his right buttock. One of his testicles was gone. Shrapnel also sheared off a two-inch piece of his tailbone, causing excruciating pain.

When North Korean boarders found the blood-soaked seaman, they tossed him on the dining table and wrapped him in the plastic table cover. Two soldiers then dragged him down passageways and over the gangplank onto the dock at Wonsan. Woelk thought he'd be heaved into the harbor.

At the Barn he was put in a cell with two other wounded sailors. With no food or medical care for the next two days, Woelk lapsed into semiconsciousness, moaning periodically for help. The only uninjured man in the room, Dale Rigby, did his best to comfort his three shipmates with no drugs or medical equipment. He had to beg the guards for an empty bottle so Woelk could urinate.

Woelk soon found himself glued to the table cover by dried blood and gore, almost unable to move. Whenever guards entered the cell, they held bandannas over their noses and mouths to keep from gagging on the stench of festering wounds.

Woelk didn't improve. After about ten days the North Koreans took him to another room and placed him on a metal examining table. They held him down and tied his hands and feet to the table. Then, without administering an anesthetic, doctors began cutting his flesh with scissors. By the time they were finished, they'd removed his other testicle and sewn up the incisions with what looked like kite string. Woelk's screams echoed throughout the Barn; other sailors thought they were overhearing a particularly gruesome torture session.

Woelk was taken to a hospital and put in a room by himself. The paint was peeling and bedbugs scuttled over his sheets. His postoperative care consisted of a doctor shoving strips of ointment-saturated gauze into his wounds with forceps. No one washed or shaved him. But each day the depth of his wounds got a little shallower as the healing process took hold. The staff gave him cigarettes, playing cards, and propaganda magazines, but no one spoke or understood English. The communists snapped frequent pictures of him; once they restaged his testicle surgery for photographers. Woelk checked off the passing days on a wall with a burned match. One was his twentieth birthday.

Eventually he was strong enough to get out of bed. The hospital room had no mirror, but Woelk saw his reflection in a glass transom above the door. His emaciation startled him: In less than two months he'd lost 55 pounds.

Woelk's Lazarus-like reappearance wasn't the only reason for the crew to rejoice. Since the move to the Country Club, systematic beatings had all but stopped. Most of the North Korean officers from the Barn had migrated with the sailors, but the guards were new. While they rarely missed a chance to kick or clout one of the Americans when their superiors weren't looking, the Country Club guards seemed to have orders to lay off. The communists already had extracted much of what they wanted from the seamen, and now apparently regarded them merely as pathetic dupes of the warmongering Johnson clique in Washington.

Life fell into a dull but relatively peaceful routine. Earsplitting electric bells jarred the prisoners awake at six a.m. They had a few minutes to splash water on their faces before assembling for calisthenics, outdoors if the weather permitted. Then they polished the floors of their cells with rags and marched to the mess hall, where they breakfasted on turnips and whatever other delicacies the North Koreans had prepared.

The rest of the morning the men were required to sit in their rooms and read propaganda magazines. They often just propped the publications open in their laps, bent their heads forward as if reading, and went to sleep. After a one p.m. lunch—more turnips—they were allowed to exercise or play sports for an hour. Then it was back to their cells to study communist "cultural materials" for a couple more hours. Supper was at six p.m.—turnips yet again—and lights-out at ten. Twice a week the men got baths.

"The typical day started in stupidity, proceeded through boredom, and ended in stupidity 16 hours later," Schumacher later wrote in a memoir.

As the North Koreans loosened their grip on the seamen, Bucher moved to reestablish his chain of command. Although officers and men were allowed to eat together, they couldn't talk, and the captain often was kept isolated from his subordinates. But the communists had assigned another enlisted man, fireman John Mitchell, to clean Bucher's room each day, and Mitchell became the courier for the captain's directives to the rest of the crew.

Mitchell did a good job keeping Bucher abreast of what was happening with his people. When someone got knocked around or fell ill, the skipper knew about it within 24 hours. If a man seemed to be buckling under the stresses of confinement, the captain made sure to whisper encouragement in his ear during an exercise session or mealtime.

Bucher urged the sailors to defy their captors in whatever ways they could. And despite his ebbing physical stamina, he led by example.

The guards still insisted that the Americans bow their heads like shamed criminals when they walked anywhere. The captain ridiculed the pose by exaggerating it, bending deeply at the waist as if he were a crippled old man. Told to cut it out, Bucher walked in a normal upright position, and after a while was allowed to get away with it.

Bucher also goaded his men to laugh, make sarcastic or obscene cracks, and otherwise express derision during the Friday-night propaganda films. One movie showed a U.S. pilot going out of his way during the Korean War to drop his entire bomb load on a little boy. "They have blinded the boy!" shrieked Fee-ture Feel-um at the climactic moment. "Fuck you!" the captain called back in the darkness.

The crewmen picked up on the captain's trick of deriding the North Koreans' authority by carrying out their orders in a preposterous way. Their antics often seemed borrowed from the TV comedy *Hogan's Heroes*, in which a group of American POWs outwitted their German captors on a daily basis. Take the sailors' slaphappy style of marching. If the North Koreans told them to turn left, they turned right. Ordered right, they went left. Directed to halt, they kept going into the nearest wall, comically plowing into one another as guards screamed at them to stop.

"Why you not march like soldiers?" a North Korean asked in exasperation. "We're Americans," came the non sequitur reply. "We just don't walk like you."

When one guard demanded that a sailor clean a spot on the wall of his cell, the man dropped to his hands and knees and furiously scrubbed the floor. Hammond made a point of trying to best his captors at every turn. The North Koreans had put him in charge of the seamen on the third floor, making him responsible for, among other things, marching them to meals and exercise. When the reveille bell went off each morning, a guard raced toward the Marine sergeant's room, shouting "Hammondie! Hammondie!" Rather than give the communist the satisfaction of rousting him from bed, Hammond got up earlier and stood inside his darkened cell, dressed and ready to go. As the guard reached his door, Hammond flung it open and charged into the hall, calling the rest of the Americans to assemble.

The main rabble-rouser, however, was Bucher. His "rascally fighting spirit," as CT Peter Langenberg described it, helped keep up morale. "He was absolutely the mastermind," recalled Langenberg. "He did a great job."

The captain and his men routinely ignored the ban on communicating with one another, whispering and passing notes during meals and calisthenics. After Schumacher was beaten for washing his socks in his room, he started doing his laundry in the latrine. Other men did the same, and soon as many as ten sailors at a time were quietly conversing as they rinsed underwear.

Often the talk was of escape. The men were convinced they could overpower the small guard detachment and get outside the compound walls, but what then? The surrounding countryside crawled with communist military personnel. A large group of Americans slogging across the snow-draped plains would be easy to spot from the air. If they somehow managed to reach the coast, could they find a boat big enough to carry all of them south? How would they evade communist patrol boats? Tim Harris proposed stealing a plane from a nearby airfield and flying to freedom. But he'd washed out of

Navy flight school, and Bucher viewed his scheme only as a desperate last resort.

Although the captain doubted that any mass breakout could succeed, he appointed a committee, chaired by Schumacher, to explore the possibilities. Word was passed to the men to put forward their best ideas. If nothing else, dreaming up escape scenarios would help distract them from the misery and ennui of prison life.

By the end of March the North Koreans apparently began to think their charges were getting too uppity. After two sailors accused a guard of filching their cigarettes, Super C cracked down.

On April 1, the colonel called the entire crew to a meeting in the room where the Friday movies were shown. He shouted that his guards didn't steal and the two complainers had insulted all Koreans. They were liars who'd committed a grave violation of the Rules of Life and deserved serious punishment.

"What should we do with these men who have lied and brought disgrace on themselves and their benefactors?" he asked the assemblage, his voice low and ominous.

Bucher, who gained a better understanding of how Super C's mind worked with each passing day, jumped to his feet. "I think these men have realized they are wrong," he said, "and I think you should give them one more chance." Taking his cue, other crewmen murmured similar sentiments.

Super C wasn't persuaded. He demanded to hear from the culprits themselves.

Communication technician Charles Sterling stood up, bowed his head, and recanted his original story. He now claimed that he, not the guard, had actually taken the cigarettes. Sterling begged forgiveness. The other accuser, fireman Michael O'Bannon, reversed his story, too, insisting he'd lost his cigarettes while exercising outdoors. He lowered his head and asked for absolution.

Their shipmates muttered faux disapproval. "You rats," said one. "How awful," exclaimed someone else. "You ought to be beaten," chimed in a third.

The act didn't work, however, and what the Americans dubbed the "April Purge" began the next day.

Guards cornered sailors in the latrine, punching them in the stomach, ribs, and back, and viciously kicking their shins. Schumacher was beaten senseless over a loose button on his jacket. A guard began yelling at Jim Kell, a cheerful, crew-cut chief petty officer who supervised the CTs, for having some rice tucked into his cheek as he left the mess hall. A moment later, a second guard slammed his rifle butt into the side of Kell's head. Kell didn't see the blow coming; he fell to one knee, his body shaking. For a week afterward he could hardly move his jaw.

"I'd never been hit like that in my life," he remembered. "The whole side of my head just exploded."

The purge ended as abruptly as it began. Acting as if nothing had happened, Super C asked Bucher whether any American holidays were coming up. The captain mentioned Easter. On Sunday, April 7, the crewmen were each granted an egg and some rice pastry to mark the day. Super C asked for a list of other American celebrations. Seeing an opportunity to improve his men's diet, Bucher scribbled out 30-odd holidays—most of them invented—including Sadie Hawkins Day, Alf Landon Concession Day, and Max Goolis Day (named for the hero of a satirical folk song by the Limeliters). But the colonel ignored the suggestions.

Super C did, however, lift the ban on talking, and even let the officers play cards and other games at night. Bucher and Schumacher began getting together in the captain's room over a chessboard. The skipper, a chess aficionado since adolescence, usually slaughtered his lieutenant. When they finished playing, the two men talked into the night, the captain entertaining Schumacher with stories of his youth, enlisted days, family, and good books he'd read. Schumacher relished the tales and listened spellbound as Bucher detailed his first few days at the Barn. The lieutenant passed along whatever news he'd picked up, and Bucher in turn relayed any orders he had for the men. A powerful bond was forming between the two officers, and the captain came to regard his intelligent young subordinate as his most trusted confidant, often bouncing ideas off him before taking them to the rest of the crew.

Super C called another all-hands assembly on April 20. With Silver Lips translating, the colonel delivered the heartbreaking news that the Reverend

Martin Luther King Jr., America's foremost civil rights leader, had been murdered. Cities across America were in flames as angry blacks lashed out at their oppressors, Super C said. The people finally were rising up against their capitalist rulers.

The North Korean revealed another startling fact: The United States was negotiating at Panmunjom to get the sailors back. He expressed disgust at Washington's refusal to apologize for the crew's transgressions. The news buoyed the hopes of many sailors, but not Bucher. The U.S. government, he was convinced, would never admit to doing something it hadn't done.

April passed drearily into May. From his window Bucher watched as spring softened the countryside. Green shoots popped up in the rice paddies. A faint scent of flowers—daisies, bluebells, and lilies of the valley, Bucher guessed—floated into his cell, along with the warbles of meadowlarks and lapwings. In the distance, peasants bent over their planting.

The bucolic sights and sounds lifted the skipper's mood. But they were mixed with the boom of artillery practice and the roar of aircraft, as military activity picked up along with the improving weather. The parachute-training tower was in action every day, and military vehicles dotted the roads.

The captain was convinced that at least some of his men would face a kangaroo court and execution—if they lasted that long on their killing diet. The portions weren't adequate to sustain a small child, much less a grown man. Moreover, the food often was larded with repulsive foreign objects. One sailor found a tooth in his bowl; others found rusty nails, stones, insects, and animal eyeballs.

"Five minutes after you ate the meal, you'd be so hungry you'd be shaking," recalled Kell. His pangs were sharpest in the mornings, when the smell of frying bacon seeped up from the first floor, where communist officers ate breakfast.

The only source of protein was sewer trout, which occasionally accompanied the turnips and rice. With its black skin and catfishlike horns, the putrid fish was particularly revolting. One CT described it as a "two-handed meal": You had to pick it up by a horn with one hand, while holding your nose with the other. The best way to eat the fish, the CT told his roommates, was to stuff a chunk in your mouth and swallow it without chewing. Hungry as they were, some sailors just couldn't choke it down at all.

The men slid into lethargy. They were eager to get outside each day and exercise in the balmy weather. But as energy ebbed from their starving bodies, jumping jacks and laps around the track became more draining than invigorating. One morning Schumacher stood watching as the enlisted men, led by Charlie Law, the sturdy quartermaster, clomped slowly along the track like exhausted dray horses. The beatings and forced confessions and daily humiliations had robbed them of much of their dignity, but they hadn't given up. Schumacher realized that the crew possessed a hidden strength: their shared suffering. What they were going through bound them together, made them stronger. No matter what happened, Schumacher sensed, these Americans would endure. Some of them flashed smiles as they loped past, and the lieutenant felt a rush of admiration for them all.

Medical problems multiplied. Boils and weeping sores broke out on the men's atrophied bodies. Some got worms; others, food poisoning. Bucher had trouble with his eyesight, and numbness in his legs. Murphy developed a painful foot infection.

The executive officer was getting acupuncture treatments from the prison physician, a plump, jovial man whom the crew naturally called "Witch Doctor." He seemed to prescribe acupuncture or a mud pack for almost any ailment the seamen came down with. They had so little confidence in his healing abilities that most stopped seeing him despite their deteriorating health. Witch Doctor had two young nurses, called Flo (for Florence Nightingale) and Little Iodine. With their stringy hair, thick legs, and flat chests, however, the women didn't even give the Americans much to fantasize about.

The North Koreans kept showing their Friday-night movies, but they decided the crew needed additional "reeducation." A number of communist officers were designated to enlighten the sailors with twice-weekly propaganda lectures. These officers became known as "room daddies," since each of them was responsible for raising the consciousness of the ideologically retarded capitalists occupying a specific cell.

The crewmen quickly anointed each daddy with a derogatory nickname. There was Robot, so named because of his automaton-like devotion to the party line; Possum, a short, rotund senior colonel who resembled a waddling marsupial; and Specs, a scholarly-looking officer who wore glasses. The propaganda officers promoted two leitmotifs: the extraordinary successes and inherent strengths of North Korea, and the fundamental corruption and fatal weaknesses of the United States. And they employed the classic propagandist's trick of using a small number of truths to lend plausibility to a large web of lies.

For instance, the room daddies made hay over America's undeniably horrendous treatment of African-Americans and Native Americans. But they twisted and distorted other episodes in U.S. history to the point of absurdity. American troops, the daddies claimed, had committed widespread atrocities during the Korean War, including massacring vast numbers of women and children and releasing clouds of disease-bearing insects on civilian populations. Walter Reuther, the great union leader, flogged autoworkers on the assembly line to increase productivity. President Benjamin Harrison honed his razor on a strop made from the skins of murdered Indians.

Sometimes the crewmen listened in silence, but other times they couldn't hold their tongues. They often challenged the room daddies' interpretations of American history and culture; the lectures evolved into excellent venues for resistance, if only verbal. When a daddy talked sadly about the impoverishment of the American working class, a sailor piped up about the nice new Chevrolet waiting for him in the garage of his three-bedroom suburban home. Impossible, declared the North Korean: Even Yankee proletarians couldn't possibly afford such things. The American insisted they could and did.

The seamen also found North Korean claims of enormous industrial and agricultural progress laughable. One room daddy insisted that his country's farms were "100 percent mechanized." But the Americans had only to look out their windows at the surrounding fields to see the primitive reality of North Korean farming methods: an old woman pulling an ox harnessed to a plow, with an old man pushing from behind.

Possum's distortions of U.S. history especially irked Harry Iredale. The shy oceanographer usually tried to keep a low profile, but he couldn't stand listening to Possum's nonsensical assertions. Iredale also worried that some of the less educated enlisted men might accept as fact what the North Korean said. One sailor in Iredale's room, for example, thought the moon physically changed shape as it went through its phases. Iredale wanted to make sure that man in particular didn't swallow too many communist falsehoods.

In his understated way Iredale went after Possum at virtually every lecture. He'd ask permission to speak and Possum's translator would reply, "Yes, Ear-a-daily?" The oceanographer then refuted everything the propaganda officer had just said. Possum would repeat his statements and ask pointedly whether Iredale understood. The American nodded. As idiotic as Possum's lies were, Iredale didn't want to push his luck.

The champion lecturer was, of course, Super C, standing spit-polished and confident as he talked for six hours or longer. He could switch gears almost instantly from shouting angrily about alleged U.S. atrocities during the Korean War to softly rhapsodizing about the beauty of the Korean countryside. "This guy could talk," said Kell. "He was programmed and he could talk and talk and talk and talk." The tireless commandant often droned on until two or three o'clock in the morning, as his listeners' eyelids fluttered with exhaustion.

Super C often found himself fencing with Bucher. The colonel once praised Karl Marx's landmark economic treatise *Das Kapital*, and commended Soviet leaders for putting Marx's theories into practice so successfully. But Bucher argued that Soviet bureaucrats had bastardized Marx's ideas for their own ends. Where the socialist philosopher dreamed of a collectivist state that would turn the means of production over to workers and then wither away, Stalin had created a permanent police state that ruthlessly kept him in power while rank-and-file Russians died by the millions in gulags and state-engineered famines. Their differences aside, Super C seemed to respect the captain and even to savor their verbal jousts.

The North Koreans weren't trying to brainwash the crewmen in the *Manchurian Candidate* sense. No one was hypnotized or injected with mind-altering drugs in an effort to destroy his basic beliefs and values. The room daddies seemed genuinely to believe their system was better, even though they had no accurate idea of what life in a Western democracy was like. They made some inroads with a handful of sailors who resented what they viewed as their country's abandonment of them. But other seamen quickly convinced the doubters they hadn't been forgotten. And so the propaganda fusillades generally fell on deaf ears.

"There was nothing to talk about," summed up Langenberg. "They couldn't sell us on their system."

Super C and his minions paid special attention to two African-American enlisted men, cook Harry Lewis and Willie Bussell, a bosun's mate. They questioned Lewis and Bussell about the riots in U.S. cities and why they hadn't participated in any. Lewis in particular baffled his captors. They refused to believe his claim that he'd bought his own car for $3,200 back in the States. Ultimately the communists gave up trying to convert the black sailors and treated them as badly as any other member of the crew, if not worse.

The weather grew warmer. The prisoners watched each morning as columns of drab-looking peasants trudged into the rice paddies, where Kim Il Sung's loudspeakers blared political slogans and exhortations of hard work and self-sacrifice from dawn until dusk.

Super C called another mass meeting on May 29. He swept into the movie room with his usual rakishness, seeming in an almost playful mood. The Americans, he declared, needed to do more work around the Country Club. They already were responsible for cleaning the two upper floors of the building, trimming trees and shrubs around it, and weeding a nearby pear orchard. But Super C wanted more. What specific jobs were they qualified to do?

Friar Tuck said facetiously that he knew how to drive tanks from his days as an Army officer. Bucher said he'd be happy to skipper a fishing boat. "Under no circumstances," said Super C, apparently getting the joke about escape opportunities. Someone else said he was a good tree cutter. Another sailor suggested the crew be given a farm to run. But nothing seemed to engage Super C's interest. Instead, he put the men to work cutting the compound's grass.

It was a chore with a peculiarly North Korean twist. The grass was to be cut not with lawn mowers or even scythes, but with penknives. Thus all 82 Americans found themselves on their hands and knees one hot day, sawing away at tufts of grass with miniature blades.

"The reason the Korcoms don't have lawn mowers is that they haven't perfected the goat yet," cracked Steve Harris, using Navy shorthand for Korean communists.

The ridiculousness of the situation was overwhelming. The sailors grinned at one another, and then began to laugh. With their self-proclaimed genius for innovation, the North Koreans had created a giggling, sunburned, 164-legged mowing machine. Soon the men were openly guffawing. To keep Super C from taking umbrage, the captain explained that his people were "delirious with delight" at being outside on such a nice day.

By late spring the guards' continuing pilferage of their paltry supplies of food and cigarettes had become a serious problem for Bucher and his men. Complaints to Super C and his officers were met with sharp reprimands for the Americans' lack of appreciation of the Korean people's generosity. So the crewmen decided to take matters into their own hands and booby-trap the goodies.

One of their targets was a habitual thief. To lure him, the sailors left out a rare treat—an apple—but not before poking small holes in it and soaking it in a bucket of urine for several hours. With the fruit properly marinated, it was placed in a spot where the sticky-fingered guard couldn't miss it. Sure enough, the apple disappeared and the thief didn't show up for the next few days. When he finally returned, said Charlie Law, "We just would look at him and grin."

Although wholesale beatings had stopped, the communists didn't hesitate to use occasional violence, or the threat of it, to keep the Americans cowed. A guard called Sweet Pea karate-chopped one sailor in the throat after he accidentally dropped a water basin in the latrine. When Stu Russell gave a guard a bored look, he pointed his rifle at Russell's head and cocked it.

The guards regularly attacked any sailor unfortunate enough to have to go to the toilet at night. This was especially hard for the men on the third floor, who had to run a gauntlet of vindictive soldiers on the way down to the second-floor head, and again on the way back up. The prisoners were required to call for a guard to escort them. And that's when the pounding started.

"They'd beat you all the way to the bathroom, knocking you in the head, knocking you down, hitting you with the rifle butt," recollected Kell. "And while you're trying to take a leak, they'd be hitting you, too. You'd come back with all kinds of bruises. It scared the hell out of you. You never knew what they were going to be doing to you."

Near the end of the May 29 meeting, Bucher stood up to speak. He wanted to take advantage of Super C's good mood and noted that the next day was Memorial Day, a national holiday for Americans to remember their war dead. Bucher was just angling for another round of eggs for his men, but the colonel hit the roof.

"How dare you bring that up!" he screamed. "You would honor the U.S. imperialist aggressors who came to kill Koreans. You insult us with that suggestion!" Instantly recognizing his mistake, Bucher tried to withdraw his request. But Super C raged on. There would be no more holidays of any kind for the Americans.

Then one day the North Koreans handed out summer uniforms: tan Chinese-style suits with wide lapels for officers; similar suits of gray for enlisted men. Everyone got Mao caps and black sneakers.

The message was clear: The Americans weren't getting out of the Country Club anytime soon.

CHAPTER 10

ALLIES AT ODDS

LBJ flew to Honolulu on April 15 for a private conference with President Park. Several months earlier, at a meeting of the two heads of state in Australia, the South Korean leader had promised to contribute 11,000 more troops to the Vietnam War effort. With fresh intelligence pointing to another enemy offensive in the summer, close on the heels of the recent Tet onslaught, Johnson wanted Park to make good on his pledge as soon as possible.

Using the Tet holidays as cover, more than 80,000 Vietcong and North Vietnamese troops had launched simultaneous attacks on cities, towns, and military bases across South Vietnam. One team carried out an audacious assault on the U.S. embassy in Saigon. While American and South Vietnamese forces had decisively beaten back the communists, inflicting enormous losses, the enemy's strength and resilience had come as a shock to the American public, which had been repeatedly assured that there was light at the end of the Vietnam tunnel and the war soon would be over. Widely televised in the United States, the savage Tet battles had stirred grave doubts among Americans about whether "Johnson's war" was winnable, or even worth fighting any longer.

From Honolulu International Airport, LBJ traveled by motorcade to

Iolani Palace, the state capitol, and gave a speech to thousands of people gathered on the palace grounds. He made a second stop at Waikiki Beach, listening to a performance of the Royal Hawaiian Band and meeting local surfers. The president then was driven to the luxurious estate of the late industrialist Henry Kaiser, where he was to stay for a few days and confer with Park.

Overlooking Maunalua Bay, the estate was a private paradise that featured a 14,000-square-foot main residence, an Olympic-size swimming pool lined in marble, sunken bars, volleyball and basketball courts, air-conditioned kennels, and a string of tropical fish ponds cascading to the sea. It must have seemed a welcome refuge to Johnson. Only two weeks before, he'd stunned the nation by announcing he wouldn't run for reelection in the fall. Instead, he said, he planned to devote his final months in office to ending the Vietnam War. His calm and unexpected act of self-sacrifice electrified ordinary Americans and left political antagonists agape. "I don't think anyone is more surprised or taken aback than I was by the announcement," said Democratic Senator William Fulbright of Arkansas, a leading critic of the administration's Vietnam policies. Outside the White House, a group of antiwar youths unfurled a banner reading, "Thanks, L.B.J." Johnson received thunderous applause when he appeared at a broadcasters' convention in Chicago and a standing ovation from parishioners at St. Patrick's Cathedral in New York.

Four days after the president's dramatic withdrawal, the murder of Martin Luther King touched off rioting, looting, and arson in dozens of cities across the country. Washington was particularly hard hit. Arsonists set more than 700 fires, creating "a pyrotechnical spectacle unmatched since British troops burned the capital in 1814." Looters cleaned out high-end clothing stores and neighborhood liquor outlets. The city's mayor pleaded for help, saying his police department was overwhelmed. LBJ called in more than 15,000 soldiers and Marines—the first federal troops to occupy the capital since the Civil War—but three days passed before order was restored. The disturbances left ten people dead and property damage exceeding $13 million—more destruction than in any other U.S. municipality. Touring the wounded city by helicopter, the president peered down at burned-out buildings that were still smoldering days later.

Preoccupied with war, riots, and a raft of other problems, Johnson was devoting less attention to the Gordian knot of the *Pueblo*. But for some members of his administration the spy ship remained a top priority. The latest letters from the crew—pleading for a U.S. apology—were under scrutiny by cryptanalysts at the Navy, CIA, and National Security Agency, all looking for coded messages. The government also brought in behavioral psychiatrists familiar with POWs to try to divine the sailors' physical condition based on what they'd written.

Oddly, the letters were postmarked not from Pyongyang but from Paris and New York. Navy intelligence speculated that communist-bloc diplomats had dropped the envelopes in Western mailboxes, perhaps because the North Koreans feared that federal agents intercepted mail from communist nations. When the Naval Investigative Service tried to trace the letters, it found only phony addresses and nonexistent senders. One missive bore the return address of "George Sand," which was, as an NIS man dryly noted, "the well-known pen name for Amandine Aurore Dupin, cigar smoking, female French novelist, of socialist orientation, who died 8 June 1876."

The Pentagon concluded that the letters were products of coercion and urged that LBJ not answer the ones sent to him. "Replying to the letters would import [sic] a significance to them which should be avoided," said a memo circulated in the White House. But the specter of Americans being executed in a communist land caused consternation in Congress, leading to scattered calls for a government mea culpa.

The Panmunjom talks, meanwhile, had produced no real dividends. By mid-April, after 14 tense meetings between Admiral Smith and his unyielding communist counterpart, the negotiations were deadlocked.

President Park, too, had much on his mind as his plane touched down in Honolulu. He was eager to see the communists crushed in South Vietnam, and two of his best infantry divisions were fighting there with notable valor. But escalating North Korean aggression—exemplified by the Blue House and *Pueblo* incidents—had caused him to reconsider his vow to commit more troops to Vietnam.

Indeed, the day before President Johnson arrived in Hawaii, Kim Il

Sung's guerrillas ambushed a U.S. Army truck a mile south of the demilitarized zone, killing two American and two South Korean soldiers. Many South Koreans expected the spring and summer to bring a new wave of violence by northern commandos. If Kim's armies suddenly surged across the border, Park didn't want to be caught with some of his toughest fighters 2,200 miles away.

His overarching fear was that America simply was losing its nerve in Asia. He'd watched in dismay as Johnson temporarily stopped bombing North Vietnam—a move Park strenuously opposed—and tried to engage its government in peace talks. Antiwar demonstrations in the United States were growing in size and intensity as more and more American soldiers returned home in wheelchairs or coffins. Park was concerned that LBJ's impending departure from the White House would lead to a sea change in U.S. policy toward Southeast Asia, with any successor devoting far less American blood and treasure to battling communists. He also was miffed that Johnson, whom he considered a personal friend, hadn't told him in advance of his intention to drop out as a presidential contender.

The South Korean leader saw signs of trouble everywhere. Washington's covert discussions with the North Koreans at Panmunjom were, in his eyes, a direct challenge to South Korean sovereignty. He'd listened to Cyrus Vance's well-reasoned appeals for restraint. He'd watched the United States put on a big show over its captured spy ship, flying in jet squadrons and forming battle groups in the Sea of Japan, while taking no real action. As a result, his thinking about South Korea's security had reached a turning point.

Since the end of World War II, his nation had grown and prospered under the protective umbrella of American military power. Fifty thousand U.S. soldiers still bulwarked its frontier with North Korea. But LBJ's cautious response to the *Pueblo* piracy convinced Park that America might not be willing to go to war again to defend his end of the Korean peninsula.

That uncertainty weighed heavily on him. He brimmed with a sense of destiny, a messianic conviction that history had chosen him to weld the two Koreas into one. He wanted to be seen as a national hero on a par with Admiral Yi Sun-sin, the sixteenth-century naval commander who defeated a Japanese invasion fleet with the help of innovative, iron-roofed "turtle ships."

Given enough time, Park might be able to achieve his dream of peaceful unification. On the other hand, he was a marked man. If war came, Kim Il Sung probably would send his special forces to hunt down and liquidate him. Gripped by "intense fear" over his and his family's safety, Park had gratefully accepted Ambassador Porter's offer for experts from the U.S. Air Force Office of Special Investigations to train his bodyguards to repel any future assaults on the Blue House. (OSI also had trained praetorian guards for the leaders of South Vietnam, Thailand, and Bolivia.) Park and his advisers believed Kim's tanks would crash through the DMZ in an attempt to conquer the south no later than 1970. Time might be running out for him to accomplish his historic mission.

Israel's blitzkrieg victory over Egypt, Syria, and Jordan in the Six-Day War had made a deep impression on Park. The Israelis seized large swaths of Arab territory and confronted the United States and other great powers with a fait accompli that no one was willing to forcibly undo. In a memo to Washington, Ambassador Porter's staff speculated that Park and his generals might be contemplating an all-out preemptive attack on North Korea in the belief that, like the Israelis, they could triumph in a "relatively short war."

Porter's people based that conclusion on an ambitious plan, drafted by Park's aggressive defense minister, for a major expansion of South Korean forces with the help of American financing and equipment. The plan envisioned converting seven rear-area security divisions into combat-ready reserve units and positioning them north of Seoul. In addition, Park's government still wanted the six squadrons of F-4 Phantom jets requested during Vance's visit (Washington had agreed to deliver only one), along with more air bases, helicopters, destroyers, landing craft, self-propelled artillery, and modern rifles. Pentagon analysts agreed that the South Korean military needed a major upgrade; most of its aircraft, tanks, trucks, and rifles dated to the Korean War, and even to World War II. But the huge quantities of new equipment the South Koreans were seeking would alter the essentially defensive nature of their military, giving it powerful offensive punch. And that, wrote a member of Porter's staff, "could lead to a military force capable of independently taking courses of action inimical to the U.S. national interest."

American policy long had been to defend South Korea while ensuring that the South Koreans didn't lash out at the north on their own, possibly starting a new war. The United Nations Command, in the person of General Bonesteel, had direct control of South Korea's armed forces, but Park was clearly straining against that short leash. In a bid for more military autonomy, he'd laid plans to manufacture his own small arms and ammunition. In addition, he was creating a two-million-member militia, training more commandos to infiltrate the north, and trying to stockpile surplus American grain as an emergency food reserve in the event of war.

Shortly after ten a.m. on April 17, the American and South Korean presidents shook hands in the library of the Kaiser estate. Each man was accompanied only by a personal interpreter. Park expressed his sorrow at Johnson's decision not to stand for reelection, describing it as a "drastic measure" that was "a shock for the Asians to hear." LBJ said he'd do everything possible to bring the Vietnam War to a successful conclusion, but he didn't know what would happen after he left office in January 1969.

Park complained that the media were "giving distorted news to the public" about the war. South Korea's army commander in Vietnam, he said, had reported that the Vietcong were "hit very badly" during Tet, losing some 60,000 fighters and "great quantities" of weapons and ammunition. Johnson agreed, but added that if the United States and its allies ultimately lost in Vietnam, the communists would only increase their pressure on South Korea, Thailand, and Laos. The time for decisive action, he said, was now. The Thais soon would be sending another infantry division into the fray. LBJ reminded Park of his promise to ante up a "light division"—11,000 soldiers—for Vietnam.

"You must give us the main strength to rout the enemy," he insisted.

Park at first dodged the issue, saying he disagreed with limits Johnson had placed on the bombing of North Vietnam. Why, he asked angrily, weren't American planes hitting Russian and Chinese supplies coming into the port of Haiphong? Even if the United States sank their freighters in Haiphong harbor, he asserted, the Russians and Chinese would do nothing.

LBJ rejoined that U.S. jets attacked Haiphong and Hanoi frequently. But no matter how often enemy targets were blasted, it was impossible to completely cut off the flow of war matériel. Attacking Russian and Chinese ships, he said, might set off World War III. With more troops from Park and a resumption of U.S. bombing, however, "I think we can take offensive action," Johnson said.

The South Korean, however, flatly refused to send the light division, saying he needed his soldiers at home. "North Korea is in a state of complete war preparedness, and we expect a considerable number of enemy guerrillas appearing in South Korea during the summer," he said. "In order to check these guerrillas, it is impossible for me to send more active soldiers to South Vietnam at present." Park said he'd be able to dispatch a combat brigade—about half the number of men he'd pledged—by July 1, but that was it.

Johnson argued that on the strength of the commitment Park made in Australia, the Pentagon had funneled $32 million earmarked for Vietnam into counterinsurgency equipment for South Korea's military. In addition, $12 million worth of gear for the promised light division had been stockpiled on Okinawa. If Park didn't spring for more troops, LBJ warned, he had no choice but to ship that critical equipment to the South Vietnamese army.

Park still wanted the Okinawa goods for his forces. The situation in South Korea, he insisted, was just as delicate and important as that in South Vietnam. "North Korea knows that whatever they do in South Korea, the U.S. will sit idly because of its troops committed to the Vietnam War," he said peevishly. "And thus there will be more incidents in Korea this year." He expected "big trouble" soon.

The two leaders decided to stop haggling for a while and eat lunch: lobster thermidor, steamed rice, Hawaiian fruit salad, and strawberry shortcake. Afterward Johnson said he needed to rest for a few hours "because of heart trouble." (A heart attack nearly killed him in 1955, and his family had a history of strokes and heart disease.)

At five p.m., LBJ took another run at his ally, employing his characteristic mix of down-home charm and thinly veiled threats. After inviting Park to visit him "anytime," Johnson reminded him that, "as your friend," he'd asked Congress to appropriate nearly $500 million in overall aid for South Korea in 1968. But, he warned, Washington lawmakers would be none too pleased if Park failed to live up to his promise to provide more soldiers for Vietnam, implying that some or all of the aid money for his country could be blocked.

Park reiterated his willingness to part with only one brigade. "Why can't he understand the true Korean situation?" he whispered irritably to Johnson's interpreter. His army, Park told LBJ, was "far inferior" to North Korea's, and his air strength was on a par with Kim Il Sung's only because of the presence of hundreds of recently arrived American jets. He asked Johnson pointedly, "At the time of the capture of the *Pueblo*, wasn't it due to your weakness that you could not give assistance to the ship?"

Park had no intention of being weak when Kim came after him; he was hurriedly erecting a multitude of new defenses. "In Seoul," he said, "pillboxes and bunkers will be built at intersections, places of work are being armed, and even some women have volunteered to join the local reserve corps." The Blue House, too, was being fortified with "electric wire entanglements" and "dozens of pillboxes." If communist invaders managed to get past all those barriers and into his innermost sanctum, the doughty little Korean told Johnson, he intended to fight to the death.

"I keep a carbine loaded with live bullets," he confided, "in my bedroom."

A week before LBJ met Park in Hawaii, Kim Il Sung greeted a delegation of Hungarian comrades at the headquarters of his ruling Korean Workers' Party in Pyongyang.

After describing how low rainfall was hurting North Korea's production of hydroelectric power, Kim turned to a subject that no doubt held more interest for his visitors: the fate of the *Pueblo*. He expressed satisfaction that the American imperialists were making less "fuss and noise" lately about the lost spy boat. Because he hadn't backed down in the face of their "threats" to bomb Wonsan and retake the vessel militarily, he said, the Americans had been forced to negotiate. And unless they relented in their arrogant refusal to apologize, they'd never see their ship or sailors again.

North Korea had to house and feed 82 capitalist layabouts in the meantime. That wasn't cheap, and Kim planned to make them work off their expenses. "We are studying what sort of qualifications the various members of the crew of the captured ship have and what sort of useful work we can make them do," he told the Hungarians, "for we are treating them too well."

Like the Soviet Union, the communist nations of Eastern Europe were keenly concerned over Kim's risky showdown with the United States, and their diplomats in Pyongyang kept a close eye on developments. Among the best-informed and most perceptive observers were those attached to the embassy of Czechoslovakia. The Czechs felt Kim had wrung all possible propaganda value from the *Pueblo* early in the crisis and that, by not releasing the ship, he was prolonging a dangerously unstable situation.

But the Czechs also realized that Kim's metronomic warnings about crazed Pentagon warmongers launching an all-out attack against North Korea were a useful internal political tool for the dictator. Although Kim had assured the Soviets he'd do nothing to provoke military conflict with the United States, his state-controlled media continued to bray to the North Korean public that war was imminent. One Czech analyst described North Koreans as living in a state of "military psychosis." The torrent of predictions of a coming death struggle with America allowed Kim's regime to demand strict obedience from its hard-pressed citizens and to stamp out any criticism of its policies. As the Czech put it: "The inescapability of war is theoretically explained, its consequences are played down, and the fear of war is countered as a display of bourgeois pacifism and revisionism."

In the past year, Kim had inflated his cult of personality to "monstrous" proportions, according to a Czech diplomatic report. The dictator had turned even his parents and grandparents into objects of compulsory veneration, complete with their own national celebrations. And his total domination of the media meant he could put his own slant on virtually all "news" consumed by North Koreans, isolating them not only from the West but from other socialist nations as well.

At some point, the North Koreans moved the *Pueblo* away from Wonsan, putting it farther out of reach of potential air or commando raids. It was a gamble, but a communist crew sailed the ship about 220 miles up the east coast to the port of Najin, not far from the Soviet border.

Whether the U.S. Navy was aware of the transfer is unclear. In any event, it made no apparent effort to interfere.

CHAPTER 11

SUMMER OF DEFIANCE

Dysentery scythed through the crew in June. Sailors collapsed in the corridors, doubled over with pain, unable to control their bowels. They struggled to reach the second-floor latrine in time, but there was only one toilet and it was constantly occupied; men often had no choice but to squat and relieve themselves on the floor. Guards angrily ordered the messes cleaned up.

The Americans were powerless to stop the terrible withering of their bodies. Charlie Law shrank from a husky 215 pounds to 125. After Jim Kell lost 70 pounds, the bones in his face protruded so sharply that an enlisted man serving as prison barber was afraid to shave him. By wolfing down rice that others no longer could stomach, Harry Iredale managed to limit his weight loss to 15 pounds. But he was as weak as the rest and could hardly lift his legs.

Big scabs formed on sailors' necks, cracked open, and became running sores. Nearly everyone had a groin rash. Witch Doctor handed out black pills for dysentery and swabbed everything else with iodine or Mercurochrome. The lack of vitamins in the seamen's diet seemed to affect certain nerves, and some men had trouble walking. More than a few were convinced they wouldn't survive unless conditions improved soon.

Summer rainstorms suffused the hot air with humidity. Bread turned moldy and the axle grease–like butter went rancid. Mosquitoes and flies buzzed through unscreened cell windows in such profusion that the crewmen staged contests to see who could kill the most. Rats flourished.

Cooped up together for months on end, the men began to get on one another's nerves. "When you see somebody every day, and you look across at them at the table, and you know every little nitpicky thing they do—the way they pick their nose, the way they fart—you know everything about them," Kell explained. "And you don't want to know everything about them."

Knowing too many nitpicky things led to arguments, and arguments spiraled into physical conflict. A brawl in a third-floor room became so violent that plaster fell off the ceiling of the cell below. A disagreement between seaman Stu Russell and Lee Roy Hayes, a radioman, escalated into a fistfight, with Hayes slugging Russell in the jaw and knocking him over a bed. When Russell stood up, Hayes decked him again. Russell got up a second time and another man finally stopped the fight.

More fisticuffs broke out in the same room when another seaman, John Shingleton, called Doc Baldridge, the veteran corpsman, an old man. Shingleton wound up with a knot on his head and Baldridge with a black eye.

CT Angelo Strano threw a cup of water in Bob Hammond's face during a set-to over religion. Another CT chattered on and on about the wonders of rapid transit systems until an exasperated roommate tried to strangle him.

Bucher began to worry that his men might descend into *Lord of the Flies* behavior. Whenever he heard of a fight, he passed word to the combatants that he was prepared to bust them in rank, but had suspended judgment pending their return to the States. "I reminded them that it would cost them a lot of money if the Navy added up their days [in North Korea] as a seaman apprentice, as opposed to a second class petty officer," he said.

The captain's concern deepened when he learned through the grapevine that several sailors were plotting to kill a roommate who'd allegedly turned snitch. The man supposedly had been overheard offering to tell the guards everything his fellow Americans said and did. Bucher sent a stern warning to the conspirators that he'd make it his solemn business to see they faced murder charges at home if they carried out their plan. No harm befell the purported informer, although the men in his room stopped talking to him and froze him out of their activities.

While the crewmen beat on one another, the North Koreans resumed beating on them. A guard called the Bear was the most feared. Nearly six feet tall, with high cheekbones and a sullen expression, the Bear seemed a born sadist. He loved to barge into a cell and stare down all the Americans until someone flinched. Then he'd order one unlucky man out to the hallway, which soon echoed with grunts, thumps, cries of pain, and pleas for mercy. When the Bear was finished, he flashed a smile and sauntered off.

The men in room five on the third floor were especially vulnerable. Their cell was at the far end of the hall, directly across from where the Friday-night movies were shown. Because of its relative isolation, the Bear and other guards felt freer to go after its occupants, especially during periods when Super C jacked up the mayhem.

Cell doors were supposed to stay closed at all times, but the door to room five had a broken latch and the wind often blew it open. Whoever tried to shut it generally was rewarded with a volley of blows from a watchful guard. To ensure an equal distribution of pain, the sailors took turns sitting in a chair next to the door, hoping to catch it before it swung open. With morbid humor, the men called this rotation the "Carousel of Death."

One day seaman Steve Ellis drew the short straw. Alert and tense, he waited for the door to move. When it did, he sprang up and grabbed the knob. But the Bear was a step ahead of him, yanking the door out of his grip from the other side. The guard stepped across the threshold and punched Ellis hard in the forehead, causing him to stagger backward but not go down. Angered, the Bear delivered a flurry of blows until Ellis crumpled. As lumps began to form on the sailor's head, the Bear grinned and strode out of the room.

The Americans seethed with hatred for their brutish captors—not just for physically abusing them, but for forcing them to be afraid, to cower and flinch. Many sailors wanted nothing more than to rip their tormentors' heads off. But fighting back would cost them at least a severe beating, and very possibly their lives, and that stark reality stopped them. So they found other ways to resist.

As usual, Bucher took the role of provocateur-in-chief.

The captain was sick during part of June. His energy sapped by the anemic diet, he seemed to slip in and out of depression. His right hip and leg still ached from repeated kicks. Sometimes Stu Russell brought meals to his cell. When Russell once asked what he thought the crew's prospects were, Bucher mumbled that he no longer cared.

But the skipper shook off his melancholy long enough to engage in an inspired piece of subversive theater. The occasion was a meeting between the crew and Super C and several room daddies. The colonel ranted for a long time before turning to Bucher, who went on and on about how much the Americans appreciated all the North Koreans had done for them. His unctuousness convinced some of his men that he'd been ordered to make the speech.

The captain kept using the word "paean," which means a fervent expression of praise. Paean is a noun and is pronounced "PEE-en." With his facility for wordplay, however, Bucher turned it into a verb and deliberately mispronounced it. The sailors, he insisted, had an obligation to "pee on" Super C for his leniency. Similarly, they should pee on the rest of the communist officers and guards for their incredible hospitality. In fact, the crew really should pee on the generous North Korean people as a whole.

Most of the seamen got the joke and burst into cheers. It took Law a minute. "Then I'm thinking of somebody urinatin' all over 'em," he remembered, "and I'm happier than shit."

Another oblique but satisfying method for Bucher and his men to express their anger was by surreptitiously killing the potted plants that sat in every room and throughout the halls. The greenery often was used as a homey accent in propaganda photos of the sailors "enjoying themselves" in prison. The North Koreans were oddly devoted to the plants, making sure they were properly watered and tended by the prisoners.

Tim Harris detested his plant as a living symbol of the North Korean nation. About four feet tall, with long branches and narrow leaves, the plant grew out of a small porcelain pot in his cell. A duty officer called King Kong had given Harris detailed instructions on caring for the plant, telling him to pour a cup of water on it each day. The first thing King Kong did whenever he came into Harris's cell was to inspect the plant.

That infuriated the ensign, who believed the communists had more compassion for shrubs than human beings. He decided to destroy their pet plant by pissing on it each day rather than watering it. The plant stood up to his onslaught for about a month. Then its leaves began to turn yellow and droop. Worried, King Kong shook a cup of fertilizer on the plant as Harris looked on, assuring him somberly that it was already getting plenty of fertilizer.

The decline couldn't be stopped. "Why plant die?" King Kong angrily demanded one day. Harris theorized that it didn't get enough sun, since his cell was on the shady side of the Country Club. King Kong wanted to know precisely how Harris was watering it. The ensign replied that he was using his teapot. "Ah," said the communist, "you should not do that." Boiled water lacked minerals; the plant obviously was undernourished. He ordered Harris to use only unboiled water, and the American dutifully complied. Between the tap water and his micturitions, the plant was drowning. When only a few leaves clung to it, Harris sensed he was close to his goal.

King Kong decided Harris might be right about the inadequate light. He had him take the plant across the corridor to Bucher's room on the sunny side of the prison. The plant smelled so bad Harris had to hold it at arm's length; he couldn't believe the North Korean didn't smell it, too. King Kong then asked the captain why the plant was in such bad shape. Bucher, who knew what Harris was up to, stroked his chin and suggested it needed pruning. "Okay, you prune," assented King Kong, who then left. Bucher and Harris opened their penknives and went to work. Off came the last few leaves. Branches were amputated next. For good measure the Americans carved up the stem. All that remained was a stricken-looking, six-inch stump.

When King Kong returned, he was dumbfounded. He summoned another duty officer nicknamed Snake. "Why you kill plant, huh?" Snake demanded. "Goddamn it, I didn't kill the goddamn plant," said Bucher, walking away. Harris was elated; he'd finally found a way to defeat the North Koreans. Gene Lacy took to urinating on the plant in his room; Schumacher knocked off three plants. Murphy, ever the contrarian, regarded his small rubber tree as a sort of companion. He took such good care of it that the communists gave him a second rubber tree to tend and, later, a lemon tree.

Almost as much as they hungered to lash back at their captors, the crewmen yearned for news of the outside world. Several of them began secretly gathering materials to build a crystal radio that could pick up stations in South Korea or Japan. Hayes sketched a blueprint and slipped it to Strano for manufacturing. Bob Chicca sculpted an earpiece from a piece of wood. Nails were collected from the playing field for a coil; a cigarette packet yielded foil for the diaphragm.

Magnetizing the nails posed the biggest technical hurdle. Dale Rigby, the ship's storekeeper, took a nail wrapped with copper wire and shorted it across an electrical switch. The cheaply made nail wouldn't hold a charge, but Rigby kept trying. At one point the lights in the prison compound flickered, and guards rushed around trying to find the faulty fuse. As his confederates tried to fabricate or steal the rest of the needed parts, Strano husbanded his growing stash under a floorboard in his room.

Meanwhile, the crew did their best to chafe the North Koreans. Law and his cellmates regularly tweaked their room daddy, Possum, after discovering how easy it was to make him lose his cool. One day they got into a big argument with him over *The Communist Manifesto*, Karl Marx and Friedrich Engels's 1848 tract that theorized how proletarians could overthrow capitalism and establish a classless society. The sailors refused to listen to Possum's views on the *Manifesto* until they'd read it for themselves. Possum searched for but couldn't find a copy. Still, he tried to convince his obstreperous wards that democratic societies were riddled with theft and other crime; by contrast, socialism bred no criminals, because everyone shared equally in material goods. But if there was no thievery in North Korea, the Americans countered, why was it necessary to lock the prison supply shed? Confronted with such impertinence, Possum frequently blew up and slapped each seaman in the face with one of his slippers.

"He never hurt anybody; it was only a little slipper," recalled Law. "Then he'd realize we got to him and he'd send us off."

By now the North Koreans' efforts to propagandize the crew had an almost pleading tone. The communists were proud of their country and sincerely believed its economic and political systems were superior to anything the West had to offer; they seemed to want the Americans merely to recognize this self-evident truth. But Bucher and his men weren't buying. On the contrary, they were fully committed to defying all further attempts to use them as propaganda shills.

The communists themselves handed the sailors their most effective weapon. On a sweltering June night the crew gathered to watch yet another turgid propaganda movie. But this one was followed by something different: a newsreel about the North Korean national soccer team playing in the 1966 World Cup championships in England. The camera tracked the waving, smiling players as they arrived at the stadium. Among the spectators was an elderly British gentleman, classically attired in a bowler hat. With great deliberation, the old man balled one hand into a fist, aimed it directly at the cameraman, and raised his middle finger. The North Korean officer narrating the newsreel appeared not to notice.

A second newsreel showed two U.S. Army helicopter pilots, shot down over the DMZ and captured by the North Koreans in 1963, as they were freed at Panmunjom about a year later. When the camera settled on a clutch of onlookers, one of them—a U.S. Navy officer—also flipped the bird. Again, no reaction from the narrator. Subdued laughter rippled among the *Pueblo* men. While the contemptuous gesture was universally recognized in the English-speaking world, the communists evidently didn't understand it.

The sailors soon began to flip off the North Koreans every chance they got. Bucher told his men, if questioned, to say they were displaying the "Hawaiian good-luck sign." To give that explanation credibility, Law dismissed the crew from calisthenics by raising his middle digit and shouting, "Good luck to everyone!" Grinning seamen returned his salute with the same sentiment.

Morale took an upswing as the Americans dissed their captors, plotted escape, built a clandestine radio, and murdered their plants. Yet even as his men's spirits improved, Bucher's deteriorated. He still was fighting dysentery and had lost 80 pounds from his precapture weight of about 205. He marched outside for exercises with "his head down, his arms at his side, and his fists clenched." He said little and didn't eat much. One day he collapsed in the latrine; a sailor dragged him back to his cell, unconscious.

On June 27, Super C ordered the crew into the movie room and informed them of problems at Panmunjom. The U.S. side, he said, had rejected his country's "just" demands, and the bilateral talks were foundering. However, the colonel reported approvingly, some high-profile Americans were publicly decrying Washington's intransigence. Among them was Rose Bucher, who, in speeches and media interviews, was denouncing the Johnson administration for not doing more to get her husband and his men back home.

It was the first news the captain had had of his family in almost five months. Hearing his wife's name, he dropped his head to his chest and began to weep—first quietly, then without holding back. The room grew still. Between sobs, Bucher stood and choked out an apology to his men for losing his composure. His first reaction to his spouse's activities was strongly negative. "Christ, there goes my career," he lamented to Schumacher. "I'm wiped out. It's the wrong thing to do." Later he reconsidered. Although he didn't fully understand Rose's motives, he came to accept her crusade. When all was said and done, she was his wife and he loved her.

Another possible threat to his career—assuming he ever made it home—was the Navy investigation that undoubtedly would follow. After all, a sailor had died on Bucher's watch, the rest of his crew had been imprisoned, and a floating surveillance platform worth millions of dollars had fallen into enemy hands. "You lose a .45[-caliber pistol] in the Navy and you're gonna have a court of inquiry," he told Schumacher over one of their nocturnal chess games.

But what would such a probe focus on? The actual circumstances that led to the *Pueblo*'s seizure or Bucher's personality clash with Murphy? The captain's pleas for rapid-destruct gear or his escapades ashore? Substantive issues or sideshows?

At the time Bucher had no reason to believe a Navy inquiry would be anything but fair, objective, and thorough. Nor did he worry that it would necessarily be fatal to his future in the service. He knew, however, that a public airing of the *Pueblo*'s dirty laundry would benefit neither him nor Murphy. The captain was firmly convinced he'd made rational, defensible decisions on the day his ship was taken, and he wanted to be able to explain them to a board of investigation without irrelevant distractions.

He also wanted to make sure his officers were on the same page if they ever had to testify before such a board. Men under fire often remember events differently, and the skipper didn't want his people contradicting one another over such basic facts as the time of capture or how many PT boats were involved. Since he'd spent so much time on the bridge during the attack, Bucher himself wasn't fully aware of everything that had transpired in the SOD hut and belowdecks, and he wanted to fill in some of those blanks.

So the captain began asking his officers what each of them remembered of the chaotic, terrifying hours on January 23 after sub chaser No. 35 signaled them to heave to. During meals, card games, and outdoor exercises, he grilled them about exactly what they'd seen and heard. He professed not to care whether their reconstructions put him in a favorable or unfavorable light, but he wasn't above pressuring them to get their stories straight. "If you got five or six guys who saw it one way, and one guy who saw it another way, well, you try to convince him," Bucher explained years later. The last thing his officers should do during an official inquiry, he told them, was "create controversy."

On July 16, Super C made an announcement that sent the crew's morale soaring. For the first time they'd be allowed to receive mail from home. Many of the letters—addressed to Pyongyang's Central Post Office, per Navy instructions to the sailors' loved ones—were months old, and it wasn't clear why the North Koreans had delayed delivery. But it hardly mattered now. The men devoured their letters, reading them over and over to themselves before reading them aloud to one another.

Murphy got joyous news of the birth of his second child, a girl. Steve Harris's mother reported writing to all 100 U.S. senators, demanding they work harder for the crew's release. Kell's wife said she'd moved to Hawaii and would wait for him there. There was tragic news, too: Strano's brother had been killed in Vietnam on the same day the *Pueblo* was forced into Wonsan harbor.

Bucher was cheered by two letters from Rose, one written in February and the other in April. She'd been careful to tell him only the most mundane details of domestic life. But holding something in his hands that she'd held in hers gave the captain a feeling of almost physical connectedness to his distant spouse. "No tender private thoughts could be conveyed, nor any of the details of the ordeal from her side, yet it was all there by some mysterious cryptography the [North Koreans] could never break," he later wrote. "It was instantly deciphered by my own heart."

Sweltering in their cells in the midsummer heat, the sailors stank like billy goats. They were permitted to bathe only once a week now, and their clothes and bedding reeked of stale sweat. They had dispensation to open their doors and windows in hopes of catching an occasional breeze, but mostly what came through were clouds of flying bugs. From their windows the men watched as soldiers loitered outside in the sun, amusing themselves by kicking skinny dogs that groveled for scraps of food.

In spite of the heat and his frail health, Bucher launched his own summer offensive against the North Koreans.

He made fun of their language by loudly mispronouncing Korean words, causing even his captors to laugh occasionally. When a guard ordered him to kill flies in his cell, he advanced toward the man waving a newspaper and slammed the door in his face.

Another time, he took off his jacket without asking permission. A guard told him to put it back on, but the skipper complained that he'd perspire too much. The guard insisted anyway. After the North Korean left the room, Bucher dumped a bucket of water over his head. The guard returned and gazed at the sodden American in disbelief.

"I told you it was gonna make me sweat," the captain explained.

Leading his sailors up a staircase one day, Bucher caught a vicious kick in the chest from a soldier on the landing above. The blow sent him reeling backward, but he kept his footing. Catching his breath, he marched back up the stairs and past the soldier as if nothing had happened.

The North Koreans began to let their captives play sports outdoors, and the Americans took full advantage of their time together. They used football huddles to exchange information and transmit the captain's orders. When a guard tried to stick his nose in, the sailors would quickly line up, hike the ball, and "run over him."

The men also organized huge, crazed games of basketball—often with 20 or more elbow-throwing players on the court—that produced a spate of injuries. Rizalino Aluague, a steward's mate, fractured his kneecap in one game; in another, Schumacher accidentally slammed into a CT and broke the other man's nose. Harry Iredale, an accomplished intramural hoops player in college despite his abbreviated size, sat out the games, both because they were so out of control and because he didn't want the communists to see him enjoying himself too much.

With injuries multiplying, the North Koreans finally banned football and basketball, allowing the Americans to indulge only in relatively nonviolent volleyball.

All the while, the guards maintained the atmosphere of intimidation, beating the seamen for even trivial offenses. But a couple of poundings resulted from a remarkably reckless public statement by U.S. Senator Stephen Young, an Ohio Democrat and member of the Senate Armed Services Committee. Young claimed in a July 12 press release that the *Pueblo*'s voyage had been a CIA operation. Although a few crewmen were Navy personnel, he said, "The majority were technicians, CIA operatives, and scientists skilled in breaking codes and in knowledge of highly sophisticated apparatus." It was likely, Young went on, that the "CIA agents in charge" of the vessel sailed it to "within 12 miles of a North Korea island" during the *Pueblo*'s ten days of radio silence.

Young's words were utterly false, but they reinforced the North Koreans' deepest suspicions. A number of sailors were called before Super C, who demanded that they confirm the CIA's involvement. When they denied it, he countered, "Are you calling one of your senators a liar?" Two crewmen were beaten for saying Young was wrong. Yet they got off easy, considering that the communists could have used his ill-considered assertions as an excuse to execute them as spies.

In some ways, however, the crewmen's worst enemy was the sheer tedium of their existence.

They talked about anything and everything to kill time. Women were a perennial topic, and the young seamen tried to outdo one another with tales of their most embarrassing romantic moments. Food was the subject of long, obsessive conversations. Law talked dreamily about his love of pork chops. Hayes was dying for a peanut butter–and-bologna sandwich. Chicca drew a picture of a hero sandwich for Russell, who kept it tucked away in a cigarette pack so he could take it out and drool over it at will. Discussions of favorite foods from home always seemed to hit a mouthwatering peak right before a barely edible prison meal was served.

Word games and brainteasers were popular with the bored swabbies, especially the intellectually restless communication technicians. Jim Shepard and Don Peppard constructed crossword puzzles for themselves and their SOD hut buddies; at one point eight puzzles were in circulation.

Bucher liked math games. One of his favorites was the "12 ball problem," which involves a dozen balls of the same size and color. One is heavier or lighter than the others. The challenge is to put the balls on a scale and figure out, in only three weighings, which of them is different, and whether it's heavier or lighter. It took Bucher 12 hours to crack the problem; a brainy CT named Charles Ayling solved it in 60 minutes.

As the prison shimmered and baked in the sun, its inmates daydreamed for hours on end. Lacy tore down and rebuilt the engine of a 1937 Ford in his head. CTs Earl Kisler and Michael Alexander constructed an imaginary sailboat and took an imaginary voyage around the world together. Steve Harris's nighttime dreams took him back to some of the most pleasant times of his life. He went bird-watching in the woods near his childhood home outside Boston. He sailed across Vineyard Sound and along the Maine coast with his father. He relived family reunions at Christmas. The dreams remained vivid for weeks at a time.

Sex became a faint memory for the men. Back in the States, chasing women would've been a primary occupation for many of them. But here in prison, terrorized at random and deprived of any feminine stimulation except for the unappetizing Flo and Little Iodine, the sailors found it difficult even to conjure a good sexual fantasy.

What was fantasized about a great deal was escape. Everyone, it seemed, had his own scheme. Ron Berens, the helmsman, thought a team of men could follow electric power lines to a dam, and then follow the river below the dam to the coast. Kisler's plan was to do the unexpected: Rather than flee south to the demilitarized zone, he wanted to head north, toward the Russian border 300 miles away. Others envisioned a breakout along the lines of a stirring World War II movie they'd seen, *The Great Escape*, in which British and American airmen tunnel their way out of a German POW camp.

But the Country Club wasn't Stalag Luft III, and North Korea wasn't northern Europe. Unlike the allied fliers in the movie, who could blend easily into European cities and towns, the *Pueblo* sailors—most of them Caucasian—would stick out like sore thumbs anywhere in North Korea. Nor were local resistance groups waiting to help them with food, guns, money, and safe houses. (And the movie was based on a real-life escape that was hardly an encouraging example. Of the 76 airmen who slipped out of the prison camp, 73 were recaptured; the Germans executed 50 of them.)

Most of the plans Bucher heard were either impractical or too dangerous or both. The only halfway realistic one came from Murphy. The XO had gotten his idea from a glossy propaganda magazine that conveniently included a detailed map of North Korea. Murphy noticed that a river stretched from the outskirts of Pyongyang to its headwaters on a mountain. On the other side of the mountain, another river flowed south to the DMZ. It might be possible for him and another man or two to slip away along the banks of the two rivers and then swim across the border. Murphy pored over the map until he'd memorized every detail: where tributaries joined the rivers, how far apart the tributaries were, and any other landmarks that might help the escapees. To help cover their tracks, the men would leave during a summer monsoon.

But Bucher decided that even this idea was too risky. The moment the prison break was discovered, he reasoned, the North Koreans would switch on their loudspeakers and sound the alarm in every village for 100 miles around. As much as heavy rain might camouflage the fleeing sailors' movements, it would also make crucial landscape features harder to recognize. Poor health was another complication. The infection in Murphy's foot, for example, got so bad that by August it was all he could do to trek to the latrine, much less the DMZ.

As summer wore on, illness and bad nutrition continued to grind down everyone. Hayes contracted hepatitis. Ramon Rosales, a young Mexican-American seaman from El Paso, Texas, got spinal meningitis and couldn't get out of bed. And Charlie Law was slowly losing his eyesight.

Law realized something was wrong when he couldn't make out Super C's face during a mass meeting. At first he thought his mind was playing tricks on him, but by early August even close-up objects looked blurry. The self-assured navigator was terrified. Perfect vision was what defined him as a Navy man, what made him special. Even after retiring from the service, he planned to earn his living with his eyes, as a navigator aboard San Diego tuna boats.

Law was afraid of Witch Doctor, so he didn't ask for his help. When Bucher found out what was happening, he insisted that the North Koreans do something. The prison physician stuck acupuncture pins behind Law's ears to "let the evil spirits out," but that didn't work. Kell loaned Law his glasses and they helped a little. But Law's condition worsened to the point that when he looked straight ahead he saw a big black circle; only his peripheral vision was intact. That made it hard for him to get around; other sailors had to take his arms and help him on stairs.

As Law struggled against encroaching blackness, the North Koreans decided to exploit their captives' longing for home as a means of pressuring the Johnson administration to roll over at Panmunjom. The communists began trying to soften up the sailors with better food. Suddenly there was canned pork, potatoes, and butter to eat. Then Super C "suggested" yet another press conference.

"Good idea, sir," Bucher replied, with pretended subservience.

Wearing fresh uniforms for the occasion, Bucher and two dozen other seamen acted out their roles before a roomful of North Korean newsmen and TV cameras on August 13. Careful as always, Super C made the captain write out answers in advance to questions the North Koreans planned to ask. The Americans spoke of how anxious they were to return to their families, and how perplexed that Washington hadn't apologized. At the end, however, Bucher stood up to say a few closing words and make his most heartfelt point.

"Good luck, everyone," he bade the journalists, middle finger triumphantly upraised.

As soon as the klieg lights died, however, the North Koreans returned to heavy-handed repression. The food worsened; beatings escalated. After Kisler refused to sign a letter to *Newsweek* magazine pleading for a U.S. apology, the Bear and Robot whipped and pounded him with a leather belt, a board, and a rubber-soled sandal until his head swelled up like a pumpkin.

Bucher was becoming dangerously weak. His orderly, John Mitchell, found him so unresponsive one day that he seemed to have fallen into a coma. Yet so disturbed was the captain by the ongoing abuse of his men that he went on a five-day hunger strike in protest. When that had no effect, he tried to scare Super C by acting like he was gravely ill, maybe even going crazy. He shivered uncontrollably. He feigned lockjaw and forced himself to vomit. When Super C addressed him, he cast his eyes downward and mumbled some nutty non sequitur. None of it worked, but the captain's histrionics on their behalf endeared him even more to his men.

"You're my kind of skipper," Kell told Bucher one day as he limped through the latrine.

"That means a lot to me, coming from you, Chief," the captain replied.

The Americans kept up their guerrilla resistance. When Super C ordered them to write another round of propaganda letters home, the men found all sorts of ways to undermine the effort. Hayes used dashes and dots above the "i"s in his letter to spell out "This is a lie" in Morse code. Peppard began a letter to his father by urging him to say hello to his old friend "Garba Gefollows" (garbage follows). Referring to the North Koreans, Kisler told his family he hadn't "met such nice people since our high school class visited St. Elizabeth's," a mental hospital outside Washington, D.C.

Murphy ignored Super C's directive that the letters be addressed to "influential Americans," sending his to a county-fair manager he knew in Northern California. Lacy wrote to a buddy on the Seattle sewer board. The North Koreans took photos of the men in their cells, spruced up with potted plants and chess sets, to include with their letters. The photographers urged them to smile and look relaxed. The sailors grinned and hoisted their middle fingers. Law suggested a group picture of the eight men in his room, and as the shutter clicked, three of them were clearly flashing the Hawaiian good-luck sign.

Law mailed a copy of the photo to his uncle in Tacoma.

Not long after the August press travesty, Super C unveiled an even grander project: an "international" news conference involving journalists from around the world, most of them communist, who'd been invited to Pyongyang to cover the twentieth anniversary of North Korea's founding. Scheduled for September 12, this dog-and-pony show was to be the biggest and most elaborate to date. The colonel boasted that he'd even invited an American newsman.

Super C warned the captives several times that their futures hinged on the success of the upcoming event. "This will be a big step toward your freedom," he said. "You must do everything to make it a success." He seemed nervous about the outcome; Bucher figured his career might be on the line.

The press conference was to be held in a classroom building across the playing field from the Country Club. All six *Pueblo* officers would participate, along with 14 enlisted men. Bucher did his best to stack the deck, recommending sailors clever enough to make the North Koreans think they were cooperating even as they signaled American viewers that the whole thing was just another coerced sham.

The communists rejected some of the suggested men and accepted others. Those selected spent two weeks memorizing scripted questions and answers; no spontaneous queries from journalists would be permitted. The sailors even had to practice walking into the room and sitting down. Those not performing were to view the show on closed-circuit TV in their barracks. Bucher warned them not to laugh at what was said, no matter how outlandish, since guards would be watching closely.

From their cell windows the skipper and his men saw TV trucks pull up and technicians run coaxial cables into the classroom building. On the morning of the conference, a fleet of small Russian- and Japanese-built cars arrived, disgorging newsmen from Poland, Hungary, Italy, the Soviet Union, India, several African republics, East Germany, Cuba, Egypt, Cambodia, and other nations. Also in attendance were several reporters from noncommunist Japanese newspapers and observers from communist embassies in Pyongyang—more than 80 people in all.

Jammed with klieg lights and cigarette-puffing journalists, the room quickly became uncomfortably hot and smoky. Super C wanted to discourage the notion that the conference was staged or coerced, and only a few soldiers guarded the doors. Bucher and his men filed in, blinking uncertainly against the dazzling lights.

Robot acted as moderator. He began by listing all the news organizations represented, including the *Guardian*, a leftist newspaper based in New York. The paper's correspondent was a plump man named Lionel Martin who smoked a pipe, wore a houndstooth jacket, and looked like a New England college professor.

Robot declared the conference open. For the benefit of the foreign reporters, the North Koreans had stationed translators around the room, and a loud babel arose as they converted Robot's remarks into a multitude of languages. Fee-ture Feel-um, the narrator of the Friday propaganda movies, served as English translator, but he couldn't handle the pressure. He stuttered and stammered and soon fell behind.

The farcical nature of the proceedings was immediately apparent. Hoping to cover up the tight scripting, Robot falsely told the journalists that all of the questions had been submitted ahead of time. As he read them aloud, one sailor after another jumped to his feet like a pop-up toy to recite an answer, although no one had been called by name.

While his men delivered their lines, Bucher scrutinized Martin, wondering whether he was a CIA agent. Had he been sent here to glean intelligence on the crew's whereabouts? The possibility intrigued the captain. Should he try to make surreptitious contact with the tweedy newsman? It was a big gamble, but it might be worth taking.

Prior to the start of the conference, the North Koreans had decided to boost the number of *Pueblo* "intrusions" from six to 17. Murphy and Law had been ordered to fabricate a chart that supposedly proved the additional violations. But the executive officer, sensing the North Korean army officers supervising him didn't understand navigation, plotted several geographically impossible coordinates for the ship.

He went over each new "intrusion" in excruciating detail for the assembled media. One set of coordinates placed the *Pueblo* in downtown Wonsan. Another set had her sailing six miles inland on the Japanese island of Kyushu. Still more coordinates had the boat traveling up mountains to a point 32 miles inland from the North Korean coast. While the communists seemed clueless, Bucher knew Navy analysts back home would realize the coordinates were faked.

The conference droned on and on. Bored by the Americans' formulaic rhetoric and puppetlike performances, the correspondents began to tune out. An African fell asleep. Robot angered some of those who stayed awake by refusing to take questions. "I wonder how much longer this shit's going to last," a Bulgarian muttered loudly in English. A diminutive Indian reporter hopped up and down in the back of the room, shouting that he couldn't hear. Watching on TV, the rest of the sailors tried to keep from cracking up.

Newsmen dozed, smoked, chatted with one another, and stared out windows. The well-rehearsed media event was fast degenerating into a circus. The more it unraveled, the more Bucher and his men loosened up. They started to ad-lib their lines, larding them with as much attitude and atrocious syntax as possible.

Asked what message he wanted to convey to the Johnson administration, CT Ralph McClintock, a Massachusetts resident, switched on his thickest Boston accent:

"Oh, how I long to walk down the quiet, shaded streets of my hometown, to swim again in the rolling surf of old Cape Cod Bay, and to indulge in the sumptuous feast of one of Mom's famous apple pies," he said. "I swear on my life that if I am ever allowed to return to my home and family, I will never again commit such a naughty crime as espionage against such a peace-loving people as these."

By now the Americans were openly enjoying themselves. They smoked and grinned as Robot struggled to maintain order. The sleepy African suddenly awoke and realized he'd missed a big chunk of the action. Super C signaled Robot to stop the conference, but the sudden halt set off an uproar.

Martin, the American correspondent, jumped to his feet and declared he had a statement to make. Reporters and TV cameramen rushed toward him, shoving and tripping over the tangle of cables on the floor. "I'd like to say that I'm convinced that the *Pueblo* crew has been treated humanely here, after hearing the testimony, the declarations of the members of the crew," he said.

"It is quite evident from the testimony of the officers and men that they were violating Korean territorial waters. I think the proof is irrefutable."

The sailors laughed as journalists pushed and elbowed one another to get close to Martin. Robot gave up trying to control the mob and resignedly cupped his chin in his hands. Seeing his distress, Tim Harris tried to imagine what a North Korean court-martial was like.

Not to be outdone, Bucher climbed atop his chair and gave his own speech. The media horde abandoned Martin and swarmed toward the captain, shouting for him to repeat what he'd said.

The press conference was a shambles. As Robot pounded his gavel in futility, even the guards had embarrassed grins on their faces. For several minutes Bucher talked about how his men missed their families and hoped they'd all be home for Christmas. The sailors cheered.

The North Koreans invited the reporters to visit the crew in their living quarters, and the delighted Americans headed back to the Country Club. In minutes Bucher's room filled with newsmen. Among them was Martin, who wanted to know what "slogan" the skipper wished to send to the people of the United States.

"Remember the *Pueblo*, sir!" he replied jauntily. "Home for Christmas!"

Before Martin's arrival, Bucher had scribbled a note on a piece of toilet paper, denying everything he and his men had said. He could easily slip it to Martin with a handshake. But now, as he stood face-to-face with him, the captain's instincts told him Martin wasn't a CIA agent. He was exactly what he seemed to be: a left-wing ideologue with a notepad.

The toilet paper stayed in Bucher's pocket.

Later, the *Pueblo* officers agreed that the press conference had been an unruly fiasco. They were certain Super C would punish them with a furious purge. But that night they learned that, on the contrary, the colonel regarded the day as an unqualified success.

So pleased was he with his prisoners' performance that he rewarded them all with a ration of beer.

CHAPTER 12

AN UNAPOLOGETIC APOLOGY

With the U.S. presidential race picking up summertime momentum, the *Pueblo* standoff was becoming a distinct liability for the Johnson administration and its Democratic allies in Congress.

LBJ had declared he wouldn't run for reelection, but both his vice president, Hubert Humphrey, and a prominent Democratic senator, Eugene McCarthy of Minnesota, were eager to succeed him. (Another high-profile Democratic senator, Robert F. Kennedy of New York, was fatally shot while campaigning in Los Angeles on June 5.) Republicans, meanwhile, realized they could use the spy-ship incident as a political tire iron against Democratic candidates for the White House and Congress. In speeches from Capitol Hill to their hometowns, GOP politicians criticized the administration's response to the seizure as yet another example of Democratic shilly-shallying in the face of communist aggression. "After a brief period of hand wringing," sniped Republican Representative Bob Wilson of San Diego, "our State Department has settled down into a rut of defeatism, puny protest, and wishy-washy talk-a-thons with the North Koreans."

Newspapers in the Republican-friendly Copley chain, including Wilson's hometown *San Diego Union*, printed boxes on their front pages showing the number of days the sailors had been held hostage. Editorial cartoonists at the zealously Republican *Chicago Tribune* showed little mercy. One *Tribune* caricature depicted a frightened Democratic donkey trying to run away from a pursuing skunk labeled "*Pueblo* Disgrace."

To Republicans as well as many conservative Democrats, the seemingly easy capture of the ship represented a devastating blow to American pride and prestige. "When the time comes that respect for America has sunk so low that a fourth-rate naval power can hijack an American military vessel from off the high seas, it's time for new leadership," declared Richard Nixon, soon to be the GOP's presidential nominee. Two thousand Republicans at a fund-raising dinner jumped to their feet and applauded when California governor Ronald Reagan warned, "Stealing the *Pueblo* and kidnapping our young men is a humiliation we will not tolerate." U.S. Senate Republican leader Everett Dirksen of Illinois contrasted President Johnson's cautious reaction with the derring-do of Commodore Stephen Decatur, who used his naval squadron's cannon to force the bey of Algiers to free American bluejackets captured during the Second Barbary War.

LBJ had no retort for his critics. The Panmunjom meetings had produced nothing but stalemate. The communists still were demanding an unconditional apology; the United States still refused to acquiesce. A rumor was circulating that Bucher had killed himself in prison, and no one in Washington knew whether it was true or not. Intelligence sources reported that North Korean divers had recovered material thrown from the boat, and captured eavesdropping equipment had been taken apart and analyzed with the aid of "foreign experts," presumably the Soviets.

While rhetorical brickbats flew in the United States, tensions on the Korean peninsula kept rising. As President Park had predicted, warmer weather attracted more infiltrators from the north, and communist saboteurs were again active in Seoul. In less than four weeks in June and July, allied forces killed 26 commandos.

On June 4, an F-4 Phantom jet, taking photos near the demilitarized zone, accidentally flew about five miles into North Korean airspace. Though the communists didn't react, the episode was unsettling enough to come to President Johnson's attention. Such mishaps, he told his new defense secretary, Clark Clifford, had to stop. On June 22, the North Koreans attacked and apparently sank a small South Korean reconnaissance boat as it tried to slip into a northern harbor in the middle of the night. Seoul hadn't notified General Bonesteel in advance of the operation, and he complained to the South Korean defense minister that it "could not have been better planned, timed, or executed to enable maximum exploitability [by] the North Koreans."

Reports filtered out of Pyongyang that Kim Il Sung still was fanning war fever, telling his people during mass rallies to prepare to "wipe out" potential American invaders. But a fresh CIA assessment of Kim's intentions came to the same conclusion American analysts had reached shortly after the *Pueblo* was taken: The dictator was more interested in fomenting a guerrilla-style "people's war" in South Korea than in launching a conventional invasion. Kim might be tempted to carry out a major raid or even to seize a piece of southern territory, according to the CIA. But no concentrations of troops or armor could be seen near the DMZ, and the north wasn't stockpiling food and medicine, as would be expected in the run-up to an actual war.

The real danger on the peninsula was the same as it had been all along: miscalculation by one side about how the other would react to a serious provocation. Such a blunder might take the form of another North Korean raid on the Blue House, or an equally rash expedition by President Park against the north. The new CIA estimate speculated that Kim and his top commanders believed the Johnson administration was unable to back up South Korea because it was so mired in Vietnam. The report added candidly, "U.S. restraint in the *Pueblo* affair probably strengthened this view."

Although American intelligence discounted the chances of a North Korean invasion, the Pentagon nonetheless drafted a set of apocalyptic plans to cope with such a contingency. One top secret scheme, eerily code-named "Freedom Drop," envisioned American aircraft or land-based rockets incinerating communist forces with nuclear warheads. The attacks could be limited to a handful of military sites, but the president also had the option of going after "all significant North Korean offensive and logistical support targets."

As LBJ groped for the right formula to defuse the Korean situation, he also kept searching for an escape hatch in Vietnam. Following months of preliminary discussions, Ho Chi Minh's government finally agreed to meet U.S.

delegates in Paris to negotiate a possible end to the war. Johnson selected veteran diplomat Averell Harriman and Cyrus Vance, fresh from his arm-twisting mission to Seoul, as his representatives. But the Paris talks, which began in May, bogged down as quickly as had those at Panmunjom. The North Vietnamese demanded an unconditional halt to aerial and naval bombardment of their territory and a pullout of U.S. troops from the south as preconditions to any peace discussions. The possibility that communist forces would take advantage of bomb-free skies to kill more GIs haunted Johnson; he insisted on a communist pledge to engage in "prompt and serious" cease-fire talks if he grounded the B-52s.

The North Vietnamese ignored him and instead used the Paris sessions as a bully pulpit to appeal to the growing American antiwar movement. Johnson, however, refused to get discouraged and break off contact with Hanoi. Clark Clifford, who despite his reputation as a Cold War hawk was emerging as the administration's leading Vietnam skeptic, advised the president there was no military solution to the war and the talks might well be the only way out.

President Park, too, was keeping a close eye on developments at Paris. But his interests were sharply different from those of his friend and protector LBJ. While the American leader was open to a political settlement in Vietnam, Park wanted nothing less than decisive military victory over the communists. His prime minister, Chung Il Kwon, told Ambassador Porter that if the Paris talks collapsed, the United States and South Korea should pour enough troops into South Vietnam to drive Ho Chi Minh from the battlefield in six months. Chung said he even favored transferring two more divisions from his endangered country to finish the job in Vietnam. With the North Vietnamese beaten, he believed, both South Korean and American units could be sent back to reinforce South Korea, ending Kim Il Sung's adventurism there.

Near the end of August the Panmunjom talks were all but defunct.

American and North Korean negotiators hadn't sat down together in more than six weeks. The smoke-blowing Admiral John Victor Smith had been succeeded by Army Major General Gilbert Woodward, a stern-faced West Point alumnus who'd once commanded the 2nd Armored Division in

Berlin. One acquaintance described him as cynical and unpleasant, but also pragmatic and "unbelievably brilliant." After just four sessions with General Pak, Woodward had lost patience with communist recalcitrance and delaying tactics. The two sides normally took turns setting dates for meetings, but the North Koreans had refused to call one since July 10. Woodward decided to get things moving. He sent word to Pak that he wanted to confer on August 27 and, without waiting for a reply, traveled from Seoul to the truce village.

Pak didn't show up.

Woodward had few cards left to play. The North Koreans already had rejected several U.S. settlement proposals. In February, Admiral Smith promised the United States would conduct an "impartial inquiry" when the crew was released and, if the results warranted, express its regrets. When the North Koreans failed to take that bait, Smith offered to let an "international fact-finding body"—made up of an American delegate, a North Korean, and a mutually agreeable chairman—undertake the investigation. Pak refused. Increasingly desperate for a deal, Washington floated the extraordinary idea of transferring the sailors to the USSR or some other North Korean ally so they could testify, supposedly without coercion, before the international panel. That, too, was unacceptable. The communist negotiator refused to budge from his original demand for "three As": Washington must *admit* to violating North Korea's waters, *apologize* for the transgressions, and *assure* Pyongyang such acts were never to be repeated.

Running out of diplomatic alternatives, the Johnson administration in mid-May turned once again to Moscow for help. Secretary of State Dean Rusk met in his private dining room with the urbane Soviet ambassador to the United States, Anatoly Dobrynin, and the USSR's deputy foreign minister, Vasily Kuznetsov. Washington had "gone as far as it is possible for it to go," said Rusk, who'd made sure the Russians received transcripts of each and every dead-end powwow at Panmunjom. He reiterated that the United States had no intention of humiliating itself by apologizing for acts it was reasonably certain it hadn't committed. North Korea, he said, still was sending commandos into the south and threatening a "possible resumption of hostilities" with Seoul. Rusk warned that the situation "could become explosive" and asked for Moscow's assistance in trying to "keep things cool."

The Soviet diplomats were noncommittal. Kuznetsov said he could give Rusk no formal reply. Dobrynin said the Soviets had seen a film in which *Pueblo* sailors seemed to corroborate North Korea's allegations of intrusion and spying. When it became clear his visitors would do little or nothing to help, Rusk made sure they understood the stakes. If Kim Il Sung was foolish enough to invade, he said in measured tones, the United States would respond with "maximum violence"—a clear signal that nuclear weapons would be used to hold back onrushing communist divisions. Perhaps taken aback by the gravity of the secretary's threat, Kuznetsov said the Soviets "strongly favor détente" in Korea and that the two superpowers should work together to prevent further exacerbation of the situation. A good first step, Rusk replied, would be the release of the *Pueblo* and its crew.

Still, North Korea didn't back down. As weeks and months ticked away with no movement at Panmunjom, LBJ's men concluded there was no way to get around Pyongyang's implacable insistence on an admission of guilt. They were surer than ever that Bucher hadn't crossed into North Korean waters. Navy analysts had taken a close look at the position logs released by the communists—the ones Murphy doctored—and realized that they placed the *Pueblo* "over 30 miles from shore on dry land" at two different points. But righteous denials of wrongdoing weren't working at Panmunjom. In utmost secrecy, Johnson's advisers began to discuss giving Kim Il Sung what he wanted—without appearing to do so.

The vehicle they talked of using was an "overwrite." There was nothing fancy about it: On a document of apology drafted by the North Koreans, a U.S. representative would write that he'd taken custody of the crew, and sign his name. Washington could then claim it had only signed a "receipt" for the men, while North Korea could crow that it had extracted an official mea culpa. "Both sides would understand this ambiguity," Under Secretary of State Nicholas Katzenbach explained in a memo to the president.

It was diplomatic legerdemain that sounded somewhat crazy, but something similar had worked in the case of the captured Army helicopter pilots. In May 1964, a U.S. Air Force general publicly signed a statement that the pilots had been spying on North Korea and no such "criminal acts" would be committed in the future. In exchange the chopper pilots were freed. The next day, the United States officially denounced the general's affidavit as "meaningless," since the pilots, as uniformed servicemen performing a military mission, couldn't be considered espionage agents under international law.

Some Americans viewed the recanted "confession" as an unpleasant expediency. But others—including some top Washington officials—regarded it as a disgraceful dodge that undercut American prestige by calling into question the trustworthiness of government pronouncements. "The feeling is that this was not an honorable course for a nation of the stature of the U.S. to pursue," an anonymous administration official told journalist Joseph Albright. General Woodward was among those who didn't think such a maneuver was a legitimate way to resolve the *Pueblo* impasse. "This country cannot indulge in lies," he firmly told his father, who'd suggested a "meaningless admission" to bring the sailors home.

But the overwrite stratagem, too, had drawbacks. For one thing, the Johnson administration had specifically promised President Park it wouldn't sign another "helicopter-type" apology to get Bucher and his men back. Park's government reminded Washington of this pledge in an aide-mémoire declaring that the "integrity, dignity and prestige of the Republic of Korea and the United States are inseparably bound." South Korea urged LBJ to "maintain a firm stand" against Pyongyang if he wanted to retrieve the *Pueblo* crew "in an honorable way."

Another difficulty was that even if Washington did sign a "receipt," there was no guarantee North Korea would let the crew go. On May 8, General Pak had presented a draft of a servile apology he wanted Woodward to sign. But when the American general asked, at their next meeting, whether Bucher and his men would be freed at the same time Woodward affixed his signature, Pak made no reply. For months afterward, Pak ducked the "simultaneity" question. State Department officials in Washington discussed whether to try to persuade the North Koreans to soften the wording of the draft apology, but finally decided against doing so. The more outlandish the rhetoric, the reasoning went, the easier it would be for the United States to renounce the document later.

Pak was no more forthcoming when Woodward tried to confirm the rumor that Bucher had committed suicide. A Japanese newsman had made that claim to American military intelligence in June, and the story soon was being whispered about in Seoul and Washington. The State Department worried that Rose Bucher might hear the rumor and go public with it. If that happened, the Johnson administration was sure to face noisy and distracting demands to push harder to get the rest of the sailors back in one piece.

The State Department instructed Woodward to press Pak at their June 27 meeting about Bucher's purported demise. But, as usual, the North Korean bobbed and weaved and refused to answer:

> ***Woodward:*** Is Commander Bucher in good health?
>
> ***Pak:*** Where did you get [such] a rumor and raise such a question? We have no knowledge of it. I don't deem it necessary to clarify every rumor that goes around.
>
> ***Woodward:*** The families of these men have had no reliable assurances that their husbands and sons are decently treated and in good health. Since February 2 you have not even made any statement to Admiral Smith or to me that they are all alive and well. . . . I'll call on you to tell me now, directly, whether or not all 82 captives are alive and well.
>
> ***Pak:*** If your side is really concerned about the fate of the crew of the *Pueblo*, you should seriously study the statement our side made at today's meeting and bring the pertinent document of apology and assurance to the next meeting, as we demanded.
>
> ***Woodward:*** General Pak, your answer was not a clear one and I ask again that you tell me whether or not the 82 captives are in good health.
>
> ***Pak:*** Refer to the statement I have already made.

A few days later, Washington again ordered Woodward to pursue the issue of Bucher's supposed suicide. "In addition [to] humanitarian considerations, we will be vulnerable to criticism if we have not made every effort [to] ascertain [the] facts in this matter," the State Department cabled. "In order to avoid unnecessary anguish for Mrs. Bucher and other families, we have tried to prevent the report about his death from becoming widely known."

(The department privately informed the captain's wife of the rumor soon afterward; she refused to believe it.)

President Park vehemently opposed the United States signing anything that even resembled an apology. Such action, he told Ambassador Porter during an August 27 conference in Seoul, would mark an embarrassing retreat from Washington's oft-stated position that the *Pueblo* had never entered North Korean waters.

The South Korean leader listened intently as Porter explained American thinking about an overwrite. Then, clearly unhappy, he peppered the envoy with questions. When Porter told him of Woodward's abortive trip to Panmunjom, Park asked why Washington was so eager for another sit-down with the communists. Their only desire, he repeated for the umpteenth time, was to demean the United States and, by extension, his country.

If LBJ apologized now, he went on, the American press and public would want to know why he hadn't done so back in February, when the communists first expressed their demands, thus sparing the sailors months of imprisonment and suffering. How would the president explain the delay? And did the State Department really believe that, by covering itself with the fig leaf of an overwrite, it could argue with a straight face that it hadn't caved in to the North Koreans' unwavering demands for an apology?

Nevertheless, Porter replied, that was exactly what the United States proposed to do. The reason for the delay was that Washington couldn't sign an overwrite until Pyongyang promised to simultaneously let the crew go. And getting the pigheaded North Koreans to say they'd do that turned out to be one of the thorniest, most time-consuming problems at Panmunjom.

The United States was well aware that North Korea only wanted to shame it, Porter said. But President Johnson couldn't afford to sit on his hands. He had to show Congress and the public that everything possible was being done to save Bucher and his men. "It [is] not practical for us to remain motionless in this matter," the ambassador told Park.

Woodward finally sat down again with Pak on August 29. The atmosphere was businesslike but charged: Each time Woodward made a statement, the North Koreans wrote it down and a courier whisked it out of the Military

Armistice Commission building. Pak seemed to expect the American negotiator to say something momentous, and he wanted to make sure his superiors in Pyongyang knew about it right away.

For his part Pak issued yet another threat: A U.S. failure to apologize, he said, would lead to "unfavorable results for the crew." The only thing he wanted to know was whether Washington was prepared to say it was sorry. Otherwise, he declared, the North Koreans had "said all we have to say to your side."

As it had done with Admiral Smith, the State Department cabled explicit instructions to Woodward on what to say to Pak. For this meeting, the general had been told to be more specific about the overwrite. In three previous sessions, Pak hadn't responded when asked whether he'd return the crew in exchange for an "appropriately amended" version of the communist-drafted apology. Now Woodward asked whether the North Koreans could accept a "receipt" for the crew. Pak didn't seem to understand the question. Woodward repeated it three times, but got no real answer. Worse, near the end of the meeting, Pak appeared to misinterpret what the American was saying.

"I have noted your statement made at today's meeting that your side is ready to sign the document of apology and assurance put forth by our side," he said.

"I take note of your statement," replied Woodward, "and only wish to reiterate that the language of my statement should be carefully studied since your last statement contains language that I did not use."

Thus the twentieth secret meeting ended in confusion and inconclusiveness.

In early September a flurry of news stories in South Korea and the United States suggested Kim Il Sung might let the crew go as part of the upcoming celebration of North Korea's twentieth anniversary as a nation. "Freeing of *Pueblo* Reported Imminent," said a headline in *The New York Times*. The evidence underpinning such stories, however, was flimsy. The North Koreans were sprucing up their side of the Joint Security Area at Panmunjom, a logical spot for a release, and the head of the Japanese Communist Party told newsmen he thought some progress was being made in the bilateral talks. But the cleanup activity could be routine and the Japanese party chief might not know what he was talking about.

American officials had no choice but to take the reports seriously. On September 8, the day before the North Korean anniversary, a U.S. military hospital ward in Seoul was cleared for the crew, and ambulances were readied to transport them from the DMZ.

Ever the pragmatist, Ambassador Porter envisioned ugly possibilities beneath the optimistic froth. Since the North Koreans' main objective was to wrest an unconditional apology from the United States, they could be planning to bring the sailors to Panmunjom, let a handful of them go—just officers, for instance—and refuse to release the rest unless Woodward signed the document they wanted. The communists could invite a large contingent of TV reporters to witness the spectacle, knowing the resulting images of newly released captives, rejoicing with bear hugs and tears—and contrasted with the fearful, anxious faces of those left behind—would sharply increase public pressure on LBJ. A second possibility was that the entire crew would be brought to the truce village and offered in exchange for an unqualified apology. All or nothing, and Woodward would have to decide on the spot.

In the eyes of much of the world, any such ploy would be seen as blackmail of the crudest, most contemptible kind. Many people would interpret an "apology" in such circumstances as the humanitarian thing to do, and make no criticism of the United States for doing it. Yet the State Department still wanted to play hardball. Even if Pak offered most or all of the sailors back, Woodward was told, he wasn't to sign an apology without including the "receipt" language.

The North Korean anniversary came and went with no relief for Bucher and his men. In Seoul, there were whispers that Woodward, at the most recent secret meeting, had agreed to an unfettered apology, and the gossip soon morphed into newspaper stories. Porter suspected President Park's government—especially the foreign minister—as the source. The rumors were uncomfortably close to the truth, and Park had a vested interest in stirring up public opposition in both his country and the United States to any expression of regret. The State Department had precisely the opposite interest, and Porter visited the foreign ministry to convey his annoyance at the whisper campaign.

On September 20, as the American ambassador accompanied Prime Minister Chung Il Kwon and several other cabinet ministers on a tour of three South Korean provinces, Chung asked whether there was anything new on the *Pueblo*.

Porter told of the difficulty of getting straight answers out of General Pak. Chung in turn urged that the U.S. government spare no effort to bring home its sailors as soon as possible. Time worked against Washington, he said; the matter would only become more volatile in the future. Porter replied that no one knew what would emerge from the closed-door negotiations. Choosing his words carefully, he asked the prime minister's opinion of how the South Korean press and public would react "if something did develop." Chung offered his best Machiavellian advice:

Whatever deal the Americans decided to make at Panmunjom, they should do it at a time when the news media were distracted by a bigger story far, far away.

CHAPTER 13

HELL WEEK

The afterglow of Super C's satisfaction with the international press conference warmed Bucher and his men well into September. More attention was paid to their medical needs; the quantity and quality of food improved. The sailors found their plates heaped with fresh fish, canned ham, bread and butter, apples. Some even began to gain back some of the weight they'd lost over the previous eight months.

A few nourishing meals weren't enough to reverse the cumulative effects of long-term malnutrition, however. About 15 crewmen, afflicted by nerve problems in their legs, still had trouble walking, and sailors still suffered from infections, chills, and fevers.

Bucher was beset by severe diarrhea, fever, a brief bout of hepatitis, and numbness in his battered right leg. One day a guard found him collapsed again—this time in the hall—and called for Charlie Law. The half-blind quartermaster scooped up his unconscious boss in his powerful arms. Weighing only 115 pounds, the skipper felt like "a bundle of feathers." Law maneuvered his way into Bucher's room and gently deposited him on his bed.

Despite their poor health, the Americans' morale was at an all-time high. CT Earl Kisler composed a tongue-in-cheek poem that reflected their heightened sense of solidarity:

Out of Japan on the fifth of Jan.
The *Pueblo* came a-steamin'
Round Kyushu's toe, past Sasebo,
You could hear the Captain a-screamin'
"XO!" he said,
"Full speed ahead! We've got us some spyin' to do!"
"Timmy, be sharp!" Then with Charlie Law's charts,
Away like a turtle we flew.

The poem went on to describe the crew's seemingly endless incarceration before concluding:

But if we get back,
No coins will we lack,
So beware all ye banks, bars, and brothels!
If some night you're pub-crawlin',
And into gutters you're fallin',
And in that gutter are 82 gaffers;
It's only the crew of AGER-2,
Otherwise known as "BUCHER'S BASTARDS."

When the North Koreans decreed that yet another round of "confessions" be written, the seamen took even more liberties than usual. Steve Harris revealed that he'd been tutored as a spy by Maxwell Smart, the hilariously clumsy, secret-agent antihero of the *Get Smart* TV series. Bucher wrote of receiving orders to "spy out" North Korea from a cartoonish cast of characters that included the villainous "Fleet General Barney Google" and CIA master spy "Sol Loxfinger," a name the captain cribbed from a *Playboy* magazine spoof of James Bond novels.

Super C also wanted the crew to submit another "petition for leniency" to his government. The captain chose Schumacher, Steve Harris, and three enlisted men to help him write it, and together they produced a small masterpiece of satirical counterpropaganda. Their statement expressed the usual contrition over violating North Korean waters, but the Americans also planted a number of linguistic booby traps the communists failed to detect.

The sailors admitted to being "super-spies" obsessed with "adding goodies to our spy bag." They were guilty, they said, of "crimes so horrible [that] they have seldom been exceeded in the history of the world." But the best line was about their ostensible intrusions into communist waters: "We, as conscientious human beings who were cast upon the rocks and shoals of immorality by the tidal wave of Washington's naughty policies, know that neither the frequency nor the distances of these transgressions into the territorial waters of this peace-loving nation matter because, in the final analysis, penetration however slight is sufficient to complete the act." The last several words of that sentence were calculated to put a smile on the face of any current or former U.S. serviceman who remembered from boot-camp lectures that "penetration however slight" was the definition of rape under military law. When Bucher read the petition aloud during a mass meeting, some of his men nearly gagged from the strain of holding in laughter. But their gullible captors accepted the statement at face value; it was broadcast on North Korean radio and printed verbatim in the English-language *Pyongyang Times* newspaper.

Super C had mysteriously disappeared from the Country Club after the international press conference. By October he was back, striding about with renewed vigor and palpable pride. Bucher soon figured out why: The four small stars on his shoulder boards that marked him as a senior colonel had been replaced by two large silver stars signifying his promotion to lieutenant general. The Americans duly upgraded his nickname to "Glorious General," or G.G. He didn't say where he'd been, but he seemed to have new plans for the crew. When he summoned Bucher for an all-night interrogation, he was in an almost convivial mood, allowing the captain to chain-smoke along with him. Bucher congratulated him on his advancement and the hard-shelled North Korean beamed with pleasure. Then he said something that made the skipper's heart leap:

"You have said you expect to be home before Christmas. Well, I say you will not be home before then, nor before your Thanksgiving, but before this month is out."

Bucher desperately wanted to believe him. But there was no way to know whether G.G. was telling the truth or not, and the captain didn't want to raise his men's hopes only to have them crushed. He decided to keep the general's prediction to himself.

Before they let their prize prisoners go—if indeed they intended to do that—the North Koreans were determined to give them a booster shot of communist culture. On October 1, the Americans were bused to Pyongyang to see a sort of propaganda opera titled *How Glorious Is Our Fatherland*. Posed in his jeep like a conquering hero, Glorious General led the way into the capital. At one point the convoy was forced to stop by a peasant farmer staggering drunkenly down the road. Honking horns and angry shouts had no effect on him. Finally, a North Korean officer got out, marched up to the farmer, and briskly slapped him in the face.

The chastened peasant stumbled off the road and the buses rolled on into the city, stopping outside a large theater with curled-up, Buddhist-style eaves. Inside it was modern and comfortable, with nearly all of the 2,000 seats occupied by North Korean army personnel. The Americans were taken to the balcony, and interpreters sat down next to every fourth man. Then the curtain rose on a large troupe of performers who energetically sang and danced their way through a musical pageant of North Korea's recent history, as scripted by the communists. With every song and scene, the interpreters leaned toward the sailors, exclaiming, "Very beautiful!" and, "Very great!"

Kim Il Sung's heroic struggle against the Japanese was acted out, along with a more contemporary tale in which actors in white U.S. Navy caps portrayed the vanquished officers of the *Pueblo*. It was all very colorful and well performed, and the crewmen thoroughly enjoyed themselves. If nothing else, it was a reprieve from the tension and tedium of their cells.

Four nights later, the Americans were taken back to Pyongyang to see a circus, complete with trapeze artists, clowns, and tightrope walkers. This show was considerably less polished. A skinny, toothless lion staged a sit-down strike, drawing an angry kick from its tamer. Then an old black bear—also lacking teeth—lumbered into the ring. When the trainer stuck his head in the animal's harmless maw, the sailors burst into wild laughter.

Even the circus had been turned into a kind of animated billboard for state ideology. One of the clowns, dressed as President Park of South Korea, loudly beat a drum marked with a U.S. dollar sign. When "Park" started to collapse, another clown costumed as an American army general jumped into the ring and reinflated him with a tire pump. The political symbolism was ham-handed but funny nonetheless. The following night, the crewmen were again bused into Pyongyang for a superb performance by the North Korean Army Chorus.

By now Bucher was convinced the seamen were going home. He made his hunch known to his officers and certain enlisted men, but some of the others had drawn their own optimistic inferences from the communist charm offensive. Why would the North Koreans spend so much time and effort entertaining them if they weren't going to be freed?

That view was reinforced when their captors made a bumbling attempt to recruit the sailors as moles for Pyongyang.

The effort began when four important-looking communists drove into the compound one day and disappeared into the building where the multinational press conference had been held. Not long afterward Doc Baldridge was summoned there. The medic was gone about three hours; the rest of the crew had no idea what was happening to him. Baldridge finally reappeared, drunk, in the mess hall at dinnertime. He had to be led to his usual seat at the head of the table, where he promptly dumped his meal on the floor, grousing that he couldn't stomach such garbage anymore. The others tried to find out what had gone on with the visiting bigwigs, but Baldridge was too blasted to explain. He lurched out of the mess hall, brusquely telling a guard at the door, "Get the hell out of my way, you dumb shit." Taken aback, the North Korean stepped aside.

Over the next week more sailors were called into what Bucher dubbed "the Gypsy Tea Room." Upon entering they found what in America might pass for a cocktail lounge combined with an all-you-can-eat buffet. Four cushioned chairs were arranged in a square; nearby tables held cold cuts, cookies, cigarettes, beer, wine, and ginseng liquor. The Americans were invited to eat and drink to their heart's content, and they didn't have to be told twice. Stu Russell polished off six beers; several others got sloshed, too.

Murphy found himself in the Tea Room with three North Koreans. One

Commander
Lloyd M. (Pete) Bucher.

★ *U.S. Navy*

The USS *Pueblo*, bristling with antennae and electronic sensors. The large rectangular box forward of the bridge encloses the SOD hut. ★ *U.S. Navy*

The spy ship's cramped galley produced meals for eighty-three officers and enlisted men each day. ★ *U.S. Navy*

Ensign F. Carl (Skip) Schumacher nearly ran the *Pueblo* aground his first time on the bridge. Fellow crewmen later lauded him as "exceptionally strong" and "an inspiration" during their imprisonment in North Korea.

★ *U.S. Navy*

Soviet surveillance trawlers often shadowed U.S. warships, studying their movements and tactics, during the 1960s. Here the *Gidrofon* paces the aircraft carrier USS *Coral Sea*.

★ *U.S. Navy*

Twenty-two-year-old Peter Langenberg joined the Navy after dropping out of Princeton.

★ *Courtesy of Peter Langenberg*

Harvard-educated Lieutenant Stephen R. Harris was in charge of the secretive communications technicians who eavesdropped on North Korean radar and radio transmissions.

★ *U.S. Navy*

Quartermaster Charles Law, the expert navigator who would lose much of his eyesight due to malnourishment in prison.

★ *U.S. Navy*

Navy shore patrolmen in the bar district of Sasebo, Japan, where Bucher spent a long night drinking and playing cards before departing for North Korea.

★ *Courtesy of Rick Juergens*

Oceanographer Harry Iredale, whose presence was intended to reinforce the *Pueblo*'s cover story as a scientific research vessel.

★ *Courtesy of Harry Iredale*

Two days before the *Pueblo* seizure, North Korean commandos tried to storm the Blue House, South Korea's presidential residence, and decapitate President Park Chung Hee.

★ *Wikimedia.org*

South Korean forces killed most of the Blue House raiders, but captured Second Lieutenant Kim Shin-jo. The attempt to murder their president left many South Koreans clamoring for revenge against the north.

★ Korea Daily

North Korean patrol boats attacked the *Pueblo* on January 23, 1968. In this frame from a North Korean propaganda film, a communist torpedo boat races past the American vessel.

★ JoongAng Ilbo

A North Korean SO-1 submarine chaser, similar to the one that blasted the *Pueblo* with cannon fire.

★ *U.S. Navy*

After their capture, Bucher and his men were paraded before an angry crowd of North Korean civilians. Some *Pueblo* veterans say this scene was a propaganda reenactment. ★ *Korean Central News Agency*

A CIA pilot flying the top secret A-12 aircraft spotted the captured *Pueblo* in Wonsan Bay. Here an A-12 refuels during a training exercise.

★ *Central Intelligence Agency*

A photo from the A-12 shows the *Pueblo* in Wonsan Bay. "Black Shield" was the code name for the January 26, 1968, reconnaissance flight that located the spy ship.

★ *Central Intelligence Agency*

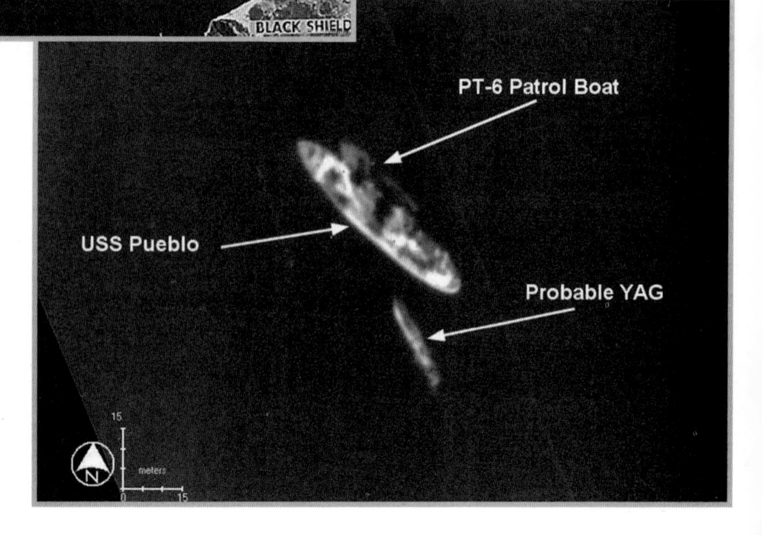

A close-up of a North Korean torpedo boat guarding the *Pueblo*. A smaller service craft is nearby.

★ *Central Intelligence Agency*

President Lyndon Johnson hoped to avoid a second Korean War over the *Pueblo*. At a White House meeting in February 1968, he was flanked by Secretary of State Dean Rusk (*left*) and Defense Secretary Robert McNamara (*right*). ★ *LBJ Library*

Diplomatic troubleshooter Cyrus Vance (*center*) struggled to restrain South Korea's Park Chung Hee (*left*) from attacking North Korea after communist infiltrators tried to assassinate him. At right is William Porter, U.S. ambassador to South Korea.

★ *National Archives and Records Administration*

Langenberg in prison. The North Koreans often added homey touches like potted plants to propaganda photos, hoping to persuade the world that their captives were being treated humanely. ★ *Korean Central News Agency*

North Korean doctors performed surgery on ship's fireman Steve Woelk without giving him any anesthetics. The communists later re-created the operation for propaganda photographers.

★ *Korean Central News Agency*

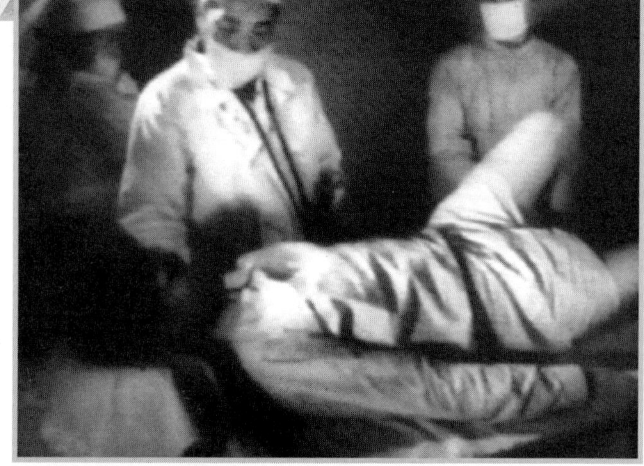

Woelk smiles at a communist doctor after his Lazarus-like recovery.

★ *Korean Central News Agency*

The sailors deliberately extended their middle fingers to ruin propaganda pictures. After *Time* magazine explained the derisive gesture, the humiliated North Koreans brutally beat the crewmen. ★ *Korean Central News Agency*

More finger salutes from communication technicians Brad Crowe (*center*) and John Shilling (*right*). ★ *Korean Central News Agency*

Marine Sergeant Robert Hammond fiercely resisted his torturers. He later was awarded the Navy Cross for extraordinary heroism.

★ *Korean Central News Agency*

Lieutenant Edward R. Murphy points out fabricated intrusions by the *Pueblo* in communist waters during the "international" press conference in September 1968.

★ *Korean Central News Agency*

The sailors found many exhibits at the Sinchon "genocide museum" hard to believe. In this 2009 tourist photo, a guide points to a depiction of a U.S. soldier torturing a boy during the Korean War.

★ *Courtesy of Raymond K. Cunningham Jr.*

Under Secretary of State Nicholas Katzenbach oversaw the frustrating secret talks with North Korea to free the crewmen. ★ *White House*

Army Major General Gilbert Woodward (*right*) signed the "prerepudiated" U.S. apology that finally convinced the North Koreans to let the sailors go.

★ *U.S. Navy*

Walking twenty paces apart, sailors cross the Bridge of No Return to freedom on December 23, 1968.

★ Stars and Stripes

Taking off his Mao cap in a final act of defiance, an emaciated but smiling Bucher reaches the allied side of the Bridge of No Return.

★ *U.S. Navy*

Gene Lacy, Steve Harris, and Skip Schumacher (*left to right*) enjoy a meal at the United Nations advance camp shortly after their release. ★ *U.S. Navy*

After eleven months of sadistic imprisonment, Bucher reunites with his wife, Rose, on Christmas Eve 1968. ★ *U.S. Navy*

Marine Sergeant Bob Chicca hugs his wife, Ann Marie, as the news media records the crew's homecoming at Miramar Naval Air Station near San Diego.

★ *U.S. Navy*

Bucher and Murphy receive Purple Hearts during a January 3, 1969, ceremony at the U.S. Naval Hospital in San Diego. ★ *U.S. Navy*

An outpouring of public sympathy buoyed Bucher and his men after their return. Here they read a ten-foot-long "welcome home" letter signed by New York schoolchildren.

★ *U.S. Navy*

Schumacher receives a plaque of appreciation from movie star John Wayne at a party in January 1969. Singer Pat Boone and "several Hollywood starlets" also entertained the sailors.

★ *U.S. Navy*

Vice Admiral Harold G. Bowen Jr. (*standing*) led the Navy's official inquiry into the *Pueblo* debacle. Seated (*left to right*) are rear admirals Richard Pratt, Marshall White, Edward Grimm, and Allen Bergner.

★ *U.S. Navy*

Captain William Newsome, chief counsel to the investigating admirals, stunned the courtroom audience by warning that Bucher might be court-martialed for giving up his ship without a fight.

★ *U.S. Navy*

Bucher with his attorneys, E. Miles Harvey (*left*) and Navy Captain James E. Keys.

★ *U.S. Navy*

Shortly before the *Pueblo* and its code machines were captured, Navy radioman John A. Walker Jr. began selling key cards for programming the devices to the Soviets. This photo was taken early in Walker's Navy career.

★ *Federal Bureau of Investigation*

After a bitter fight with the Pentagon, Bucher and his men were awarded the Prisoner of War Medal during a 1990 ceremony in San Diego.

★ © U-T San Diego/*Zumapress.com*

For years, the *Pueblo* has been a floating tourist attraction in Pyongyang. In this 2010 photo, North Koreans raise their fists at a rally marking the sixtieth anniversary of the Korean War's outbreak.

★ *Korean Central News Agency*

was an army captain who'd interrogated Murphy early in his captivity. The other two, in civilian clothes, appeared to be political officers. They made small talk as two sweater-clad girls brought in trays of apples, sausage, candies, and—perhaps in deference to the executive officer's teetotaling—soft drinks. One girl wore a green sweater and matching skirt; the other wore all red. Murphy thought of them as "Merry" and "Christmas."

The Koreans talked with creepily detailed knowledge of Murphy's two children and schools he'd attended. They asked whether he'd like to return to their country someday. Trying to sound as "sincere" as possible, the XO said he would, but only after spending time with his family in the States. Was Murphy willing to receive a North Korean "visitor" at his home in America? Oh, yes, the lieutenant said archly; he promised to give anyone from North Korea a welcome "he would long remember."

The communists probed for receptiveness among other sailors, too. Some men gave compliant answers to their questions; others blatantly insulted their hosts. Asked whether he'd open his home to someone from North Korea, Baldridge replied, "Are you kidding? Why the hell should I, anyway?" Friar Tuck said the only way he wanted to see North Korea again was through a bombsight. Russell, happily soused, agreed not only to take a visitor into his Southern California home, but to escort him to Disneyland, Knott's Berry Farm, maybe even Tijuana.

The Gypsy Tea Room apparently yielded little, if anything, of value to the North Koreans, and they decided to give the crew one last propaganda immersion. On October 10, the sailors were told to pack toothpaste, soap, and other personal items for a short trip. Buses took them back to Pyongyang, where they boarded a train for a place they'd never heard of: Sinchon.

Located about 40 miles southwest of Pyongyang, Sinchon was a sort of national historic site dedicated to hatred of Americans. North Korea claimed that during the Korean War, rampaging U.S. troops turned the Sinchon area into a vast slaughterhouse, massacring more than 35,000 civilians. To memorialize the alleged butchery, Kim Il Sung erected his own version of a Holocaust museum in Sinchon; it was there the sailors were to be taken.

Glorious General had first mentioned the museum when the crewmen were at the Barn. "Someday I hope you may visit Sinchon," he said. "Then you will really understand why we Koreans hate you Americans." Throngs of North Koreans, including many schoolchildren, made pilgrimages to Sinchon each year. Some of the guards had mentioned with pride that they'd lost relatives in the Sinchon "genocide."*

The crewmen arrived in Sinchon on the morning of October 11. Buses took them to the museum, a boxy, two-story structure of light-colored stone that was once the local Communist Party headquarters. There they were met by a guide, a thin young woman with stringy black hair, and, as always when a propaganda photo op presented itself, a TV crew.

The museum was a hive of small exhibit rooms, each containing "artifacts" of the horror American soldiers supposedly wreaked on the local populace in late 1950. The displays were far from convincing. The first was a glass case that held only a lock of hair, which the guide said belonged to "a patriotic hero of the war who was murdered by the U.S. imperialist aggressors." The hair, of course, could have come from anyone, living or dead. The sailors moved on to another exhibit featuring an old, rusty knife that had been used to "chop off the head of a patriotic Korean soldier." Another glass case contained the shoes of people purportedly drowned in a river by homicidal U.S. troops. A framed photograph of the river hung above the case, but there were no bodies in the water.

Many of the claimed atrocities were attributed to a "Lieutenant Harrison," first name unknown. He'd supposedly been captured during the war and confessed to hundreds of crimes. Among other things, he was said to have dragged 30 innocent women and children to their deaths behind a U.S. military vehicle; one of the display cases bore a length of rope Harrison al-

---

*The author knows of no credible evidence that American troops committed war crimes in Sinchon. Bruce Cumings, a University of Chicago historian and a leading scholar of the Korean War, has written that, following a 1987 visit, he became convinced that "a terrible atrocity had taken place" there, although he wasn't sure who was responsible. Cumings cites the work of South Korean dissident writer Hwang Sok-yong, who interviewed people who said they witnessed massacres in the area. In his novel *The Guest*, Hwang suggests that after United Nations troops occupied Sinchon County during the war, right-wing youth groups and Christians from South Korea moved in and murdered many northern civilians. Hwang also says marauding communist guerrilla bands killed "anyone who got in their way."

legedly used in this deed. A large painting depicted him and other American military men sitting around a conference table, plotting villainous acts. When Murphy asked which one was Lieutenant Harrison, the guide pointed without hesitation to a soldier with corporal's stripes on his uniform. Throughout the tour the TV crew filmed the Americans' reaction to their tragic national shrine; some of the crewmen, though trying to act contrite, couldn't resist flipping off the camera.

It was all a bit much for Bucher, who could barely keep from laughing out loud at the hokey displays. "How ghastly!" he declared in mock abhorrence as he stared at a rusty nail that the evil Harrison was said to have pounded into the heads of Korean women.

The crewmen were led downstairs to a dungeonlike chamber where, the guide insisted, 900 Koreans had been burned to death. Since the room was hardly big enough to hold 82 sailors, the claim was inherently suspicious. The captain asked whether all the victims were incinerated at the same time. Yes, replied the guide. "Unbelievable!" Bucher burst out. She pointed at the ceiling, saying carbonized skin was still visible there. To the sailors the dark spots looked like mold. Feeling himself on the verge of an uncontrollable guffaw, Bucher suffered another of his "lockjaw" attacks. "I can't take any more," he rasped through gritted teeth, as some of his men nearly went into convulsions at his antics. Silver Lips was so pleased with the skipper's apparent distress at the evidence of U.S. atrocities that he told the camera crew to move in for a close-up. Bucher mugged obligingly, jaws firmly clamped.

Some of the Americans had hoped the trip to Sinchon was to be the first leg of a freedom ride to Panmunjom. But that wasn't the case. When the museum tour ended, they were shipped back to the Country Club. Not long afterward, the North Koreans' recent benevolence evaporated. All talk of repatriation stopped. Robot and other room daddies began demanding to know more about the Hawaiian good-luck sign. Bucher was confined to his cell for long periods. His orderly was taken away, cutting off his communication with the crew. Bucher worried whether the abrupt change in attitude was his fault, whether he'd gone too far with his lockjaw routine and other shenanigans. Had he crossed some fatal line with the communists?

He couldn't find out from Glorious General; the prison commandant had again vanished. When he returned a few weeks later, he displayed nothing but icy disdain toward the Americans.

G.G. ended all special privileges. No more Ping-Pong and card games. Watery turnip soup again became the dietary staple. The number of guards on each floor multiplied from two to 12; the seamen were again forced to bow their heads in their captors' presence.

There were other ominous signs. The Bear had disappeared for a while, too, but now he was back, and he and other guards became rougher. One day the Bear pulled a sailor out of his room and smashed him into a wall for no apparent reason. Law and two men from his cell were brutally worked over. A squat, shaved-headed North Korean colonel in charge of day-to-day discipline—called Odd Job for his resemblance to the brutish, bowler-hurling foe of James Bond—strutted up and down the halls with a knowing smirk on his face.

The escalating violence revived talk of escape. By mid-November snow had started to fall again and some crewmen doubted they'd survive another marrow-chilling winter in this abominable sinkhole. A spiking fever left seaman Ramon Rosales unable to move on his bed. When Bucher demanded medical attention for Rosales, G.G. just laughed.

The latest escape discussions made it imperative to finish the illicit radio. No one wanted to risk his neck trying to break out if the Panmunjom talks were close to bearing fruit. And the only way to find out was to tune in to U.S. Armed Forces Radio or a South Korean news station. Strano had almost completed the crystal set. He finally succeeded in assembling a crude battery and discovered an antenna attached to the wall just outside his cell window, solving another technical problem. The device lacked only an earphone, and Hayes thought he could build one from parts pilfered from the prison movie projector.

One evening G.G. summoned the *Pueblo* officers. He seemed on the verge of exploding in rage. "Do you play us for the fool?" he screamed. On a table before him lay a copy of the Far East edition of *Time* magazine. It was open to a photo of the eight unsmiling occupants of Law's cell, three of whom had their middle digits outstretched. In dead silence Bucher and his officers read the caption:

> The North Koreans are having a hard time proving to the world that the captive crewmen of the USS *Pueblo* are a contrite and cooperative lot. Last week Pyongyang's flacks tried again—and lost to the U.S. Navy. In this class-reunion picture, three of the crewmen have managed to use the medium for a message, furtively getting off the U.S. hand signal of obscene derisiveness and contempt.

Ironically, the photo had made it into *Time* because of Law. The Tacoma uncle to whom he'd sent a copy turned it over to his local newspaper. From there the picture was picked up by the Associated Press and distributed to hundreds of news organizations around the United States. Not all editors understood it. The *Detroit News*, for instance, asked some of its press operators, who were deaf and read sign language, to interpret the finger gestures; the pressmen concluded that the sailors were signing the word "help." Both *The New York Times* and the *Washington Post* printed the picture on their front pages and let the extended digits speak for themselves. But *Time* spelled out their meaning, and now the crewmen were facing the consequences.

Murphy stared at the magazine, mesmerized. He knew the North Koreans had lost face before the entire world. He imagined the Soviets and Chinese chuckling and shaking their heads at their dim-bulb allies. The North Koreans knew they'd been had, too; they were sifting through all of the film footage and still photographs they'd shot of the crew, looking for telltale finger salutes. Bucher felt triumphant, tremendously proud that his men had succeeded in conveying to the world their refusal to knuckle under to communist coercion.

On the other hand, he knew they were in for some serious payback.

Glorious General began bombarding the Americans with shrill accusations, some wildly off the mark. He claimed the crossword puzzles they'd exchanged were coded messages. He charged them with handing "pages of secrets" back and forth; in reality, the pages were part of an amateur porno novel written by one of the enlisted guys. But some of the general's accusations were on target. Many of the sailors had indeed lied during interrogations and penned "insincere" letters home. At the end of his tirade G.G. dismissed everyone except Bucher. The communist harangued him for several more hours, saying he was now certain to face trial and swift execution.

Bucher trudged back to his room convinced he didn't have much time to live. He passed word to his men to ditch the radio and all other contraband.

"The shit's hit the fan," he said. "We're heading into rough waters."

Frigid winds raked the prison during the first week of December; patches of ice glittered in the rice paddies beyond.

The Bear beat up several men on December 7. Chief Engineman Monroe Goldman caught the worst of it. The communists' dislike of the wiry Californian, who'd served on a ship that planted mines in Wonsan harbor during the Korean War, seemed to run unusually deep. Bucher was shocked when he encountered Goldman later. The chief's eyes were swollen shut, his face was covered with bruises, his mouth was badly cut, and he was nearly unable to walk. Goldman had buckled during the ferocious beating, confirming the true meaning of the Hawaiian good-luck sign.

"Captain, I'm sorry, but they know about [it]," he whispered. "Just couldn't hold out any longer."

"I understand that, Chief," Bucher answered. He put out the word that the crewmen were to tell the truth if questioned about the gesture; no one else should suffer trying to protect the blown secret.

G.G. called an all-hands meeting on December 10. He was furious. The Americans, he said, would now pay for their insincerity. First they must confess all the crimes they'd committed in captivity, plus those of their shipmates. This was their last chance to be truthful. Tables were set up and the men immediately began writing a new round of confessions. Back in his cell, Tim Harris could see Bucher in his room across the corridor, staring dejectedly at a wall.

The next morning the Americans heard the foreboding sounds of furniture being rearranged. Guards were clearing out certain rooms to open up more space for interrogations. Sailors not actively writing confessions were forced to sit in chairs, heads deeply bowed, hands clenched on thighs. No moving, talking, or sleeping allowed. The heat was turned off. Lights stayed on day and night, with guards posted in every cell to keep them on. If a sailor wanted to stand, get a drink of water, or go to the head, he had to ask permission.

The long waking nightmare the men would call "Hell Week" was beginning.

Tim Harris heard a racket in the hall and looked up just as Odd Job and Silver Lips barged into Bucher's room. The captain was at his desk, writing. He started to get up, looking surprised, when Odd Job slugged him in the mouth. Bucher stayed on his feet, but Silver Lips belted him, too, knocking the captain onto his desk. The translator pulled Bucher to his feet and punched him again. The sight horrified Harris. Odd Job kept hitting Bucher as Silver Lips yelled, "You CIA man!" The captain finally admitted instigating the Hawaiian good-luck sign. Silver Lips shoved him back into his chair and the two Koreans strode out of the room. Half-conscious, the skipper slid to the floor.

Similar mayhem erupted throughout the prison. Law was taken to a newly emptied cell where Odd Job and a translator sat behind a desk. Although the North Koreans had pegged him as a key rabble-rouser, the quartermaster had escaped serious harm during past purges. He thought he could bluff his way through this one, too: maybe absorb a few kicks and punches and soon be back in his room.

Odd Job began firing questions as soon as he sat down. The communist demanded to know which member of the crew was the CIA agent. Law chose to indict himself. "There's no point in going through this," he said, throwing up his hands in evident defeat. "I am." Odd Job acted as if he hadn't heard Law's admission. Bucher was the agent, wasn't he? No, replied Law, again shouldering responsibility.

"Why you afraid of Bucher?" Odd Job asked.

Law decided to play along and see where this line of inquiry went. "I'm afraid of him because he can make it real rough for me," said the quartermaster.

"Why you afraid of Schumacher?"

"He went to college and uses big words."

Getting angrier and angrier, Odd Job kept demanding the real identity of the CIA operative aboard the *Pueblo*. After he'd spent more than an hour on the hot seat, Law's back began to ache. He flexed his arms to relieve the tension, but that set off the North Korean colonel. His fist slammed the desk. "You son of a bitch!" he screamed. He stalked out of the room but returned a short time later with the Bear and another guard.

Law was ordered to his knees. The Bear punched him hard below his right ear, but the burly sailor only swayed. The Bear grabbed him by the hair and slugged him three or four more times, then kicked him in the stomach. Law grunted and doubled over. The thuggish guard then picked up a five-foot-long rod of weathered wood and began bashing Law across the back and shoulders. The pain was almost as bad as being bullwhipped. Law fell forward onto the floor.

"Shit on you!" he blurted.

That only caused the Bear to flog him harder. He clubbed the prostrate sailor over and over and over. The force of the blows broke the rod in two, one piece of it flying across the room. Law was close to losing consciousness. The Bear stabbed him in the ear with the jagged piece of stick he still held; tears flushed Law's eyes. For the first time in prison he feared for his life. The North Koreans seemed out of control, like they didn't give a damn whether he lived or died. The Bear beat Law with the shortened rod until it broke and then hit him with the remaining piece until that snapped, too. Temporarily exhausted, the guard paused and then kicked the downed sailor in the belly again.

Law lay on his side, sobbing and struggling to breathe.

Odd Job told him to get back into the chair and asked whether he was ready to be sincere. Though the quartermaster feared being beaten to death, he shouted, "Every goddamned thing I told you was a lie, you bastard!" With his fist the Bear clouted Law on the side of the head, dumping him out of the chair. Another guard entered the room carrying a wooden board that looked like a four-by-four. "God, you can't hit me with that!" Law wailed. The guard whacked him across the back, knocking him onto his face.

Law lay sprawled on the floor, his body pulsing with pain. He choked back the urge to vomit. Odd Job ordered him to his feet. The sailor staggered upright and was led next door to Bucher's cell.

The skipper was kneeling in the center of the room, his scrawny frame shaking. Standing over him was Silver Lips. The interpreter looked like a crazy man, his hair and uniform disheveled.

"Aren't you a paid spy?" Silver Lips screeched.

"Yes, yes!" the frightened captain replied.

"Aren't you going to tell us the instructions you passed to Law?"

"Yes, yes!"

Silver Lips then demanded of Law, "What instructions he give you?"

Still stupefied, Law replied, "Pardon me?"

The interpreter belted him in the jaw. "Pardon me!" he shouted sarcastically. "Pardon me!" Two guards started pummeling the quartermaster as if they were working out on a speed bag. Trying to ward off the blows, Law crossed his arms in front of him. A guard kneed him in the groin, flooding his belly with nausea and pain.

Law was forced back to his interrogation room. Silver Lips told him to reveal his escape plans. When the American mumbled that he didn't have any, Silver Lips made him get down on his knees. A guard slugged him several times in the head, trying to topple him over. But the sailor remained upright, so the guard kicked him in the stomach. Law slumped to the floor in the fetal position. The guard kicked him in the back and rump, and then hauled him back into the chair.

"Escape plans!" Silver Lips demanded again.

His head spinning, Law blurted a fictitious tale of how he, Bucher, and several others planned to steal a truck and drive to Panmunjom. The scheme was preposterous, but Silver Lips listened intently, as if it made perfect sense.

"You using crossword puzzles to pass messages?" Silver Lips asked.

"I don't know about that," Law replied. A guard whacked him on the head. "Yes!" the sailor corrected himself, instantly conforming to his captors' preconceptions. "We were passing the puzzles back and forth. They were messages on the plan."

At that point Law had been alternately walloped and questioned for five hours. Pain fogged his mind. Told to write a confession, he scrawled anything that came into his head—he'd thumbed his nose at duty officers behind their backs; he'd peed out his cell window. He printed in big block letters to fill more space, covering fifty pages with his crimes. About ten p.m. Odd Job came in, glanced at the confession, and said he already knew about the petty offenses; he wanted the serious stuff. Law scribbled wearily through the night. If he paused, a guard hit him. At six a.m. on December 13, he was given soup and a slice of bread, his first food in almost 20 hours, and he gobbled it hungrily. His confession was taken away. He sat throbbing in the interrogation room until ten a.m., when Odd Job came back.

"You are starting," the North Korean said approvingly, "to become sincere."

Over the next several days Bucher was beaten twice during daylight hours and at least once each night. Soon, he wrote later, "my ribs felt cracked, my guts ruptured, my testicles ready to burst, and my face a pulp with all my front teeth loosened and almost falling out." Lying gingerly on his bunk between thrashings, the captain could hear the groans and screams of his men getting worked over. It was as if they'd somehow time-traveled back to the pitiless days of January. Again Bucher was urinating blood in a latrine spattered with the blood and vomit of his mauled sailors. Again he was agonizing over not being able to shield his men, even as he whispered encouragement to them:

"At least we've rattled these bastards by making them look stupid to the outside world. That's something we can all be proud of!"

His pain was so bad and the situation so dire that he contemplated another suicide attempt. He wasn't the only one. After a vicious assault by the Bear, Howard Bland, the young fireman, tried to dive out a second-floor window, only to be snagged by guards. Law's low point came when he was made to scoop feces out of a clogged toilet with his bare hands.

Despite his efforts to keep his head down, Harry Iredale found himself in the North Koreans' crosshairs like everybody else. In an interrogation room one morning he found himself facing Possum, his room daddy, plus three other officers and a guard. "Who is the CIA agent?" Possum demanded. "Who made you try to fool us?" When Iredale said he didn't understand the question, the officers rapidly filed out of the room and the guard set to beating him. Possum and his retinue came back later and asked the same question. Iredale again said he didn't understand. Enraged, an officer punched him in the mouth. Fear flashed through Iredale's belly. No officer had ever hit him before; the communists seemed to be panicking. Iredale was told to write a confession identifying the CIA man and all his shipmates' plots.

The oceanographer wrote for the rest of that day and all through the night. Scared as he was, he was fed up with being bullied. Back in January, an interrogator had chided him for being "weak" and caving in too fast, and the remark still stung. Not this time, Iredale resolved. This time he'd give the Koreans nothing.

"I'm English," he explained many years later. "I got stubborn."

By the time he finished, his "confession" was little more than a rehash of past statements. He didn't finger anyone as the CIA agent and revealed nothing about the crew's resistance activities. In the morning someone came by to pick up his work. A few hours later, the guard who'd worked him over the previous day returned. Iredale was punched and kicked so vigorously that he flew out the door into the corridor.

That afternoon he was brought to a bigger room where the Bear and three other guards waited. They made him kneel and jammed a thick wooden pole behind his knees. Two guards jumped up and down on the ends of the pole several times while the Bear screamed threats at the top of his lungs. The communist bruiser then produced a wooden hammer handle and began whacking Iredale around the crown of his head. The oceanographer shrieked as loudly as he could, trying to convince the Bear he was inflicting too much pain.

Iredale soon looked as if he'd just lost a one-sided prizefight. His lower lip had swollen to three times its normal size; angry red welts were rising all over his battered scalp. His left eye was swollen shut and a bloodred halo encircled his right pupil. His ribs, hips, and knees ached. But he hadn't caved.

He was told to draft yet another confession, and this time he added the tidbit that he'd once sailed on the *Banner.* At dusk an officer came in and ordered Iredale to wash his own blood off the floor and walls with a rag. The oceanographer had to stand on a chair to reach the highest spatters.

Around four a.m. the next day—after 39 hours of beatings and grilling, with no food, water, or sleep—he was sent back to his cell. His cellmates groggily asked whether he was okay. He mumbled something about still being alive and collapsed on his bed.

With his history of unbending defiance, Bob Hammond figured he'd be singled out for special abuse, and that made him "damn scared." The Marine sergeant wasn't sure he could take much more. As guards wreaked havoc on his shipmates, Hammond thought of ways to kill himself. He'd hurl himself out a window or attack a North Korean and get himself shot.

But, with a wife and two small children, he couldn't bring himself to do it. He decided instead to bluff the North Koreans with a fake suicide try. Even though they were beating the daylights out of the Americans, the communists evidently wanted to keep them alive, and Hammond hoped to turn that desire to his advantage.

One night he broke a mirror and tried to cut his wrists. He sawed vigorously with a shard of glass but drew hardly any blood. Then he tried another method. Getting into bed, he placed the sliver against his stomach and rolled over hard on it, opening a wound so big he worried that he'd gone too far. But the bleeding stopped after a while and Hammond fell asleep.

The next morning he stayed in his rack, smeared with dried blood, until guards came around. Shocked, they took him to a duty officer, who asked why he cut himself. Yelling like a maniac, Hammond demanded that the officer shoot him and called him "chicken" for not doing so. A communist colonel later gave the Marine a fatherly lecture, ticking off all the reasons for him to stay alive. But Hammond's gambit apparently worked; the North Koreans didn't touch him again.

Hell Week abruptly ended on the morning of December 19. The beatings stopped and Glorious General's enforcers withdrew. The halls grew quiet, and a feeling of uncertain reprieve settled over the battered, worn-out Americans.

CHAPTER 14

BRIDGE OF NO RETURN

In Washington, Nicholas Katzenbach had reached the bottom of his bag of diplomatic tricks.

The rangy, balding under secretary of state, Dean Rusk's right-hand man, had been directly supervising the U.S. side at Panmunjom since the secret talks began in February. Now it was early December, and the North Koreans had systematically ridiculed and rejected every negotiating gimmick Katzenbach and his team had come up with.

Katzenbach was no stranger to trying to get his government out of a tight spot. A Rhodes scholar and Yale Law School graduate, he'd joined the Kennedy administration in 1961 and soon became a key member of Attorney General Robert Kennedy's "riot squad" that worked to enforce civil rights laws in the Deep South. In one memorable episode, Katzenbach led a band of federal marshals as they struggled to carry out a court order to enroll a black former Air Force sergeant, James Meredith, at the University of Mississippi in 1962. For several hours, about 400 marshals holding a defensive line outside the registrar's office withstood a deadly hail of bricks, Molotov cocktails, and gunshots from as many as 5,000 enraged whites. Mobs attempted to run down the marshals with a bulldozer and blast them with jets of water from a fire truck. Katzenbach ran a makeshift command center inside the registrar's office; at one point, a marshal was carried in with a hemorrhaging gunshot wound to the neck. Katzenbach and the besieged lawmen finally were relieved by rushed-in Army and National Guard troops.

The North Koreans, Katzenbach had discovered, were no less intractable than rampaging racists at Ole Miss. At almost every meeting with the Americans, General Pak repeated his charges that the *Pueblo* had violated North Korean waters while committing espionage. His demand for a U.S. apology never wavered. But for months Pak had refused to guarantee that if General Woodward signed a mea culpa satisfactory to North Korea, Bucher and his men would be released at the same time. Then, at a meeting on September 30, Pak suddenly reversed course, agreeing to simultaneous release.

Woodward, however, had never offered to sign an unvarnished apology. He told Pak time and again that he was prepared to put his name only on a handwritten "receipt" acknowledging that 82 Americans had been turned over to him—the overwrite gambit. Katzenbach brooded over the possibility that Pak's abrupt, almost glib acceptance of simultaneity meant he didn't understand the difference between "acknowledging receipt" and simply signing a communist-drafted apology. If the overwrite didn't come into focus for the North Koreans until they saw it at the signing ceremony, they might angrily walk out—and take their prisoners with them. To avoid such a calamity, Woodward was instructed to explain the overwrite to Pak in detail.

The American general had done so on October 10. Pak listened carefully and then said nothing for more than half an hour as he formulated a reply. He finally muttered that the Johnson administration had "taken an insincere and arrogant attitude, frustrating the agreement." At the next get-together, two weeks later, Pak cross-examined Woodward about exactly what an overwrite would look like. When Woodward showed him, scrawling the receipt language diagonally across the text of the apology, Pak exclaimed sarcastically, "Ha!" One of his aides commented that the American was trying to "cancel the text." "Understandable!" snapped Pak. During an October 31 meeting, Pak declared that the overwrite was "far beyond discussion" and warned yet again that the crewmen would "pay appropriate costs" unless Washington bowed down.

Pak stayed away from the bargaining table for the next six weeks. In the

United States, the lack of progress triggered complaints that President Johnson—who had said nothing publicly about the *Pueblo* for months—"was not sufficiently engaged in this problem." Americans were further stirred up by another blizzard of letters from the seamen, who now urged family and friends to lobby Washington to give the communists what they wanted.

To avoid further complicating the Panmunjom talks, LBJ in late October postponed a joint military exercise with South Korea. Under the operation, code-named "Focus Retina," 2,500 U.S. paratroopers were to fly to South Korea for maneuvers with 4,500 American and South Korean soldiers. Focus Retina was meant to reassure President Park that the United States could rapidly reinforce him if war broke out. But Johnson was concerned that the North Koreans might feel they were being strong-armed into settling at Panmunjom.

The communists, however, had no qualms about conducting real military operations amid the talks, as their commandos attacked along the demilitarized zone and the South Korean coast. On November 3, about 50 guerrillas came ashore near the town of Ulchin and made their way inland over mountainous terrain—the largest incursion in the south since the 1953 armistice. The infiltrators took over a village and held a propaganda rally in broad daylight. When one peasant tried to escape, the communists beat and stabbed him to death, warning other villagers to expect the same if they said anything to police. The peasants sounded the alarm anyway, and more than 5,000 South Korean troops and combat police rushed to the area; within days 40 commandos had been killed and the rest were on the run.

Having lost contact with the communists at Panmunjom, Katzenbach and his aides ransacked their brains for a way to gain some leverage over them. At the time a Dutch firm was building four fish-processing ships for North Korea at a cost of nearly $28 million. That gave Katzenbach and his people an idea. If they could plant rumors that the U.S. Navy might commandeer the factory ships on their long journey between Rotterdam and the Far East, the communists might soften their position on the *Pueblo*. Fish provided much of the animal protein in the North Korean diet, and each of the ships—described as "by far the biggest fish freezing installations in the world"—was capable of processing 125,000 fish per day. As overfishing depleted North Korea's coastal waters, the communist fishing fleet was ranging farther from shore, making the refrigeration ships vital.

"If for some reason we could inject [the] thought that [the] U.S. might obstruct their delivery to North Korea," Katzenbach cabled the American ambassador at the Hague, "this might have [a] salutary effect."

Doing nothing about the vessels, the State Department believed, was not an option. Congress had learned of the Dutch shipbuilding contract and was likely to demand some sort of action. Ambassador Porter countered that Kim Il Sung might react to any hint of Navy intervention by refusing to let the *Pueblo* crew out of his grip until his fish ships were safely moored in North Korean ports. One of Katzenbach's deputies, James Leonard, cabled Porter that Washington was aware of that danger. But, he added, the moment the North Korean vessels put to sea there would inevitably be public cries for their seizure. A little rumor-mongering, Leonard said, was preferable to a potentially violent confrontation on the high seas. Such a clash could result in Bucher and his men being held longer, or even executed.

American diplomats in Europe began quietly spreading the story. They persuaded the Dutch government to convey Washington's "great interest" in the ships to the North Koreans through an executive of the Verolme shipyard in Rotterdam, where the vessels were under construction. The British government was enlisted to pass a similar message to Lloyd's of London, which was insuring the craft, in the hope that the firm also would put a bug in the North Koreans' ears.

Despite all the innuendo, the United States had no intention of actually hijacking the communist ships. "It was a bluff," Katzenbach acknowledged in an interview more than 30 years later.

The disinformation campaign imploded, however, when *The New York Times* revealed it in a front-page story on November 26. The newspaper also ran an editorial opposing a revenge seizure, saying it was "inconceivable that the world's foremost champion of freedom of the seas would stoop to such a form of retaliation, no matter how worthy the cause." The episode became a major political embarrassment to the Dutch government, with nationalist critics charging that it underscored the country's "servility" to Washington.

With their government seemingly unable to make headway with North

Korea, ordinary Americans began to volunteer their services as international deal makers.

In a letter to President Johnson, an Illinois salesman, Glenn A. Karl, offered to go to Pyongyang and negotiate face-to-face with Kim Il Sung. "I believe that possibly an average American as I am, a salesman all my life, that sent by my President and my country to talk directly to the leader of North Korea, I just might be persuasive enough and just possibly might be the answer to the *Pueblo* crew's release," Karl wrote.

A former Oklahoma congressman, Victor Wickersham, went further, flying to South Korea and offering to become a hostage of the communists if they'd free the sailors. U.S. military officers escorted him to Panmunjom, where he told journalists the secret negotiations should be opened to the press and conducted around the clock. He also recommended that General Woodward be replaced by a prominent private citizen such as evangelist Billy Graham or Harrison Salisbury, a *New York Times* reporter who'd covered many stories in the communist world.

Wickersham—a Democrat then campaigning to win back his old seat in Congress—favored a U.S. apology and thought making himself a hostage might reassure the North Koreans that it wouldn't be retracted as soon as the crewmen were let go. But when the politician was taken to observe a session of the Military Armistice Commission, the experience sobered him. "He evidently had no real conception of [the] harshness of [the] meeting atmosphere and [the] tenseness at Panmunjom itself," Porter cabled Washington.

An even more determined effort to co-opt the Panmunjom talks was made by Bruce Noland, a Virginia contractor and onetime Navy officer.

Noland's odyssey began in Washington, where he'd gone in July to investigate for himself what was being done to help Bucher and his men. Concluding that there was "no genuine interest at any governmental agency," Noland set off to ransom the crew.

He traveled first to Moscow, but had no success in meeting resident North Korean diplomats. From there he went to New Delhi, but wasn't allowed to speak to anyone at the local North Korean embassy. His next stop was Hong Kong, where he hoped to make contact with Kim Il Sung's representatives through the Communist Chinese. That attempt, too, proved futile.

Noland moved on to Tokyo, meeting with Kenji Miyamoto, head of the Japanese Communist Party. Miyamoto recently had attended North Korea's twentieth-anniversary festivities, and Noland was convinced he had good contacts in Pyongyang. Although Noland had no such funds at his disposal, he blithely offered to pay $50 million to North Korea and another $1 million to Miyamoto's organization in exchange for the *Pueblo* crew. With that potential windfall to tempt him, Miyamoto agreed to transmit the offer to Pyongyang.

Noland turned up in Washington again in late October, asking for State Department help in carrying out his plan.

He was given an appointment with Dalton V. Killion, of the department's East Asia desk. Noland said his conversations abroad had convinced him the Panmunjom talks were doomed because the North Koreans had come to "dislike and distrust" General Woodward. Noland also claimed he was waiting for a telegram from Miyamoto confirming the North Korean government's approval of the ransom deal. He was certain he could persuade a U.S. bank to put up the $51 million he needed. Killion, he said, should accompany him to Tokyo to hand the money over to the Japanese communists.

Killion, however, was wary of the peripatetic businessman, describing him to colleagues as naive, "very high-strung," and "unstable." Politely but firmly, he told Noland his scheme had no merit: The North Koreans had never demanded ransom, and even if they had, the U.S. government would face "obvious problems" in swapping cash for imprisoned servicemen.

Two days later, Noland phoned Killion to say that, despite their discussion, he was flying to South Korea. He then wired LBJ, asking his blessing for the ransom project. In Seoul, Noland claimed to U.S. embassy officials that the State Department had pledged Woodward's help in setting up a meeting for him with the North Koreans at Panmunjom. Noland added that Woodward was supposed to provide him with a car, an interpreter, and an armed escort to the village.

Embassy staffers told him they had no such instructions and, in any event, such a meeting was out of the question. The talks were strictly government-to-government; no private citizen could represent the United States.

Unfazed, Noland returned to Tokyo. He took a cab to a large villa hidden behind high walls and met with someone who claimed to represent the North Korean foreign office in Japan. But that person only repeated what the State Department had told him: North Korea was not interested in a payoff; the *Pueblo* crew would be freed only if Washington apologized.

The absence of movement at Panmunjom was also a source of deep frustration to State Department officials, who plunged into internal debate and soul-searching over whether the United States should give in and apologize.

Katzenbach opposed doing that. The mere thought of his country groveling before the North Koreans stuck in the under secretary's craw. He'd been a prisoner of war himself during World War II and knew full well the urgency of getting the sailors out. As a navigator on a B-25 bomber, he was shot down over the Mediterranean and sat in German and Italian POW camps for more than two years, though under conditions not nearly as grim as those faced by Bucher and his men.

In a December 3 memo to President Johnson, Katzenbach acknowledged that the idea of the government holding its nose and signing a false apology "appeals to many reasonable men." Nevertheless, he argued, giving in to communist blackmail—even for humanitarian purposes—was too high a price to pay in terms of its damage to America's good name. The under secretary puckishly noted, "Most foreign governments and even many Americans are puzzled by our reluctance to utter untruths, but they respect us for this eccentricity."

Among those who shared Katzenbach's scorn for an apology were the parents of CT David Ritter, who laid out their reasoning in a brief letter to LBJ.

"David and the rest of the crew, we are sure, would feel their work had been for naught if because of [thoughtless] public pressure, an apology was tendered for something that has not been conclusively proven," Elizabeth and Caspar Ritter wrote.

"We wish there was some way to facilitate the release of the prisoners with honor and dignity because we know that our son would want it that way. He is a career man in the Navy, or was until this episode, and he was extremely proud of his contribution to the United States' efforts." The Ritters closed by offering Johnson their "heartfelt sympathy . . . for the decisions you must make." So touched was Dean Rusk by the couple's words that he responded with a personal note, telling them that "the President and I will face our responsibilities with more confidence because of your reminder of what sort of people we are privileged to serve."

In the absence of an apology, however, would the crew ever come home? The dilemma ate at James Leonard, who ran the Korea desk at the State Department. Like Katzenbach, Leonard didn't want to resort to the device that had sprung the helicopter pilots—a false admission followed by a loud renunciation. That maneuver, he felt, was inherently deceptive and beneath a great nation's dignity. But what was the alternative?

One Sunday in late November, Leonard was discussing the problem with his wife at their Bethesda, Maryland, home. Eleanor Leonard suggested a variation on the helicopter scenario: Why not publicly repudiate the apology *before* General Woodward signed it, rather than after? That way no credible allegations of trickery could be made, and the United States could walk away from Panmunjom with a clear conscience.

It seemed like a nonsensical idea, akin to offering a kidnapper a voided check to let his victim go. Jim Leonard didn't think the North Koreans would buy it. On the other hand, Washington had tried almost everything else, and so the next day he brought his wife's idea to Katzenbach. The under secretary didn't think it would work either, but he agreed to present it to the White House. "I called up the president," Katzenbach recalled. "I said, 'This may sound nutty to you,' and I told him, and he said it was. It did sound nutty and he couldn't believe it could happen. I said, 'Well, can I try it?' He said, 'If [Woodward is] willing to do it, I'm willing to do it.'"

Unlike the Washington skeptics, Woodward embraced the ploy. He thought the North Koreans would go for a "prerepudiated" apology because it gave them what they'd demanded all along: a ranking American official's signature on a document that portrayed the United States as genuflecting before Pyongyang. Most North Koreans, the general figured, would never learn that he'd disavowed the apology in advance; their government's propaganda machine would see to that. Woodward would have to swallow his pride to make the deal, but that was a small matter compared to freedom for the 82 *Pueblo* survivors.

Katzenbach knew LBJ wanted the crew back by Christmas, in the waning days of his presidency. In order to make it home on time, the sailors had to be released no later than December 23. Katzenbach instructed Woodward on December 9 to offer General Pak a take-it-or-leave-it choice between the overwrite and the prerepudiated apology. A time limit would apply: If Pak didn't say yes to one of the proposals and promise to let the crew go before Christmas, both offers would be withdrawn and no new ones put on the table. Pyongyang then would have to take its chances with the incoming administration of Richard Nixon, who'd narrowly beaten Hubert Humphrey for the White House the previous month.

Woodward demanded an immediate sit-down with Pak, but the North Korean didn't reply for several days. He finally appeared at Panmunjom on December 17. Woodward explained that Christmas was a national holiday of great emotional power for Americans, symbolizing family togetherness, and President Johnson was "prepared to go very far indeed" to reunite the captured seamen with their loved ones by then. The U.S. negotiator said that if Pak chose the prerepudiated apology, Woodward would sign it, but only after publicly stating there was no convincing evidence that the spy ship had encroached on North Korean waters; that its surveillance activities were perfectly legal; and that the U.S. government couldn't apologize for an action without solid proof it had actually taken place—points that blatantly contradicted the contents of the communist-crafted apology.

Pak called a recess to study the offer. Fifty minutes later, he returned and demanded to know precisely where Woodward would sign the apology after renouncing it. The U.S. general said his name would appear above the signature block, in the American manner. Pak wanted Woodward's name to the right of the block, Korean style.

"If you sign on the right of your name," he said, "we are agreeable."

Woodward said that was fine and a tentative agreement was struck. The two men met again on December 19, hashing out numerous logistical details. Bucher and his crew would be freed at the Bridge of No Return, which spanned the Sachon River not far from Panmunjom. The 250-foot-long bridge had gotten its name at the end of the Korean War, when thousands of POWs from North Korean, Chinese, and U.N. forces were brought there and asked whether they wanted to go back to their home countries. If they did, they were allowed to cross over to either the allied or communist side, never to return. Pak said the North Koreans planned to deliver the body of Duane Hodges first. Then Bucher would cross the bridge alone. After him would come the rest of the crew, in inverse order of rank, walking 20 paces apart. Murphy would be the last man over.

Hodges's coffin, Pak said with no evident irony, didn't have to be returned.

Before the seamen could be released, Woodward had to sign. He'd do that in the same conference room in which he'd bickered for months with Pak. Civilian journalists would be barred from the signing, in case something went awry. "We are . . . perturbed by [the] possibility of [a] last-minute hassle over what is being signed, and prefer not to have [the] press as witnesses," the State Department explained in a cable to its Seoul embassy. Instead, newsmen were to be corralled on a hill near the southern end of the bridge, viewing the carefully choreographed freedom walk from a safe distance.

Ignoring Woodward's repeated objections, Pak insisted on a two-hour lag between when the apology was inked and the prisoners set loose. Another sticking point was whether the two sides could announce that a deal had been reached. Woodward wanted to be able to issue a brief statement, but Pak didn't concur. It was left unclear what information, if any, either side could put out—an ambiguity that would come back to haunt Woodward.

Throughout nearly five hours of point-by-point haggling, Pak refused to set a date for letting the sailors go. Woodward pushed for December 20. Pak wouldn't budge and didn't even agree to talk again until December 22. But within minutes of the start of that meeting—the 28th since the *Pueblo* was taken—the communist general pledged to emancipate the crew the next day. Woodward would sign the apology at nine a.m. on December 23; the men would be let go at eleven a.m.

One sensitive issue was barely discussed: the possibility of a fracas at the bridge. What if the sailors somehow antagonized the North Koreans—by, say, giving the Hawaiian good-luck sign one last time as they crossed—and the communists tried to stop the repatriation? What if North Korean soldiers started shooting at the crewmen?

Both sides had a vested interest in a calm and orderly handover of the sailors. But an unanticipated incident couldn't be ruled out. U.S. military officials quietly laid plans to pump troops into the area if anything went wrong on the bridge.

Two North Korean officers entered Bucher's cell on December 22 and ordered him to strip. A third officer, nicknamed Major Rectum, joined them and subjected the captain to a body-cavity search that was "not entirely medical in character." Satisfied that his orifices bore no contraband, the communists issued Bucher a new lightweight uniform—gray cotton jacket and trousers, white shirt, black sneakers—that was wholly unsuited to the Korean winter.

Since the end of Hell Week three days earlier, the North Koreans had schizophrenically flip-flopped yet again and were acting like they actually cared about their prisoners' well-being. The food improved, the sailors could eat together again, and exercise privileges were restored. Witch Doctor applied hard-boiled eggs and poultices of hot paraffin to the most severely beaten Americans in an effort to clear up black eyes and facial bruises.

As soon as he put on the fresh uniform, the captain was escorted to an all-crew meeting in the movie room. He was startled to see all of his men dressed exactly like him. The new outfits had to mean something, but what? Freedom? A mass trial of the crew?

Glorious General strode in with a self-satisfied expression on his face. "As I knew and told you from the beginning of this shameful imperialist intrigue against our peace-loving Korean people," he said, "it has ended with the warmongering United States on its knees apologizing to us and assuring that no such provocation and intrusions into our sovereign territorial water shall occur again!" Then he got to the real news. In exchange for Washington's just atonement, the crew was to be freed the next day. Bucher's mind spun. Had the United States really caved in to Kim Il Sung? He couldn't believe it. Were he and his men really to be repatriated after all these months? He hoped so, but he couldn't exclude the possibility of a ruse.

First, of course, a final press conference had to be staged. About a dozen correspondents showed up, all North Koreans, and they mostly wanted to know how the Americans felt about going home. The crewmen answered with complete sincerity that they couldn't wait to leave.

The sailors had an early supper. As the evening wore on, Glorious General was quiet and reserved. He told the Americans he was happy they were going home at last. He even gave them the finger, maybe to show he got the joke. Bucher stood up, expressed his thanks, and said that although he thought little of socialism, he had to recognize a fine officer who did his job well. G.G. made no reply. He glanced at his watch.

"Come," he said. "I don't want you to miss the train."

The men were issued quilted blue overcoats and blue Mao-style caps. At about eleven p.m. they boarded buses and rode to the Pyongyang railroad station, where they stepped onto a comfortable, well-heated train. Duty officers from the Country Club accompanied them. Glorious General stayed behind.

The train rolled south all night, but most of its passengers were too keyed up to sleep. Murphy thought of his wife and children. Steve Harris tried to stretch out on his bunk, but his legs were stiff from malnutrition and his calves ached painfully. Bucher fretted that the communists might pull the plug on the repatriation for some arbitrary reason. The train made frequent stops, and each time it halted, the captain sat up with a "terrible sinking feeling" in his chest.

Along with the residual pain of his Hell Week injuries, Schumacher felt deep satisfaction. Through eleven long months of horrendous brutality, he and his shipmates had held up in important ways. The North Koreans had beaten phony confessions out of them, but the lieutenant believed little if any information of genuine value had been given up. Certainly the sailors had squabbled and even clashed physically. But that was due more to boredom and the friction of living in close quarters than to their captors' ability to turn them against one another. Forged in a crucible of soul-piercing hardship, the men's bonds of loyalty—to one another, their leader, their country—were intact and strong. They'd preserved their identities and sense of humanity in the face of fearsome physical and psychological pressures. Best of all, they'd made the communists look like fools by turning their own propaganda against them.

Near daybreak the train stopped. Its windows were covered, but Bucher pulled aside a screen and saw that they were on an empty siding. The sailors ate a last breakfast of turnips. At about eight a.m. they climbed onto three antiquated green-and-yellow buses.

Although he was wearing three pairs of socks, Murphy shivered.

The old buses motored along hilly, snow-dusted roads. Bucher and the lowest-ranking enlisted men rode in the lead vehicle; the other officers and petty officers were in the last. Feeling ridiculous in their Mao caps and padded jackets, the Americans said little. Murphy felt as if he were in some sort of dreamworld in which "to speak was to risk waking." Perhaps to brighten the collective mood, someone said, "Maybe we'll all get medals when we get back." Law wearily dismissed that suggestion.

"No, you get medals for charging machine-gun nests," he said. "You don't get medals for this."

After about fifteen minutes the buses stopped near the Bridge of No Return. The duty officers gave the Americans detailed instructions on how to cross. They must not run. They must not talk or look back. Above all, they must not make "gestures." Anyone who did would be shot.

Huddled against the cold, the men sat and waited. Tension filled the buses; what if for some reason the North Koreans changed their minds? The eleven a.m. deadline for their release came and went. Still they waited. In spite of the cold, Ralph McClintock, the communication technician from Massachusetts, was sweating heavily. His heart pounded. He thought he was going to dissolve in a crying jag.

If the communists sent them back now, he was convinced, the Americans were sure to be killed.

Woodward sat down across the narrow table from Pak at nine a.m. sharp. In front of the American general lay two copies of the apology, one in English, the other in Korean. Before he signed them, he read a statement declaring that their contents were hogwash.

The U.S. government had maintained all along that the *Pueblo* was doing nothing illegal, he said. Nor was there any plausible evidence that the ship had trespassed in North Korean waters. Woodward said he understood those facts were at odds with the apology, and he was putting his name to it for one simple reason: "I will sign the document to free the crew and only to free the crew."

Pak ignored the refutation and, as communist cameras rolled, milked the moment for maximum propaganda value. "The documents admitting the criminal acts of the crew of the *Pueblo* and apologizing for them," he said, "will remain forever together with the shameful aggressive history of the U.S. imperialists."

Woodward slid the signed papers across the table. "Put the date," Pak demanded. Then he heaved a monkey wrench into the works.

Earlier, the State Department had issued a one-sentence announcement that the two sides had reached final agreement and the crew would be let go at the bridge. Pak denounced the statement as a "perfidious act" that violated a supposed promise by Woodward not to publicize the release beforehand. With the shivering sailors yearning for deliverance on their buses, the North Korean general now said he'd punish the United States by holding them longer.

Woodward couldn't believe his ears: "I felt like saying, 'What the hell are you trying to prove?'" The deal on publicity, as he understood it, was that if either side made an announcement prior to the signing, the other side was free to say whatever it wanted. Woodward glared in contempt at his antagonist but kept his voice even: "If you now repudiate this agreement and do not release the crew as you agreed, at 1100 hours, you will have repudiated your solemn agreement."

Pak threw himself into another long tirade, crowing over the apology and lambasting Washington for covering up its "crimes" until "the very last moment." Then he declared his penalty for the allegedly premature U.S. announcement:

The crew must sit on the buses an extra half hour.

Snow was falling over the Bridge of No Return. On nearby hillsides communist riflemen watched and waited. Odd Job called Bucher out of his bus to identify the remains of Duane Hodges. Wrapped mummylike in gauze, the fireman's body had been brought to the bridge in an ambulance. Attendants wearing white surgical masks lifted the lid of the wooden coffin and pulled aside the bandages so the captain could see the corpse's face.

"Yes, that is Duane Hodges," he said, turning away in grief and revulsion.

Odd Job led Bucher back aboard the bus. Then he and other duty officers handed out mimeographed copies of Woodward's apology. Bucher couldn't believe what he was reading:

> The Government of the United States of America,
>
> Acknowledging the validity of the confessions of the crew of the USS "Pueblo" and of the documents of evidence produced by the representative of the Government of the Democratic People's Republic of Korea to the effect that the ship, which was seized by the self-defense measures of the naval vessels of the Korean People's Army in the territorial waters of the Democratic People's Republic of Korea on January 23, 1968, had illegally intruded into the territorial waters of the Democratic People's Republic of Korea on many occasions and conducted espionage activities of spying out important military and state secrets of the Democratic People's Republic of Korea,
>
> Shoulders full responsibility and solemnly apologizes for the grave acts of espionage committed by the U.S. ship against the Democratic People's Republic of Korea after having intruded into the territorial waters of the Democratic People's Republic of Korea,
>
> And gives firm assurance that no U.S. ships will intrude again in the future into the territorial waters of the Democratic People's Republic of Korea.

At eleven thirty a.m., Bucher was ordered off the bus again. He was escorted toward a guardhouse incongruously decorated with painted doves; just beyond was the magical sight of the bridge. A high-ranking North Korean officer began loudly haranguing him. It was General Pak, and he inveighed against U.S. imperialist aggression for twenty minutes as the captain stamped his sneaker-clad feet to keep them from freezing. When

Pak finally finished, Odd Job said sternly, "Now walk across that bridge, Captain. Not stop. Not look back. Not make any bad move. Just walk across sincerely. Go now!"

Gaunt and hollow eyed, his brown hair turned steel gray after nearly a year of sadistic imprisonment, the skipper limped for home. He'd led his men into this ordeal, and now he was leading them out. Behind him crept the ambulance bearing Hodges's body. A loudspeaker boomed a recording of Bucher's final confession: "Eleven months to the day ago, we were captured in the act of committing espionage. . . ."

One by one, the others were called off the buses, warned not to get out of line, and steered toward the bridge. Soon the span was filled with nervous Americans walking twenty paces apart. Some had to suppress a powerful urge to run like jackrabbits; others resisted a strong desire to spit in the faces of soldiers they passed.

Law, his eyes damaged beyond repair, turned the wrong way as he stepped off his bus. Rough hands spun him back toward the bridge. As he started across he struggled to remember a Bible verse he'd learned long ago in Sunday school. Finally it popped into his head: "Yea, though I walk through the valley of the shadow of death, I will fear no evil, for Thou art with me." He trudged on, mouthing the words, tears dampening his cheeks.

When McClintock heard his name, he shouted, "Here!" and started down the aisle of his bus. Near the door stood a duty officer the crewmen called Fetch, for his willingness to get them things at the Country Club. Fetch seemed to regard McClintock and some of the other Americans as his only friends at the prison. He loved to chat about women and sex, and was particularly fascinated by bikini-wearing Hawaiian women. As McClintock was about to exit, Fetch reached out and clutched one of the sailor's hands in both of his.

"I come to visit you in Hawaii when it's socialist," he said eagerly.

"Don't hold your breath," rejoined the American, heading for the bridge.

McClintock felt as if he were exiting the twilight zone. As far as he was concerned, the months in prison were dead time; they'd never happened. Today was his first day after being captured. He wasn't euphoric about getting out; the wait had been too long and there'd been too many false hopes. He even found it difficult to hate the guards who'd beaten him. They weren't born cruel and brutal; they'd been indoctrinated since childhood to despise and fear Americans.

Halfway across the bridge, heedless of the duty officers' warnings, McClintock stopped and turned around. He began to laugh. The problem with North Korea was communism, not the people. He felt only pity for those who had to live under such a dehumanizing system. He took a last look at the wintry countryside. After a few moments he began walking again.

The soldiers did nothing.

As Bucher neared the far end of the bridge, he too committed a final act of defiance, whipping the Mao cap off his head. He'd be damned if he'd wear communist clothes a minute longer than necessary. A wide grin bloomed on his weather-beaten face. "Welcome back, Commander Bucher!" shouted a cheerful U.S. Army colonel who was checking off the arriving sailors' names on a clipboard. Bucher marveled at how warmly dressed the man looked.

The North Koreans began releasing the rest of the men on the last bus. An injured Gene Lacy hobbled down the aisle. "Ensign Harris!" a duty officer called, and Tim ran for the door. "Schumacher!" someone shouted; Skip bolted after him. Only Murphy remained. "What if your name isn't called?" asked a duty officer, smiling. Murphy didn't trust himself to reply. The loudspeaker had fallen silent. Several minutes crept by.

"Murphy!" a North Korean finally called, and the executive officer practically flew out the door.

Schumacher struggled to put one foot in front of the other without breaking into a panicked run. The crossing took only two or three minutes but it seemed like a thousand years. At the other end Bucher stood waiting for the last of his men. Schumacher saluted his commanding officer, and then shook his hand.

"We made it, Captain," he said softly.

CHAPTER 15

A CHRISTMAS PRESENT FOR THE NATION

Bucher was nearly overcome with excitement. What should he do first as a free man? Grinning Army officers and military policemen crowded around, shaking his hand, clapping his back. Their job was to get the newly liberated sailors away from the demilitarized zone as fast as possible. Standing with them was an expensively dressed civilian; Bucher assumed he was from the State Department.

Warm army parkas were handed out to the crewmen, along with Red Cross packets of cigarettes and candy. Then they were hustled aboard three olive-drab buses that rapidly departed for a United Nations advance camp four miles to the south. General Bonesteel greeted them at the base, heartily shaking each man's hand. The sailors were ushered into a Quonset hut where army cooks had whipped up an authentic American feast: piles of juicy steaks, hamburgers, mashed potatoes, and apple pie. But a military doctor took one look at the men's shrunken frames and decreed a more digestible menu: chicken noodle soup, bologna sandwiches, and milk. Several crew members proclaimed it the best meal they ever ate.

Bucher entered the mess hall last; his men jumped to their feet and gave him a loud, happy ovation. Then the well-dressed civilian approached the captain and asked whether they could talk privately. Richard Fryklund wasn't from State; he was a high-ranking Pentagon public-relations officer who'd been instructed to find out right away whether the *Pueblo* had entered North Korean waters. Much was riding on the answer. If Bucher said the intrusion allegations were false, the U.S. government would flash his denial to the world's media, countering North Korean propaganda. Fryklund already had set up a press conference, with more than 80 journalists waiting eagerly in a nearby room to hear from the captain.

Though Bucher and his men weren't aware of it, the Navy had been carefully planning their homecoming for months. How it was to be handled had been the subject of much bureaucratic infighting. At one point, planners envisioned flying the crew from South Korea to the Marine Air Station at Kaneohe Bay in Hawaii, where they'd be held virtually incommunicado while undergoing intensive intelligence debriefings lasting days or even weeks.

That idea was scuttled when Navy officials realized the public-relations fiasco that would ensue when anxious wives and parents, rushing to the base from across the country, were turned away at the gate. It was decided instead to bring the sailors to the U.S. Naval Hospital in San Diego, where loved ones could visit as doctors examined the men. Intelligence debriefs would begin only when the medical screenings were finished. The secret repatriation plan was code-named "Breeches Buoy," after a device used to rescue shipwreck victims.

Fryklund escorted Bucher outside the mess hall to an army sedan and, as they rode around, the two men talked. Even this encounter had been scripted beforehand in Washington. Navy lawyers worried that if Bucher was asked, without benefit of legal counsel, whether he'd violated North Korean waters, any subsequent disciplinary proceedings against him might be tainted. Fryklund therefore had been told to get Bucher talking in the hope that he'd raise the issue on his own. As the main architect of Breeches Buoy noted, the captain was "known to be voluble" and probably would open up without much prompting.

Bucher did exactly that, denying his ship ever crossed into communist waters. "That's what we thought," replied Fryklund, "but I'm relieved to hear it from you." He mentioned the press conference he'd arranged and asked whether Bucher would make a statement. The captain said it'd be a pleasure "to talk to real newspeople for a change."

Thus, less than two hours after hobbling across the Bridge of No Return, Bucher found himself facing a roomful of newsmen keen on knowing why he'd given up his ship without firing a shot in its defense. The skipper looked awful. To one journalist he appeared a decade older than his 41 years; to another, 20 years older. With his drawn face and reddened eyes, he seemed to be under tremendous strain. Cameramen beckoned him to wave and he obligingly did so. He'd never seen so much television equipment in his life.

The stakes were high for Bucher as well as the Navy, and the journalists sensed the drama. There'd been no time to coach the captain, and the Navy had no idea what he might blurt out under the reporters' gruff questioning. As Bucher mounted a small platform to speak, the faces of Fryklund and other government PR spinners "were a study in agony and suspense."

For Bucher the risk was saying something he'd later regret if the Navy pressed charges against him. No defense lawyer worthy of the name would've permitted a client to put his neck in such a potential legal noose, but the skipper seemed oblivious to the danger. He welcomed the chance to explain himself to an American public that, while sympathetic, also had questions about his actions. And considering his condition and lack of preparation, his statement to the media was remarkably lucid.

He began by praising his men, saying they were "simply tremendous" and "never once lost their spirit or faith in the United States of America." He insisted—three times—that the *Pueblo* hadn't penetrated North Korean waters. "We were attacked on the open sea and we were captured on the open seas," he said. "This is pure and simple and as plain as that." The navigation records showing intrusions, he said, were "completely doctored." He also gave a frank explanation of what happened after the communist gunboats surrounded him: "We—I surrendered the ship because there was nothing but a slaughter out there, and I couldn't see allowing any more people to be slaughtered or killing the entire crew for no reason."

Bucher modestly claimed he was beaten "less than anyone else," but added that on many occasions "I didn't think I was going to make it." He described Hell Week as "the most concentrated form of terror that I've ever seen or dreamed is possible." When a reporter asked how much classified material the crew was able to get rid of, Bucher replied, "We made an attempt to destroy everything." Then he added, "Well, truthfully, we did not complete it."

A Navy official cut off the questions when the captain appeared to be tiring. But he'd made a good impression on the media. His hesitations, repetitions, and occasionally unsteady stance made his words seem unrehearsed and genuine. As he left the stage, some of the newsmen applauded him—a rare tribute from such a hard-nosed bunch. The haggard commander, one reporter was to write, "emerged as a man who seemed to place responsibility for his crew above linguistic national loyalty or 'service' loyalty to the Navy."

After the press conference, helicopters shuttled Bucher and his men to a U.S. Army hospital about ten miles east of Seoul. Awaiting them was a crowd of 500 hospital patients, employees, and MPs, whistling and waving enthusiastically. At the hospital the sailors got X-rays, blood tests, and hot showers. They gladly shed their communist uniforms and put on blue submarine-style jumpsuits with "USS *PUEBLO*" printed on the back. Someone handed the captain a telegram from President Johnson, who declared the crew's release "a source of the deepest satisfaction to me and to all of your fellow countrymen."

Bucher was taken to a ward reserved for *Pueblo* officers. Lacy, Schumacher, and Tim Harris were already there, talking excitedly. Steve Harris lay on a bunk, staring at the ceiling while Murphy spoke in low tones to him. Someone rustled up eggnog and brandy, and the officers toasted their freedom. Bucher then toured five wards occupied by the enlisted men, downing more spiked nog at each stop. By the time he got back to his own ward, he was pleasantly buzzed. The officers were so wound up they needed sedatives to get to sleep that night.

The Navy called another news conference the next day. The sole speaker was Admiral Edwin Rosenberg, a genial Navy doctor. Assigned to personally escort the crewmen to San Diego, Rosenberg had talked with many of them about their experiences and was impressed not only by their stoicism and resistance in prison, but by their high morale and cohesiveness as a crew.

The Navy, he told reporters, expected to convene a "routine" court of inquiry in San Diego to look into the circumstances of the ship's capture. That piqued the newsmen's interest. They wanted to know how the Navy regarded what was known of the sailors' behavior at sea and in captivity. Were they suspected of violating any regulations for giving up their ship and participating in North Korean propaganda efforts? Rosenberg had in front of him a prepared statement filled with careful, understated phrases. But, perhaps caught up in the excitement and pride of the moment, he put it aside and spoke off the cuff, portraying the sailors in glowing terms as "heroes" and Bucher as "a hero among heroes."

"As far as the U.S. government and the Navy are concerned," declared the admiral, "these men have acted honorably."

Rosenberg's words undoubtedly were heartfelt. But he'd gone too far and the journalists knew it. The admiral sounded like he was exonerating the crew of any possible wrongdoing before the Navy's investigation even began. Indeed, his unconditional praise was a major public-relations stumble that helped set the stage for a severe public backlash against the Navy when it actually convened the court of inquiry.

Predictably, Rosenberg was asked whether his comments had the effect of prejudicing public opinion in favor of the crew. Rosenberg denied that, clearly annoyed by the question. Another newsman wanted to know how often the Navy dragged "heroes" before a board of investigation. That happened "all the time," the admiral insisted.

A flag officer labeling the sailors as heroes and men of honor, however, couldn't help but tilt public attitudes toward them. Rosenberg's remarks were widely circulated in the U.S. media. At a time when many Americans were trying to decide whether Bucher and his crew were exemplars or collaborators, Rosenberg had given them what looked like an official Navy seal of approval.

Later that day Bucher was visited at the hospital by the South Korean prime minister, Chung Il Kwon, trailed by several other cabinet ministers and still more reporters. His face flushed with emotion, the captain told Chung of the falsity of North Korean propaganda about the south and said he hoped that "at no time did we ever embarrass your country."

"There were methods used that made us sometimes ashamed of ourselves," said Bucher. "But we tried to give you at least some evidence that we didn't believe a word of what we were doing."

"Our experience in the Korean War taught us the value of freedom [is] more than life," replied Chung.

"Freedom is worth more than anyone's life," agreed the captain. "You have a splendid country. I hope your republic stands a thousand years, at least."

As he spoke, Bucher clasped both of Chung's hands in his for several minutes. The gesture had a strong impact on the premier and his party. Watching the scene, Ambassador Porter was struck by the skipper's composure and his "measured and eloquent" words. "He is an unusual individual," Porter cabled Washington, adding that Bucher's "affection for [his] crew came through clearly," and that the captain obviously enjoyed his men's respect and admiration.

At the White House, Walt Rostow forwarded Porter's "heartening report of Captain Bucher's graceful performance" to LBJ.

Cleared by military doctors to travel, the sailors were taken that afternoon to Kimpo airport outside Seoul. As an Air Force band blared "California, Here I Come," they boarded two cavernous C-141 Starlifter jets for the long flight to San Diego.

The transports landed at Midway Island to refuel at two a.m. Despite the late hour, the Navy post exchange was opened and everything was on the house. The sailors wolfed hamburgers and read about their release on the front page of the *Honolulu Advertiser.* The next-biggest story was the Apollo 8 astronauts heading for the moon.

On hand at Midway to greet the crew was Admiral John Hyland, commander in chief of the U.S. Pacific Fleet, who'd flown over from his Hawaii headquarters. He made the same mistake as Rosenberg, hailing the sailors at a press conference as "a group of young heroes." The encomium carried even more awkward implications coming from Hyland, since it was his responsibility to appoint the members of the *Pueblo* court of inquiry. Bucher also spoke to the reporters, but by now he was running on fumes. He earnestly tried to take responsibility for the entire spy-ship debacle in a statement so embarrassingly disjointed that newsmen didn't even quote it.

The captain spent the rest of the flight "in fitful sleep and jittery talks with my men." He awoke with a start at dawn. The crewmen had left South

Korea on Christmas Eve but, by crossing the international date line, they'd gain a day and still arrive in San Diego on December 24. The prospect of spending Christmas with their loved ones was thrilling and nerve-racking at the same time. Bucher's head filled with thoughts of his wife. He'd regained some weight in his last weeks in North Korea but still weighed only 127 pounds, nearly 80 pounds less than before his capture. Would Rose even recognize her stick-thin husband?

Then there was the matter of the Court of Inquiry. Many crewmen had no idea how they'd be received at home. Some expected mostly contempt and derision from the public, and probably punishment from the Navy. As he'd done in prison, Bucher again emphasized to his men that they should tell Navy investigators more or less the same story about their capture and confinement.

"You guys are gonna get a lot of questions, and I'd like to be reasonably close to being on the same page," he told the sailors on one plane. "It'll save us a lot of agony." At Midway the skipper switched aircraft and made the same speech to the rest of the crew.

Anticipation and stress spread through the cabins of the two jets as they raced over the Pacific. Sailors were combing their hair and otherwise preening. When the pilot announced an estimated touchdown in San Diego at two p.m., Bucher got goose bumps. Then someone peered out a window and yelled, "Land to starboard!"

By early afternoon on Christmas Eve, a restless crowd had gathered at the edge of a runway at Miramar Naval Air Station, ten miles north of downtown San Diego.

Wives, children, parents, and siblings of the seamen had flown in from all over the nation, some arriving only that morning. Summoned by electrifying phone calls from the Navy just two days earlier, family members had dropped everything—work, holiday preparations, *everything*—to make travel plans. Since the Navy was allowing no one except immediate kin through the base gate, only about 200 people were at the airfield. But outside, traffic had backed up for miles as thousands of well-wishers spontaneously converged on the base to witness the homecoming, which was to be televised live on all three networks.

At the front of the throng stood Rose Bucher, elated and on edge. She wore white gloves and a tailored brown dress suit, a big white orchid pinned to the shoulder. With her were her two teenage sons, Mark and Mike. Around them, anxious young mothers cooed to infants in strollers as older children—little girls in ribbons and boys in their Sunday best—giggled and fidgeted. Rose chatted with other relatives while casting hopeful glances at the western sky.

Finally two black dots appeared on the horizon, getting bigger by the moment. "They're coming in!" someone shouted. The Starlifters circled the airfield and seemed to land in slow motion. The big jets taxied toward the waiting families and cut their engines. A tense stillness settled over the crowd as uniformed sailors unrolled red carpets up to the aircraft. Then a hatch on the lead plane popped open, and Pete Bucher wobbled down the staircase, worn-looking but smiling.

To his amazement a Navy band was playing "The Lonely Bull."

"It's so great!" he exulted. "You'll never know how great it is!"

A moment later he and Rose were locked in a fierce embrace, their tear-streaked faces crushed together.

"I love you, Rose," the skipper said simply.

His men ran into the hungry arms of their loved ones. "Oh, Anthony! Oh, darling, I'm so happy!" cried a gray-haired mother as she embraced her son. An older man in a checked vest pumped away at his boy's hand, saying, "Well, Merry Christmas, Merry Christmas. By golly, it's good to see you." One wife supported a pale, gaunt husband who seemed too weak to stand on his own; another pressed her head hard into her man's chest, drawing comfort and strength from his presence. A sailor held his infant son for the first time, regarding him with pride and wonder.

"This was the nation's Christmas present," a local newsman summed up, "and the emotion was almost too big to handle."

Like two small islands of grief amid this ocean of joy stood Duane Hodges's parents. Jesse and Stella Hodges were plain, deeply religious people from Oregon with faces out of a Dorothea Lange photograph. The Navy had never officially explained how their son died, and so they came to San Diego seeking the truth from his shipmates. Rose brought the bereaved couple over to meet her husband, and placed a steadying hand on his back as he struggled to get out some words of comfort.

"Mr. Hodges, I—I can't tell you what a tremendous job your son did for us," Bucher said, looking intently into the retired millworker's tear-dappled face. "I'm so, so sorry that he couldn't return alive with us."

"Captain, I'm so glad you got back," replied Hodges, gripping Bucher's hand.

The stricken skipper wrapped his arms around both parents and told of the North Korean shell that hit their son and his death in a shipmate's arms. "What were his last words?" Mrs. Hodges asked. Bucher said he wasn't there at the time and didn't know. But he promised to put her in contact with the sailor who'd cradled her boy in his final moments.

Bucher was led to the speaker's podium, flanked by military and political dignitaries. Governor Reagan spoke to him briefly, recalling the captain's role as an extra in Reagan's 1957 movie *Hellcats of the Navy*, filmed in part aboard one of Bucher's old submarines, the *Besugo*. The captain congratulated him on his excellent memory and turned to face a brace of microphones. TV lenses zeroed in on his tired face.

He spoke of his obsessive worrying in prison about "the embarrassment that we caused the United States by losing one of its very fine ships to the North Koreans." He described the *Pueblo* getting shot up at "point-blank range." When he mentioned Duane Hodges's mortal wounding, he choked up. His jaws moved but no sound came out. An admiral patted his shoulder.

Moments later, six Navy pallbearers in dress blues and white helmets carried Hodges's flag-draped coffin from a Starlifter to a gray hearse. An honor guard snapped off crisp rifle volleys at the winter sky. As muted trumpets played taps, Bucher and his men came to attention and saluted their fallen comrade. Reagan made some welcoming remarks, as did the mayor of San Diego, who also offered Bucher a key to the city. But the jittery politician kept extending and withdrawing the key, doing so three or four times. Finally he finished his speech, dropped the key in his pocket, and walked away. Bucher had his first really good laugh since leaving North Korea.

The crewmen and their families climbed into eight buses for the short ride to the U.S. Naval Hospital at Balboa Park, in the gentle hills overlooking downtown San Diego. Rolling through the base gates, the sailors met a completely unexpected sight: multitudes of cheering San Diegans lining the route to the hospital, standing three and four deep in places. The civilians pounded car horns, whistled, flashed thumbs-up, and shook handmade "welcome home" signs.

Bucher grinned and waved at the crowds like a barnstorming senator. The wild outpouring of public joy, however, unnerved some of the others.

Gazing out a window, Schumacher wondered for the thousandth time whether he could've done more to resist the North Koreans. Steve Harris's mother, Eleanor, an effervescent Boston-area schoolteacher, noticed that most of the wan-looking sailors on her bus weren't waving back.

"Wave to them!" she urged. "You should all wave to them!"

Her son tried to restrain her. "Mother, we're not heroes," he said mildly. "We're just a bunch of ordinary guys who were in the right place at the wrong time."

The buses passed a little boy, clad only in faded brown shorts, jumping up and down as he waved a small American flag. For many passengers the sight of the dirt-streaked kid and his guileless patriotism was too much. "Slow tears came upon faces all along the aisle, parents and sons alike," Eleanor Harris wrote later. "An older sailor across from me—at least his hair was gray—was crying into thin, gnarled hands."

The convoy arrived at the hospital. With 2,600 beds and more than 300 doctors, the Balboa complex was the largest military medical facility in the world. The sailors lugged their white ditty bags into a four-story pink stucco building normally inhabited by Navy hospital corps students. Dubbed the "Pink Palace," it was to be their home for the next few weeks. Murphy was impressed by the luxuriousness of the two-man suites: carpeting, writing desks, and beds long enough to accommodate American frames. The only drawback was that he had to share his digs with Bucher.

By now the captain was bleary with fatigue. His head was ready to burst from the day's excitement and stress. Fewer than 55 hours had passed since he crossed the Bridge of No Return. He limped over to the adjacent enlisted men's club to have dinner with his sailors, only to be mobbed by their exuberant, grateful families. "Some of the handshakes I received from fathers and brothers of my crew nearly broke my hand," he was to write of the experience. "Mothers and wives hugged and kissed me. It was overwhelming." After dinner he and Rose sneaked to the back of the room for a semiprivate reunion with kisses, hand-holding, and tender words.

The Navy was working hard to satisfy the needs of the crewmen and their kin. It had paid for last-minute plane tickets to San Diego for scores of family members. Phones were set up so sailors could make free calls to friends and relatives all over the country. "An *admiral* just fetched me a cup of coffee," a bemused enlisted man told Murphy. By the same token, the crewmen were confined to the hospital grounds for at least the next several days. They had orders not to talk to the media, not even about the weather. The Navy wanted to be sure no military secrets leaked, and no one said anything that might later jeopardize himself legally. Armed sentries were posted to keep news reporters away from the Pink Palace.

On Christmas morning, the crew went on a shopping spree at the Balboa post exchange. With $200,000 in back pay in their collective pockets, they snapped up cameras, watches, appliances, coats for their wives, and toys for their kids. Bucher moved easily among his men, joking and wishing them a merry Christmas. That evening, under the Navy's liberal definition of "next of kin," more than 500 people jammed the dining room, feasting on turkey, rainbow trout, beef prime rib, French onion soup, and tomato bisque. Catholic and Protestant services were held before an altar jury-rigged out of a table, a sheet, and two candles; the faithful took Communion in the soft, flickering light.

"When we sang 'Joy to the World,'" one mother said, "you never heard anything like it."

The happy homecoming triggered a widespread catharsis. "Never, in 35 years, have I been so burstingly proud to be an American," a San Diego man wrote to a local newspaper. "Standing on 10th Avenue, with many others, to welcome home the *Pueblo* crew was an overwhelming experience." America's first television-age hostage crisis—a phenomenon that would become distressingly familiar in the future—had ended remarkably well. The survivors were safe, they were in one piece, and—thanks to the Johnson administration's dogged diplomacy—they were back home with loved ones just in time for Christmas.

LBJ was widely praised for not succumbing to the temptation to unsheathe military force during the long standoff with Pyongyang. *The New York Times* hailed his "wise decision . . . to accept some sacrifice of American pride." Even some hawks applauded the gentler approach. "Many of our members called for speedier and forceful action immediately after the *Pueblo* was illegally seized," the national commander of Veterans of Foreign Wars wrote to the White House. "Many more became most impatient as the months dragged by. In retrospect, however, the Nation's restraint and patience have paid off."

Amid the exultant chorus of hosannas, however, were strident notes of dissent.

Soon after the sailors were safely across the bridge, Dean Rusk had publicly characterized the Panmunjom deal as "a strange procedure" with "no precedent in my 19 years of public service." He described General Woodward's signature as "worthless" and said only the North Koreans could explain why they accepted the "prerepudiated" apology.

Flushed with holiday spirit, many Americans seemed inclined to savor the gratifying ends and overlook the slippery means. But some conservatives derided the settlement as an odious sellout of American honor. "If a formal apology is signed but a verbal repudiation made, what can one believe?" asked a *St. Louis Globe-Democrat* editorial. "This is the propaganda predicament into which Red Korea has finessed the United States." Columnist James J. Kilpatrick concurred: "All this is being served up to the American public as a glorious achievement. It seems a far cry, somehow, from Stephen Decatur and John Paul Jones." Critics also questioned whether the sailors deserved all the public adulation. "They were heroes in the sense that they survived the imprisonment, but they did sign a great many statements that didn't reflect to my mind any great heroism," sniffed Senator Richard Russell, the powerful Georgia Democrat who chaired the Senate Armed Services Committee.

North Korea wasted no time in capitalizing on the Panmunjom pact. "U.S. Imperialists Bend Their Knees Again Before Korean People," gloated the *Pyongyang Times*. In spite of Woodward's disclaimer, the newspaper trumpeted his signature as an "ignominious defeat" for America. Other Eastern bloc nations jumped on the bandwagon. Given the Johnson administration's disavowal of its apology, the East German news agency questioned whether the United States could be trusted to stand by any international treaty or agreement it signed. The *San Diego Union* acknowledged the potency of the communist campaign with an editorial cartoon that managed to combine a racist caricature with a racially mocking double entendre. It depicted a North Korean military officer with huge buckteeth holding a piece of paper marked, "U.S. *Pueblo* 'Confession' Propaganda." "We sank you!" the officer crowed, with a bow and a grin.

Washington swiftly returned fire. Having finally had a chance to confer directly with the crew, the Navy held a press conference at the hospital the day after Christmas to refute the key allegation that the *Pueblo* had trespassed in North Korean waters. The main attraction was Ed Murphy, standing in for Bucher, who was confined to bed with fever and chills from an upper respiratory infection.

Murphy told a roomful of newsmen that, as navigator, he was certain his ship had never come closer than 12 miles to the communist shore. Smiling and appearing rested, the executive officer told of how the North Koreans forged navigation charts and logs to make it look as if the *Pueblo* had intruded, and how he'd inserted errors in the forgeries to make them look inane. On the same day, Admiral Thomas Moorer, the chief of naval operations, told reporters in Washington that the Navy knew early on the charts were faked, but decided not to say so publicly for fear of further endangering Bucher and his fellow captives.

Meanwhile, Navy doctors began examining the crew. Malnourishment was the main diagnosis. Seven men, including Bucher, reported pain in their hands and feet, probably caused by a loss of fat supporting peripheral nerve sheaths. Schumacher still had "considerable pain" in his back, sternum, and thorax from Hell Week, though his overall prognosis was good. Despite the vicious beatings that left him unconscious on several occasions, Hammond exhibited "no residual injuries."

Bucher had been running a fever since his release, and his vision was still fuzzy. He was transferred to a single room and confined to bed rest for several days. A Marine guard stood watch outside his door, but the captain talked his way past him several times to use a pay phone in the hall.

Bucher's vivid descriptions to the media of the crew's treatment in prison caused general repugnance in the United States, and President Johnson ordered an "urgent investigation" of what had happened in North Korea.

The Navy hastily complied. Investigators showed the crewmen dozens of still photos of communist officers and guards, extracted from news footage of Super C's propaganda pageants. The sailors dutifully pointed out Robot, Possum, Odd Job, and others. Police-style "identi-kits" were used to reconstruct the faces of North Koreans who didn't appear at news conferences, such as those in the Gypsy Tea Room. The crewmen also gave affidavits detailing how they were beaten and otherwise abused. The statements, the men were told, were to be sent to the United Nations, along with Washington's formal protest.

But that never happened. The bottom line, as the Balboa hospital commander told the press, was that "no serious injuries" had been inflicted on the sailors. (He apparently overlooked Law's ruined eyes and Woelk's loss of his testicles.) The worst beatings had been reserved for tough guys like Hammond and Kisler, who served as bloody warnings to the rest of the Americans not to resist. The survival of all 82 crewmen, Navy investigators concluded, suggested the North Korean government had "consciously and carefully controlled" the levels of violence. In any event, there was little Washington could do about it, short of a military strike, and the results of the inquiry were quietly shelved.

Their physical exams completed, the sailors were handed off to a team of Navy psychiatrists led by Captain Raymond Spaulding, chief of psychiatry at Balboa and an expert on POW psychology. Spaulding and his cohorts interviewed each member of the crew, often for several hours at a time. To no one's surprise, they determined that being imprisoned and brutalized by a communist dictatorship for nearly a year had been hard on the men's psyches. Sixteen sailors exhibited symptoms of severe depression while incarcerated, including feelings of despair and thoughts of suicide. Forty others experienced "significant anxiety," largely due to their captors' capricious violence. Twenty developed anorexia. Plagued by guilt over their forced confessions, some sailors fantasized about the United States bombing the prison and killing everyone—guards and captives alike.

But Spaulding also found the seamen had drawn psychic strength and comfort from one another's company. Living together in cells became a form of group therapy as they discussed their lives, aspirations, sexual adventures, and favorite foods. Natural leaders emerged in each room, helping shipmates resist "thought reform" efforts by discussing what the room daddies said and "destroying their logic." "'Brainwashing' techniques were unsuccessful in converting any man to Communism or even in persuading him to reject any American principles," Spaulding reported in an article for the *American Journal of Psychiatry.*

Upon their return to the United States, many sailors expected to be "punished and ridiculed" and were confused by their enthusiastic reception, Spaulding wrote. While they professed remorse over being used as propaganda puppets, most had "ready rationalizations" for their behavior, noting that they'd often undermined the North Koreans' message with the Hawaiian good-luck sign and other tricks.

An exception to the rationalizers was Schumacher, whom other crew members regarded as "exceptionally strong and an inspiration," according to Spaulding. The young lieutenant had hidden "considerable mental anguish" in prison, including anxiety nightmares, thoughts of suicide, and "feelings of guilt over not having lived up to the military Code of Conduct."

One of the psychiatrists on Spaulding's team, Commander C. W. Erwin, interviewed 15 enlisted men, whom he viewed as "unusually bright" compared to typical enlistees. Not only did they not suffer any lasting mental harm, Erwin said, but most described their time in North Korea as a "profound, life-changing experience" that gave them significant insight into themselves and others. Many cited "major religious experiences" and other personal epiphanies that convinced them to work harder at their marriages or go back to college when they got home. They didn't feel bad about surrendering, since they were convinced that fighting back "would have been suicide." And although the communists had tortured and humiliated them, the sailors believed they'd triumphed in the end by simply surviving.

Certified by the hospital as relatively healthy in body and mind, the men were ready for the most sensitive part of Breeches Buoy: the intelligence debriefings. Months before, in a secret planning document, the Navy had declared these interviews "a matter of the highest priority." The government badly wanted to find out what classified information and equipment—especially code machines—had been lost or compromised as a result of the *Pueblo*'s capture. The answers would be incorporated into what was known in intelligence circles as a "damage assessment."

Underscoring the assessment's importance was the sudden appearance in San Diego of nearly 300 members of a special team—interviewers, technical experts, transcribers, report writers, and administrators—drawn from the National Security Agency, CIA, Defense Intelligence Agency, Naval Intelligence Command, and FBI. The NSA contingent arrived the day after Christmas aboard a chartered plane from Baltimore, some members a bit tipsy from martini consumption along the way.

The team's interrogation protocol had been carefully worked out in Washington; the goal was to extract as much information as possible from each seaman. But actually doing so was expected to be a tricky business.

Intelligence officials were concerned that as crewmen became aware they could be liable for stiff punishment, they might clam up in the debriefings. To allay their anxiety, the Navy took the unusual step of erecting a legal firewall between the debriefers and the Court of Inquiry. Each seaman was given a written guarantee that whatever he said in the debriefs was privileged and couldn't be used against him in disciplinary proceedings of any kind. Debriefers were instructed to avoid coming off like prosecutors; they were to establish a "relaxed atmosphere" and a "sympathetic relationship" with the crewmen. If a sailor displayed any sign of distress or confusion, the interview was to be terminated and medical assistance summoned. If anyone inquired about his legal rights, he was to be provided with a Navy lawyer at no cost.

For crewmen not connected to the SOD hut, the debrief sessions had the comfortable feel of a conversation between friends. For the communication technicians, the experience was more intense. Michael Barrett underwent 15 interviews; another CT endured 26. But, protected against legal fallout from their revelations, many sailors spoke frankly. As one NSA debriefer recalled: "We told them, 'I don't want to hear about the fight. I don't want to hear anything about the battle. I don't want to hear nothing about who got shot. I don't want to hear nothing about who was on their hands and knees and praying. . . . All I want to know is, what did you take aboard that ship when you went?' And the kids became pretty free in telling me that."

At the end of each day, behind-the-scenes technical experts pored over transcripts of the interviews and drew up a list of more specific questions for debriefers to ask the next day. The process yielded a huge amount of material: 270 miles of interview tapes and enough written reports to fill a number of large filing cabinets. Everything was boxed up and flown to Washington, where another group of analysts was to go over it in minute detail inside a locked vault at Naval Security Group headquarters. The results of the damage evaluation wouldn't be known for weeks.

In the meantime, the citizens of San Diego—arguably the most Navy-friendly town in America—continued to treat the crew like kings. The Chamber of Commerce raised more than $52,000 to defray the cost of hotel rooms and food for out-of-town relatives. The owner of an Italian restaurant offered sailors and their families a free meal for each day of captivity. When Stu Russell announced his impending marriage, local women's groups volunteered to sew his bride's gown, bake the wedding cake, buy flowers, and organize the reception. Smiling strangers came up to Steve Harris's wife and told her approvingly, "You belong to the *Pueblo* family."

As the days passed the Navy loosened its leash on the men. On New Year's Day, 19 of them were allowed to ride a chartered bus up to Pasadena to see the Rose Bowl. CT Don McClarren got married in Las Vegas, with a casino singer picking up the tab for champagne, flowers, and a bridal suite at the Riviera Hotel. Bucher's health gradually improved and, on January 3, 1969, he, Murphy, and eight others were awarded Purple Hearts for wounds received in action. For some unfathomable military reason, "This Is the

Army, Mr. Jones" played on the public-address system during the medal-pinning ceremony in a sunny hospital courtyard.

On January 12, actor John Wayne, singer Pat Boone, and "several Hollywood starlets" entertained the awestruck sailors at a party in a local hotel. About 100 other well-wishers crowded into the bash, which was organized by local pro-*Pueblo* groups and began with Bucher and his men marching into the room to the strains of "The Lonely Bull." Wayne presented the captain with a plaque saying Americans would always remember the *Pueblo* crew with gratitude. To Rose the movie star gave two dozen long-stemmed roses, gallantly telling her, "With one Rose as lovely as you, we don't need the other 23."

Rose had saved armloads of newspaper and magazine clippings about the *Pueblo*, and she gave them to her husband to read while he recuperated at the hospital. He hadn't known how big the story was in the United States. He began to understand its full dimensions when he saw a painting of himself, in white captain's hat and dress blue uniform, on the cover of *Time* magazine.

Some of the articles, however, made for uncomfortable reading. A good portion of the Navy's command hierarchy, it was clear, was furious at Bucher. The captain had soiled the most hallowed tradition of the most tradition-steeped branch of the armed services: He'd surrendered without a fight.

The Navy's self-image was built on heroic tales of sea commanders who fought against long odds or otherwise tempted fate with their derring-do. There was John Paul Jones, who captured the faster and much better armed British frigate *Serapis* after a ferocious night battle, then watched from its decks as his own badly shot-up vessel, the *Bonhomme Richard*, slid beneath the waves of the North Sea. There was David Farragut, who led his squadron into a Confederate minefield protecting Mobile Bay by calling out, "Damn the torpedoes! Full speed ahead!" For generations a banner had hung in the U.S. Naval Academy at Annapolis as an inspiration to cadets. It bore the last words of a mortally wounded commander, James Lawrence, during an 1813 battle off Boston harbor: "Don't give up the ship." In the minds of many naval officers, that brave exhortation carried the gravity and immutability of sacred writ.

By contrast, Bucher's most aggressive act had been to hurl expletives at the North Korean gunboats. "There had better be a good explanation," one

Navy officer told the *Los Angeles Times* after the *Pueblo*'s seizure. "You don't just give up the ship because somebody asked you to." Others insisted Bucher should have at least scuttled or blown up his boat. Asked what he'd have done in the same circumstances, Admiral William Raborn, who at different times in his career had run the Navy's Polaris missile program and the CIA, snapped, "I would have shot the hell out of them. I would have made those North Koreans pay a high price." Another captain said that while many officers felt compassion for Bucher because of his prison travails, "I haven't heard of anyone who is sympathetic with his decision to give up the ship."

To Bucher the handwriting was on the wall. If the Navy was looking for a scapegoat in the upcoming court of inquiry, he was the leading candidate.

CHAPTER 16

BUCHER'S GETHSEMANE

As the crew jetted toward Miramar on Christmas Eve, a Navy lawyer named William Newsome drove out to the airfield in his Volkswagen Beetle to see how ordinary San Diegans would receive them.

Newsome's motive was more than idle curiosity. The previous summer the Navy had designated the balding, 45-year-old captain as chief counsel for the *Pueblo* court of inquiry. Newsome was given a private office at the Navy amphibious base on Coronado Island, just across the bay from downtown San Diego, where the inquest was to be held. The office soon filled with boxes of sensitive documents: sailors' personnel files; urgent messages flashed among various Navy commands during the seizure crisis; the background investigation that revealed Bucher's dalliances in Japan.

The son of a Brooklyn postal worker, Newsome was a serious, driven man. After serving aboard a mortar-firing assault boat during the World War II invasions of Okinawa and other Pacific islands, he earned a law degree from New York University. He studied so hard for a postgraduate course in military law that he ended up in the hospital with bleeding ulcers. (Despite his illness, friends kept bringing homework to his bedside so he wouldn't fall behind in class.) He'd been involved in hundreds of military cases and had served as a military judge. Yet for all his experience Newsome worried that he wasn't up to handling the *Pueblo* court, which promised more raw drama than any military judicial proceeding since the 1925 court-martial of General Billy Mitchell, an outspoken proponent of airpower, for insubordination.

Contrary to what its name might suggest, a court of inquiry isn't an arena for a trial. It's a fact-finding body, similar to a civilian grand jury, designed to get to the bottom of naval disasters that result in loss of life or property. Courts of inquiry have investigated some of the most wrenching episodes in Navy history: the mysterious explosion that sank the USS *Maine* in Havana harbor in 1898; the lack of preparedness on the part of top Navy and Army commanders prior to the Japanese attack on Pearl Harbor in 1941; and the sudden flooding and sinking of the submarine *Thresher* off Cape Cod in 1963. A court's importance is proportional to the number of admirals who sit on it. One admiral signifies a relatively simple, low-level investigation; more indicate a complex, higher-profile probe. Five admirals—the maximum—would sit on the *Pueblo* court.

Courts of inquiry can recommend but not impose punishment. As court counsel, Newsome's job wasn't to prosecute Bucher and his men but to elicit enough facts from them and other witnesses to enable the court members to understand the circumstances that led to the *Pueblo* calamity.

Some of those facts, Newsome knew, might reflect badly on the sailors, and bringing them to light in open hearings could put him in an unenviable position. The crewmen already were riding a wave of public sympathy, and two admirals—Rosenberg and Hyland—had publicly crowned them as heroes. At the same time, public opinion was turning against the Navy and the rest of the military over the Vietnam War. By asking tough, potentially embarrassing questions of Bucher and his men, Newsome could easily become the villain in a high-visibility morality play. If that happened, so be it. But the attorney wanted to get a sense of what he was in for. And so he drove out to Miramar.

The scene at the airfield shook him badly. As the freed seamen staggered off their planes, the waiting crowd exploded in cheers, screams of joy, and tears—not just the men's families, but hundreds of regular people standing outside the base gates as well. *They're acting like they just saw Lindbergh touch down in Paris*, Newsome thought in alarm. He could guess what that meant: When the court of inquiry got under way, many Americans would view him as the guy throwing mud at a bunch of national idols.

For a wild moment, all he wanted to do was run away.

"I honestly thought of getting in my Volkswagen and filling it up with gas, and going as far east as I could, and filling it up with gas again, and going as far east as I could again, and never coming back to this thing," Newsome recalled, "because I was scared to death."

But he didn't take off. He kept going to work at his Coronado office each day, methodically preparing for the biggest case of his life.

Bucher didn't feel ready for the rigors of a public inquiry, but the Navy wanted it to begin before too many crewmen's enlistments expired. By the middle of January 1969, 25 sailors would be eligible for discharge. If they reverted to civilian status and left town, it might be difficult, if not impossible, to get them to return as witnesses. So the Navy placed 90-day "medical holds" on the men, forcing them to stay in San Diego for the duration of the court, which Newsome expected would be no more than three or four weeks. When Bucher asked for a delay, the Navy said his men with expired enlistments couldn't go home until the inquest had concluded. The captain reluctantly agreed to a January 20 start date.

On January 10, a Navy doctor told the press Bucher's "emotional condition is now good." In fact, it still was quite iffy. The captain suffered fierce headaches—a common symptom of post-traumatic stress disorder—and often wept at the mere thought of his prison experiences. "Emotions just leaked out of me like I was a sieve," he remembered. "God, I felt like a damn fool. But I just [couldn't] control myself."

The court hearings were to be held in a small auditorium at the Naval Amphibious School on Coronado. Extra seats were installed to accommodate the expected passel of newsmen. The five admirals would sit on a raised stage behind a long table covered with green baize. A few feet in front of the stage was a small table for Bucher and his attorneys, and a solitary chair for witnesses. A scrambler phone with a direct line to Washington hung on a wall. Some court sessions would be open to the public and others closed; testimony involving classified matters would be heard in an identical room next door. Technicians swept both chambers for hidden bugs. Marine guards posted inside and outside the auditorium would provide security.

Admiral John Hyland, the Pacific Fleet commander and convening authority for the court, chose each of its members as carefully as if he were selecting a bride. All were Annapolis graduates, and four of the five had seen combat in waters near Wonsan during the Korean War. Collectively they represented all major subdivisions of the Navy: surface ships, naval aviation, amphibious warfare, and submarines.

For the "horrible chore" of serving as court president, Hyland picked a close friend, Vice Admiral Harold G. Bowen Jr., commander of U.S. antisubmarine warfare forces in the Pacific. Hyland admired Bowen as "one of the brightest guys . . . that ever graduated from the [Naval] Academy." Hyland knew Bowen didn't want the job, but he didn't think he had anyone else who could handle it.

His reluctance aside, the 55-year-old Bowen was a natural choice. As the son and son-in-law of vice admirals, he was Navy royalty. Patrician-looking and fit from frequent games of squash and tennis, he'd graduated fourth in his class at Annapolis in 1933 and had gone on to earn a master's degree in metallurgical engineering. He commanded a destroyer in the South Pacific during World War II and a destroyer division in the Korean War. For his coolheaded leadership in a deadly artillery duel between his flagship, the destroyer *Maddox*, and enemy shore batteries near Wonsan, Bowen was awarded the Legion of Merit. Later he ran the Navy's nuclear power division. He talked softly and with an engineer's dry precision, but the lanky admiral had a charismatic presence. "When he spoke, everybody listened," recalled Newsome. He also had a good trial judge's knack for cutting through thickets of verbiage and getting to the heart of a matter, which would serve him well during the complicated *Pueblo* probe.

Bowen's four court colleagues also were pillars of the Navy establishment.

A brusque ex-submariner whose teeth often were clamped around an unlit cigar, Rear Admiral Allen Bergner headed the big San Diego naval training center. In 1939, he'd captained the Naval Academy football squad that beat Army 10–0. Called "Big Bear" by teammates, Bergner played tackle both ways. He also was captain of the Annapolis wrestling team and lettered in boxing and lacrosse. As a newly minted ensign, he found himself assigned to the USS *West Virginia* on December 7, 1941, when the battleship was sunk in Pearl Harbor by Japanese attackers. Later in World War II, as executive officer of the submarine *Gar*, he won a Bronze Star. At 53, the white-haired Bergner was the youngest member of the court.

Rear Admiral Edward Grimm, 58, was the oldest. A veteran of 35 years in the Navy, he headed the Pacific Fleet training command, based in San Diego. As navigator of the cruiser *Birmingham* during World War II, he was badly injured when his ship pulled alongside the carrier *Princeton* to fight fires touched off by a kamikaze strike. Like Bowen, Grimm had skippered a destroyer that bombarded targets near Wonsan. In 1952, he obtained a master's degree in business administration; his subsequent career alternated between sea commands and shore jobs as a Navy budget expert. With a faint smile often playing on his face, Grimm seemed more sympathetic toward Bucher than any other court member.

Soft-spoken and scholarly-looking, Rear Admiral Richard Pratt, commander of amphibious training in the Pacific, had been both a star athlete at the Naval Academy and a war hero. The nephew of a chief of naval operations, he quarterbacked the Navy football squad three years in a row in the 1930s and also captained the baseball team. During the hellish struggle for Okinawa in 1945, he commanded a destroyer that put fire hoses aboard a burning aircraft carrier and saved it. Pratt's medals included two Navy Crosses, the service's highest decoration for heroism; a Silver Star; and a Bronze Star. In his spare time he enjoyed attending art exhibits and other cultural events.

The last member of the court, Rear Admiral Marshall White, was a flier and former skipper of the aircraft carrier *Hornet*. A Bronze Star winner during the Korean War, he now commanded the Navy missile test range at Point Mugu, California. He spoke with a Missouri drawl and, as the court dragged on, occasionally sighed about neglecting his weekend gardening.

Together, the court members had served 184 years, won 77 medals and decorations, and, in a number of ways, embodied the best of Navy tradition. Hyland directed them to investigate "all the facts and circumstances" of the

Pueblo's capture and the detention of its crew, and the admirals seemed determined to do so.

Bucher was impressed by Bowen and his distinguished cohorts and believed they'd give him a "full, fair, and impartial" hearing, as Navy regulations required. The captain was willing to shoulder some of the blame for the disaster off Wonsan, but he also felt that nothing he had or hadn't done on January 23, 1968, would have changed the outcome after the gunboats surrounded him. He believed the investigating admirals would want to know about how ill-prepared the Navy had left him, and he envisioned a long line of brass hats from Washington being called on the carpet to explain why they turned down his requests for a rapid-destruct mechanism and other necessary hardware.

But the skipper didn't know the Navy had quietly placed strict limits on how far Bowen could go with his investigation. According to a secret internal agreement struck before the court began, Bowen couldn't take testimony in several key areas. For one thing, he was prohibited from examining the actions of the court's convener, Hyland, even though Hyland's command might have made important decisions involving the *Pueblo*. Nor could Bowen call anyone in "higher authority" as a witness, meaning no one from Admiral Moorer's office, the Joint Chiefs of Staff, or the White House could be compelled to explain their actions, or lack thereof.

Bucher spent the weekend before the court began sequestered with his lawyer, E. Miles Harvey, a dapper young partner in a white-shoe San Diego firm. Harvey had helped Rose Bucher with various matters during her husband's captivity. He initially turned down the captain's request to represent him before the admirals, saying he wasn't qualified. Harvey was a top-drawer business attorney, brokering complex real estate deals and corporate mergers and acquisitions. But he'd never tried a case in court and knew almost nothing about military law.

"I didn't know what a court of inquiry was," he admitted years later.

Harvey did know something about the Navy, however. He was a commander in the Navy Reserve, specializing in intelligence. He agreed to represent Bucher partly because the skipper also would have the services of an experienced Navy lawyer, Captain James E. Keys. Regarded in naval circles as a superb, even brilliant legal mind, the crew-cut, soft-voiced Keys had participated in numerous military trials and served as a military judge in Vietnam. He knew the Uniform Code of Military Justice backward and forward. But he had a major liability: He was a heavy drinker. "By noon he was through half a fifth of scotch," recalled Harvey, "and by two o'clock he was through the fifth." Keys also would fail Harvey at a critical juncture in the court hearings, by Harvey's account. (The author was unable to locate Keys to ask for his response.)

Harvey was optimistic about Bucher's chances in court; he thought the skipper could even wind up with a medal. The notion that Bowen and his court colleagues might recommend serious disciplinary action, up to and including a court-martial, didn't cross his mind. Though handicapped by his unfamiliarity with military law, Harvey was shrewd and imaginative. After years of hard bargaining with CEOs and other high-powered business types, he wasn't the least bit intimidated by the prospect of facing a few admirals. Plus, he had Keys to help him, or so he thought.

Since Harvey didn't have nearly enough time to get up to speed on the intricacies of military law, he asked Bowen to suspend the rules of evidence, as permitted under the flexible regulations governing courts of inquiry. Harvey expected to be turned down, but Bowen assented to his request. Among other things, the court president's decision meant witnesses could testify without being interrupted by lawyers' distracting and time-consuming objections. And that cleared the way for Harvey to pursue a clever public-relations strategy.

The attorney correctly sensed that the media would play a crucial role in the court's outcome, and he wanted journalists to "come on board with Bucher." He hoped to nudge them up the gangway by having the captain narrate, from beginning to end, his astonishing story of capture on the high seas, barbaric imprisonment, brave resistance, and eventual freedom. As soon as they heard the full saga, Harvey believed, newsmen would be more likely to identify with the earthy, careworn skipper than with the five admirals, whom Harvey described as looking "as pompous as they possibly could" with their copious gold braid and medal-bedecked chests. To Harvey's delight, Bowen also agreed to let Bucher be the leadoff witness.

Newsome had some interesting cards to play as well. Thanks to the Naval Investigative Service, he already knew about Bucher's bar habits and womanizing. The NIS gave the court counsel a copy of its investigation of Bucher as the court was getting started. But, reading through the file, Newsome realized it created a dilemma for him as much as it provided potential ammunition against the *Pueblo* commander.

Certainly the NIS material could be used against Bucher, if that became necessary. But publicly dredging up sordid personal information about the skipper could backfire, making Newsome—and by extension, the Navy—look sleazy and ruthless. Despite the tactical advantage the dossier might give him, Newsome didn't want to use it in court. By the same token, he didn't want Harvey to get too carried away extolling Bucher's virtues to the admirals. So he privately warned the captain's attorney that he had the NIS report.

"You can make him John Paul Jones," Newsome remembered telling Harvey, "but don't make him John the Baptist."

Cold rains inundated Coronado on Monday, January 20, the court of inquiry's first day. The amphibious school auditorium was jammed with spectators, most of them news reporters. Ever since their release, Bucher and his men had been a media sensation, and the court was to receive extensive coverage from newspapers, magazines, television, and radio.

The admirals filed in and took their seats promptly at nine a.m. Sitting a few feet away were Bucher and Harvey. The captain assured the court he was in "very good physical condition," having gained 18 pounds since his return. But his appearance belied his words. He wore black-rimmed glasses to improve his vitamin-deficient eyesight; when he stood up, his uniform sagged on his undernourished frame.

Bucher took the witness seat and, over the next four days, told his epic tale from start to finish. He began, slowly and solemnly, by itemizing the *Pueblo*'s many deficiencies. Its ancient steering system broke down continually on the way to Japan, he said, though it was largely fixed by the time he left for North Korea. A request for a collision alarm was denied. He never got the dedicated phone circuits he wanted to better communicate with his navigation and damage-control teams. He made "two or three" requests to the chief of naval operations' office for a rapid-destruction system, but was turned down. While mounts were installed for three machine guns, only two were delivered. Camouflaged under frozen tarpaulins, the weapons took agonizing minutes to be brought into action; Bucher's men once needed a full hour to get one working. The guns were unshielded and prone to jamming; the captain never expected them to be very effective.

Without explicitly saying so, Bucher left the strong impression that the Navy regarded the AGERs and their crews as expendable. Bowen had no intention of letting that perception go unchallenged, however. Under Navy regulations, a captain had the right to refuse to weigh anchor if he believed his vessel unprepared for its mission. The court president listened to Bucher's complaints and then asked whether the *Pueblo* hadn't been ready, drawing a telling response from its commander.

"There was no question in my mind that the ship and myself, as well as the crew, were prepared to carry out the mission assigned successfully," he said.

Thus, with a single incisive question, Bowen neatly boxed in the captain. Had Bucher answered that he wasn't prepared to depart, but did so anyway, he'd have appeared negligent. His acknowledgment that he was ready tended to undercut his criticisms of the Navy for not properly equipping him.

Under further questioning, Bucher also admitted he'd been less than diligent in drilling his men for emergencies. While they'd practiced going to general quarters and abandoning ship during their storm-lashed passage to North Korea, they didn't exercise in repelling boarders or destroying classified materials.

On his second day of testimony, Bucher described his frustrating, unproductive transit of the communist coast. Looking tense and sipping frequently from a glass of water, he told of drifting from one North Korean port to another as the CTs tried to zero in on radio and radar signals. The admirals questioned him closely on the possibility of navigational error—What charts had he used? Was his loran accurate?—but Bucher insisted the *Pueblo* had never left international waters.

Then came the calamity off Wonsan: the sudden appearance of the sub chaser; the sharklike circling of the PT boats; the terrifying hail of shells and bullets as the *Pueblo* tried to run. In short order, said the captain, he found himself "completely and hopelessly outgunned." The tarps on his machine guns were frozen solid; anyone trying to pry them loose and set up the weapons would have been quickly cut down.

"I saw no point," said Bucher, explaining why he hadn't manned the guns, "in senselessly sending people to their deaths."

The skipper recounted the MiGs roaring overhead and Dwayne Hodges's intestines spilling on the deck. He didn't mention what he remembered as Lacy's frenzied demand to stop the ship and Murphy's deck-hugging under fire. As the *Pueblo* coasted to a halt, the North Koreans ceased firing. "I felt that any further, or any, resistance on our part would only end up in a complete slaughter of the crew," the captain stated.

The admirals' next round of questions reflected their skepticism of Bucher's rationale for surrendering. The cigar-chewing Bergner led the charge, demanding to know whether small arms had been broken out.

No, the captain replied.

What had his damage-control parties reported before Bucher stopped the ship? Bergner asked.

"No fires, no flooding, and no material casualties," the captain calmly answered.

Apparently taken aback, Bergner then asked, "For clarification, what significant event occurred just prior to your making the decision to stop?"

"No particular action took place," said Bucher. "My feeling was that we would be hopelessly riddled and perhaps sustain an inordinate number of casualties, which would interfere with the destruction of the classified matter."

Bowen weighed in with another penetrating question:

"Did you ever consider that you might [be] attacked and, if so, what would you do?"

"No, sir," responded the captain. "I never considered that I would ever be attacked on this mission. It never occurred to me." (These remarks were contradicted by Bucher's discussions, in Hawaii as well as Yokosuka, about what help he could expect if the North Koreans went after him.) He also admitted he hadn't fully grasped the dangerously large volume of secret publications aboard, which he estimated would have taken up to 12 hours to burn.

Bucher testified that the "one thing I wanted to accomplish without fail" was the destruction of classified materials. But Newsome, who soon began to sound more like a prosecutor than a neutral fact finder, used that assertion to lure the captain into a trap.

"Commander, certainly one of the most classified elements on this ship were the personnel, was that right?"

"Yes, sir."

"So that in making the decision to surrender your ship, and surrender the personnel, you also made the calculated decision that you would also surrender the additional classified element of your ship, the personnel?"

"Yes, sir. That is correct."

Newsome had all he needed. On the afternoon of Bucher's third day in the witness chair, the court counsel abruptly cut off his testimony and Bowen adjourned the court. Shortly afterward, the admirals reconvened and Newsome officially warned Bucher he was suspected of violating Article 0730, a Navy regulation that forbade a commander from letting a foreign power search his vessel or remove any of his sailors "so long as he has the power to resist." Anything Bucher said from that point on, Newsome added, could be used against him "in a subsequent trial."

The warning stunned the courtroom audience. It was the first time the Navy had so forcefully raised the possibility of court-martialing Bucher. Harvey was caught completely off guard. He was furious at Keys for not advising him this might happen. But the suave corporate lawyer showed no outward sign of distress. He got to his feet, declared, "[O]bviously we anticipated the situation that we find ourselves in at the present moment," and asked his client one question:

"At the time the North Koreans set foot on your ship, did you any longer have the power to resist?"

"No, I did not," the captain responded firmly.

That issue—whether or not Bucher had the ability to fight back at the time he surrendered—was the central legal conundrum facing the court of inquiry. On its surface, "the power to resist" seemed like a convenient rhetorical yardstick for measuring whether a skipper had lived up to the don't-give-up-the-ship ethos. As far as many naval officers were concerned, if Bucher could have fought back but didn't, he was a coward, a disgrace to the service. But could the power to resist be quantified? If so, how? By number of fighting men? By number and type of weapons? By degree of courage and determination?

At the moment Bucher gave it up, his ship was generally intact and most of his men unscathed. But he was encircled by six enemy gunboats—capable of shelling and torpedoing his vessel from a safe distance until it came apart at the seams—while two MiG fighters menaced from above. What were his chances, realistically, of breaking out of that tactical vise? If the answer was slim to none, did he have a moral responsibility to surrender without wasting his subordinates' lives? Few would argue that a man with a derringer surrounded by six men with shotguns possesses, in any practical sense, the power to resist. Was there a point at which resistance regardless of the odds becomes an act not of bravery but of recklessness, even idiocy?

Bucher wanted to keep testifying in spite of the Article 0730 notification. On day four of the court, he recounted his mind-bending first hours in North Korean custody. He described the fat general angrily calling him and his officers spies and saying they'd all be shot at sundown. He testified about demanding to be executed so his crew could go free. He told of Super C screaming at him to sign the pretyped "confession" and, when he refused, ordering one of his goons to count down from two minutes and blow his brains out.

As he related that part of his story, the captain stood before an easel holding a large diagram of the Barn. He used a pointer to indicate the room in which the pistol was cocked near his ear.

"It occurred to me that being shot at this point would be a blessing," he told the admirals. "So I knelt there on the floor and during the entire two minutes . . ."

He stopped, unable to continue. He sipped water from a yellow goblet. His hands trembled and his shoulders drooped. A microphone around his neck carried the sound of his labored breathing throughout the auditorium.

"Would the commander like a recess at this time?" Newsome asked solicitously.

"No, sir." Bucher tried to go on but faltered again after a few words. "Sir, I would rather get this over with right now, if I may." He wiped his forehead. Fighting for control, he stood there for long moments before trying to speak again.

"Sir, during the entire two minutes that I was laying on the floor I repeated over"—another long pause, more sips—"merely the phrase 'I love you, Rose,' and thereby kept my mind off what was going to happen."

Sitting in the front row of the packed courtroom, his wife cupped a hand over her eyes.

The captain began quietly to weep. A Navy doctor, assigned to observe him for signs of excessive stress, rushed to his side. The admirals turned away.

Gathering himself, Bucher went on: "At the end of the two minutes the colonel asked me again, was I ready to sign, and I told him, 'I will not sign.' So the officer who was standing in front of me was ordered to move aside, presumably so that when I was shot, the bullet, if it would have passed through my head, would not have also hit this officer."

But the North Koreans were only playing him with an unloaded gun. When he refused to sign a second time, Super C ordered him beaten into unconsciousness.

The skipper testified that as the night wore on, the communists kept upping the pressure, trying to break him quickly. He told of being taken to the dungeon and blacking out after seeing the gruesomely tortured stranger. He related the threat to shoot his men one by one, and his desperate attempt to drown himself in his water pail.

When he finished his horrific testimony, the admirals seemed not to know how to react.

"What was your objective in not eating?" Bergner asked awkwardly.

White posed a question whose answer seemed painfully obvious: "Why didn't you sleep?"

Observing from the audience, Trevor Armbrister, a reporter for the *Saturday Evening Post*, felt a rush of conflicting emotions. "An aura of unreality pervaded the courtroom that afternoon," he later wrote. "Listening to such questions, one felt, at first, a surge of anger and then, surprisingly, deep compassion for these five honorable, lonely men who had entered the shadows of Bucher's despair and had not known what to say."

Mercifully, Bowen called a recess. Newsome put a gentle hand on Bucher's shoulder. Harvey led the skipper out a side door and, as light rain fell, walked slowly around an athletic track with him.

Though as potential witnesses Bucher's men were barred from the hearing room, they soon found out about the Article 0730 warning. At one point on day four, Tim Harris darted through the front door and slipped the captain a handwritten note from the entire crew.

"Dear Captain," it read, "We've made it this far together and we'll finish it together." The note was signed, "Bucher's Bastards." The men's plainspoken expression of loyalty and solidarity with their beleaguered leader was written up on the front page of the next day's *Washington Post.*

His sailors weren't alone in their feelings for Bucher. His heartrending story resonated with many Americans. And as his grueling first days in the witness chair ended, an extraordinary public outcry arose.

Newspaper commentators, members of Congress, and average citizens vociferously criticized the Navy for supposedly trying to blame the captain for errors made by higher echelons. Bucher was called a martyr and compared to Alfred Dreyfus, the French Army captain falsely accused of treason, and Lord Jim, the British seaman who redeems himself after a moment of weakness in Joseph Conrad's eponymous novel. A *Boston Globe* cartoonist depicted Bucher lashed as if crucified to the prow of an antiquated sailing ship, labeled "U.S. Navy." Many Americans rejected the Navy's repeated assertions that the court of inquiry was necessary and routine, regarding it instead as an exercise in inquisitorial cruelty. Max Lerner, a New York columnist, characterized the Coronado courtroom as "Bucher's Gethsemane," a reference to the garden near Jerusalem where Jesus was betrayed.

Bucher hadn't deliberately tried to turn the tables on the Navy. While his dramatic testimony had been confrontational to some extent, he still considered himself a loyal officer and hoped one day to command another ship. But the captain strongly believed the Navy bore much of the responsibility for what had happened to the *Pueblo*, and many of his fellow citizens felt the same way. "The Navy Is on Trial, Not Bucher," proclaimed the *Christian Science Monitor*, calling Newsome's admonition of a possible court-martial an "appalling demonstration of inhumanity, ill-timing, pompousness, and poor taste." The *Los Angeles Times* echoed that sentiment with a cartoon showing three admirals, bug-eyed with fear, standing in a wobbly rowboat while trying to fend off a floating mine labeled, "Bucher's '*Pueblo*' Testimony." U.S. Representative Richard Ottinger, a New York Democrat, sent a letter to President Nixon's newly appointed defense secretary, Melvin Laird, charging that the Navy's Article 0730 warning was "a clear attempt to intimidate the *Pueblo*'s commander into withholding the full story of the intelligence ship's failure."

More than 3,000 letters poured in to the Navy's public information bureau at the Pentagon, many of them blisteringly critical. Other letters and telegrams went directly to Admiral Bowen, including one addressed to "Bowen and his pimps." Bag after bag of angry mail arrived in Coronado:

"How can you crucify that man, when all he did was try to save the lives of his crew?"

"It's an obvious frame-up."

"Hang the higher-ups, not Bucher."

Admiral Moorer found himself sucked into the cyclone of scorn, too. A man from Glen Rock, New Jersey, telephoned the chief of naval operations' office and vented that "the Navy stinks . . . and Admiral Moorer is a horse's ass and the Navy was torturing Commander Bucher and the man should not be made to suffer for the Navy's mistakes." In a letter to John Chafee, Nixon's new secretary of the Navy, the mayor of New Haven, Connecticut, described the court of inquiry as "cruelty of the most intolerable kind."

"I protest for thousands of Americans," Richard C. Lee went on. "I would hope that this harassment would be halted before it goes any further and kills this man. He has gone through too much to be treated in this fashion by navy brass who apparently have no concern except to fix the blame, somehow, on someone other than the establishment." Another Connecticut resident asked the Navy's chief chaplain in a telegram, "What do they expect of a wounded man with no guns responsible for 82 men? Who is the admiral responsible for this fiasco?"

At the same time, Bucher and his wife received hundreds of supportive letters and wires.

"We are with you, Commander," someone scrawled on a pro-Bucher editorial torn from their local newspaper. Declared another fan: "You're a hero to us here in Boston, Cmdr. Bucher, and you always will be." The six members of an Orange, Connecticut, family—Russell, Nancy, Roger, Marjorie, Eileen, and Bonnie Ziontz—opened their letter with a hearty, "Welcome home!"

"We want you to know," the Ziontzes continued, "that we consider you a very brave and humane man. The kind our country needs a lot more of. To do what you have done—save the lives of all your captured crew and endured the hell you have been through—you must be made of pure hero material."

As hundreds of U.S. soldiers perished every month in the futile meat grinder of Vietnam, many Americans applauded Bucher's decision to avoid a potential massacre of his crew. Fighting back against the North Korean gunboats, wrote *Miami Herald* columnist Jack Kofoed, "made as much sense as a circus midget trying to slug Cassius Clay," the champion heavyweight boxer who had renamed himself Muhammad Ali. "To die for no reason except to uphold 0730 of Naval regulations," Kofoed added, "makes no sense." Orien Fifer, a *Phoenix Gazette* columnist, concurred: "If he'd resisted with his two machineguns or pistols, he and his entire crew would have been blown to Kingdom Come."

Through no fault of his own, Bucher was fast becoming America's newest antiestablishment hero, a freethinking rebel who refused to sacrifice his men merely to uphold outmoded martial values. That portrayal, of course, was an almost comical distortion of the skipper's true self: an aggressive, salute-snapping career officer thoroughly steeped in Navy convention. Fans in the media nevertheless embraced him as a paragon of conscience and humaneness, a new kind of military leader who strove to preserve life rather than destroy it. "In a time when ancient rituals of 'national honor' could trigger a nuclear Sarajevo, Bucher chose indignity over insanity, humanity over heroics," wrote *New York Post* columnist James Wechsler, referring to the Serbian capital where World War I metastasized. "In a better time he may become a legend."

Even as the Navy put Bucher on notice that he might face a court-martial, critics sternly advised the Navy to back off. "If those five admirals think the people will sit still for making Cmdr. Lloyd Bucher the scapegoat for what went wrong in the *Pueblo* fiasco, they're in for a big surprise," declared U.S. Representative Samuel Stratton, a New York Democrat and member of the House Armed Services Committee. Added columnist Fifer, "I would estimate that 90 percent of the people in all walks of life would say the Navy deserves a torpedo-sized hole in its image if it puts the commander on trial. What gives anyway?"

The message wasn't lost on the new men in the White House. "Bucher comes off a decent and honorable officer," wrote two aides to President Nixon in a January 23 summary of TV coverage of the court of inquiry. "All three networks reflected sympathetically on Bucher and adversely on Navy." In a margin the president, himself a Navy veteran, penned a note to Defense Secretary Laird: "Don't let Navy make a fool of itself."

In the undeclared public-relations war with the Navy, Bucher had won a decisive victory after only a few days. Harvey's strategy was working; the press was firmly on the captain's side. So was much of the public. "In essence, Harvey was running the court," Captain William J. Crowe Jr., an aide to Admiral Moorer who'd drafted the Breeches Buoy repatriation plan, would later write. Crowe exaggerated the lawyer's influence, but his point was well-taken. Harvey, added Crowe, "was winning decisions and positioning Bucher in just the right public spotlight."

The press loves an underdog, and reporters gravitated naturally to the skipper in his high-stakes battle with the Navy. "He was standing up against authority—everybody likes that," remarked Bernard Weinraub, who covered the court of inquiry for *The New York Times*. "Also, you felt for him. He was very emotional. He was gutsy. And he was putting himself on the line. You never disliked him . . . but you realized that he was a flawed person."

While many newsmen liked and sympathized with the *Pueblo* commander, their attitude toward the admirals of the court was very different. Some reporters became so disdainful of Bowen and his colleagues that they refused to stand when "those punks" entered the courtroom. Others displayed no disrespect, but sensed an undercurrent of social caste running through the inquiry.

George C. Wilson, a *Washington Post* military reporter, wrote that the hearings pitted "five glittering admirals" against a "mustang," Navy slang for an officer who has risen from enlisted ranks. Weinraub discerned the same dynamic at work. "There was this distinct class difference," he said. "The admirals were Annapolis [products] . . . and they were treating [Bucher] like an enlisted man of a low grade. They weren't treating him like an officer. It was a tone. They weren't treating him as one of their own. It was just evident."

The furious backlash against the Navy became a serious concern to Admiral Moorer. On January 25, he tried to calm the roiling waters with a speech before the American Bar Foundation in Chicago.

Saying he was "deeply troubled" that the Article 0730 notice had been "widely misinterpreted," Moorer reminded his audience of attorneys that Bucher was not on trial in Coronado. "The Navy is searching for facts, not scapegoats," the admiral insisted. He asked the public "to be patient, not to prejudge, and to have full trust and confidence that the [court of inquiry is] being carried out by experienced men of great integrity who have only the welfare of our country at heart."

At an impromptu news conference two days later, Harvey and Bucher sought to reinforce Moorer's assurances of evenhandedness. Harvey told reporters that Bucher felt his treatment by the admirals so far had been "eminently fair." His remarks were purely voluntary, but many people assumed the brass had pressured him. As a result, noted a chagrined Ed Murphy, "the public thronged to [Bucher] in even greater numbers."

Bowen closed the courtroom doors to the press and public following Bucher's lengthy testimony, ostensibly to discuss sensitive matters of national security. Public relations may have been on his mind as well, because over the next four days a parade of high-ranking officers discussed key Navy assumptions about the spy-ship mission that turned out to be horribly flawed.

Among those taking the witness chair were Admiral Frank L. Johnson, the onetime commander of U.S. naval forces in Japan, and several of his staff officers.

The 61-year-old Johnson was a highly decorated war veteran. As skipper of the destroyer USS *Purdy* during the Okinawa invasion, he'd won not one but two Navy Crosses. One was for his extraordinary actions in saving the USS *Mullany*, another destroyer abandoned after kamikazes badly damaged it. As fires burned near the *Mullany*'s magazine, which could have exploded at any moment, Johnson brought his vessel alongside. His crew managed to extinguish the blazes, allowing the *Mullany* to be salvaged. But many years had passed since Johnson's days as a dashing wartime destroyerman. Now, with his white hair, chubby cheeks, and bland manner, the admiral came across more like a cautious small-town banker.

Johnson and his former subordinates described how they'd developed a schedule of nine missions over six months in 1968 for the *Pueblo* and the *Banner* and then bucked it up the chain of command for approval. Johnson's area of operations was enormous; his surveillance ships could be sent anywhere from the East China Sea to the Bering Sea. But winter storms put the northernmost destinations out of bounds, and the State Department had made it clear, ever since the *Banner* had been harassed off China, that it wanted the snooping shifted to other locales.

That left the Sea of Japan and the Tsushima Strait. Soviet warships patrolled continuously in the strait, and COMNAVFORJAPAN had photographed most of them already. So Johnson's staff decided to focus on North Korean coastal defenses and naval activity in the Sea of Japan. A young lieutenant who worked for Johnson did much of the initial mission planning.

The Navy didn't have exclusive control over the AGERs, however. It had to share their "tasking" with the National Security Agency, and that generated some tension. The NSA wanted to collect information on "national" intelligence targets, while the Navy was more interested in data of tactical value to its fleet commanders. It was agreed that the two agencies would divide up the nine AGER missions, with the Navy designing the first one, to be carried out by the *Pueblo*.

After Johnson signed off on the schedule, he forwarded it to the Honolulu headquarters of Admiral Hyland, commander of the Pacific Fleet. Hyland approved and sent it a few miles down the road to his boss, Admiral Ulysses S. Grant Sharp, commander of all U.S. forces in the Pacific. From there it went to Washington, where the Joint Chiefs of Staff green-lighted it.

The AGER proposal also had to pass muster by the 303 Committee, a little-known arm of President Johnson's National Security Council. The 303 Committee—so named because its civilian members formerly met in room 303 of the Executive Office Building—had the final say on all eavesdropping expeditions by American aircraft, surface ships, and submarines around the globe. At the time the *Pueblo* mission was approved, the group's members were national security adviser Walt Rostow, CIA Director Richard Helms, Under Secretary of State Nicholas Katzenbach, and Deputy Secretary of Defense Paul Nitze.

As part of the planning process, each echelon in the chain of command made its own estimate of risk for a specific AGER mission. Admiral Johnson testified that he considered several factors, including the degree of political tension between the United States and the target country, and whether that nation had tried to interfere with American ferrets in the past. None of the *Banner*'s 16 previous missions in the Sea of Japan and East China Sea had drawn a risk assessment higher than "minimal," even though several trips proved to be somewhat dangerous. Chinese patrol boats or armed trawlers had trained their guns on the *Banner* on four separate occasions, and a Soviet intelligence collector, the *Anemometer*, had once "shouldered"—deliberately bumped—the U.S. ship.

Johnson's command was less worried about North Korea. The *Banner* had lain off Wonsan on two trips—for 11 hours in 1966 and 36 hours in 1967—without the North Koreans trying to bully it away. Johnson thought the *Pueblo* was likely to encounter the same evident forbearance. Like most Navy officers involved in the AGER program, he believed with almost mystical conviction in the abstract protections of international maritime law and custom. No U.S. Navy vessel had been attacked on the high seas in more than a century and a half, and he saw no reason to think that time-tested precedent wouldn't hold true for the *Pueblo* as well.

"If you were a betting man," he told the court members, "I would suggest that a [bookmaker] would give you such fantastic odds that such an incident would not happen . . . that maybe somebody even as rich as Howard Hughes could not pay off on it."

But North Korea's track record was more complex than Johnson made it out to be. While Kim Il Sung's commanders hadn't reacted to the *Banner*, they could be very sensitive about foreign ships and aircraft approaching their shores, and that touchiness had led to violence in the past. In 1965, two North Korean jets opened fire on an American RB-47 reconnaissance aircraft flying in international airspace about 50 miles east of Wonsan. Though severely damaged, the plane was able to limp back to its base in Japan. In 1967, communist coastal batteries had sunk a South Korean patrol boat, *PCE 56*.

Ever since the Korean War, Pyongyang had been broadcasting strident warnings to South Korean fishing boats and "U.S. imperialist aggressors" to stay clear of its claimed waters, especially near the demilitarized zone. Southern fishermen, however, frequently motored across the seaward extension of the demarcation line in search of bigger catches. North Korea's navy sometimes responded by seizing or shooting up interlopers. Just two weeks before the *Pueblo* was captured, a pair of North Korean patrol craft slashed into a fleet of 200 fishing boats, ramming and sinking one and forcing three others to go north. In 1967, North Korea had kidnapped a total of 353 southern fishermen aboard 50 boats.

The communists often accused the United States of using southern fishing fleets as a screen to infiltrate surveillance ships into their waters. Indeed, on January 11, 1968—two days before the *Pueblo* first arrived off Wonsan—Pyongyang radio had promised to take "determined countermeasures" against American "spy boats." Johnson's headquarters had been aware of these threats, but wrote them off as routine communist saber rattling of the sort that had been occurring since the early 1950s.

There were other red flags as well, but Johnson—along with everyone else in the chain of command—paid little heed. The number of clashes between allied and North Korean troops in the DMZ was rising dramatically; the U.N. Command reported a more than tenfold increase in border incidents from 1966 to 1967. The biggest warning flag of all was the Blue House raid, which took place less than 36 hours before the *Pueblo* reached Wonsan for the fateful second time. Prudence should have dictated that the spy ship be given plenty of protection or pulled back until things cooled down. Instead, the Navy allowed it to cruise ever closer to disaster, clinging to the hollow assurance of a "minimal" risk rating.

Though Johnson had operational responsibility for all *Pueblo* and *Banner* missions, he had no combat ships or planes to send to their rescue in an emergency. His only option was to request long-distance help from the Seventh Fleet or the Fifth Air Force. But Johnson's closed-door testimony revealed the illusory nature of that "on-call" arrangement.

The admiral had pushed the on-call button on two occasions when Chinese boats confronted the *Banner*, summoning distant U.S. destroyers to drive off the harassers. In both instances the *Banner* slipped away to safety long before the destroyers arrived. The reality was that the Seventh Fleet could help only if its vessels were close enough—which they usually weren't, since most fleet assets were tied up by the Vietnam War.

Air Force assistance was no less problematic. Johnson was so convinced the *Pueblo*'s maiden mission would be a cakewalk that he hadn't asked for jet fighters to be placed on "strip alert," meaning they'd be armed and fueled and their pilots set to go if trouble developed. And even if he had requested an alert, American warplanes were anything but readily available in the Far East.

The handful of U.S. jets in South Korea—those closest to the *Pueblo* when it came under attack—were reserved for use in a nuclear war against the Soviets. And General Bonesteel, the commander of all allied forces in the south, wasn't inclined to permit the South Korean air force to go to the aid of an American ship for fear of touching off an uncontrollable clash with the communists. Indeed, Bonesteel wouldn't let the South Koreans help their *own* naval vessels, as he demonstrated when he refused to allow their jets to break up the attack on *PCE 56*.

Nor was it a simple matter to launch U.S. aircraft based in Japan. A secret status-of-forces agreement required American commanders to "consult" with the Japanese government before mounting combat strikes from Japanese soil—a time-consuming and politically uncertain process. Asked whether jets from the *Enterprise* even could have refueled in Japan en route to helping the spy ship, Johnson replied that doing so without Japanese concurrence would have created "a diplomatic uproar."

Bowen quickly grasped the main implication of Johnson's testimony.

"Would you say then that essentially there was no means to protect this ship if she got into a situation such as she did?" he asked.

Johnson answered bluntly: "There was no means and no procedures established to prevent the *Pueblo* or the *Banner* from being seized on the high seas."

Johnson also made it clear he didn't approve of installing machine guns on AGERs. Such light weapons, he told the court, didn't significantly improve the boats' capacity to defend themselves against anything bigger than an armed junk. Johnson was especially concerned about what might happen if an American snooper with guns manned confronted a communist ship in the same mode. He acknowledged telling Bucher before he left Japan to keep his guns covered so as not to "provoke" hostile vessels. But the admiral insisted he'd placed no restrictions on using the .50-calibers if the *Pueblo*'s survival was threatened. He added that Bucher was specifically instructed to bring the machine guns into action against would-be boarders.

Although Johnson had been ordered to verify the *Pueblo*'s ability to get rid of its classified material, his inspection was cursory at best. He testified that he personally examined the ship's topside incinerator, but not its fire axes, sledgehammers, and ditch bags. Neither he nor his staff tested how much time might be needed to burn, shred, or pulverize all of the electronic equipment and publications. He also noted that multiple commands, including his, had delivered secret documents to the ship willy-nilly, with no single authority limiting the overall volume.

The bottom line on Johnson's testimony was devastating: The little spy tub, jammed with sensitive documents and electronics, had been sent into dangerous waters with no air or sea cover and virtually no means to defend itself. Navy planners assumed that a solitary intelligence ship hard by the shores of one of the world's most heavily armed and unpredictable regimes would be safe at a time when that regime could reasonably be expected to be on high military alert, deeply fearful of possible retaliation for the Blue House raid. And no one in the Navy had given much thought to destroying a mountain of top secret material in a hurry.

The level of complacency and heedlessness was appalling.

To Bowen's credit, Johnson was recalled to the witness chair two days later to repeat in open court much of what he'd said behind closed doors. Johnson then dug himself an even deeper hole by testifying that he hadn't raised the mission's risk assessment even though he knew of North Korea's attacks on the South Korean patrol boat and the American RB-47, as well as the sharp rise in violence along the DMZ.

The admirals of the court hadn't been pleased with Johnson's secret testimony, and they sharpened their criticism in the public session.

"So, when we add it up, then, we really had a contingency plan to use [rescue] forces which do not exist," said White, summing up the on-call arrangement.

Bowen piled on Johnson with "ill-concealed disgust." "You have referred frequently to the on-call concept, which I believe is somewhat misleading, since nothing was on-call," said the court president.

Johnson's cheeks reddened as the humiliation sank in. A few feet away sat Bucher, biting his lip. Johnson's testimony had been embarrassing, but it was the truth.

CHAPTER 17

EVERYONE'S WORST NIGHTMARE

Having all but torn off the hapless Admiral Johnson's epaulets, Bowen and his cohorts turned their attention to the *Pueblo*'s crew. And the court members soon discovered that the seamen's preparations to defend their ship and its top secret contents left much to be desired.

Since no one had ever told them what their true mission was, some sailors actually believed the cover story that the spy ship was conducting scientific research. Few if any had given much thought to the possibility of being attacked. "This never really entered my mind," testified Law. Said Schumacher, "I honestly believed the worst that might happen to us would be perhaps a dent or some scratched paint."

Bob Chicca, the Marine translator, testified that he'd informed his superiors at the Kamiseya communication station that his Korean language skills were very rusty, but he was ordered aboard the spy ship anyway. When he reported for duty, the SOD hut commander, Steve Harris, never asked about his proficiency. Harris testified that he realized after leaving Japan the ship wasn't carrying enough ditch bags to dispose of all the classified documents, but he didn't warn Bucher. Jim Kell, Harris's number two, admitted in closed session that he didn't even know where the bags were stored.

Crewmen gave contradictory testimony about the ship's destruction bill, a vital directive specifying which CT was responsible for getting rid of what secret material in an emergency. The bill was supposed to have been posted in the SOD hut for all to read. (The *Banner*'s four-page bill was so detailed that it prescribed a certain sequence for destroying individual documents stashed in shipboard safes.)

Harris said the *Pueblo*'s bill had been properly displayed, but at least four CTs testified that they never saw it. Bucher said he signed the bill somewhere "between Pearl Harbor and Yokosuka," but didn't know whether it was ever posted. CT Donald Peppard testified that he typed the document and put it up at Harris's request a few hours before the attack. Kell insisted it wasn't posted until 15 minutes after sub chaser No. 35 began circling the *Pueblo*.

One of the few moments of levity in the courtroom came when Captain John Williams, an icily correct officer from Naval Security Group headquarters in Washington, took the witness seat. As Williams poured himself a glass of water, accidentally spilling some on his pants, Miles Harvey asked whether he had any experience in submarines. "I do now," he said in chagrin, as guffaws erupted in the audience. But Williams went on to contradict Steve Harris on a key provision of the destruction bill. Harris had believed that classified material couldn't be dumped in less than one hundred fathoms—six hundred feet—of water. Williams, however, said there were no specific depth requirements and it was the captain's call whether the water was deep enough to make salvage difficult or impossible.

Questions also were raised about Harris's leadership during the attack. In closed-door testimony, three CTs said the lieutenant gave them no guidance as they struggled to annihilate classified materials. (Indeed, it was Kell, not Harris, who'd given the order to initiate emergency destruction.) Two CTs said they never saw Harris laying waste to anything himself. Asked who was in charge of the overall elimination effort, one CT replied, "I don't know. It seemed like no one was, actually."

The CTs described scenes of confusion and chaos in the SOD hut, where about ten men had tried to destroy whatever they could. After only fifteen minutes or so of burning documents, someone ordered them to stop. But no one seemed to know who issued that command or why, and the North Koreans didn't board the ship for at least another hour.

Kell said CTs tore up documents by hand after the order to cease burning. But the chief petty officer also admitted he didn't know the ship carried two shredders and that the source of the stop-burning command might have been him, although he couldn't remember for sure. He testified that he hadn't spoken to Harris at any point during the destruction work. Asked to evaluate Harris as an officer, Kell responded, "Nothing outstanding, nothing bad, sir. Just average." (Kell later asked to revise his testimony, saying he hadn't known the lieutenant long enough to form a meaningful opinion.)

The spook chief took a beating from the media, too. *Time* magazine ran a sneering profile, calling Harris the "villain" of the *Pueblo* story and deriding his physical appearance. "Pale and skinny, he is the antithesis of the recruiting-poster image of a Navy officer," the article said. "His face has a furtive cast to it, his chin is narrow, and when he takes his glasses off, he has a wide-eyed, rabbity look." The magazine even used Harris's looks to imply he was a coward, saying he "gives the appearance of being a timorous man, one who might well lose control under fire."

In his own testimony, Harris acknowledged the destruction process had been "painfully slow" and "considerably less than efficient." Part of the problem, he said, was the sheer mass of material. "We went out to sea with what I consider an immense amount of junk on board, which was of no use to us whatsoever," he told the admirals in one closed session. Harris believed up to nine hours would've been needed to get rid of everything—far more time than he and his men had. The reason some CTs didn't see him in the SOD hut, he explained, was because he'd gone aft to burn papers from a safe outside the captain's cabin.

Yet Harris insisted that despite the obstacles, he and his men had been very successful, reducing classified documents to "confetti" and electronic equipment "virtually to powder." By the time the CTs were dragged off the ship, he said, none of their instruments was usable.

But had the manic destruction effort really been so thorough?

At the time of the sailors' joyous homecoming, Americans were led to believe the intelligence material that fell into enemy hands wasn't worth losing much sleep over. "Some of the equipment North Korea seized and some of the documents aboard were secret, but so far as we know they were not regarded as any great loss," NBC News anchor David Brinkley told his viewers on December 23, 1968. Such a conclusion wasn't surprising, given how the Johnson administration downplayed the severity of the loss. A National Security Agency official told *Newsweek* magazine, for example, that the crew had done "an excellent job" of getting rid of "nearly all the secret gear and papers."

The truth, however, was that government officials had received a number of confidential reports during 1968 indicating that the communists had gotten their hands on a good deal of valuable paraphernalia.

In May, naval intelligence informed the Joint Chiefs of Staff that the seizure had caused "the probable compromise of a considerable amount of U.S. classified material." The CIA reported in August that North Korean divers had "recovered the gear tossed overboard by the *Pueblo* crew prior to capture." At a closed-door congressional hearing in September, CIA chief Richard Helms said the North Koreans "have been dismantling the antennas and by now have probably completed their exploitation of the ship's equipment."

Ever since the crewmen were debriefed in San Diego, NSA and Navy intelligence specialists had been working to put together a detailed picture of how the *Pueblo*'s capture affected national security. At Naval Security Group headquarters in Washington, about 75 analysts sifted through the sailors' voluminous statements in an effort to figure out exactly what codes, code machines, and other material had been compromised.

By late February 1969, the first of several top secret damage assessments was finished. The cumulative conclusion: The actual intelligence loss was far graver than originally believed. (These reports remained secret for many years. At the author's request, the National Security Agency declassified all or parts of three damage assessments. The declassification took more than seven years.)

Of the 539 classified documents and pieces of equipment aboard the ship, up to 80 percent had been compromised, the National Security Agency reported in one assessment. Only 5 percent of the electronic gear had been "destroyed beyond repair or usefulness." As an NSA historian later wrote of the

Pueblo seizure: "It was everyone's worst nightmare, surpassing in damage anything that had ever happened to the cryptologic community."

NSA experts characterized the crew's stabs at destruction as "highly disorganized" and carried out "in almost total confusion." Steve Harris was faulted for not drilling his men beforehand. The lieutenant had told his debriefers he was "pretty confused" and "a little bit scared" as his men struggled to tear apart their gear. But instead of directly supervising and helping them, Harris spent his time anxiously overseeing radio transmissions to Kamiseya.

"I didn't pay any attention to the emergency destruction," he said in a startling admission quoted in one damage estimate. "I would like to have, but I felt that there should be no unauthorized information transmitted because this was being watched very closely by high-ranking people."

Bucher, too, came in for criticism. Although the captain had tried in Bremerton and Japan to obtain a rapid-destruction system, an NSA report blamed him for not following through and "ensuring that his men knew what to do in an emergency."

NSA investigators conducted an experiment to test the effectiveness of the CTs' adrenaline-fueled attempts to demolish code machines. Hefting sledgehammers and fire axes, they bashed similar encryptors with the same force and frequency described by the CTs. The metal-walled devices were remarkably strong. Tightly wired circuit boards, the NSA team discovered, were largely immune to pounding. Even after being smashed apart, some components could be reassembled in as little as 30 minutes.

Moreover, the CTs had neglected to get rid of spare parts. The NSA reported it was "highly probable" that communist electronics experts, using spares and scarcely damaged circuit boards, were able to assemble working copies of at least three of the four types of code machines aboard the spy ship. North Korea's acquisition of the devices was "a major intelligence coup without parallel in modern history," according to an NSA study written in 1995.

The CTs had tried to destroy as many operating and maintenance manuals for the code machines as they could. To an enemy specialist, such handbooks could provide important insights into how the encryptors worked, if not partial blueprints for them. But wastebasket fires had consumed few of the manuals and the two slow shredders weren't even used. Sailors tossed some books into ditch bags and mattress covers, intending to jettison them when the fleeing ship reached the 100-fathom curve. Since it never did, an "undetermined number" of manuals were captured intact, the NSA reported. (One bag was heaved overboard, but the North Koreans retrieved it.) Publications stored outside the SOD hut had been "largely overlooked in the frantic destruction efforts."

The damage evaluators had a hard time figuring out precisely what fell into communist clutches because the sailors failed to keep track of what they did burn or tear up. For example, no one was sure what had become of the "key cards"—IBM-style punch cards used to program code machines each day. NSA investigators established that of 36 key card booklets aboard, only two had been fully destroyed. The rest, they were forced to assume, had been compromised.

It was clear the loss included all code cards for the months of November and December 1967, which the crew should've burned within a few weeks of using but hadn't. These were particularly valuable, because an enemy that had intercepted and taped encrypted messages during those two months could use the captured cards to unscramble them. While the North Koreans probably didn't have the technical savvy to pull two months of worldwide U.S. radio traffic from the airwaves, the Soviets did.

Indeed, Moscow seemed to have benefited nicely from the spy-boat debacle. According to NSA sources, the North Koreans arranged for Soviet technicians to examine materials from the *Pueblo* "immediately after the seizure." A group of electronic-surveillance specialists from Soviet military intelligence inspected the vessel, and some electronic components were taken back to the USSR for closer study.

American intelligence officials also were concerned about the possible compromise of about 8,000 messages radioed to Bucher's ship as part of the Navy's fleet-wide operational intelligence broadcasts in the Western Pacific. Transmitted from Guam, these so-called GOPI broadcasts carried detailed reports of U.S. air and ground combat in Vietnam, along with results of American intelligence-gathering efforts throughout Southeast Asia.

Many GOPI messages pertained to electronic monitoring of North Vietnamese air defenses. U.S. eavesdroppers knew, for instance, when enemy jets and antiaircraft missiles were being readied for launch—and swiftly relayed warnings to approaching American bombers to switch on electronic jammers or take evasive action. If the North Vietnamese learned the extent of this penetration, they'd tighten their communications security. That would not only impede U.S. intelligence-collection operations, but it would put aircrews at greater risk.

As of early 1969, however, no heightened security measures had been detected. Nor had the North Vietnamese gained any noticeable advantage in the war as a result of the *Pueblo* incident. But the "great danger," as the NSA's director, General Marshall Carter, told Congress behind closed doors on March 10, was that the Soviets and Chinese, alerted to the sophistication of American surveillance, would find ways to better protect their secret transmissions.

NSA investigators discovered, too, that captive CTs had been an unexpectedly bountiful source of information for the North Koreans. CTs had been interrogated as many as 20 times in sessions lasting as long as several hours. While some of them dismissed the North Koreans as "stupid" and unable to grasp technical subtleties, others admitted the communists were highly knowledgeable about electronics and "could not be deceived."

The North Koreans had quickly zeroed in on CTs who operated code machines, questioning them extensively. Under the pressure of beatings and fear of beatings, the NSA noted, some young technicians proved to be "more talkative and cooperative than originally imagined."

One SOD hut denizen was intensively interrogated about the KW-7, an encryptor widely used by U.S. and NATO forces. The man initially tried to give up as little information as possible, drawing a diagram of the device that lacked detail and contained errors. But the North Korean grilling him pointed out the "mistakes" and demanded a better sketch. When the CT tried to claim he had a poor memory, the communist pulled out a captured maintenance manual and continued to ask on-point questions. The American eventually gave up a full explanation of how and when KW-7 code changes were made; a second CT described the machine's complicated operating procedures.

The North Koreans sweated another CT about the KWR-37, which deciphered "fleet broadcast" messages sent to all Navy warships. As the American tried to explain its workings, an impatient interrogator interrupted to say he already understood the basics; he wanted more advanced data. The CT ended up diagramming the machine's electronic brain, or "logic"—circuits that used algorithms to generate random codes—in great detail. The communists used tidbits extracted from one CT to confirm those coughed up by another, and they didn't hesitate to clobber anyone they felt wasn't giving correct information. The NSA believed the CTs' explanations saved the North Koreans many months of arduous trial and error to figure out how the code machines worked.

The North Koreans also showed great interest in CTs who intercepted and translated Soviet naval traffic. A North Korean colonel fluent in Russian supervised the questioning of these men. While being debriefed in San Diego, one CT admitted that due to his "terrified condition," he'd fingered "Russian linguists, intercept operators, and cryptographic personnel" among his shipmates. NSA analysts believed that some CTs, out of shame or fear of possible punishment, hadn't told their debriefers the whole truth about what classified information they gave up, making an accurate accounting more difficult.

Yet even with the enormous loss from the *Pueblo*, U.S. intelligence and military officials didn't lose faith in the fundamental security of their clandestine communications. For although the North Koreans and Russians might now possess American code machines, they still lacked the codes needed to program them. The ciphers were changed daily as a security precaution. In fact, the NSA designed its encryptors on the assumption that a foreign power would someday steal them or capture them on a battlefield. Thousands of KW-7s, for instance, were then in use by American troops, combat ships, and air squadrons around the globe, not to mention by the armed services of a dozen or more allied nations. By 1969, at least four KW-7s were thought to have been acquired by hostile forces. But as long as the enemy didn't have the corresponding codes, encrypted messages were believed to be safe.

Unfortunately, what no one in the cryptographic community knew at the time was that a U.S. Navy radio specialist named John Anthony Walker Jr. recently had begun selling codes to the Soviets. Walker went to the Soviet embassy in Washington, D.C., in late 1967 and offered to sell a broad range of secret documents related to Navy operations. The Soviets quickly accepted. In early January 1968, shortly before the *Pueblo* hijack, Walker left a package of KW-7 codes for the Russians at a dead drop in the Virginia countryside.

Walker went on to assemble the most devastatingly effective spy ring in American history, recruiting his son, a communication technician aboard an aircraft carrier; his brother, a retired Navy officer; and his best friend, a fellow Navy radioman, to help him steal sensitive Navy documents.

The ring remained active for an extraordinary 17 years, until Walker's ex-wife tipped the FBI and he was arrested in 1985. The damage he inflicted on national security was "incalculable," according to Robert Hunter, who led the FBI team that finally cornered Walker at a Virginia motel. Thanks to the traitorous radioman, the Russians knew the tactics American aircraft carriers would use in wartime and how to sabotage U.S. spy satellites. He sold the locations of underwater listening devices used to track Soviet subs and information on GI movements in South Vietnam. At the time he was caught, Walker was, incredibly, trying to hand the Soviets authentication codes needed to launch U.S. nuclear missiles.

Since so many American military units relied on the KW-7, the NSA decided not to replace it despite the *Pueblo* seizure. Instead, the NSA modified the machine, thinking the changes plus daily code switches would suffice to keep it secure. When the NSA distributed a new technical manual outlining the modifications, Walker sold a copy to the Soviets.

Walker had a diabolically fruitful partnership with his closest friend, Jerry Whitworth, a mild-mannered chief warrant officer over whom Walker seemed to have Svengali-like influence. Whitworth photographed technical manuals for the KW-7 and KWR-37 and turned the film over to Walker for delivery to the Soviets. Whitworth also took pictures of code lists and technical publications for five other cryptographic systems, providing the Russians with schematics for almost every U.S. code device. "For more than 17 years, Walker enabled your enemies to read your most sensitive military secrets. We knew everything!" Boris Solomatin, chief of the KGB station in Washington, once exulted.

Cunning and ruthlessly manipulative, Walker also recruited his son Michael and older brother Arthur. (He tried but failed to lure a daughter serving in the Army Signal Corps, where she, too, had access to secret ciphers.) He met his KGB handlers in Vienna, Austria, nearly a dozen times over the years, passing on rolls of microfilm. On one trip he brought along his mother, taking her on a side visit to Italy. On the flight home he persuaded her to wear a money belt containing $24,000 in KGB payoff cash. Unaware of its contents, Walker's mother wore the belt as she passed through U.S. Customs, where she could've been arrested for violating federal currency-control laws.

Working in communication centers aboard two nuclear subs, and later at Atlantic Fleet headquarters in Norfolk, Virginia, Walker stole all manner of valuable material. "A Kmart store has better security than the U.S. Navy," he later crowed. Facing a routine FBI background check, he forged his own security clearance so agents wouldn't talk to his hard-drinking wife, Barbara, who knew how he was earning up to $4,000 a month over his $725 salary as a Navy warrant officer. (He subsequently urged the KGB to "eliminate" her.) The Soviets code-named Walker "Agent No. 1" and made him an honorary admiral.

After Walker was arrested, a high-ranking KGB defector, Vitaly Yurchenko, told his American debriefers that with Walker's help, his country had deciphered more than one million U.S. military messages. So much information flowed in that a special building had to be constructed in Moscow to house all the analysts needed to process it, he said. "It was the greatest case in KGB history," asserted Yurchenko. "If there had been a war, we would have won it."

In custody Walker vehemently denied that his dealings with the Soviets set the *Pueblo* capture in motion, and no persuasive evidence has yet surfaced to contradict him. Nearly 30 years after he was exposed, it remains unclear whether the Soviets were able to synthesize the material Walker delivered with whatever they may have gleaned from the *Pueblo*. But that could be a moot question, since the Walker ring itself supplied the two critical tools—

codes and code machine schematics—that may have enabled Moscow to crack America's elaborate military encryption system.

The court hearings were taking a visible toll on Bucher. He didn't look well as he sat at his table, swallowing pills and peering at documents through a magnifying glass. He took frequent drinks of water and occasionally trembled. To one journalist he looked like "a desperate, cornered man." When he testified, his manner was a little too forceful, a bit irritable, as if he sensed the admirals didn't believe him. A Navy doctor called a three-day recess to give him a rest.

Away from the pressures of the courtroom, the captain became his old self. The hunch went out of his shoulders. He was animated and laughed easily. When his crew played flag football against another Navy team, Bucher gave his guys noisy encouragement from the sidelines. In the evenings, he sometimes joined Schumacher, Lacy, and Tim Harris for drinks at the Mexican Village, a loud, lively restaurant and bar on Coronado that attracted crowds of fliers from the North Island Naval Air Station and young women who didn't mind meeting them.

The rest of the crew spent little time in court, though they were on 24-hour call as witnesses. Other than keeping their barracks clean, they had no duties. "Like sheep awaiting the slaughter, we innocent peons do nothing but wait our turn in court," Peter Langenberg wrote to his mother, sarcastically referring to the hearings as "the Great *Pueblo* War Criminal Trial."

To pass the time, the men golfed, went sightseeing, hit bars, and chased women. San Diego businesses were still showering them with freebies; the sailors ate on the cuff everywhere from pizza joints to the best restaurants in town. A group of them glided over San Diego in a Goodyear blimp; others took day trips to Disneyland or Tijuana.

Charlie Law got married. His wedding was a rowdy blowout held at the Beach Boy, a local bar where he'd met his future wife, a secretary for a landscaping firm, just five weeks earlier. "We were in there yahooin' and drinkin' and raisin' hell, and I saw this good-lookin' bitch come in one day and went 'wow'!" Law recollected. He and his bride arrived for the ceremony in a chauffeured limousine, courtesy of a local cab company owner. A popular blues musician, C. C. Jones, entertained the guests, whose ranks included Bucher,

Rose, and about 30 *Pueblo* sailors, as camera crews from three local TV stations recorded the nuptials. Law made his entrance from the men's room, and he and his new wife later sliced a towering wedding cake. The quartermaster downed so many Velvet Hammers that he couldn't remember whether his best man made a toast or how he got back to his hotel room. He woke up the next morning on the floor.

Harry Iredale spent his time "just partying." His usual coconspirator was Friar Tuck, with whom he was living in bachelor officer quarters at the naval air station. Their routine was to get up for morning roll call, jump back in the sack for a few more hours of shut-eye, and rise again for lunch. At night they'd hit some nightclubs, have a late dinner, and stay out until closing time. Sometimes they hung out at a topless dance joint called the Body Shop.

For some crewmen, however, the good times weren't enough to blot out the self-doubt and remorse.

The men suspected they'd violated at least some tenets of the Spartan-tough Code of Conduct, which prohibited any cooperation with the enemy. Yet the sailors had confessed to trumped-up espionage charges, written propaganda letters home, taken part in anti-U.S. press conferences, and, on Bucher's order, signed a group apology to North Korea. When they arrived at Miramar, some of them expected to be marched straight to the brig.

(They needn't have worried. Though some of the acts it prohibited could be prosecuted under military law, the code itself had no legal force: It was intended only as a guide. In an official opinion issued a few days after the crew returned home, Navy lawyers said breaking the code carried no criminal penalties.)

Still, some crewmen harbored doubts about their performance during the attack and in prison, and the court of inquiry exacerbated those feelings. The sailors followed the hearings in local newspapers, and it was obvious that the admirals were none too impressed with the way the crew had dealt with the North Korean gunboats. Snide comments were sometimes aimed their way in bars. At night, sleeping uneasily in their barracks, some sailors let out screams that petrified a young Navy sentry on patrol outside. "I don't know if they thought I was a North Korean guard or what," he related, "but I had no trouble staying awake during my watch." With their haggard appearances and thousand-yard stares, the sentry said, the crewmen reminded him of dazed prisoners he'd seen in old newsreels of newly liberated Nazi concentration camps.

Visiting their quarters, Bucher saw some enlisted men "drinking themselves into oblivion" and taking drugs. "Some guys were feeling just really bad about the whole thing," he recalled. "It was getting to them, there's no doubt about it."

Despite the court testimony about their mistakes and shortcomings, the skipper and his men still enjoyed strong public support. In a Harris Poll published in early February, 83 percent of the respondents said the crew "showed real courage in the face of physical and mental torture." (Only 2 percent disagreed.) Perhaps more significantly, 65 percent of those polled disagreed with the statement that "the honor and integrity of the U.S. are more important than the lives of any servicemen."

By early March the court of inquiry had dragged on for six weeks. Now it wasn't just Bucher showing the strain; everyone was. Harvey was putting in 14- and 15-hour days; Newsome was working even longer. When the testimony ended each afternoon, the court counsel often had to interview the next day's witnesses until midnight or one a.m. Newsome would get home at two and be back in his office at six a.m. The burden was heavy on the admirals, too. Not only did they have to sit through each day's dense, often emotionally draining proceedings, but they were also responsible for running their regular commands. It wasn't uncommon to see one of them on the night ferry back to San Diego, sitting in his car with the overhead light on, reading a sheaf of official papers. "It was damn near a 24-hour-a-day job," recalled Grimm.

The stress triggered occasional bouts of binge drinking. One Friday night after a difficult week, Harvey headed for the Mexican Village to unwind. Later that evening, Bowen walked in with a retinue of younger officers and all of them proceeded to get smashed. Around midnight, with the place jumping, someone asked Harvey to take the incapacitated admiral home.

"I literally picked him up and took him back to his quarters at the amphibious base and put him in bed," Harvey said. "I thought the media would have a great time if they saw me loading this body in the car and it happened to be the president of the court."

Harvey also remembered bailing a senior Navy public-relations officer out of jail after his arrest in nearby Escondido for drunk driving. Problems developed in the lawyer's own family as well. With their father away from home so much, the only time his three daughters got to see him was on TV news. Harvey's middle girl, then fourteen, began experimenting with LSD. "I had to go pick her up one time at the city hoosegow and bail her out," he said.

Jim Keys, Bucher's Navy lawyer, spent many court sessions in an alcohol haze, according to Newsome.

"He was asleep so much that the [court] members would get upset and they'd say to me, 'Isn't there something you can do?'" Newsome said.

But he and the admirals had little latitude to interfere with the composition of Bucher's legal team, and Harvey felt stuck with Keys. Trying to replace him at this late date would be too difficult, Harvey believed; the Navy had offered up Keys only after rejecting Harvey's top three or four choices for a cocounsel. And if Keys was suddenly yanked from the courtroom, and the real reason leaked out, wouldn't much of the press and public jump to the conclusion that the Navy had tried to sabotage Bucher by saddling him with a boozehound for a lawyer? From Bowen's perspective, that would be a very bad outcome.

Bucher got a much-needed break from the exigencies of the court when he took his family sailing on March 8. It was a glorious, late-winter Saturday, sunny and brisk, and the captain had rented a 29-foot boat for the occasion. Bundled in a thick sweater, Rose lost her balance as she stepped aboard, falling into her smiling husband's arms. With his two sons working the jib sheets, Bucher took a helm for the first time since the *Pueblo*'s capture and steered out into the swells of San Diego Bay.

Scudding past the submarine base, he spotted one of his old boats, the *Ronquil*, and was granted permission to come on board. "Welcome home, Captain," said a swabbie standing atop the long dark hull. Bucher later chewed the fat with a few cronies at the Ballast Tank, the submariners' club where his raiding party had nabbed the voluptuous nude.

If Bucher's stock was declining in the eyes of the admirals, it stayed high with journalists. Indeed, the captain was joined on his sailing holiday by the *Washington Post*'s George C. Wilson, who wrote a sentimental feature that ran on the paper's front page the next day. The story, accompanied by no fewer than five photographs of Bucher and his family, highlighted the skipper's desire to go back to sea when the court finally adjourned.

On the same day the *Post* article appeared, Bucher was the subject of an admiring cover story in *Parade* magazine, inserted in numerous Sunday newspapers across the United States. He was reported to have received "many lucrative offers for books, articles, TV, radio, and club appearances." A Hollywood agent who seemed eager for his business suggested the captain could earn as much as $2 million for the film rights to his story. "Bucher's biography," the agent told *Parade*, "has all the ingredients for a great motion picture: adventure, humor, tragedy, love, danger, and, best of all, a happy ending." With the captain's good looks and brains, the agent said, he'd be a strong candidate to play himself in the movie.

Wary of being accused of muzzling the crewmen, the Navy decided that all 82 of them should take the witness chair and tell their stories. Most of the time Bowen and his colleagues listened attentively and respectfully. But sometimes their irritation and disapproval showed.

When a bosun's mate described reflexively catching and securing a line thrown from a PT boat so communist soldiers could board the *Pueblo*, Admiral White asked him, almost beseechingly, "But didn't you have the urge to throw it back?"

Nor was White pleased when a CT testified that he hadn't fired a Thompson submachine gun out a porthole at the boarders because he wasn't tall enough.

"Well," said the admiral, his cheeks coloring with suppressed anger, "I think I could have tippy-toed up and peeked out of there with that gun and mowed them down."

More sailors broke down as they related their horrific prison experiences. But their chokes and tears and hot shame were met with coolness from the admirals. When Monroe Goldman, the veteran engineman, wept as he described being forced to strip naked and crawl around a cell as guards kicked him, the court members studied the walls and ceiling. Tim Harris got little more reaction when, telling of his futile attempt to kill himself and his "extreme hatred" of the communists, he suddenly covered his face and cried so hard his body shook.

Newsome asked the seamen-witnesses what they thought of Bucher as a leader. Many sailors regarded the man who refused to sacrifice their lives at sea and shepherded them safely through the ordeal of prison as something approaching a demigod. They praised him to the heavens.

"He is the greatest skipper I have ever served under," declared Harry Lewis, the cook.

"I would consider it a privilege and an honor if I could serve with him again," stated engineman William Scarborough.

"He's just a great man; I just admire him tremendously," said Law.

The only lukewarm assessment came from Murphy. "Under the circumstances, he did his job as well as any commanding officer could be expected to do," the XO said.

Policarpo Garcia, a Filipino storekeeper, told of serving as the crew's barber at the Country Club. Each time Bucher sat down for a shave or haircut, Garcia saw the awful amount of weight he was losing, the way his skin was tightening on his skull. Garcia also had witnessed the soldier kick Bucher down the stairs. Yet for all the ill treatment and degradation he suffered, the captain always had an encouraging word for Garcia.

"He tell me every time, 'Don't lose your faith; the United States will do something,'" Garcia said to the admirals. "The only thing I can say about the commanding officer is, without the commanding officer, I don't think I could make it."

The crew clearly understood what it had cost their skipper to protect them from harm, both on the ship and in prison.

Larry Strickland, a fireman, cried unabashedly as he testified. "I feel that we owe quite a bit to the captain and all the things that he did to get us through. He was willing to sacrifice himself and his career to see to it that we made it through the whole ordeal."

The testimonials moved Bucher deeply. He tried to hold back his emotions, but the words of Ramon Rosales, the young seaman from Texas, finally sent him over the edge.

Asked whether the communists had tried to undermine his faith in American values, Rosales talked about a room daddy who insisted in his lectures that God didn't exist.

"I stood up and told him that there was a God," said Rosales, smiling gently at the court members. "And he says, 'Do you see Him?' and I told him that I saw Him every day. I told him that I saw Him in the flowers and the trees and everything around, that God was alive. He got kinda shook up."

Hearing this, Bucher bowed his head. In prison, when Rosales developed a high fever, the captain had tried to get him medical care, but Glorious General just laughed at him.

Admiral Pratt then asked Rosales what most helped him get through captivity. The seaman flashed his serene smile again. "Well, I think the help was my faith in God and my country and the decisions of my commanding officer, sir."

Bucher put his head down on his table and wept convulsively. Harvey grasped his right arm and whispered to him, but the skipper continued to shed tears for several minutes. Harvey finally led him out of the courtroom.

"It's the cumulative effect that's gotten to him," the attorney later told reporters. "He's listening to all these kids and it's bringing back too many memories."

Bucher had tried to run from the gunboats while simultaneously destroying his classified materials. But he hadn't fired back or resorted to other forms of resistance, like disabling his engines or scuttling the *Pueblo*. The admirals wanted to hear his reasons.

The ship's gunner's mate, Ken Wadley, testified that he and his gun crews had been fully prepared to man the .50-caliber machine guns and do battle with the communists. Law and other witnesses, however, said that would have been suicidal; no one could have survived the withering enemy fire as they ran across open decks to unshielded machine guns and struggled to pry off half-frozen tarpaulins, pop open ammunition boxes, and thread in ammo belts.

"We of course had 83 personnel who could have gone up [to the guns]," Murphy told the admirals, "but I feel that they had 83 or more bullets that could have easily caused fatal injuries to each one of us."

Bucher also could have tried to break away from the North Koreans by leaving his shell-shattered bridge and steering from the relative safety of the engine room. He hadn't done that either, and the admirals asked several witnesses whether it would have been feasible to guide the ship from belowdecks.

Murphy said yes. "We not only could have, but we had many times when we actually had to go through this drill for actual practical purposes. We found that the ship responded fairly well." Monroe Goldman, the chief engineman, agreed, saying the *Pueblo* could have been conned from below even with its entire bridge shot away.

Testifying all day on March 11, Bucher laid out the rationale behind his actions. He looked nervous and physically weak but he spoke evenly, and sometimes with heat.

The captain made it clear that he hadn't had much to work with. The Navy turned down his repeated requests for a rapid destruction system, leaving his men, while under fire, with nothing but hand tools, two inadequate shredders, and a small incinerator to get rid of hundreds of pounds of paper and numerous steel-encased electronic devices. And he had only two unprotected and unreliable machine guns to hold off six enemy combat vessels and two jet fighters.

So he did the best he could with what he had. His first impulse was to flee back out to sea, buying as much time as possible for his men to eliminate classified materials. Although the Navy had no plan to rescue him, a radio operator in Japan held out the prospect of salvation—LAST I GOT WAS AIR FORCE GOING HELP YOU—if only Bucher could fend off the North Koreans long enough. The skipper considered scuttling but decided not to, he told the admirals, because he didn't want to be wallowing dead in the water, with no power or maneuverability, if American warplanes suddenly showed up. For the same reason, he decided not to disable his engines. (At another point in his testimony, he conceded he hadn't crippled his twin diesels as the communists rushed aboard because that "just didn't occur to me.")

Bucher lit off his engines and tried to outrun the boarding party on the PT boat. He stopped when he realized that sub chaser No. 35, hammering the *Pueblo* with cannon fire, probably would blow it out of the water if he kept going. He was surrounded and massively outgunned. The slow-moving spy boat had no way to defend against shelling by the sub chaser and, potentially, torpedoes from the PTs and rockets from the MiGs. If his men returned fire, the captain figured, the communists would only ratchet up the intensity of their attack. And as more sailors were killed or wounded, he'd have less manpower to get rid of his secret materials.

Bucher said he hadn't tried to repel the boarders for a couple of reasons. For one, he thought they might have mistaken the *Pueblo* for a South Korean vessel and would depart once they realized their error. (This explanation was undercut by the fact that Bucher had hoisted the American flag before the attack began.) He also felt that shooting at the boarding party would violate Admiral Johnson's order not to provoke the North Koreans. He was convinced his ship would be demolished if he tried to fight off the communists jumping aboard.

In defending his decision to surrender, Bucher made the ludicrous claim that he hadn't really surrendered. "I preferred to feel that, in that I never struck my colors, I never did actually surrender the ship," he testified. "We were seized. The Koreans hauled our colors down when we got into port." Yet surrender was precisely what he'd done: He relinquished control of his ship to an enemy under compulsion.

But several of Bucher's officers—including Murphy—backed the captain's contention that, at the time he halted the *Pueblo*, he lacked the power to hold off the communists any longer. Although the XO wasn't consulted about the decision to give up, he said he would've done the same thing had he been in command.

"They were going to board us and we had no way of stopping them," Murphy testified.

The admirals seemed uncomfortable with Bucher's explanations. At one point, Pratt asked another witness, Captain Pete Block, one of Bucher's former submarine bosses, whether he thought the *Pueblo* skipper was "abnormally concerned" about the men under him. Block denied that. But the question—with its implication that Bucher lacked the stomach for the blood sacrifices command at sea sometimes demanded—hung in the air.

Pratt's exchange with Block also underscored that the *Pueblo* court of inquiry was more than just a dramatic clash between the Navy and one of its officers: It also represented a collision of deeply held and sometimes contradictory values. While Bucher's impulse to save his men's lives had been a humane one, the Navy was in the fundamentally inhumane business of spending men's lives to help win America's wars. It was a fighting organization, first and foremost, and loss of life was the inevitable by-product of combat.

As sensible as Bucher's surrender might appear, the Navy couldn't condone its commanders giving up without a fight. The annals of U.S. military history were replete with examples of men fighting hard in the face of lousy odds. The opening words of the Code of Conduct embodied that proud, gutsy tradition: "I am an American fighting man. I serve in the forces which guard my country and our way of life. I am prepared to give my life in their defense." If surrendering to preserve sailors' lives became the norm, the Navy couldn't do its job; it would fall to pieces.

Officers who failed to fight therefore had to be punished. That was especially true where such failure placed a boatload of top secret code machines and documents in enemy hands. So far, there were no indications the North Koreans or Soviets were intercepting U.S. military messages with the help of material purloined from the *Pueblo*. But who knew what they'd do with it in the future? What price would the United States one day pay?

However, these were the views of America's tarnished warrior class. Ordinary citizens didn't necessarily see things the same way. Indeed, many apparently didn't mind that the captain gave up without firing a shot. When pollsters asked whether Bucher "did a disservice to this country in trying to save his own life," 68 percent of the respondents said no; only 9 percent said yes.

The captain certainly hadn't drenched himself in martial glory during the attack. With the North Koreans blasting him from all sides and a trusted subordinate yelling at him to stop the ship, he froze. But he recovered quickly and did what he could to give his men more time to destroy their secret paraphernalia. He went on to provide superior leadership in prison under dire circumstances.

The truth was that many everyday Americans understood and empathized with Bucher's decision to spare the lives of his men. They felt he'd been placed in a no-win position. The ultimate logic of Article 0730 was that commanders must fight on until all of their men were wounded or dead, and then die themselves. Naval regulations offered no guidance on the point at which a captain could honorably give up. Was it after he'd lost 25 percent of his men? Fifty percent? Ninety percent? The public found such calculations distasteful, if not crazy. What could Bucher have accomplished by fighting back, except to get more of his people killed? No rescuers came, and his chances of breaking free of the North Koreans on his own were poor. Men who'd done their best to resist the enemy deserved to live.

Americans embraced Bucher for the reason that he hadn't thrown away lives for the sake of some quixotic notion of military honor or tradition. The more thoughtful ones understood, too, that regardless of the court's outcome, Bucher for the rest of his days was condemned to mentally replay the events of that ferocious afternoon in the Sea of Japan, doubting and second-guessing himself, wondering whether he'd been tough enough, searching his innermost self for some mortifying streak of yellow.

And that was a harsher and more crippling sentence than anything the Navy could dish out.

On the evening before the last day of court, the admirals, lower-ranking officers, journalists, and some crewmen got together at a local hotel for a party marking the occasion. Bucher stepped up to Admiral Bowen at one point and nervously shook his hand. "He still loves the Navy so much," one of the captain's shipmates observed to a newsman as they watched the scene. "But the Navy sure doesn't love him."

The next day, March 13, Bucher made his last remarks to the court, stating "unequivocally" that he hadn't had the power to resist. Harvey followed with an eloquent closing argument.

The lawyer began by noting the inherent cruelty of a court of inquiry. Fresh from a disaster at sea, traumatized men were pummeled with probing, sometimes humiliating questions. Their actions and behavior under extreme duress were mercilessly dissected in public; they were forced to relive experiences that forever would haunt them. But if the inquiry at times resembled an inquisition, it also served vital purposes: Lessons must be learned from the misadventure, and military leaders must be held accountable for their decisions.

"On the sea there is a tradition older even than the traditions of our nation, and wiser in its trust than our 'new morality,'" said Harvey. "It is the tradition that with authority goes responsibility, and with both goes accountability."

Bucher had accounted for his actions, but for what should he be held responsible? As Navy experts testified behind closed doors, the *Pueblo* incident had led to extensive modifications of the two surviving AGERs. They now carried far less classified material, and sensitive documents were printed on paper that dissolved in water. Explosives capable of scuttling the vessels in 15 minutes had been installed, along with thermite for rapidly melting electronics. Itemizing these improvements, Harvey portrayed Bucher as "either a prophet or a man ahead of his time."

"He knew what was needed on an AGER. The [new] destruct gear has been described by the experts with great pride; Commander Bucher would have settled for three cans of TNT. We've seen a demonstration of water-soluble paper; Commander Bucher would have settled for a reduced publications allowance. . . . The .50-caliber guns have been removed; Commander Bucher thought they were inappropriate when put aboard."

Harvey emphasized that the *Pueblo* wasn't a combat ship and couldn't possibly have fought a pitched battle at sea. He went over the Navy's faulty assumptions about North Korean reactions, the absence of air or surface support, the admonition to Bucher not to "start a war out there."

"As the North Koreans closed his ship, Commander Bucher did everything in accordance with his previous instructions. He identified his nationality, maintained his right to be where he was, attempted to depart the area in a dignified manner, maintained course and speed when the Koreans tried to divert him, kept his guns covered, did not appear aggressive or provocative, and made the required reports to his command. When the North Koreans became serious about seizing or sinking the *Pueblo*, the commanding officer had no credible power to resist."

A commander, Harvey pointed out, is the only person in a position to know whether his men have the capacity to fight back. "It has been stated, although not in this courtroom, that it might have appeared better for the Navy if 15 or 20 [sailors] had been killed, rather than only one," he said. "This type of irresponsible statement only accentuates the horrible decision that the commanding officer was confronted with in determining how long he could hold out."

Whether the captain could have done things differently, his attorney continued, would always be a matter of speculation. But he insisted there was "not one shred of evidence" that Bucher had had the physical power to prevent the seizure. The skipper's performance, he added, "was, under the circumstances, outstanding."

Bucher also shone in the way he led his men in prison, Harvey told the admirals. "The chain of command was maintained, leadership was exerted, escape plans formulated and evaluated," he said. "Every method was used to resist the North Koreans. None accepted favor or parole; each kept faith with the others."

Harvey revisited the crew's successes in discrediting communist propaganda and urged that every man injured in prison be awarded the Purple Heart. The sailors signed propaganda statements and participated in enemy press conferences only under the "grossest . . . coercion and duress imaginable," he said, adding pointedly that "such coercion and duress must have far exceeded that imposed upon our nation to obtain the false confession that resulted in the repatriation of the crew."

Rather than condemn Bucher, the admirals should applaud him, Harvey concluded. "We have been privileged to see a man, a real man, who has been tried by his enemies, been found to be successful, who was returned to his homeland and accounted fully for his actions. His greatest reward would be to be returned to full duty and to occupy his rightful position in a normal Navy career pattern."

The lawyer sat back down. The admirals remained expressionless, offering no clue to their reactions.

Newsome declined to present a final summation. Bowen asked if the court members had any questions and, hearing none, closed the proceedings. After eight grueling weeks, Bucher's latest ordeal was over.

The captain stepped outside into the rain to face the TV cameras. Rose stood beside him, holding his hand. "I love the Navy," said Bucher. "I want to stay in, if they'll let me." He would await the admirals' verdict, he said, with "considerable apprehension."

CHAPTER 18

BALM OF MERCY

With the court hearings behind him, Bucher went into seclusion. Newspeople were driving him nuts, calling his house so often that he wanted to disconnect the phone. One of Miles Harvey's law partners offered the use of his vacation home in Borrego Springs, a small resort town in the desert northeast of San Diego, and the captain gathered up his wife and sons and went there for a week to recuperate. The family also spent several days in Acapulco.

Though Bucher was on edge about his legal prospects, Harvey remained optimistic. One hundred and four witnesses had appeared before the court, generating almost 3,400 pages of testimony. The admirals now had to review that voluminous record and draft their official findings and recommendations. Their report was expected to reach Admiral Hyland's desk in the next few weeks.

While the court members pondered his fate, the captain embarked on a series of trips, basking in unbridled public adulation wherever he went.

His first stop was the small Colorado city of Pueblo, his ship's namesake town, where more than 500 enthusiastic citizens flocked to the airport to meet him and his family.

The Buchers rode into town in a convertible escorted by a police car and

Shriners on motorcycles. At City Hall the captain was surrounded by news reporters as a high school band played. The mayor hailed Bucher as "one who has demonstrated outstanding valor" and presented him with a plaque. The following evening, he and Rose were the guests of honor at the annual chamber of commerce dinner, packed with a sellout crowd of 600.

Then there was a triumphant visit to Boys Town, which the skipper described as "the most glorious day of my life."

As he stepped off his plane in Omaha on April 23, 1969, more than 900 boys—the juvenile refuge's entire population—greeted him with cheers, whistles, and a sea of waving American flags. The Boys Town band belted out "Anchors Aweigh." Some of the kids got so excited they vaulted a fence bordering the airfield to pound Bucher's back, shake his hand, and tell him he was their hero. The beaming commander—tanned and 40 pounds heavier since leaving North Korea—ambled along the fence, pumping scores of outstretched hands. His voice cracked as he tried to thank every boy individually.

"I'm glad to be home," he said, over and over. "This is my home."

The youngsters rushed back to Boys Town on buses while the Buchers wound through the streets of Omaha in a 30-car motorcade. At the gates of Boys Town, the kids gave Bucher a second exuberant welcome, complete with fireworks and wailing sirens. Engulfed by fresh-faced admirers, Bucher and his family sauntered down a flag-bedecked street with Monsignor Nicholas Wegner, Boys Town's director. That night, Bucher ate with the youths, who gave him one standing ovation as he entered the dining hall, another when he rose to speak, and yet another when he finished.

The captain was the featured guest the next evening at a dinner that filled Boys Town's cavernous Field House with 1,200 people. Among them were Nebraska's governor, both U.S. senators, and a congressman who'd recently introduced a bill to award Bucher the Medal of Honor. With an enormous "Welcome Home, Pete" banner hanging from a wall, the event was a giant lovefest for the skipper.

"You're a courageous man, a man of character, a man of duty," Father Wegner told Bucher in front of the adoring audience. "You'll always be a hero in the eyes of these young men, and in fact in the eyes of the entire nation.

You deserve every honor this nation can confer upon you." Governor Norbert Tiemann described the captain as "one of the most gallant men this country has ever produced." Senator Roman Hruska, noting that the Navy hadn't yet reached a decision on Bucher's future, declared, "As far as the American public is concerned, the verdict has already been returned. It is a verdict of commendation and tribute and honor for a courageous and honorable sailor and his intrepid shipmates." Hruska later called the dinner "one of the most moving events of my life."

A few days later Bucher went to Chicago, sightseeing along the Loop and dining at the famed Pump Room, where the house orchestra serenaded him and Rose as other diners stood and applauded.

At the Sherman House the following night, the captain delivered a corker of a speech to more than 800 Notre Dame alumni, assailing communists, campus radicals, and "vipers in our midst spreading anti-Americanism."

Bucher wasn't supposed to comment publicly on the *Pueblo* court of inquiry before the Navy made a final ruling, but he couldn't resist a few pokes at the military. "I feel the United States let me and my men down. I personally had assurances from high officials in the U.S. Navy that, were we attacked by enemy forces, planes would come to our aid. No planes came." (In fact, Bucher had been told the opposite in Hawaii: that if attacked, he probably was on his own.)

The skipper also faulted the Nixon administration for not retaliating against North Korea over its latest atrocity: the April 14, 1969, shoot-down of an unarmed American reconnaissance plane over the Sea of Japan. Thirty-one U.S. airmen perished.

The downed craft was an EC-121, the military designation for a converted Lockheed Constellation, an aging, propeller-driven airliner packed with six tons of electronic listening gear. It had been flying about 90 miles southeast of the port of Chongjin when two MiG fighters pounced on it.

For President Nixon, the incident must have seemed like an awful case of déjà vu. During his campaign for the White House, he'd criticized Lyndon Johnson for allowing the *Pueblo* to be captured by "a fourth-rate military power like North Korea" and pledged that if elected, he would "not let this happen again." Now, as commander in chief, Nixon faced a nearly identical crisis, except with a graver loss of American lives and fewer options for responding.

The United States immediately suspended all eavesdropping flights near North Korea, and American search planes and ships rushed to the area where the EC-121 went down. The Soviets, evidently caught off guard again by their bellicose allies in Pyongyang, dispatched two destroyers to help look for survivors. A U.S. plane reported seeing dim lights on the water at night, but only three bodies of EC-121 fliers were recovered.

The situation was even more complicated than the *Pueblo*, because National Security Agency intercepts indicated the attack might have been a mistake, the product of miscommunication between one of the MiG pilots and his ground controller. Nonetheless, North Korea quickly claimed responsibility for the outrage, boasting that its jets had "scored the brilliant battle success of shooting [the EC-121] down with a single shot."

Cries for vengeance weren't long in coming. On Capitol Hill, U.S. Representative L. Mendel Rivers, a conservative South Carolina Democrat who chaired the House Armed Services Committee, proclaimed, "There can be only one answer for America—retaliation, retaliation, retaliation!" Nixon's national security adviser, Henry Kissinger, pressed for a U.S. counterstrike on North Korean air bases. Nixon himself viewed the shoot-down as an act of cold-blooded mass murder; among the responses he considered were a military attack on North Korea and seizure of one of the Dutch-built fish-processing ships, then sailing near Cape Town, South Africa, on its way to North Korea.

However, the new Republican president, like his Democratic predecessor, had his hands full with Vietnam. Nixon's secretaries of defense and state both counseled against hitting North Korea. As with the *Pueblo*, any major retaliation ran the risk of triggering an invasion of South Korea by Kim Il Sung's forces and escalation to general war. William Porter, the ever-prudent ambassador to Seoul, warned that President Park might interpret a U.S. airstrike as permission to invade the North. And aside from hawks like Rivers, Americans seemed to have little stomach for another hard-to-exit military adventure in Asia.

For three days, Nixon took no action as his advisers debated what to do.

There was nothing to negotiate the return of, since the EC-121 crew was dead and the plane destroyed. (The United States lodged a complaint at Panmunjom, but North Korea's representative responded with only an insolent question: "Whom does the aircraft belong to?") Since a United Nations protest coupled with no other action might make him look weak, the president eventually chose a face-saving middle course: He announced that American snooper flights would resume, but with armed protection. Like LBJ, he also sent an armada into the Sea of Japan: 40 ships, including the *Enterprise*, three other aircraft carriers, three cruisers, 22 destroyers, five submarines, and the famed battleship *New Jersey*.

But, again like Johnson, Nixon ordered no punitive actions and the mammoth naval squadron ultimately withdrew. For the second time in little more than a year, Kim Il Sung had sucker punched Uncle Sam and walked away unscathed. A secret CIA report speculated that the North Koreans' decision to open fire on the EC-121 probably was "strongly influenced" by Washington's failure to avenge the *Pueblo*.

Even before the court of inquiry ended, Congress had concluded that the admirals weren't adequately addressing some of the biggest questions arising from the *Pueblo* affair. Who'd given final approval for the mission? Why was no concerted effort made to rescue the ship?

The House Armed Services Committee impaneled a special subcommittee to investigate. Its chairman was U.S. Representative Otis Pike, an irreverent, often cantankerous Democrat who represented much of Long Island, New York. Pike had flown 120 missions as a Marine dive-bomber and night-fighter pilot in the Pacific during World War II and was well versed on naval matters. Elected to Congress in 1960, he was known for a sharp tongue that he enjoyed honing on recalcitrant bureaucrats—including those of the military variety—who appeared before him. He once killed a bill to give flight pay to deskbound admirals by demonstrating, on the House floor, how difficult it was to fly a desk.

Pike inaugurated his hearings on March 4, 1969, calling a who's who of top Pentagon and intelligence officials to testify. Unlike Admiral Bowen, with his limited power to call high-ranking witnesses, Pike could subpoena virtually anyone in the government. Among those he called were General Earle Wheeler, chairman of the Joint Chiefs of Staff; Admiral Moorer, the chief of naval operations; Admiral Sharp, former commander of all U.S. forces in the Pacific; and Rear Admiral Horace Epes, the cautious air commander of the *Enterprise*. The parade of witnesses also included the heads of the CIA, National Security Agency, and Defense Intelligence Agency.

One of the first orders of business was to find out who at the top had green-lighted the *Pueblo* mission.

As the court of inquiry already had learned, Admiral Johnson's staff in Japan concocted the voyage. Sharp's command in Honolulu subsequently endorsed it. On December 23, 1967, Sharp's headquarters forwarded the mission proposal to the Joint Chiefs in Washington. The JCS staff then bundled the *Pueblo* with more than 800 other sea- and airborne reconnaissance sorties planned around the globe during the month of January 1968, and delivered the whole package to the chiefs for review.

But, with the holidays looming, the January reconnaissance "book" wasn't handled in the usual fashion.

The Joint Chiefs normally met three times a week in "the tank," a large Pentagon conference room dominated by a heavy walnut table surrounded by 16 red leather chairs. Before the meetings, each chief was supposed to be briefed about every item on the agenda, including recon schedules. If the chiefs had a question about a specific mission, they could ask for a detailed explanation from Air Force General Ralph Steakley, head of the Joint Reconnaissance Center, an arm of the JCS that coordinated all U.S. eavesdropping forays worldwide.

When the January book came up for review, however, only two of the five principals were in town. General Wheeler was away on leave. General Harold K. Johnson, the Army chief, was in Southeast Asia. And the Marine commandant, General Wallace Greene Jr., was retiring in a few days.

So instead, the chiefs' operating deputies approved the recon schedule on December 29—the same day they received it. Members of the civilian 303 Committee—who had the final say on all intelligence-collection missions—also received and endorsed the book on December 29.

Under questioning by Pike's subcommittee, Wheeler characterized the

JCS review as "comprehensive and deliberate." Moorer seconded that, saying military and civilian experts put in "literally hundreds of man-hours" preparing and evaluating reconnaissance schedules before they ever reached the JCS level. But Pike didn't buy the brass's assessment, saying their review of the big January book appeared "necessarily cursory and perfunctory." And Moorer conceded that he didn't recall "having delved into" the *Pueblo* mission specifically.

On the day the Washington agencies gave the go-ahead, the National Security Agency transmitted an unusual piece of advice to the Joint Chiefs. In deliberately bland language, the NSA challenged the lackadaisical assumption that the *Pueblo*'s first mission would be nearly risk-free.

"The North Korean Air Force has been extremely sensitive to peripheral reconnaissance flights in this area since early 1965," the message said. It continued:

> The North Korean Navy reacts to any Republic of Korea [South Korean] Navy vessel or Republic of Korea fishing vessel near the North Korean coast line. (This was emphasized on January 19, 1967, when a Republic of Korea Navy vessel was sunk by coast artillery.)
>
> Internationally recognized boundaries as they relate to airborne activities are generally not honored by North Korea on the East Coast of Korea. But there is no . . . evidence of provocative harassment activities by North Korean vessels beyond 12 nautical miles from the coast.
>
> The above is provided to aid in evaluating the requirement for ship protective measures and is not intended to reflect adversely on CINCPACFLT deployment proposal.

In other words, while the North Koreans hadn't yet molested any foreign ships outside their territorial waters, the Joint Chiefs might want to rethink not protecting the *Pueblo* in light of the recent attacks on the RB-47 plane and the South Korean patrol boat *PCE 56*. An earlier draft of the message was much less diplomatic, according to former NSA officer Eugene Sheck, who helped plan AGER missions. He didn't testify before the Pike subcommittee but made his remarks years later in an oral history. According to Sheck, a junior NSA staffer who regarded the *Pueblo* mission as too dangerous wrote the original warning:

"This young fellow had a message drafted that said, 'Boy, you people have got to be complete blithering idiots to put that ship off North Korea, because all kinds of bad things are going to happen. Therefore, cancel [the mission].'"

Since the *Pueblo*'s first outing was a Navy operation, NSA officials didn't want to appear to be interfering. So higher-ups rewrote the young analyst's warning, watering it down considerably, Sheck said. Following the spy ship's capture, he added, the NSA's director, General Marshall Carter, admonished subordinates not to mention the message to anyone outside their agency.

"He said, 'I don't want anybody in this room to call or to bring to anybody's attention the existence of this message,'" recalled Sheck. "'That they will find out themselves. And when they do, they will be sufficiently embarrassed about the whole situation that I don't have to worry about that and you don't have to worry about that. But I consider that message as kind of saving our ass.'"

As tepid as the warning was, most of its intended recipients never laid eyes on it, according to testimony before Pike's subcommittee. None of the Joint Chiefs even received the message. Instead, their staff rerouted it to Admiral Sharp's headquarters in Honolulu. Sharp's staff didn't bring it to his attention, either. A copy was sent to Admiral Moorer's office in Washington, but never delivered to him. Admiral Johnson in Japan didn't see the warning until two or three weeks after the *Pueblo* was captured.

Sharp insisted to the subcommittee that his staff and other military planners already had considered all of the information the NSA cited before classifying the mission as minimal risk. But Pike and his colleagues condemned the Pentagon's slipshod handling of the warning.

"At best, it suggests an unfortunate coincidence of omission," said the subcommittee's final report. "At worst, it suggests the highest order of incompetence." The congressmen noted that despite the throng of high-ranking government executives that testified before them, no one mentioned the existence of the NSA message. The subcommittee characterized the collective silence as "a deliberate effort to bury" the warning.

Pike also wanted to find out why no rescue attempt was mounted from the *Enterprise*, which had been only about 500 miles south of the *Pueblo*, putting its fighters closer to the scene than any other readily usable aircraft.

To get at that issue, Pike summoned Sharp, Johnson, and Epes. And what was most striking about the three admirals' testimony was their ambivalence and confusion about how to respond to the *Pueblo* emergency.

Despite the carrier's relative nearness, Johnson hadn't asked for its help. He testified that he didn't think he had the authority to do so. But Epes told the subcommittee Johnson could have requested carrier jets. It was an unsettling moment: two top commanders disagreeing over such a fundamental point.

Sharp testified that the *Enterprise* radioed it was prepared to launch aircraft on the afternoon of the seizure, but never asked for actual permission. (He didn't mention that neither his command nor any other in the Pacific ever *ordered* a launch.) The Pike hearings shed light on another critical event that day, too. At 3:06 p.m. Korean time, Admiral William F. Bringle, commander of the Seventh Fleet, told the *Enterprise* to take "no overt action until further informed." That order, the subcommittee declared, effectively eliminated "any opportunity or intention" on the part of the *Enterprise*'s air commander, Epes, to try a rescue.

Pike wanted his hearings held in public as much as possible, but to his dismay several witnesses insisted on answering some questions—often the most sensitive ones—behind closed doors. Nor would the Navy cough up all the documents he wanted. "I am so tired of Navy classifying everything so I can't ask them any questions about it," he groused. The chiefs of the CIA, NSA, and Defense Intelligence Agency not only spoke in executive session, but their entire testimony was deleted from the hearing transcript. But that didn't prevent Pike from inserting revealing highlights from other witnesses' closed-door remarks into the public record.

Admiral Sharp, for instance, said during a lengthy executive session that he'd objected when, early on the day after the hijacking, the Joint Chiefs ordered the *Enterprise* and other warships racing toward Wonsan to halt and hold their positions. The admiral said he transmitted a "protest sort of message" to Washington, arguing that at least one destroyer should go to Wonsan to demonstrate America's right to traverse sea lanes in the area. The Joint Chiefs, he said, never replied.

The subcommittee's counsel, Frank Slatinshek, asked whether Sharp had ever urged his superiors to let him carry out retaliatory strikes. "Oh yes," emphasized the admiral; his staff forwarded plans for "a whole series of strikes" to Washington. Pike then asked for clarification.

"Did you recommend those strikes?" he inquired.

"Well, I don't remember whether I did or not, to tell you the truth," the admiral replied.

Sharp's memory lapse perhaps was attributable to his ambivalence about actually tangling with the North Koreans. He questioned whether "two or three . . . or four or five airplanes" from the *Enterprise* could have run off the *Pueblo*'s attackers. And once the spy ship had been forced into Wonsan, he said, any major U.S. counterstrike risked setting off a new war in Asia—something he didn't want to be responsible for.

"To say the least, I was lukewarm to starting a second war out there," he told the subcommittee.

At one point in an open hearing, U.S. Representative William Bray, an Indiana Republican, got under the admiral's skin with a loaded question about Pentagon policies on hot pursuit. Could U.S. warplanes have chased the North Korean gunboats into Wonsan harbor, the congressman asked, "if somebody had had the courage and foresight to order them?"

"Mr. Bray, are you in any way implying that I didn't have the courage?" Sharp bristled. "Because if you are, I would like to talk to you privately."

One of the last witnesses was General Seth McKee, the bulldog Fifth Air Force commander who held the subcommittee in thrall with his gripping tale of scrambling F-105 fighters from distant Okinawa.

At first McKee scoured the Far East by telephone, looking for any available aircraft. Believing the *Enterprise* to be closer than any of his land-based warplanes, McKee called his boss in Honolulu, General John Ryan, and "urgently" requested the carrier be contacted. But apparently that never happened.

McKee also considered using South Korean aircraft, which were closer than even the *Enterprise*. But when his aides called the headquarters of General Bonesteel, the U.N. commander, they were advised in no uncertain terms "not to contact the South Korean air force."

Undeterred, McKee decided to try to do the job with Major John Wright's 18th Tactical Fighter Wing on Okinawa. Knowing Wright's jets would have dry tanks over Wonsan if they flew there directly, McKee ordered the pilots to land at Osan Air Base in South Korea, refuel, and take off again to "strike in support of the *Pueblo*"—if they could reach it before dark.

The first pair of F-105s screamed away from Okinawa at 4:11 p.m., just 83 minutes after McKee gave the order. At 4:45 p.m., Admiral Sharp's command estimated that the *Pueblo* had entered Wonsan harbor and McKee "came to the unhappy conclusion" his fighters couldn't get to the doomed spy boat in time. The first F-105s arrived at Osan at 5:35 p.m.; nightfall came at 5:53 p.m.

Slatinshek posed a question: If McKee's aircraft had arrived in time, could they have altered the outcome of the incident?

"I think one of three things would have happened," the general answered. "We would have changed it; I would have gotten my aircraft shot down; or we would have started another war. I don't know which."

"Maybe all three," murmured Republican U.S. Representative Robert Stafford of Vermont.

Though he wasn't able to extricate the *Pueblo*, McKee's boldness and decisiveness drew the only praise that the subcommittee members bestowed on any of the witnesses.

"It was kind of nice," said Pike, "to see that somebody was making some decisions."

Back in Coronado, Bowen and his colleagues gathered in private to pass judgment on Bucher.

The admirals first had to draft their official "findings of fact, opinions, and recommendations," based on the testimony they'd heard. Written in cool, precise language by Captain Newsome, the 184-page report itemized Bucher's alleged failures in great detail.

The admirals acknowledged the *Pueblo* had been burdened with too much classified material, and that those who planned its maiden mission had been largely blind to danger signs emanating from North Korea. Still, they laid much of the blame for the fiasco at Bucher's feet.

The captain, said the admirals' report, failed to anticipate that he might have to battle the communists and didn't prepare his crew for that possibility. Although he diligently tried to find some dynamite, he didn't appreciate the large volume of secret equipment and papers on board; nor did he drill his men in disposing of it quickly. When enemy gunboats began closing in, Bucher should've engaged in "radical maneuvering," changing course and speed rapidly in an effort to shake them, the admirals said. (They didn't explain how any amount of zigzagging would have allowed him to elude pursuers capable of traveling up to four times faster.)

Crucially, the court members determined that Bucher still had the power to resist at the time he surrendered. With the North Koreans firing in a sporadic and controlled manner, his ship was generally intact and fully operational. There were no onboard fires and no flooding. Except for Hodges, Woelk, and Chicca, the crew had suffered only a handful of minor injuries. The admirals concluded that the *Pueblo* could've been steered from belowdecks, with its bridge personnel protected from gunfire. When the boarders came over the side, Bucher's men could have blasted them with small arms. But the captain ordered no such action.

"He just didn't try—this was his greatest fault," the admirals' report declared.

The court members also rejected Bucher's contention that his ship had been seized rather than surrendered. They said he had indeed surrendered when he stopped the *Pueblo* and then followed sub chaser No. 35 toward Wonsan, as the communists demanded. That happened before the boarding party set foot on the spy boat, the admirals noted.

Their report had sharp words for Murphy and Steve Harris as well. Harris "completely failed as a leader" in the frantic rush to demolish the SOD hut's contents. By not piling documents in a compartment, dousing them with diesel fuel, and setting them afire, Harris demonstrated a lack of initiative and imagination, the admirals said. The lieutenant also hadn't understood the rules on jettisoning secret materials and failed to inform the captain of the Marine translators' lack of Korean fluency.

Describing Murphy as "completely overshadowed" by Bucher, the admirals faulted the executive officer for not leading the crew and making "no apparent effort" to ensure that emergency destruction was carried out properly.

Schumacher and Lacy were found to have performed "satisfactorily" on the day of capture. By exposing himself to gunfire while incinerating documents near the smokestack, Tim Harris "performed most creditably" of all the officers.

The admirals were considerably more complimentary about the crew's behavior in prison, saying many men "showed real courage" in the face of torture and brutality.

After "his initial breakdown," Bucher rebounded and "upheld morale in a superior manner," inventing all sorts of ways to ridicule and harass his captors. He repeatedly demanded that his men be kept together, given medical attention, and treated according to the Geneva convention, and he never stopped protesting the beatings. Although his advice to his men sometimes didn't conform strictly to the Code of Conduct, it was always meant to undermine communist propaganda and to get the sailors out of prison in one piece, the admirals said. As a result, morale stayed high, discipline was good, and North Korean efforts to convince the Americans of socialism's superiority went nowhere.

Schumacher was singled out for his strong leadership and creative harrying of the North Koreans. Law was praised as instrumental in maintaining the chain of command and for taking punishment on behalf of shipmates; Hammond for his extraordinary resistance to his tormentors.

The admirals concluded that Murphy, Steve Harris, Lacy, and Tim Harris "were undistinguished during detention and provided no discernible leadership to the enlisted men."

The court members' work didn't end with the completion of their report. They also had to recommend a punishment that fit Bucher's alleged transgressions. For two days, sequestered in an office adjacent to the *Pueblo* courtroom, they argued back and forth, dividing into two factions.

Bowen, Bergner, and White were adamant that the captain should be court-martialed for not doing more to hold off the enemy gunboats. The three hard-line admirals "had fought ships, they had Purple Hearts and Navy Crosses, they were fighting machines," recalled Newsome. "They would have hung Bucher with his own rope."

The other two admirals—Grimm and Pratt—weren't so sure. Grimm felt that although Bucher hadn't prepared his crew to cope with the attack, he proved a superlative leader in prison. Indeed, Grimm thought the skipper deserved a medal for his courage and devotion to his men.

By the end of the first day of deliberations, the admirals were split three to one in favor of a court-martial, with Grimm opposed and Pratt undecided. Bowen wanted a unanimous decision and the five men agreed to go home and think it over that night.

The admirals in the majority continued to work on the holdouts the next day. Bowen's bloc argued that a public trial was Bucher's best chance to clear his name. At the same time, a court-martial recommendation would signal the officer corps that the hallowed precept of never giving up without a fight remained unsullied and fully operative.

Grimm countered that Bucher wasn't the only person at fault. Many higher-ups, he argued, were also culpable for stacking too many intelligence publications aboard and for not giving Bucher adequate means to destroy them. If the skipper was to be pilloried, Grimm believed, so should a pack of brass hats. But Grimm and Pratt eventually acquiesced to the insistent polemics of the majority.

Bowen signed the court's findings on April 10. The admirals unanimously recommended that Bucher be court-martialed for five purported offenses: permitting his ship to be seized while he had the power to resist; failing to take immediate and aggressive measures when his ship was attacked; complying with the North Koreans' orders to follow them into port; failing to complete destruction of classified materials and allowing them to fall into enemy hands; and failing to properly train his crew for emergency destruction.

The court members said Steve Harris should stand trial on three counts: not informing Bucher of deficiencies in the support capabilities of the CT detachment; not drilling the CTs properly in emergency destruction; and not destroying all classified materials.

Murphy, the admirals said, should receive a letter of admonition, a relatively mild nonjudicial punishment, for failing to organize and lead the crew on the day of capture, especially in wrecking classified gear.

Perhaps in deference to Grimm's concerns, the court also advised that letters of reprimand be issued to Admiral Johnson and Captain Everett Gladding, head of the Naval Security Group, Pacific. Johnson was cited for not planning "effective emergency support forces" for the *Pueblo* and not verifying the ship's ability to rapidly destroy its secret material. Gladding, the admirals charged, hadn't developed "procedures to ensure the readiness" of the CTs or made sure that other agencies and service branches provided adequate intelligence support to the *Pueblo*.

The recommendations were forwarded to Admiral Hyland, who held the firm belief that a captain is solely responsible for everything that happens on his vessel. Hyland was appalled that Bucher hadn't broken out small arms to drive off the boarders and had let them capture his classified papers and equipment. That loss, the admiral believed, could one day cost many American lives. He wanted Bucher punished.

Hyland endorsed Bowen's call for a court-martial and notified Washington of his decision. But the hardheaded realists at the top of the Navy's chain of command knew putting Bucher on trial wasn't a practical possibility; the public simply wouldn't stand for it. Admiral Bernard Clarey, the vice chief of naval operations, and two aides got on the phone with Hyland, explaining how politicized the case had become and urging him to alter his views. Finally, "grumbling and dragging his heels," Hyland hung up.

But the Pacific fleet commander got the message. He quietly withdrew his earlier court-martial endorsement. In a fresh memo, he said Bucher and Harris should receive only letters of reprimand, and agreed that Murphy's punishment should be a letter of admonition. He wrote that the charges against Johnson should be reduced to failing to establish the *Pueblo*'s capacity for rapid destruction. Gladding, he said, shouldn't be sanctioned at all.

In Washington, Admiral Moorer quickly concurred with the softened recommendations.

One of the Navy's biggest hot potatoes in years finally landed on the desk of Navy Secretary John Chafee, appointed to his post only three months earlier by President Nixon.

Rangy and athletic, Chafee was a Rhode Islander, descended from one of the wealthy "five families" that once ran the state before Irish and Italian immigrants changed its demographics and politics in the 1930s. When World War II broke out, Chafee dropped out of Yale and joined the Marines, seeing action on Guadalcanal and Okinawa. He later enrolled at Harvard Law School and, in 1951, was recalled to active duty and served as a Marine company commander in Korea.

A moderate Republican, Chafee was elected governor of Rhode Island in 1962. In 1968, he abandoned his campaign for a fourth term after a horse fatally kicked his 14-year-old daughter in the head. A few months later, Chafee was named Navy secretary even though he'd backed Governor Nelson Rockefeller of New York, a fellow moderate, over Nixon in the GOP presidential primaries.

Chafee took over the Navy at a time when its reputation was more tattered than at any other in modern memory. Like the other armed services, the Navy had suffered from the public's growing distaste for the Vietnam War. Racial tensions in the ranks were flaring. But the Navy had its own unique problems as well, including horrifying fires that broke out on two aircraft carriers. In January 1969, the month Chafee took office, an inferno on the *Enterprise* left 26 sailors dead and 85 injured. In 1967, an even deadlier fire had swept the USS *Forrestal*, killing 134 men. A nationwide poll commissioned by the Navy found its prestige had fallen to "a very poor fourth" among the services, behind the Army, Air Force, and Marine Corps.

The *Pueblo* only aggravated the situation. Chafee was savvy enough to recognize that any missteps in the final disposition of the case had the potential to badly burn both him and the Navy. In ruling on his admirals' conflicting recommendations, he had to tread a narrow path between imposing too much punishment on Bucher—thereby infuriating a sympathetic press and public—and imposing too little, which would anger many old-line Navy officers. If he disciplined the captain but no one of higher rank, he'd doubtless be accused of scapegoating the easiest target.

Sitting in his Pentagon office, with its sobering views of the Iwo Jima Memorial and Arlington National Cemetery, the fledgling secretary considered what to do. He assigned his special counsel, Rear Admiral Merlin Staring, to read and summarize the entire court of inquiry transcript. The task took Staring a full week. But by early May, Chafee was ready to act.

He called a press conference for the morning of May 6. He opened it by revealing the court of inquiry's recommended charges against Bucher and the four other officers, and Hyland's proposed reductions of those charges. Chafee candidly admitted that mistakes and miscalculations by the Navy had led to what he called the *Pueblo*'s "lonely confrontation by unanticipatedly bold and hostile forces."

The secretary said he wasn't in a position to judge "the guilt or innocence of any of the officers." The most important factor in the debacle, he said, was the "sudden collapse" of the premise that the *Pueblo*'s presence in international waters would protect it. It was an assumption that had been shared up and down the chain of command, from Bucher to the Pentagon. Thus the consequences of the ship's seizure, Chafee said, "must in fairness be borne by all, rather than by one or two individuals whom circumstances had placed closer to the crucial event."

Because of this collective responsibility, the secretary said he was overruling his admirals. Bucher and his men had endured a great deal of punishment in North Korea and they'd face no further judicial action by the Navy.

"They have suffered enough," said Chafee. Reporters raced for the phones.

Chafee was widely praised for his wisdom and compassion. With a shrewd compromise, he'd guided the Navy past a dangerous political shoal. By publicizing the court of inquiry's allegations, he'd paid homage to the Navy establishment's strong disapproval of Bucher's surrender. Yet the secretary also acknowledged the Navy's errors and spread a balm of mercy over what had appeared, to many observers, to be unduly severe legal proceedings against the captain. Moreover, Chafee had firmly shut the door against a new round of court hearings that might well expose more details of slipshod Navy planning and provoke an even more rancorous backlash from the public, press, and Congress.

A few hours after Chafee's news conference, Bucher and Harvey held one of their own. The reporters wanted the captain's reaction to Chafee's ruling.

Angry thoughts clogged Bucher's mind. His respect for the Navy—particularly its leaders and their sense of justice—had been "dashed to pieces." The admirals of the court, he believed, wanted him keelhauled for refusing to make his men commit suicide. Bucher could hardly speak due to a bad case of laryngitis, and he was afraid of what might pop out of his mouth anyway. He deferred to Harvey, who read a short statement.

"As far as we're concerned," said the lawyer, "Commander Bucher has been cleared."

But he hadn't been cleared. At best, he'd been preemptively pardoned. Since the admirals' allegations would not be formally lodged against him, he had no legal right to publicly refute them before a court-martial. A cloud of unresolved doubt—about his competence, his courage—now hung over him. And he might never be able to make it go away.

CHAPTER 19

A DAY IN THE SUN

The next couple of years were difficult ones for Bucher.

In September 1969, the Navy gave him a sought-after billet at the prestigious Naval Postgraduate School in Monterey, California, where the captain intended to take a year of management classes.

Things went well at first. Bucher and his family lived in a comfortable house with a brick fireplace and a soothing screen of pine trees. His classes were tough and Bucher sometimes had to study all night to make sense of subjects, like calculus, that he'd never done well in. But he held his own, getting an A, two Bs, and a C in his first term.

The superintendent and several instructors went out of their way to make him feel welcome, and he experienced no overt hostility from the faculty or fellow students. But wherever he went he sensed appraising eyes on him. When he passed two people conversing, he imagined, with a touch of paranoia, that he was their subject.

"I didn't really get any static from any of those people up there, but I could see them talking about me," he remembered. "And I often wondered, 'What the hell are they saying?' I couldn't walk anywhere without people looking at me."

After only a few months, his health began to fray. Shattering headaches lasting up to three days plagued him. His right hip and leg, where he'd been kicked so many times, still bothered him; blind spots in his right eye were an enduring legacy of malnutrition. He had to undergo surgery on his nose, which Silver Lips had broken during Hell Week.

At night, he was visited by terrible dreams. In one, he was back in North Korea, again listening helplessly as his men screamed and moaned in nearby cells. Bodies crashed into walls; guards shouted and cursed and cocked assault rifles—Bucher's mind writhed with terrifying sounds and images.

Another dream was pure fantasy but somehow even more frightening.

After the captain and his men finally made it home, a high-ranking official of the American government told them an awful mistake had been made. The repatriation wasn't done correctly; the crew must go back to North Korea. Horrified, the captain ordered his men to flee into the rugged backcountry of San Diego County. They collected guns and food, kissed weeping wives and children good-bye, and began a desperate exodus.

Hurrying over the sere hills, the men lost their way. Night fell; some of them drifted off the trail and vanished in the dark. Their frightened leader couldn't figure out where he and his remaining sailors were or how to get to a safe hiding place. How close were the pursuing federal agents? The exhausted fugitives knew it was only a matter of time before they'd be caught and forced back to the brutality and degradation and bladder-voiding fear of a communist hellhole, where God only knew what new torments awaited them. . . .

Shuddering awake, Bucher would find his face moist with sweat. He'd slip out of bed, careful not to wake his sleeping spouse. Padding into the living room, he tuned the radio to a classical music station. In the blackness he listened to the calming melodies of Schubert and Mahler, sitting still as a statue until his panic subsided.

Weighed down by physical and psychological troubles, he fell further behind in his studies and eventually dropped out of the Postgraduate School.

But he didn't falter on another project: his memoirs. Aided by a professional writer, Bucher cranked out a riveting narrative titled *Bucher: My Story*, which hit bookstores in August 1970 and rapidly became a bestseller.

While painting Schumacher, Law, and others in a flattering light, *My Story* was predictably hard on Murphy, portraying him as feckless, cowardly, and disliked by the crew. The following year, Murphy struck back with his own memoir, *Second in Command*, which was little more than a lengthy counterattack on his ex-boss. Its unrelenting spitefulness made some reviewers recoil. "We now have a book castigating *Pueblo*'s skipper, Commander Lloyd M. Bucher, as a drunk, a coward, a liar, a hypocrite, a chiseler, a skirt-chaser, a misfit, an oddball, a poor leader, and a 'lousy ship handler,'" wrote one critic, adding that Murphy's screed contained "so many caustic remarks about Bucher's character that readers may find some of the pages downright embarrassing to digest." The reviewer noted that it was only fair for Murphy to have a right of reply to Bucher's book, but expressed hope that "perhaps now we've heard an end to the name-calling."

My Story also provoked a public quarrel between Bucher and Gene Lacy over which of them had actually stopped the *Pueblo* under fire.

Captain Newsome first raised that issue during the court of inquiry, but Bucher claimed he couldn't remember.

> **Q:** With respect to stopping the ship, the first time, it is not quite clear whether it was at your direction or Mr. Lacy's suggestion that the ship stop. Did he suggest that the ship stop and you approved it, or was it at your direction that the ship stop?
>
> **A:** Well, sir, that particular sequence is not clear in my mind. I did not personally ring up the order to stop the ship the first time. I have given a great deal of thought to that, as to just who did do it, and what the sequence of events were, and I cannot with any degree of certainty recall the exact sequence. Nevertheless, the ship was stopped . . . and it must have been with my, at least, passive approval.

By the time his book came out, however, Bucher's foggy memory had cleared up. He wrote that just after a cannon shell whizzed through the pilothouse, almost hitting Lacy's head, the chief engineer shot him a "wild-eyed look" and screamed, "Are you going to stop this son of a bitch or not?" Without waiting for an answer, the captain's book said, Lacy racked the annunciator to all-stop, cutting the engines.

In that moment, wrote Bucher, he realized that "my most experienced officer, my most trusted friend aboard this ill-starred little ship, had robbed me of the last vestige of support in my efforts to save the mission, leaving me alone with an Executive Officer who had proven to be unreliable and two very young and inexperienced junior officers on my bridge."

The captain failed to tell his readers, however, that there was nothing to prevent him from restarting the engines. Nor did he mention the lie-detector test he took before beginning work on his memoir in an attempt to reassure himself that his recollection of "controversial issues" wasn't faulty. (He passed, he said.)

The dispute broke into public view when *The New York Times* got hold of a prepublication copy of *My Story*. The newspaper reported that while Bucher denied ordering Lacy to stop, two other sailors on the bridge at the time—Law and Tim Harris—backed Lacy's account that he'd acted on the captain's command. "I don't know whether he's grasping at straws or what the hell the deal is on it," Lacy told the paper.

Bucher insisted he hadn't mentioned Lacy's purported actions to the court of inquiry because he didn't want to embarrass him or appear to be blaming a subordinate. But when it came time to pen his memoir, the captain said, he wanted to be "as accurate and forthcoming as I could" in telling the *Pueblo* story. Lacy no doubt felt blindsided and humiliated by his onetime friend. In a letter to the engineer after *My Story* was published, Bucher apologized for not including Lacy's version of events. And in an interview many years afterward, the captain said he wished he'd never pointed an accusatory finger at his buddy.

"I regret having done it," he conceded. "It really hurt Gene a lot. . . . It was years before we were able to have a conversation."

The autumn of 1970 found Bucher in San Diego again. He desperately wanted to get back to sea. Instead, the Navy stuck him with a dead-end shore job checking the training records of reserve officers throughout Southern California. Frustrated and bored silly, he spent his days driving to various reservist centers and thumbing through personnel files.

"This job with the Reserves is unbelievable," he wrote an acquaintance. "I am lost all the time."

He felt like a pariah. At age forty-three, his career was over, he believed; the Navy would never give him a decent job again. His emotions veered between stubborn, visceral affection for the service and deepening anger and resentment at the brass for having ignored his pleas for help in the Sea of Japan. "I have tried not to let myself become bitter and become a crotchety old man," he told one reporter, "but the bitterness keeps creeping through." It positively burst through in an interview with the *Washington Post*:

"The *Pueblo* was the result of a tremendous amount of stupidity and poor planning by supposedly responsible officials in and out of the Navy," Bucher said. "Many of them are still in the same jobs doing other things just as poorly—without ever having been held accountable for their actions. . . . It would have satisfied a great many, in and out of the Navy, if my crew had been completely wiped out. Then there would have been nobody to come back and haunt them. It would have been marvelous if we had stood up and committed suicide."

In November 1970, Bucher failed a physical exam, raising the possibility of his forced retirement. Even if the Navy didn't push him out, he decided to put in his papers after one more year. Yet the captain never wavered in his conviction that he'd done the right thing in giving up his ship. He had more than his share of nightmares, but at least he didn't have the ghosts of dead sailors slipping into his bedroom every night to stare at him in silent anger and reproach. If he'd wasted lives trying to fight his way past the North Korean gunboats, he felt, he'd have much more to answer for. "I can shave and look right at myself in the mirror every morning," he told an interviewer. "I know that I made the right decision."

On the streets of San Diego, he still was a hero. Everywhere he went people recognized him: in restaurants, on airplanes. Strangers walked up to shake his hand and get his autograph; some well-wishers broke into tears. He was urged to run for public office. But his fondest desire was to be reassigned to sea duty "in any capacity on any ship afloat."

With profits from his book, the skipper bought a comfortable ranch-style home in the small, semirural community of Poway, about 25 miles northeast of downtown San Diego. Set back from the road amid avocado and citrus trees, the house became a sanctuary for him and Rose. In his spare time he played chess with her and read extensively. He dreamed of coaching a football team after he retired, or maybe getting hired by *National Geographic* to sail to distant parts of the world and take photographs. Endlessly reliving the capture in his mind, he came to believe the North Koreans had mistaken the *Pueblo* for a South Korean intruder and, after realizing the vessel was American, grabbed it anyway.

Over time, some of his ailments went away. His vision problems lingered, but he no longer suffered from hand tremors or skull-cracking headaches. In July 1971, a medical board returned him to full duty. The Bureau of Naval Personnel, however, rebuffed his pleas for a job more suitable than babysitting reservists.

"Everybody was scared to death of me," he recalled. "It was like I had the plague or leprosy or something."

Finally, Bucher appealed to the top. He wrote a letter to the new chief of naval operations, Admiral Elmo Zumwalt, who had a reputation for trying to make enlisted life less regimented. (Among his more memorable reforms were letting sailors grow beards and mustaches and installing beer-dispensing machines in barracks.) Bucher included his résumé and insisted that nothing in his record should preclude him from getting an assignment commensurate with his rank and experience. Zumwalt responded by summoning him to Washington. Bucher chatted about his future with the CNO and figured things were going his way when Zumwalt began calling him "Pete."

"He says, 'Pete, you go on back to San Diego and tomorrow you'll have an offer for a job,'" Bucher recalled.

Sure enough, the Bureau of Naval Personnel called with three attractive choices, all chief of staff billets. Two were in San Diego, the third on Guam. Mostly to escape his own notoriety, Bucher picked Guam. He was sick and tired of answering questions from reporters and scribbling autographs for strangers. He didn't want airline pilots eagerly asking him about the attack or people pointing at him in restaurants. "Every place I went—*everywhere*—it was always on my tail about my service in the *Pueblo*," he said. The skipper just wanted it all to stop. Maybe if he moved to an island in the North Pacific, it would.

In September 1971, he took up his new duties as chief staff officer for a Guam-based minesweeper squadron. Mine Flotilla One later would clear mines from Haiphong harbor as part of the peace deal with North Vietnam that ended American involvement in the war. But Bucher's new gig had a very unpleasant downside: cold shoulders and insults from some of his brother officers.

The sniping started even before he arrived. The commander of MINE-FLOTONE wasn't happy to have the infamous *Pueblo* skipper as his number two and tried hard to keep him off the island. Bucher found out about his new boss's displeasure when an old submarine buddy, then on the Seventh Fleet staff, slipped him copies of protesting messages from the minesweeper chief to other commands. But, backed by Zumwalt, the captain moved into his new position anyway.

A more direct snub took place when Bucher boarded a helicopter to join his squadron's flagship at sea. As he sat down next to an admiral he'd never seen before, the other man "pointedly got up and moved his seat to the other end of the damn [aircraft]," Bucher said. "I thought that was a little tacky."

The hassling followed him into a rowdy, country-western-style officers' club on the huge U.S. naval base at Subic Bay in the Philippines. The bar was usually jam-packed as off-duty officers drank, laughed, and egged on the Filipino singers trying to imitate Johnny Cash and Merle Haggard onstage. Bucher liked the place and visited as often as he could. One night a waitress came over and handed him a note from another patron asking "what ships did I surrender today, or something like that," remembered Bucher. "There was no name on it or anything, so I didn't know where the hell it came from."

Yet the captain wasn't completely shunned. One day a three-star admiral poked his head into Bucher's office and asked him to take a walk. As they strolled, the flag officer told him that "he thought I'd handled myself with honor and integrity, and my service had been everything that I could have done." It was the first time since the skipper came home that a high-ranking officer had spoken such comforting words to him, and he was deeply appreciative.

Despite the occasional hazing, Bucher enjoyed the Guam job and postponed his plans to retire at the end of 1971. Technically, there was nothing in his record to prevent him from moving up in rank. As a practical matter, he knew his chances were nil. Everyone in the Navy was aware of the court of inquiry's recommendation that he be court-martialed. That was a political brick wall he'd never get around. By 1973, he was ready to leave. He put in his retirement papers on June 1, 1973; the Navy approved them in "about two minutes," he said.

Separated after 27 years from the service he loved, Bucher concentrated on what to do next with his life. For a while he worked as a paid speaker, regaling rapt audiences with stories of his *Pueblo* and North Korea experiences. He also tried his hand at writing a humorous novel, based on the antics of a trouble-prone torpedoman Bucher knew who ended up in jail in nearly every port he visited. But, although the captain hadn't had much difficulty producing an autobiography with the help of a professional writer, composing a work of fiction on his own proved much harder.

He eventually gave up and tried to ease into a quiet, low-profile existence in Poway. To stay fit, he walked three miles a day and played an occasional round of golf. He watched sports on TV and played poker at the officers' club at Miramar Naval Air Station. Once a month he took Rose out for seafood in downtown San Diego.

The controversies engendered by the *Pueblo* were never far away, however. In 1974 or 1975, he made a trip to St. Louis to see Schumacher and his new wife. During the visit, the former lieutenant took Bucher to dinner at the home of an old friend, a local businessman. The evening started off amiably, but when Bucher talked about surrendering the *Pueblo*, the businessman exploded in anger, yanking the tablecloth off the dining table and sending plates and glasses crashing to the floor.

"He said, 'Commander, I don't care what the situation was, you just don't give up the ship!'" recalled Schumacher.

Having dropped the idea of becoming a novelist, Bucher cast about for something else to do. His speaking engagements paid well, but public interest in him probably would diminish over time. He'd had a couple of job offers, including one in public relations for Boise Cascade, a company that made wood and paper products. But he declined, figuring he'd never be able to discard his *Pueblo* baggage in such a visible position.

One thing Bucher had always enjoyed was art. Whenever he went ashore in a new port, he made a point of visiting local art museums. He checked out an armload of how-to books from the Poway public library and, over the course of a year, taught himself to draw and paint. When he presented a portfolio of samples to the Art Center College of Design, an elite school in Los Angeles, he was granted admission.

Bucher rented an apartment in L.A. Not only was he the sole incoming student without an undergraduate art degree, but he'd never even taken an art class. On top of that, he was the oldest student. The others, most in their twenties, called him "grandpa." He turned 50 while attending the Art Center in 1977. On weekends, he commuted home to Rose behind the wheel of a powder-blue Porsche he'd bought after returning from North Korea.

The captain turned out to be a natural. He liked oils and watercolors, and ships and serene landscapes were among his favorite subjects. *Time* magazine heard he was at the school and photographed him in a drawing class. In later years, he'd become an accomplished artist, selling his pieces for top dollar. (One of his most popular images was a watercolor of the *Pueblo* under way.) Besides, painting helped to calm him after a night of bad dreams about North Korea, an increasingly common occurrence.

He wasn't alone. In 1978, Captain Raymond Spaulding, the Navy psychiatrist who'd screened the *Pueblo* sailors upon their release, published a psychological study of the crew, based on questionnaires answered by 41 men. It concluded that some of them displayed symptoms consistent with "concentration camp syndrome," a collection of mental and physical disorders that afflicted survivors of Hitler's death camps. About half of those responding to the questionnaire reported having nightmares, feeling "weak all over," and sometimes wondering "if anything is worthwhile." Seventy-one percent of the respondents admitted to "difficulty in controlling their temper." Fifty-six percent reported "emotional instability," "depressive episodes," and "loss of initiative." Nine men said they'd been partially disabled by their *Pueblo* experiences; eight said they could no longer work in their usual occupation.

Busy with his art classes, Bucher cut back on lecture tours, though he continued to give a talk now and then. One sponsor was the Reverend Sun Myung Moon, controversial founder of the Unification Church. In 1980, Moon brought the captain to South Korea, where he gave speeches and received several medals from the government. In 1988, the South Koreans invited him back. He met with the president, spoke at three universities, and took part in a big parade.

Yet even two decades after the capture, the Navy establishment still viewed Bucher as an outcast. To mark the twentieth anniversary of the *Pueblo* incident, in 1988, the editors of *Naval History* magazine—a prestigious journal with a wide readership among active-duty and retired officers—published excerpts from oral histories of five admirals who'd played a part in the spy-ship drama. Three of them took potshots at the captain, including John Hyland, the former Pacific fleet commander who'd been arm-twisted into not advocating a court-martial for Bucher.

"I guess Bucher looked around his ship and saw this man bleeding like hell, so he decided that the jig was up," said Hyland. "He thought he was in a hopeless situation, so he surrendered. He never fired a shot. He never manned the guns. He didn't go to general quarters until he'd already been fired upon and sustained some casualties." Hyland said Bucher "had all kinds of opportunities to observe what was a very threatening movement against his ship," but didn't do anything to avoid it. He gave the captain "a completely failing grade."

Bucher was permitted a reply in the next issue of *Naval History*. In an eloquent statement that stretched over seven pages of the magazine, he retold the melancholic tale of the *Pueblo* and vigorously rebutted Hyland, making several points he hadn't during the court hearings. Most significantly, he underlined the contradictory nature of the Navy's orders and expectations of him.

On one hand, he'd been instructed not to provoke the North Koreans, to deny them any pretext for starting another war. On the other, he was expected to uphold the don't-give-up-the-ship tradition, to fight back with all his might. As Bucher wrote, "We could not have it both ways." His remark echoed the findings of the Ball Committee's secret report to President Johnson in 1968.

Regarding his "failing grade" from Hyland, Bucher asked rhetorically, "What grade can be given to the many commanders, such as [Hyland], who were not prepared for our emergency?" What grade, the skipper asked, should be assigned "to the naval and air forces close at hand who did not respond to our plight?" What grade for the intelligence analysts who so badly underestimated the danger of the mission?

"The story of the *Pueblo* in a nutshell," wrote Bucher, "is one of a naval officer, his crew, and his ship, sent to do a job; things went bad, and the Navy abandoned them. Our country and our Navy were served honorably and loyally by all the officers and men of the *Pueblo*—and, if I may say so, one hell of a sight better than they were in turn served."

Bucher claimed in the article that his ship had carried "only a few pieces of classified equipment." It was an assertion he'd make again in the future in an attempt to downplay the seriousness of what actually had been a colossal compromise of code machines and other highly sensitive materials. (The captain also erroneously wrote that three aircraft carriers had been within easy flying range of the *Pueblo*; in fact, only the *Enterprise* had been relatively close.)

Bucher ended by saying he'd "answered all the questions put to me" in the previous 20 years. He challenged the admirals quoted in *Naval History* to meet him at the U.S. Naval Academy, in an auditorium full of midshipmen, and answer some questions from him. "I am ready!" he declared.

The skipper's spirited self-defense left some naval officers unmoved. "Even if we assume that all of Commander Bucher's complaints about failure on the part of his seniors to act are true, one fact remains," said one retiree in a letter to the editor. "Commander Bucher was the first U.S. Navy captain to surrender his ship without firing a shot."

But others had begun to see the *Pueblo* in a different light. "Commander Bucher's article was quite a shock to me," wrote Daniel M. Karcher, a retired captain. For years, Karcher related, he'd been embarrassed when friends in the Army or Air Force chided him over Bucher's "cowardly performance" as a Navy officer. "But now," he continued, "there seems to be more to this incident than previously known. . . . I think it is time to reevaluate Commander Bucher's performance as commanding officer of the *Pueblo* considering the circumstances under which he found himself, and to establish who is really responsible for this operation."

In 1988, Bucher turned 61. It was an age at which he should've been slowing down, golfing and traveling more, enjoying his leisure with Rose and his sons, now in their mid-thirties. Instead, he went to bat for his sailors once again. For even as he dueled with admirals in the pages of *Naval History*, he began a bitter public struggle with the Pentagon after it refused to give his men the newly created Prisoner of War Medal.

It wasn't the first time the skipper had sought medals for his men. In 1973, based on his recommendations, the Navy decorated 18 crewmen for bravery during the attack. The following year, 78 men won medals for their actions in communist prisons. Hammond was awarded the Navy Cross; Schumacher got a Silver Star.

The POW medal, however, was unique. No nation ever had decorated its fighting men specifically for being captured and incarcerated by an enemy. Public support for such a medal had begun to swell following North Vietnam's release of American POWs in the early 1970s. The Pentagon initially opposed the award, arguing that it wouldn't take into consideration the circumstances of a recipient's capture. Men who'd willingly thrown up their hands would be just as eligible as those who'd fought valiantly or had been badly wounded or unconscious when taken prisoner. Nonetheless, Congress, after a number of unsuccessful attempts, finally authorized the award in 1985. No one convicted by a military tribunal of misconduct during captivity could receive it. About 142,000 veterans of the two world wars, Korea, and Vietnam were eligible.

Struck in bronze, the medallion bore the proud but somber image of an American eagle encircled by barbed wire and bayonet points. When the Pentagon started issuing the POW badge in the spring of 1988, many veterans believed it was long overdue. "I have a couple of medals tucked away in a drawer, fading and maybe a little rusty, but with meaning," a New Jersey veteran of

World War II told a newspaper interviewer. "But this one I have earned and paid for in ways that I just can't describe." A gunner on a B-17 bomber, the man had been shot down over Germany and imprisoned there for nine months. As the Soviet army advanced on his camp, the Germans ordered the POWs on a forced march westward that many didn't survive. The veteran said his haunting memories of that time had never dimmed, adding that the POW medal might be "a way of just easing the pain."

Some *Pueblo* sailors, now in their forties, had similar feelings. Bucher estimated that half of them had been at least partially disabled as a result of beatings and torture. Howard Bland—the young fireman whom the North Koreans threatened to execute as a way of pressuring Bucher to sign his first "confession"—had felt for years as if his heart were about to explode. John Mitchell, who'd served as Bucher's prison orderly and courier, suffered back pain and excruciating migraines. Stu Russell, who'd gotten happily sloshed in the Gypsy Tea Room, endured terrifying nightmares. Ed Murphy couldn't move at times because his back "was totally redesigned by rifle butts and boot kickings."

In September 1988, the military arranged for 320 veterans to be presented with the Prisoner of War Medal at the Marine Corps Recruit Depot in San Diego. The *Pueblo* crewmen weren't included. When asked to explain, a Pentagon spokesman said they didn't meet the criteria set forth by Congress: They'd been "detainees" rather than prisoners of war. Many crewmen were furious and deeply hurt, and their exclusion caused widespread outrage among veterans' groups. The Veterans of Foreign Wars, American Legion, Disabled American Veterans, and Jewish American War Veterans all wrote letters of protest. Some of those scheduled to receive decorations threatened to return them or give them to Bucher.

Publicly, the captain insisted the snub was no big deal. The military had classified his men as ex-POWs for purposes of medical benefits, and that was what really mattered. Privately, he was incensed. Two decades after the crew's bondage—after they boldly flipped off their torturers before the eyes of the world; after a bloody CT grinned in spite of a vicious beating; after they all marched to freedom across the Bridge of No Return—Bucher still felt a strong sense of responsibility for the men. How dare the Pentagon deny them a slug of base metal after all of the blood, sweat, and tears they'd shed in hellish communist prisons? "This was such a slap in the face to them," he remembered. "I thought, 'By God, I gotta get that son of a bitch, one way or another.'" One of the things Bucher had always admired about the Navy was that it took care of its own. The crewmen were the skipper's own, and he'd be damned if he didn't take care of them now. During an interview more than a dozen years later, he got so choked up over the issue he could hardly speak.

Bucher began writing to every government official he could think of, asking them to demand that the Defense Department change its mind. He wrote to senators, congressmen, the secretary of defense, the secretary of the Navy, the chief of naval operations.

The cause was taken up by U.S. Representative Sonny Montgomery, an influential Mississippi Democrat who chaired the House Veterans Affairs Committee. Montgomery asked the Pentagon to formally explain its reasons for not awarding the *Pueblo* crew the medal. To qualify, a service member had to have been captured while "engaged in an action against an enemy of the United States" or "engaged in military operations involving conflict with an opposing foreign force."

In a letter to Montgomery, Kathleen A. Buck, a Defense Department attorney, said the sailors met neither test.

Buck described the *Pueblo*'s intelligence-collection mission as a "passive" activity that "hardly qualifies . . . as an 'action,' a term that denotes violence in the employment of weapons." She also said North Korea wasn't an enemy of the United States, since the two countries had signed an armistice in 1953.

Addressing the second criterion, the Pentagon lawyer wrote that while the *Pueblo*'s voyage "could arguably" be categorized as a military operation, its bloody capture didn't involve "conflict as that term is normally construed," since the spy boat "offered no resistance." At a minimum, she added, "there must be a fire fight of some kind."

Bucher couldn't believe it. The Pentagon, he felt, was resorting to pretzel logic to keep his guys from getting their medals. He was convinced that the real reason for the denial was his embarrassing revelations at the court of inquiry. In November 1988, he fired off his own letter to Montgomery, angrily refuting Buck's arguments: "I don't know what [the Defense Department's] definition of conflict is, but one hell of a lot of conflict occurred that noon in international waters in the Sea of Japan."

In a separate letter to the chief of naval operations, Bucher pointed out that he and all of his men previously had been awarded the Combat Action Ribbon. How could the Pentagon now say they hadn't engaged in action against an enemy? The captain also noted that since the Korean War ended with a truce, not a peace treaty, the United States technically still was at war with North Korea. If North Korea wasn't an enemy, what was it? He denied that the *Pueblo* hadn't resisted capture, and rejected Buck's argument that the POW medal couldn't be granted in the absence of a "fire fight." And he was right: The law authorizing the decoration made no mention of a firefight as a prerequisite.

His pleas fell on deaf ears, however.

Temporarily stymied, the skipper took a trip with Rose to visit a friend on Prince Edward Island, off Canada's east coast. On the way they stopped in Boston to see another friend, a local TV news reporter. Agreeing that something needed to be done about the POW medals, the journalist put Bucher in touch with a longtime acquaintance, U.S. Representative Nicholas Mavroules, a Democrat whose district lay in the suburbs north of Boston.

The son of Greek immigrants, Mavroules happened to be chairman of the Subcommittee on Investigations of the House Armed Services Committee. He knew his way around the Pentagon and he knew what buttons to push. Mavroules had led the congressional investigation into the 1983 bombing that killed 241 U.S. Marines, sailors, and soldiers in a Beirut barracks, and he'd challenged President Ronald Reagan's controversial "Star Wars" missile-defense program. He was no particular friend of the Navy. His subcommittee had exposed cost overruns on Navy aircraft and soon would look into the deadly 1989 gun-turret explosion on the battleship *Iowa*, which killed 47 seamen.

Mavroules gave Bucher an hour one Sunday morning at his campaign office in Massachusetts. The skipper related his experiences aboard the *Pueblo*, in North Korea, and at the hands of the Navy afterward. Mavroules sympathized. From his probe of security problems at the bombed Beirut barracks, he knew military higher-ups occasionally sought scapegoats in the wake of a high-profile disaster. He also thought that, in view of the *Pueblo* sailors' struggles to evade the North Koreans at sea and to resist them in prison, the Pentagon had made a mistake in not giving them the POW decoration. "The thing that really gnawed at me was that I wondered what they would have done—that is, the head of the Pentagon, or whoever is making decisions—if they were in that same situation," Mavroules recalled. "I truly think they would have made the same decisions as Pete." The congressman promised to bring the matter before his subcommittee soon.

Mavroules was as good as his word. Back in Washington, he convened a hearing on June 23, 1989. Among the invited witnesses were Bucher, Schumacher, and Harry Iredale.

The chairman made it clear in his opening remarks that his goal was to change the law so the *Pueblo* crew was eligible for the POW medal.

"Due to the wording of the law, the crew of the *Pueblo* were technically ineligible since the *Pueblo* was engaged in an intelligence gathering mission and not in a military engagement," Mavroules said. "However, in my judgment, that was an oversight. The crew members of the *Pueblo* made great sacrifices and it is important to recognize their accomplishment." He proposed an amendment that would award medals to men who'd been "held by hostile forces under circumstances which the Secretary of the Navy considers comparable to their being held captive during a period of armed conflict."

Bucher testified, as did a Kansas congressman whose constituents included Steve Woelk, the sailor who'd undergone surgery without anesthesia in North Korea. But the most anticipated witness was Vice Admiral Jeremy M. Boorda, the chief of naval personnel. Boorda surprised the other witnesses by quickly stating, "Navy supports the award of the medal."

The admiral acknowledged that a case could be made for decorating Bucher and his men under the existing statute. But the Navy, he said, believed the law should be changed so that the *Pueblo* sailors were explicitly eligible.

"I personally feel that we as a nation should recognize the sacrifices made by these crew members," Boorda told the subcommittee. "We, as elected and appointed officials of our government, have an obligation to do the right thing and, in this case, that means to do what is necessary to permit the award of the POW medal to each *Pueblo* crewman. They have earned it."

Congress passed the *Pueblo* amendment in November 1989, and President George H. W. Bush signed it into law. The following spring, Bucher got a call at home in Poway. His men would get their medals at a public ceremony in San Diego on May 5, 1990. The date was only two weeks away.

By now, the crewmen were scattered across the country. Knowing some of them couldn't afford a trip to San Diego, the captain set out to raise money to cover their expenses. He phoned a bond broker he knew, hoping to squeeze $50 or $100 out of him. When the man pledged $1,000, Bucher was stunned. "I couldn't speak and neither could he," remembered the captain. "We stood there on the phone, listening to each other breathe. I couldn't say anything, I was so emotionally choked up. And he got choked up because I was choked up, so we sat there holding on to the phone for about a minute or so."

Emboldened, Bucher started putting the arm on other people. Helen Copley, wife of the publisher of the *San Diego Union*, which had editorialized in favor of POW medals for the crew, gave $5,000. The owner of the San Diego Padres kicked in $1,000. Stu Russell collected $350 from friends in Eureka, California, where he lived. In ten days Bucher and company raised a phenomenal $40,000. The owner of a travel agency the captain had met on a trip to Russia contributed free plane tickets for six crewmen living in New England. Each donor received a framed copy of Bucher's watercolor of the *Pueblo* at sea.

Bob Chicca, the former Marine linguist who was now selling graduation rings to high school students in the San Diego area, called some of his old shipmates to invite them to the ceremony. Some of the men "just broke down and cried" at the news. The Veterans Administration, not the Navy, was put in charge of the event. The VA wanted a "neutral site" for it and selected the lawn in front of the San Diego County Administration Building.

May 5 was a gorgeous Southern California Saturday. The city fathers had proclaimed it "USS *Pueblo* Day." About 400 people gathered outside the county building, enjoying a panoramic view of the azure waters of San Diego Bay. Sixty-four of the 79 living sailors showed up, yellow carnations in their lapels. Reporters and TV cameramen wandered around, interviewing people. Anchored in the distance was the USS *Ranger*, one of the aircraft carriers dispatched to the Sea of Japan during the *Pueblo* crisis. On its flight deck stood its entire complement of 3,800 officers and men, perfectly spaced, in brilliant white uniforms. The carrier ran up signal flags congratulating the *Pueblo* crew.

A Navy band played the national anthem, and the director of the local VA office acted as master of ceremonies. "It is, I hope, a bad day for the ghost of the *Pueblo*," he said. "We all hope that this is the day that that ghost is laid to rest." Several dignitaries spoke. Barbara Pope, an assistant secretary of the Navy, read a proclamation from President Bush and declared that, with the presentation of the POW medals, the *Pueblo* sailors "rightfully join the ranks of all the nation's sons who have suffered, on our behalf, the bitter trials of enemy captivity."

Congressman Mavroules also spoke, striking a humbler note. "I apologize for all the citizens of this nation," he said, "because it has taken us so long to recognize your bravery and your service."

That was all the aging ex-seamen really needed to hear. The medal was, after all, just a trinket, a bronze disk an inch and three-eighths in diameter. But it represented an important piece of their lives. It was both symbol and acknowledgment of their suffering, their comradeship, their valiant struggle to stand up to cruel, ruthless foes who'd tried to crush them. It attested to their dogged will to survive. The medals would be taken home and slipped into desk drawers and shoe boxes. But they'd never be forgotten.

The *Pueblo* men leaned forward in their chairs, eager to catch every word of every speech. Then it was time to receive their decorations. An admiral and a Marine general, resplendent in dress uniforms, handed them out one by one. Among the sailors there were grins and backslaps, bear hugs and damp eyes.

Bucher was too overcome to make a speech. But when he stood up in the sunshine to accept his medal, his men cheered like there was no tomorrow.

EPILOGUE

In the late 1990s, the North Koreans gambled again with the *Pueblo.* They disguised it as a freighter and sailed it around South Korea to the west coast of North Korea, and then up a river to Pyongyang. The ship chugged through international waters for nine days. American and South Korean forces, although presumably monitoring communist ports and sea lanes, again made no apparent move to intercept the vessel.

Not long after its arrival in Pyongyang, the *Pueblo* was opened to the public as a combination war trophy and tourist attraction. Moored on the Taedong River in the heart of the communist capital, it drew large numbers of visitors, including Americans and other Westerners. Tourists were shown a video declaring that the captured ship "will testify century after century [about] the crimes of aggression played by U.S. imperialists against the Korean people." Escorted by English-speaking guides in snappy military outfits, visitors got to see battered code machines in the SOD hut and a framed copy of General Woodward's apology (lacking any mention of his "prerepudiation," of course). They mugged for photos at the ship's wheel, gleefully swiveled machine guns back and forth, and gawked at clusters of large-caliber bullet holes—helpfully circled in red paint—in the bulkheads.

The North Koreans were said to be intensely proud of their prize and, despite its age, the *Pueblo* seemed well preserved. Strolling its decks in 2001, a U.S. Navy veteran met a North Korean guide who said he was part of the 1968 boarding party. The aging communist offered regards to the *Pueblo*'s crewmen and promised to "care for [their] ship until he dies."

Near the end of 2012, the *Pueblo* suddenly vanished from its dock. But several months later, the ship reappeared, anchored outside a renovated war museum as a permanent anti-imperialist exhibit.

As of this writing, the *Pueblo* has the unhappy distinction of being the only commissioned U.S. Navy vessel in the hands of a foreign power. Yet the U.S. government has made no visible effort to get the ship back since the crew was repatriated 45 years ago. As a Navy spokesman explained, Washington faces far more pressing problems with North Korea, especially trying to curtail its determined efforts to build nuclear weapons.

And so the *Pueblo* languishes, with no influential constituency to demand its return. Many Americans have either forgotten about the ship or never heard of it. Its surviving sailors, now mostly in their sixties, want the *Pueblo* brought home as closure to their ugly experiences in 1968—memories of which haunt them to this day. ("It would give all us crew a peace of mind if we knew it was on our home ground," Alvin Plucker, a young quartermaster who later managed a Colorado turkey farm, told a journalist.) But the ex-crewmen have virtually no voice in Congress or at the White House. Their only committed allies seem to be residents of the small, rough-and-tumble city for which the ship is named: Pueblo, Colorado.

Located in the high desert about 110 miles south of Denver, the city of 105,000 was once an important steel-making center. Now home to Professional Bull Riders, Inc. (motto: "The first rule is just to stay alive") and an annual car show put on by the National Street Rod Association, it's the kind of place that takes its military heritage seriously. In 1993, the city dubbed itself "the Home of Heroes," since four Medal of Honor winners have hailed from Pueblo—more per capita than any other city in the nation. ("What is it, something in the water out there in Pueblo?" asked President Dwight D. Eisenhower as he presented the medal to one local man, Raymond G. Murphy, in 1953.)

The local newspaper, the *Pueblo Chieftain*, has campaigned for years for the ship's return. It runs stories every year marking the anniversary of the capture. It editorializes for North Korea to do the right thing and give back the ship. Its publisher, Bob Rawlings, chairs the "Puebloans for the Return of the *Pueblo*" committee. Other citizens have taken up the cause, too. At one point, an enterprising businessman planned to build a memorial park featuring an eight-foot-deep pond, in which the *Pueblo* could one day float. The city's elected representatives in the Colorado legislature routinely introduce resolutions calling on North Korea to return the ship; Colorado's representatives in Congress sponsor similar pleas.

Some Coloradans regard Washington's failure to recover the ship as a national disgrace. Others view the vessel's release as a long-overdue act of goodwill by North Korea that could open big doors of potential cooperation with the West. After all, a series of Ping-Pong games in 1971 helped pave the way for the United States to establish diplomatic relations with China.

For a while, it seemed as if a breakthrough were possible. Following a 2002 visit to North Korea, Donald Gregg, a former U.S. ambassador to South Korea, said he received a "cryptic note" from Pyongyang's deputy foreign minister that Gregg interpreted as a sign of the communist regime's willingness to release the vessel. But any possible deal fell through when the Bush administration later revealed that the north was trying to produce uranium-based nuclear weapons. The North Koreans again hinted at a possible rapprochement to Gregg in 2005 and to another American visitor, New Mexico Governor Bill Richardson, in 2007. But no agreement ever materialized.

Hope also flickered in 2007 when U.S. Senator Wayne Allard, a Colorado Republican, called for the return of a Korean battle flag seized by American sailors and Marines who stormed a Korean fort in 1871. The blue-and-yellow flag, belonging to the fort's commander, General Uh Je-yeon, had been displayed at the U.S. Naval Academy, along with 300 other captured foreign battle flags, ever since. (About 350 Korean warriors died defending their turf against the smaller but much better armed U.S. landing party; many Koreans today regard the Battle of Kanghwa Island as their Alamo.) Allard and other *Pueblo* supporters thought giving back the 13-by-13-foot pennant might prompt Pyongyang to release the ship as a reciprocal gesture. But the north didn't reply to the offer; instead, the South Korean government promptly sent a delegation to Annapolis to retrieve the treasured banner.

North Korea's traditional intransigence has only seemed to worsen in recent years. In 2012, a Colorado lawmaker who'd cosponsored the legislature's annual bring-home-the-*Pueblo* resolution received a postcard with a return address in Pyongyang. The postcard said that "never, not in a million years" would the ship be returned. Its sender dared State Representative Keith Swerdfeger: "Come and get it! The Korean People's Army is ready to offer you full hospitality!" On the postcard's flip side was an illustration of two North Korean soldiers battering a terrified American serviceman with rifle butts. It wasn't clear whether the postcard came from the communist government or just an angry citizen.

On the other hand, the North Koreans can be jaw-droppingly unpredictable. (Who could ever have imagined their current leader, Kim Jong-un, hugging ex–Chicago Bulls star Dennis Rodman like they were best friends?) It's not outside the realm of possibility that they might abruptly hand back the ship, based on some internal calculus of political or economic gain in the future.

In the final analysis, however, asking North Korea to return the *Pueblo* may be as futile as asking the British Museum to return the Elgin Marbles. Pyongyang's leaders have as deep an attachment to the ship as the museum's overseers have to the famous sculptures and other marble artifacts Lord Elgin removed so controversially from Greece's Parthenon early in the nineteenth century.

It's hard to imagine the *Pueblo* ever coming home except as part of a grand bargain between North Korea and the United States in which Pyongyang agreed to permanently halt its nuclear weapons program in exchange for, say, large deliveries of fuel oil and food for its chronically underfed populace. But it's unlikely that American negotiators would push very hard for the *Pueblo* if it meant upending a potential deal with North Korea to stop building nuclear warheads and missiles that can deliver them far from its territory.

With such limited prospects of getting the ship back, three ex–*Pueblo* sailors and the captain's wife decided to seek another kind of justice. In 2006, they sued North Korea under the Foreign Sovereign Immunities Act, which permits U.S. citizens to seek damages from foreign governments for torture.

The lawsuit, filed in federal court in Washington, D.C., was organized by William T. Massie, a onetime machinist's mate. His fellow plaintiffs were Friar Tuck, the ex-oceanographer; Don McClarren, the former communication technician; and Rose Bucher, standing in for her husband, who died in 2004.

A farm boy from Illinois, Massie had enlisted in the Navy at 18, hoping to see the world while serving aboard a nuclear submarine. Instead, he was assigned to the *Pueblo*. Like other crew members, he was beaten remorselessly in North Korea. Guards wearing heavy combat boots kicked him over and over in the back, groin, knees, arms, elbows, and ankles. "My ankles were raw—they were actually bleeding," he says. "They just kept it up, and kept it up, and kept it up."

One day, after Massie was caught whispering with a shipmate, the Bear jammed the muzzle of an assault rifle into his mouth. "He took the clip out, and all this time he was yelling at me in Korean. He showed me the bullets and he slammed the clip back in and put his hand on the trigger and showed that the safety was off. And he just kept yakking at me. Finally, my knees were shaking so bad he pulled the rifle . . . out of my mouth and whacked me upside the head with it. Knocked me to the floor."

Back in his hometown after his enlistment ended, Massie worked variously as a road paver, mechanic, and truck driver. He got married four years after coming home but suffered from nightmares and sexual dysfunction. His wife divorced him after only six months.

"I had a short temper. I wasn't the same guy I was before I left. I was kind of moody. I'd have these dreams at night that would startle me in the middle of the night. I'd wake up screamin' or sweatin' or whatever. It was a hard situation for somebody to live with."

In his dreams he was being punched and kicked and bashed all over again, and the sensations were so real, the pain so intense, he thought it was actually happening. Sometimes he envisioned himself breaking out of prison, knifing or shooting a guard to death in the process, and running for days through the hostile countryside, disoriented and terrified. Eventually the North Koreans caught up to him, riddling his body with gunshots and then dragging him through the streets as civilians shrieked at and kicked him.

By the mid-1990s, he was sweating through such dreams four or five nights a week. Exhaustion set in. His weight ballooned from overeating. When he thought of Duane Hodges's bloody death and the injuries to his shipmates during the attack and in prison, he'd "just burst out and cry." In 1997, he started his own heating and air-conditioning business, but persistent aches and pains made it increasingly difficult to work. "My back was killing me, my legs and ankles from when I was kicked and beaten overseas. At times, I couldn't hardly walk."

Massie never sought help because he didn't want to be "a burden" on taxpayers. Finally, during a crew reunion, Bucher all but ordered him to seek treatment from the Veterans Administration. Massie received a disability rating of 100 percent due to post-traumatic stress disorder. Now, at 65, he takes several medications a day for anxiety and depression, and sees a VA psychiatrist at least once a month. He receives about $3,000 a month in government disability benefits. He never remarried and lives alone in the one-story house he grew up in.

"I'm just to the point now where I don't get out of my house. I pretty much am a hermit here. I don't like getting outside the house, really. I don't like that much to get involved with people. With friends, and all the things that I used to really enjoy, I don't anymore."

Massie doesn't try to sugarcoat his motive for suing North Korea: revenge, pure and simple. He wanted to punish the communists by prying as much money as possible out of them for what they did to him and his shipmates. But the court action also was his way of honoring Bucher, with whom he became close.

"I didn't want to reach the Pearly Gates and have Pete up there waitin' on me and ask me what the hell I was doin' because I hadn't done anything on the *Pueblo*'s cause," he says. "I knew I had to do something to carry on, or try to carry on, part of his legacy, of our legacy."

Massie approached a local lawyer, Daniel T. Gilbert, to draft his lawsuit. Gilbert had successfully sued Iran over the hijacking of TWA Flight 847 in

1985. His clients were six U.S. Navy construction divers who'd been passengers on the plane, which was en route from Athens to Rome when Hezbollah terrorists commandeered it. The hijackers killed another Navy diver, Robert Stethem, dumping his body on the runway when the plane landed in Beirut.

Gilbert won a $309 million judgment against Iran, demonstrating in federal court that it was a state sponsor of Hezbollah. He and his clients later collected $9 million out of Iranian assets frozen by the U.S. government. But Gilbert was reluctant to take on the *Pueblo* case. Squeezing money out of North Korea, he knew, would be much more difficult. He told Massie the case would be long and frustrating, and stood little chance of success. But Massie persisted and Gilbert ultimately agreed to help.

When the suit went to trial, no one appeared to defend North Korea. The sailors gave emotional testimony about what the Bear and other guards did to them, and how it had marred their lives. In December 2008, U.S. District Judge Henry H. Kennedy Jr. ruled in their favor, ordering North Korea to pay nearly $66 million: $16.75 million each to Massie, Tuck, and McClarren for their time in prison and subsequent pain and suffering; $14.3 million to Pete Bucher's estate; and $1.25 million to Rose Bucher.

Kennedy noted that the sailors underwent "extensive and shocking" abuse in prison and "suffered physical and mental harm that has endured." Massie and his coplaintiffs were particularly pleased by the judge's statement that Bucher surrendered the *Pueblo* only after "recognizing there was no chance of escape."

To date, however, the former crewmen and Rose Bucher haven't seen a cent. Gilbert is working with a Chicago law firm to uncover North Korean funds that could be attached. So far, they've found none.

"We have been continuously looking," the attorney says. "I really can't go into any other details than that. We've not been successful, unfortunately. But we're constantly seeking to find the assets that would be available." Gilbert adds that "it's totally unpredictable" whether the plaintiffs will ever see any money.

Massie deeply misses Bucher, whom he credits with saving his life on the high seas and easing his pain at home. He was among about two dozen ex-sailors who attended the captain's funeral after his death, following years of declining health, at 76. During a funeral mass at St. Michael's Catholic Church in Poway, a priest told mourners the trials that marked Bucher's life paralleled those of Jesus, "who was also betrayed, abandoned, discouraged, spat upon, preyed upon." Actor Hal Holbrook, who portrayed Bucher in an acclaimed 1973 TV movie, sent a message describing him as "a beautiful man, a patriot who loved his wife and his country and the men who served and endured with him." Holbrook added, "I salute him from my heart."

Several hundred people attended the captain's burial with full military honors at Fort Rosecrans National Cemetery in San Diego. The Navy that once tried to court-martial him provided a 21-gun salute. Two young sailors presented Rose Bucher with the American flag that had covered her husband's casket, and his remains were slowly lowered into the ground.

The cemetery sits atop Point Loma, a windswept finger of land that curves protectively around San Diego Bay. It's a lovely spot. To the east, you can see sailboats flitting across the bay, with the city's sun-gilded skyline in the background. To the west is an even more spectacular view of Bucher's first love, the vast, merciless Pacific Ocean.

ENDNOTES

ABBREVIATIONS

NA National Archives at College Park (Archives II), College Park, Maryland

LBJ Lyndon Baines Johnson Library & Museum, Austin, Texas

GF Gerald R. Ford Library, Ann Arbor, Michigan

NHHC U.S. Naval Historical & Heritage Command, Washington Navy Yard, D.C.

VU Vanderbilt University Television News Archive, Nashville, Tennessee

AMHI U.S. Army Military History Institute, Carlisle Barracks, Pennsylvania

HI Hoover Institution, Stanford, California

NSA National Security Agency, oral history series, Fort Meade, Maryland

WW Woodrow Wilson Center, North Korea International Documentation Project, Washington, D.C.

RG Record Group

NSF National Security File

RP Record of Proceedings of a Court of Inquiry, Convened by Order of Commander in Chief, United States Pacific Fleet, to Inquire into the Circumstances Relating to the Seizure of the USS *Pueblo* (AGER 2) by North Korean Naval Forces Which Occurred in the Sea of Japan on 23 January 1968

CA Classified Annex to Record of Proceedings of a Court of Inquiry, Convened by Order of Commander in Chief, United States Pacific Fleet, to Inquire into the Circumstances Relating to the Seizure of the USS *Pueblo* (AGER 2) by North Korean Naval Forces Which Occurred in the Sea of Japan on 23 January 1968

Inq Inquiry into the USS *Pueblo* and EC-121 Plane Incidents, Hearings Before the Special Subcommittee on the USS *Pueblo* of the Committee on Armed Services, House of Representatives, 91st Congress, First Session, 1969

PROLOGUE

1 **The Russians buried Dunham:** Larry Tart and Robert Keefe (*The Price of Vigilance: Attacks on American Surveillance Flights*, Ballantine Books, New York, 2001), 29.

2 **Reconnaissance aircraft were shot down:** Figures on the shoot-downs are drawn from Tart and Keefe, ibid., and LBJ, "Memorandum for the Record," 16 Feb. 1967, NSF, Country File, Asia and the Pacific, Korea, *Pueblo* Incident, Events Leading Up To, box 264.

3 **"Provocative incidents":** NA, "Encounters Between US and Soviet Ships and Aircraft," RG 59, General Records of the Department of State, Office of the Executive Secretariat, Korea Crisis ("*Pueblo* Crisis") Files, 1968, Entry 5192, Lot 69D912, box 5, folder: Misc. *Pueblo*, 2/1/68-68, Book II of II (folder 1 of 2).

3 **Russian captain rushed:** ibid.

CHAPTER 1: SPIES AHOY

8 **He didn't get drafted:** Author interview with F. Carl (Skip) Schumacher Jr.

9 **"Where'd you come from?":** F. Carl Schumacher Jr. and George C. Wilson, *Bridge of No Return: The Ordeal of the U.S.S.* Pueblo (Harcourt Brace Jovanovich, Inc., New York, 1971), 46.

9 **"Intellectual barbarian":** Author interview with Lieutenant Commander Allen Hemphill, U.S. Navy, retired. Hemphill was a onetime shipmate and longtime friend of Bucher's.

10 **Operation Clickbeetle:** For a fuller account of Operation Clickbeetle, see Trevor Armbrister, *A Matter of Accountability: The True Story of the* Pueblo *Affair* (Coward-McCann Inc., New York, 1970), 81–87.

10 **"Pipe-smoking characters":** Lloyd M. Bucher and Mark Rascovich, *Bucher: My Story* (Doubleday & Co., Inc., Garden City, New York, 1970), 14.

11 **462 mechanical and design deficiencies:** Armbrister, op. cit., 149.

12 **"Overzealous":** Bucher, op. cit., 14.

12 **Fourth century B.C.:** Author interview with Peter Langenberg.

12 **Steering engine had failed 180 times:** Bucher, op. cit., 81.

13 **Missive found its way:** Ibid., 30.

14 **Harrowing attack:** For two very different views of the *Liberty* incident, see James M. Ennes Jr., *Assault on the* Liberty*: The True Story of the Israeli Attack on an American Intelligence Ship* (Random House, New York, 1979) and A. Jay Cristol, *The* Liberty *Incident: The 1967 Attack on the U.S. Navy Spy Ship* (Brassey's/Potomac Books, Washington, D.C., 2002). Ennes, who was on board the *Liberty* when it was hit, concludes that Israel attacked deliberately. Cristol, a federal bankruptcy judge in Florida, argues that the attack was a tragic case of mistaken identity, as Israel maintained.

15 **"A little unfair of me":** Schumacher, op. cit., 47.

16 **"The Lonely Bull":** Author interview with Lloyd M. Bucher.

17 **Double-fingered whistle:** Schumacher, op. cit., 58.

18 **Great Naked Art Heist:** Details of the temporary theft of the painting are drawn from Bucher, op. cit. 105, and Ed Brandt, *The Last Voyage of USS* Pueblo (W. W. Norton & Co., New York, 1969), 18.

19 **"The captain of all captains":** Armbrister, op. cit., 154.

20 **Dropped out of Princeton:** Langenberg, op. cit.

21 **A shy academic:** Biographical details of Steve Harris are drawn from Schumacher, op. cit., 56, and Armbrister, op. cit., 107.

21 **"Wish you were dead":** Langenberg, op. cit.

22 **Lost electrical steering:** Mitchell B. Lerner, *The* Pueblo *Incident: A Spy Ship and the Failure of American Foreign Policy* (University Press of Kansas, Lawrence, Kansas, 2002), 40.

23 **"Contingency plans . . . are written and approved":** Bucher, op. cit., 113.

23 **Despite his pique:** Edward R. Murphy Jr. and Curt Gentry, *Second in Command* (Holt, Rinehart and Winston, New York, 1971), 72.

26 **"Boosted morale about 600 percent":** Armbrister, op. cit., 162.

26 **Plunged into the frigid ocean:** Murphy, op. cit., 15–16.

27 **Murphy sipped a ginger ale:** Bucher, op. cit., 37.

28 **Pass on the mincemeat:** Murphy, op. cit., 73.

29 **They were laughing:** Bucher, op. cit., 121.

CHAPTER 2: DON'T START A WAR OUT THERE, CAPTAIN

30 **"Put together like a plate of hash":** Trevor Armbrister, *A Matter of Accountability: The True Story of the* Pueblo *Affair* (Coward-McCann Inc., New York, 1970), 86.

31–32 **Destroyer steaming at 30 knots:** Armbrister, ibid., 122.

32 **"All kinds of signals":** Author interview with Dick Fredlund.

32 **24 hours to lock on:** Lloyd M. Bucher and Mark Rascovich, *Bucher: My Story* (Doubleday & Co., Inc., Garden City, New York, 1970), 129.

33 **"Boom-yakle-yakle":** F. Carl Schumacher Jr. and George C. Wilson, *Bridge of No Return: The Ordeal of the U.S.S.* Pueblo (Harcourt Brace Jovanovich, Inc., New York, 1971), 51.

35 **Angry and embarrassed:** Author interview with Lloyd M. Bucher.

37 **Landed an agent:** Bucher, ibid.

37 **"I admired them":** Bucher, op. cit.

38 **Zech couldn't reverse his decision:** Armbrister, op. cit., 105.

40 **Stack the excess:** Edward R. Murphy Jr. and Curt Gentry, *Second in Command* (Holt, Rinehart and Winston, New York, 1971), 78.

40 **Electronic warfare policy:** NA, RG 526, Records of the Naval Criminal Investigative Service, box 13, folder: US6500, USS *Pueblo,* Feb 1–7, 1968.

41 **At least a dozen code machines:** NA, RG 526, Records of the Naval Criminal Investigative Service, box 13, folder: US6500, USS *Pueblo,* Jan 1–25, 1968.

41 **Told him to shape up:** Armbrister, op. cit., 177.

42 **No time to replace them:** Ed Brandt, *The Last Voyage of USS* Pueblo (W. W. Norton & Co., New York, 1969), 21.

42 **A presail briefing:** Details of the briefing are drawn from Bucher, *Bucher: My Story,* op. cit., 138; Murphy, op. cit. 95; and Armbrister, op. cit., 203.

43 **"You're not going out there to start a war":** Bucher, op. cit., 140.

CHAPTER 3: ALONG A DREAD COAST

45 **"Sir, but I've got to puke":** Lloyd M. Bucher and Mark Rascovich, *Bucher: My Story* (Doubleday & Co., Inc., Garden City, New York, 1970), 46.

47 **It wasn't his fault:** Edward R. Murphy Jr. and Curt Gentry, *Second in Command* (Holt, Rinehart and Winston, New York, 1971), 110.

47 **"Jesus Christ, mister!":** Bucher, op. cit., 149.

48 **Terse language:** The text of the sailing order can be found in Bucher, op. cit., 420–22.

49 **That delighted the quartermaster:** Author interview with Charles Law.

50 **"A sailor first and foremost":** "Bremerton—An Anecdote," online essay by Stu Russell, http://www.usspueblo.org/Background/Bremerton/Bremerton-P1.html.

51 **Movies were shown:** The list of film titles is from NA, RG 526, Records of the Naval Criminal Investigative Service, box 12, folder: *Pueblo* #2.

51 **"What the hell's going on up there?":** F. Carl Schumacher Jr. and George C. Wilson, *Bridge of No Return: The Ordeal of the U.S.S.* Pueblo (Harcourt Brace Jovanovich, Inc., New York, 1971), 77.

52 **Black mountains:** "Colder and Getting Colder—An Anecdote," online essay by Stu Russell, http://www.usspueblo.org/Pueblo_Incident/This_is_Not_Real/Cold_colder.html.

52 **Crosshatch the navigation charts:** Trevor Armbrister, *A Matter of Accountability: The True Story of the* Pueblo *Affair* (Coward-McCann Inc., New York, 1970), 24.

53 **"Unproductive":** Schumacher, op. cit., 72.

54 **"Eat our livers":** Stu Russell, op. cit.

56 **Slipped past soldiers from the U.S. 2nd Infantry Division:** LBJ, NSF, National Security Council Histories, *Pueblo* Crisis 1968, Vol. 14, Telegrams to Seoul, tabs 20–22, box 33.

56 **A suspicious Seoul policeman:** Daniel P. Bolger, "Scenes from an Unfinished War: Low-Intensity Conflict in Korea, 1966–1969" (Leavenworth Papers No. 19, Combat Studies Institute, U.S. Army Command and General Staff College, Fort Leavenworth, Kansas, 1991), 63.

57 **"Extreme tension":** *Korea Times* newspaper, Seoul, South Korea, Jan. 26, 1968.

57 **Decided to concentrate on the Blue House:** LBJ, NSF, National Security Council Histories, *Pueblo* Crisis 1968, Vol. 15, Telegrams to Seoul, tabs 9–17, box 34.

58 **Only two were believed made it home:** Joseph S. Bermudez, *North Korean Special Forces* (Naval Institute Press, Annapolis, Md., 1998), 85.

CHAPTER 4: SOS SOS SOS

61 **"Balmy winters":** Lloyd M. Bucher and Mark Rascovich, *Bucher: My Story* (Doubleday & Co., Inc., Garden City, New York, 1970), 46.

61 **Unbeknown to the captain:** The flight of the C-130 reconnaissance plane was described to the author by a former crewman who asked to remain anonymous because he'd signed a lifetime Air Force secrecy pledge.

62 **"We have approached the target":** Transcripts of this and subsequent radio messages from the North Korean gunboats are contained in LBJ, NSF, Country File, "Korea, *Pueblo* Incident, Vol. I, Part A (thru Jan.)," box 257.

64 **A searching look:** Bucher, op. cit., 182.

65 **"I'll be goddamned":** Bucher, op. cit., 184.

65 **"For God's sake, stop!":** Edward R. Murphy Jr. and Curt Gentry, *Second in Command* (Holt, Rinehart and Winston, New York, 1971), 131.

67 **"SOS. SOS. SOS. SOS. . . .":** Inq, 671.

68 **"Everybody on your feet!":** Bucher, *Bucher: My Story,* op. cit., 191.

69 **A sharp kick in the rear:** Bucher, op. cit., 189.

69 **"Answer the fucking phones!":** Author interview with Lloyd M. Bucher.

69 **"I'm going to have to get busy":** Ed Brandt, *The Last Voyage of USS* Pueblo (W. W. Norton & Co., New York, 1969), 48.

70 **"A wild-eyed look":** Bucher, op. cit., 191.

73 **Three pounds of paper at a time:** Murphy, op. cit., 139.

74 **A slab of human flesh:** Bucher interview.

75 **"AIR FORCE GOING HELP YOU":** Inq, 671.

77 **Afraid he'd burst into tears:** F. Carl Schumacher Jr. and George C. Wilson, *Bridge of No Return: The Ordeal of the U.S.S.* Pueblo (Harcourt Brace Jovanovich, Inc., New York, 1971), 99.

77 **Strike aircraft:** Inq., op. cit., 898.

78 **"Creature-comfort admiral":** Reminiscences of Vice Admiral Kent L. Lee, U.S. Navy (Retired), Vol. II (U.S. Naval Institute, Annapolis, Maryland, 1987–88), 479.

78 **Port city's air defenses:** Inq, op. cit., 916.

79 **"No overt action":** Inq, ibid., 1672.

79 **McKee fired question after question:** Author interview with Seth McKee.

80 **But only four planes were available:** It's unclear exactly how many U.S. fighters were in Japan that day, and how many were flyable. Although General John McConnell, the Air Force chief of staff, told President Johnson there were 24 planes, General Earle Wheeler, chairman of the Joint Chiefs of Staff, put the figure at 77. Defense Secretary Robert McNamara told congressional leaders "40-odd" aircraft were in Japan at the time. General Seth McKee indicated in congressional testimony that, in any event, none of the planes were combat-ready and immediately available.

80 **Configured for nuclear bombs:** NA, RG 59, General Records of the Department of State, Office of the Executive Secretariat, Entry 5192, Korean Crisis ("*Pueblo* Crisis") files, 1968, Lot file 69D219, stack 150/69/17/07, box 1.

81 **Tip South Korea into war:** AMHI, General Charles H. Bonesteel interview, Senior Officers Oral History Program, 1973, Vol. 1, 342.

81 **"The goddamn Navy":** Author interview with John Wright.

82 **"What's happening to them?":** McKee interview.

CHAPTER 5: WE WILL NOW BEGIN TO SHOOT YOUR CREW

83 **"I protest this outrage!":** Lloyd M. Bucher and Mark Rascovich, *Bucher: My Story* (Doubleday & Co., Inc., Garden City, New York, 1970), 208.

85 **"Tell your colonel":** Bucher, ibid., 213.

86 **"Share the wealth":** Ibid., 216.

87 **"Inside my rectum":** CA, Vol. III, 1312–29.

88 **He, too, bravely refused:** Stephen R. Harris and James C. Hefley, *My Anchor Held* (Fleming H. Revell Co., Old Tappan, New Jersey, 1970), 13.

88 **"You have no military rights":** Bucher, op. cit., 220.

90 **"Compromised for ten years":** Author interview with John Wright.

92 **"Captain, you first":** F. Carl Schumacher Jr. and George C. Wilson, *Bridge of No Return: The Ordeal of the U.S.S.* Pueblo (Harcourt Brace Jovanovich, Inc., New York, 1971), 9.

93 **Sterile and lonely:** Harris, op. cit., 16.

94 "How you feel?": Bucher, op. cit., 229.

97 "You will be shot this afternoon!": Details of the tribunal were drawn from memoirs by Bucher, Murphy, Steve Harris, and Schumacher.

99 "Sign this confession!": Bucher, op. cit., 237.

100 "Without more unpleasantness": Ibid., 239.

101 No ejected dud hit the floor: Details of the mock execution are drawn from *Bucher: My Story* and the Bucher interview.

102 A horrifying sight: *Bucher: My Story*, op. cit., 243.

104 "I will sign": Details of this scene are drawn from *Bucher: My Story* and the Bucher interview.

CHAPTER 6: A MINEFIELD OF UNKNOWNS

106 Bucher's admission: The full text of the captain's "confession" was published in the January 25, 1968, edition of *The New York Times*.

106 "Look very closely at his record": LBJ, Tom Johnson's Notes of Meetings, Jan. 24, 1968, 1 p.m., *Pueblo* II, National Security Council, container #2. Johnson did not take verbatim notes of what was said at LBJ's meetings, but instead paraphrased participants. The author has chosen to quote short sentences from his notes as the closest reconstructions of President Johnson's otherwise unrecorded words during *Pueblo* crisis meetings that are ever likely to be available.

108 "The only thing I could think to do": "The Capture," *Naval History*, Fall 1988, 54.

109 "Drop the atomic bomb": LBJ, National Security-Defense, ND 19, CO 151/1-30-68, box 205.

109 "Coward": LBJ, National Security-Defense, ND 191, 5-25-65, CO 151/1-28-68, box 205.

110 "792 pounds of cargo": LBJ, Tom Johnson's Notes of Meetings, Jan. 25, 1968, 1:26 p.m., *Pueblo* 5 luncheon meeting, container #2.

111 "The fullest justification": LBJ, NSF, Files of Bromley K. Smith, Meeting of the *Pueblo* Group, 1/24/68, 10:30 a.m., box 1.

112 "An act of war": "U.S. Pressing Ship's Release," *Washington Post*, Jan. 25, 1968.

113 "Putting prestige factors in the refrigerator": LBJ, NSF, Files of Bromley K. Smith, op. cit.

114 CIA pilot Jack Weeks: A number of published accounts credit another CIA pilot, Frank Murray, with locating the *Pueblo* after its capture. But a declassified CIA history of the A-12 reconnaissance aircraft program, "Finding a Mission," says it was Weeks who discovered the ship in a small bay north of Wonsan on January 26, 1968. About four months later Weeks disappeared while flying a Mach 3–plus A-12 over the Pacific Ocean near the Philippines. His body was never found. https://www.cia.gov/library/center-for-the-study-of-intelligence/csi-publications/books-and-monographs/a-12/finding-a-mission.html

114 No concentrations of troops and tanks: LBJ, NSF, National Security Council Histories, "*Pueblo* Crisis 1968, Vol. 4, Day to Day Documents, Part 5," box 28.

117 "Just crazy enough": Author interview with John Denham.

118 KGB agent in India: LBJ, NSF, Country File, Korea, *Pueblo* Incident, Vol. I, Part B, box 257.

119 FBI men in Washington and New York: Information about the communist nations' plans at the United Nations is taken from Lloyd Mark Bucher's FBI file, File No. HQ 100-370055, Section 5, obtained by the author through the Freedom of Information Act.

120 "We going to have to do something": LBJ, Recording of Telephone Conversation Between Lyndon B. Johnson and Arthur Goldberg, Jan. 28, 1968, 11:38 a.m., Citation #12613, track 3, Recordings and Transcripts of Conversations and Meetings, White House Series, WH6801.02.

121 "Is that clearly understood?": LBJ, Tom Johnson's Notes of Meetings, Jan. 26, 1968, 7:29 p.m., *Pueblo* Backgrounder with Hugh Sidey, container #2.

121 "I am neither optimistic or pessimistic": Ibid.

123 NIS men grilled hostesses: Details of the Naval Investigative Service probe of Bucher are contained in multiple documents located at NA, RG 526, Records of the Naval Criminal Investigative Service, US6500, Jan. 26–27, 1968, box 13. In an interview, Bucher conceded that he "may have chased around a couple of those little girls over there in Yokosuka."

124 "Too involved with his men": LBJ, NSF, National Security Council Histories,

Pueblo Crisis 1968, Vol. 4, Day by Day Documents, Part 5, box 28. The author obtained a partially redacted copy of the CIA profile of Bucher through the Freedom of Information Act.

124 Nine submarines: NA, RG 218, Records of General Earle Wheeler, chairman of the Joint Chiefs of Staff, box 29, tab 4.

125 Men hastily built bunkers: AMHI, General Charles H. Bonesteel interview, Senior Officers Oral History Program, 1973, Vol. 1, 353.

125 "A rather serious loss": LBJ, NSF, Meeting Notes File, Jan. 31, 1968, meeting with congressional leaders, box 2.

126 "I just don't see any value at all": Executive Sessions of the Senate Foreign Relations Committee (Historical Series), Volume XX, Ninetieth Congress, Second Session, 1968 (made public in 2010), 157.

127 "When you send out a spy": LBJ, op. cit.

127 "Tension bouncing off the walls": Author interview with Joseph A. Yager, former deputy director of the Korean Task Force.

128 Ten possible courses of action: NA, RG 59, General Records of the Department of State, Central Foreign Policy Files, 1967–1969, Political and Defense, Lot File 69D219, Stack 150/69/17/07, box 1.

CHAPTER 7: SUICIDE IN A BUCKET

130 Profound sense of shame: Author interview with Lloyd M. Bucher.

132 Drenched and defeated: Author interview with F. Carl Schumacher Jr.

134 "You must be aware of the tortures": Lloyd M. Bucher and Mark Rascovich, *Bucher: My Story* (Doubleday & Co., Inc., Garden City, New York, 1970), 263.

137 He'd decided to adhere rigidly: The full text of the Code of Conduct can be found at Inq, 937.

139 "You're a weakling": Author interview with Harry Iredale.

140 "I was determined": CA, Vol. III, 1006–86.

140 "A brief confession": LBJ, NSF, Memos to the President, Walt Rostow, Vol. 112, Dec. 26–31 (1 of 2), container 44, "Statement of Robert James Hammond."

141 Scowling grimly: The Rules of Life are quoted in Bucher, op. cit., 281.

143 Stepped into a sunken tub: Ibid., 284.

144 "You will be given a special treat!": Ibid., 287.

145 Schumacher sent back a note: Trevor Armbrister, *A Matter of Accountability: The True Story of the* Pueblo *Affair* (Coward-McCann Inc., New York, 1970), 282.

147 "That's nonsense": NA, RG 59, General Records of the Department of State, Office of the Executive Secretariat, Korean Crisis ("*Pueblo* Crisis") Files, 1968, Entry 5192, Lot 69D219, box 5, folder: Miscellaneous—*Pueblo*, 2/1/68–8/68, Book II of II, transcript: "Officers of the Armed Spy Ship '*Pueblo*' of U.S. Imperialist Aggression Army Were Interviewed by Newspaper, News Agency, and Radio Reporters."

147 They debated the exact meaning: Bucher, op. cit., 304.

150 Some signed hesitantly: Details of the collective signing are taken from Bucher's and Schumacher's memoirs and the author's interview with Bucher.

CHAPTER 8: AT THE MAD HATTER'S TEA PARTY

151 People in the capital heard artillery: LBJ, NSF, National Security Council Histories, *Pueblo* Crisis 1968, Vol. 19, Telegrams to Posts Other Than Seoul (1 of 2), container 36.

151 "Tens of thousands of hand grenades": NA, RG 526, Records of the Naval Criminal Investigative Service, Stack 630A/1/2/1, box 12, folder: *Pueblo* #2.

152 An East German diplomat: WW, Memorandum on an Information of 1 February 1968, Embassy of the GDR in the DPRK, Pyongyang, History and Public Policy Program Digital Archive, MfAA C 1023/73. Translated by Karen Riechert. http://digitalarchive.wilsoncenter.org/document/113741.

153 "Fat revisionist pig": Obituary of Kim Il Sung, *Daily Telegraph*, London, July 11, 1994.

153 Their own request: LBJ, NSF, National Security Council Histories, *Pueblo* Crisis 1968, Vol. 12, CIA Documents [1], box 32.

154 Bulldozed and defoliated: Daniel P. Bolger, "Scenes from an Unfinished War: Low-Intensity Conflict in Korea, 1966–1969," Leavenworth Papers No. 19 (Combat Studies Institute, U.S. Army Command and General Staff College, Fort Leavenworth, Kansas, 1991), 49.

154 Digging in for war: NA, RG 218, Records of the U.S. Joint Chiefs of Staff, Records of Chairman (Gen.) Earle G. Wheeler, 1964–1970, box 29, folder: Korea (*Pueblo*) 091, 21 Feb. 1968, Vol. III.

155 "Seriously disturbed": NA, RG 526, Records of the Naval Criminal Investigative Service, box 13, tab 15, folder: US6500, USS *Pueblo*, Jan. 26–27, 1968.

156 "Sir, this is the break": LBJ, NSF, Country File, Korea, box 57, folder: *Pueblo* Incident, Vol. Ia, Part A.

156 "Results could be explosive": LBJ, NSF, National Security Council Histories, *Pueblo* Crisis 1968, Vol. 15, Telegrams to Seoul, tab 9–17, box 34.

157 Berger's retort to Porter: LBJ, NSF, Memos to the President, Walt Rostow, Vol. 58, Jan. 25–31, 1968 (2 of 3), container 28.

157 Park already had alerted his generals: LBJ, NSF, National Security Council Histories, *Pueblo* Crisis 1968, Vol. 16, Telegrams from Seoul, tab 8, box 34, "Final Vance Meeting with President Park," Feb. 17, 1968.

158 "Getting nowhere": Reminiscences of Vice Admiral J. Victor Smith, U.S. Navy (Retired), (U.S. Naval Institute, Annapolis, Maryland, 1977), 422.

158 "Putrid corpse": LBJ, NSF, Country File, Asia and the Pacific (Korea), Korea cables and memos, Vol. V, 9/67–3/68, box 255.

159 LBJ was disappointed: NA, RG 59, Records of Secretary of State Dean Rusk, Rusk telephone transcripts, telephone call from Walt Rostow, Feb. 2, 1968, 10:13 a.m.

160 "[Smith] is not psychologically suited": LBJ, NSF, National Security Council Histories, *Pueblo* Crisis 1968, Vol. 16, Telegrams from Seoul, tabs 1–5, box 34.

160 "I'd sit up watching": Author interview with Marion Smith.

161 A bridge leading to Panmunjom: Details of the students' protest are drawn from wire service accounts printed in the *Virginian-Pilot* and the *News and Courier* (Charleston, South Carolina), Feb. 8, 1968.

162 "Appeasement, indecisive, disappointing": LBJ, NSF, National Security Council Histories, *Pueblo* Crisis 1968, Vol. 16, Telegrams from Seoul, tabs 1–5, box 34.

163 Arrested and paraded: Don Oberdorfer, *The Two Koreas: A Contemporary History* (Basic Books, New York, 1997), 10.

163 "I resolved to uproot": Park Chung Hee, *The Country, the Revolution, and I* (Hollym Publishers, Seoul, South Korea, 1970), 61.

163 "Ringleader of a Communist cell": *New York Times*, May 20, 1961.

164 "An almost psychopathic fear": NA, RG 59, General Records of the Department of State, Office of the Executive Secretariat, Korea Crisis ("*Pueblo* Crisis") Files, 1968, Historical reports relating to diplomacy during the Lyndon Johnson Administration, 1963–1969, box 4, folder: Vol. 6.

164 **"Forceful, fair and intelligent":** Edward C. Keefer et al., *Foreign Relations of the United States, 1961–1963, Vol. XXII, Northeast Asia* (U.S. Government Printing Office, Washington, D.C., 1996), 543.

164 **"Upheaval, division, and probably bloodshed":** NA, RG 59, op. cit.

165 **Drinking heavily:** Karen L. Gatz, editor, *Foreign Relations of the United States, 1964–1968, Vol. XXIX, Part 1, Korea* (U.S. Government Printing Office, Washington, D.C., 2000), 377.

166 **"We're doing very well":** Author interview with Kent L. Lee.

166 **"No, I am not":** LBJ, Appointment File (Diary Backup), 2/1/68–2/9/68, Feb. 2, 1968, container 89.

167 **"Flat on our ass":** Gatz, *Foreign Relations of the United States*, op. cit., 554.

167 **Ball destroyed all hard copies:** George W. Ball, *The Past Has Another Pattern: Memoirs* (New York, W. W. Norton & Co., 1982), 436. A copy of Ball's report in draft form, however, found its way to the LBJ Library, and the author had it declassified. The draft can be found at NSF, Intelligence File, "*Pueblo* (Jan. 1968)," box 11, document #2.

168 **The United States "will not . . . humiliate itself":** LBJ, NSF, National Security Council Histories, *Pueblo* Crisis 1968, Vol. 14, Telegrams to Seoul, tab 1–12, box 33.

168 **"A pirate and a thief":** NA, RG 59, General Records of the Department of State, Central Foreign Policy Files 1967–1969, Political and Defense, Pol 33-6 Kor N.–U.S., 2/1/68 to 2/15/68, box 2276, folder: 2/8/68.

168 **Emergency powers:** LBJ, NSF, National Security Council Histories, *Pueblo* Crisis 1968, Vol. 12, CIA Documents [2], box 32.

170 **Only a few hours:** *New York Times*, Feb. 16, 1968.

171 **"An absolute menace":** Gatz, *Foreign Relations of the United States*, op. cit., 377.

171 **"We are not helpless":** LBJ, NSF, National Security Council Histories, *Pueblo* Crisis 1968, Vol. 14, Telegrams to Seoul, tab 20–22, box 33.

173 **"Gasped, sputtered":** LBJ, NSF, Memos to the President, Walt Rostow, Vol. 62, Feb. 14–16, 1968 (2 of 2), container #29 (1 of 2).

173 **Fortifying themselves with whisky:** Author interview with Abbott Greenleaf.

174 "Not strong enough": LBJ, NSF, National Security Council Histories, *Pueblo* Crisis 1968, Vol. 16, Telegrams from Seoul, tab 8, box 34.

176 "Profoundly disturbed": Ibid.

177 "Going on for some time": Gatz, *Foreign Relations of the United States*, op. cit., 378.

177 "A weak reed": Ibid., 382.

178 "Will fight together": Sergey S. Radchenko, *The Soviet Union and the North Korean Seizure of the USS* Pueblo*: Evidence from Russian Archives*, Cold War International History Project, Working Paper #47 (Woodrow Wilson International Center for Scholars, Washington, D.C., undated), 65.

178 "A defensive character": Ibid., 66.

CHAPTER 9: THE ENDURANCE OF MEN

180 "Welcome to your new home": F. Carl Schumacher Jr. and George C. Wilson, *Bridge of No Return: The Ordeal of the U.S.S.* Pueblo (Harcourt Brace Jovanovich, Inc., New York, 1971), 162.

180 Pondering various ways: Author interview with Lloyd M. Bucher.

181 "I have broken into tears many times": *Time* magazine, April 12, 1968.

182 "Time is running out": NA, RG 59, General Records of the Department of State, Central Foreign Policy Files 1967–1969, Political and Defense, Pol 33-6 Kor N.–U.S., 4/1/68 to 5/1/68, box 2270, folder: 4/15/68.

184 His emaciation startled him: Details of Woelk's experiences are drawn from an author interview with Woelk; an online essay he wrote, "D.P.R.K.'s Glorious Medicare Care," www.usspueblo.org/Prisoners/Medicare_Care.html; and Ed Brandt, *The Last Voyage of USS* Pueblo (W. W. Norton & Co., New York, 1969), 71.

185 "The typical day started in stupidity": Schumacher, op. cit., 174.

185 "They have blinded the boy!": Ibid., 166.

186 "We just don't walk like you": Trevor Armbrister, *A Matter of Accountability: The True Story of the* Pueblo *Affair* (Coward-McCann Inc., New York, 1970).

186 "Rascally fighting spirit": Author interview with Peter Langenberg.

187 "You ought to be beaten": Brandt, op. cit., 139.

188 "My head just exploded": Author interview with Jim Kell.

189 "So hungry you'd be shaking": Ibid.

191 **"100 percent mechanized":** "My *Pueblo* Nightmare," *Boston Globe* series, May 1969, episode 11.

192 **"Talk and talk and talk and talk":** Kell interview, op. cit.

193 **"They couldn't sell us on their system":** Langenberg interview, op. cit.

193 **Bought his own car for $3,200:** Brandt, op. cit., 141.

194 **"They haven't perfected the goat":** Stephen R. Harris and James C. Hefley, *My Anchor Held* (Fleming H. Revell Co., Old Tappan, New Jersey, 1970), 101.

194 **"Delirious with delight":** "Day 221: Mid summer, time to mow the lawn!" essay by crewman Ralph McClintock, copy in author's possession.

194 **"Look at him and grin":** Author interview with Charles Law.

195 **"It scared the hell out of you":** Kell interview, op. cit.

195 **"How dare you bring that up!":** Brandt, op. cit., 148.

CHAPTER 10: ALLIES AT ODDS

197 **Description of Kaiser estate:** LBJ, Appointment File (Diary Backup), April 15–17, 1968, Hawaii, container 96.

197 **"A pyrotechnical spectacle":** *Time* magazine, April 19, 1968.

198 **Under scrutiny by cryptanalysts:** NA, RG 526, Records of the Naval Criminal Investigative Service, folder: US6500, USS *Pueblo*, April 1968, box 13.

198 **"Replying to the letters":** LBJ, Papers of Clark Clifford, folder: *Pueblo*—March 1, 1968–January 20, 1969, box 23.

199 **His overarching fear:** LBJ, NSF, International Meetings and Travel File, Korea, President Johnson's Meeting w/ President Park, 4/68, container 21.

199 **A turning point:** LBJ, NSF, National Security Council Histories, *Pueblo* Crisis 1968, Vol. 21, Airgrams, misc., box 37.

199 **A sense of destiny:** Ibid.

200 **Gripped by "intense fear":** LBJ, NSF, International Meetings and Travel File, Korea, President Johnson's Meeting w/ President Park, 4/68, container 21.

200 **A "relatively short war":** LBJ, NSF, Country File, Korea, Memos and Cables, Vol. VI, 4/68–12/68, box 256.

200 **"Inimical to the U.S. national interest":** Ibid.

201 **"A shock for the Asians":** LBJ, NSF, National Security Council Histories, *Pueblo* Crisis 1968, Vol. 7, Day by Day Documents, Part 14, box 30.

201 "You must give us the main strength": Ibid.

203 "Loaded with live bullets": Ibid.

203 "We are treating them too well": WW, Report, Embassy of Hungary in North Korea to the Hungarian Foreign Ministry, 27 April 1968, http://www.wilsoncenter.org/sites/default/files/Crisis-Conf.Doc_reader-Pt1.pdf.

204 "Bourgeois pacifism and revisionism": WW, Presidium of the Central Committee of CPCZ, Information about the Situation in Korea, February 5, 1968, http://www.wilsoncenter.org/sites/default/files/NKIDP_Document_Reader_New_Evidence_on_North_Korea.pdf.

204 220 miles up the east coast: NA, RG 59, General Records of the Department of State, Central Foreign Policy Files 1967–1969, Political and Defense, Pol 33-6 Kor N.–U.S. 4/1/68 to 5/1/68, folder: 4/15/86, box 2270.

CHAPTER 11: SUMMER OF DEFIANCE

206 "Every little nitpicky thing": Author interview with Jim Kell.

206 "It would cost them a lot of money": Author interview with Lloyd M. Bucher.

206 He'd make it his solemn business: Ibid.

208 Bucher mumbled that he no longer cared: Ed Brandt, *The Last Voyage of USS* Pueblo (W. W. Norton & Co., New York, 1969), 151.

208 "I'm happier than shit": Author interview with Charles Law.

209 "Goddamn it, I didn't kill the goddamn plant": Brandt, op. cit., 145.

210 Strano husbanded his growing stash: Ibid., 152.

210 "He'd realize we got to him, and he'd send us off": Law interview. op. cit.

211 "His head down": Trevor Armbrister, *A Matter of Accountability: The True Story of the* Pueblo *Affair* (Coward-McCann Inc., New York, 1970), 308.

212 "Christ, there goes my career": Ibid., 309.

212 "You lose a .45[-caliber pistol] in the Navy": Author interview with F. Carl (Skip) Schumacher Jr.

213 "If you got five or six guys who saw it one way": Bucher interview. op. cit.

213 "No tender private thoughts could be conveyed": Lloyd M. Bucher and Mark Rascovich, *Bucher: My Story* (Doubleday & Co., Inc., Garden City, New York, 1970), 335.

214 "I told you it was gonna make me sweat": Armbrister, op. cit., 309.

214 "Run over him": Interview with Donald Richard Peppard, Library of Congress, Veterans History Project, Oct. 29, 2002.

215 "The majority were . . . CIA operatives": NA, RG 59, General Records of the Department of State, Central Foreign Policy Files, 1967–1969, Political and Defense, Central, Pol 33-6, Kor N–U.S., 7/1/68, box 2272, folder: 7/1/68.

215 Two crewmen were beaten: HI, unpublished excerpt from *Bucher: My Story*, Bucher Papers, box 17.

216 The "12 ball problem": F. Carl Schumacher Jr. and George C. Wilson, *Bridge of No Return: The Ordeal of the USS* Pueblo (Harcourt Brace Jovanovich, Inc., New York, 1971), 177.

216 Harris's nighttime dreams: Stephen R. Harris and James C. Hefley, *My Anchor Held* (Fleming H. Revell Co., Old Tappan, New Jersey, 1970), 100.

217 The infection in Murphy's foot: Edward R. Murphy Jr. and Curt Gentry, *Second in Command* (Holt, Rinehart and Winston, New York, 1971), 267.

218 "Let the evil spirits out": Armbrister, op. cit., 318.

218 "Good luck, everyone": Brandt, op. cit., 164.

219 "That means a lot to me": Kell interview. op. cit.

221 Still more coordinates: Murphy, op. cit., 269.

222 "Oh, how I long to walk": "Text of *Pueblo* Crew's Press Conference," as prepared by the Korean Central News Agency, Sept. 16, 1968, 12.

223 "The proof is irrefutable": Ibid., 16.

223 What a North Korean court-martial is like: Brandt, op. cit., 182.

223 Toilet paper stayed in Bucher's pocket: Bucher, *Bucher: My Story*, op. cit., 346.

CHAPTER 12: AN UNAPOLOGETIC APOLOGY

224 "Defeatism, puny protest, and wishy-washy talk-a-thons": *Congressional Record*, July 22, 1968, pp. H7168–7169.

225 Such mishaps . . . had to stop: LBJ, NSF, Country File, Korea memos and cables, Vol. VI, 4/68–12/68, box 256.

226 "Maximum exploitability": NA, RG 218, Records of Gen. Earle Wheeler, chairman of the Joint Chiefs of Staff, box 29, folder: 091 Korea, 5/1/68–4/31/69.

226 "Wipe out" potential American invaders: *Washington Post*, June 1, 1968.

226 "U.S. restraint in the *Pueblo* affair probably strengthened this view": NA, RG 59, General Records of the Department of State, Policy Planning Council, Korea through Philippines 1967–1968, box 306, folder: Korea, 1967–1968.

226 Code-named "Freedom Drop": NA, RG 218, Records of Gen. Earle Wheeler, chairman of the Joint Chiefs of Staff, box 29, folder: Korea 091, 1 May 1968–31 April 1969.

228 Cynical and unpleasant: WW, 15 April 1969: 11:00 p.m., Telephone conversation between National Security Adviser Kissinger and Dr. Kramer, http://www.wilsoncenter.org/sites/default/files/Crisis-Conf.Doc_reader-Pt1.pdf.

229 "Maximum violence": LBJ, NSF, Memos to the President—Walt Rostow, Vol. 76, May 9–14, 1968 (1 of 2), box 34.

229 "Over 30 miles from shore on dry land": LBJ, NSF, Papers of Clark Clifford, *Pueblo*, March 1, 1968–Jan. 20, 1969, box 23.

229 "Both sides would understand this ambiguity": LBJ, National Security File, Memos to the President—Walt Rostow, Vol. 78, May 20–24, 1968 (2 of 2), box 34.

230 "This country cannot indulge in lies": *Virginian-Pilot* newspaper, undated. A copy is in the author's possession.

230 "Republic of Korea and the United States are inseparably bound": NA, RG 59, General Records of the Department of State, Central Foreign Policy Files, 1967–1969, Political and Defense, Pol 33-6 Kor N-US, 5/1/68 to 7/1/68, box 2271, folder: 5/20/68.

230 The more outlandish the rhetoric: Ibid., folder: 7/1/68.

230 A Japanese newsman: NA, RG 526, Records of the Naval Criminal Investigative Service, Stack 630A/1/2/1, box 12, folder: "*Pueblo* No. 1."

231 "Is Commander Bucher in good health?": LBJ, NSF, National Security Council Histories, *Pueblo* Crisis 1968, Vol. 18, Telegrams from Seoul, Tab 1 [1 of 2], box 35.

231 "We will be vulnerable to criticism": LBJ, NSF, National Security Council Histories, *Pueblo* Crisis 1968, Vol. 15, Telegrams to Seoul, box 34, tabs 4–8.

232 "It [is] not practical for us to remain motionless": NA, RG 59, General Records of the Department of State, Central Foreign Policy Files, 1967–1969, Political and Defense, Pol 33-6 Kor N.–US, 7/1/68, box 2271, folder: 7/1/68.

233 Pak didn't seem to understand: LBJ, NSF, National Security Council Histories, *Pueblo* Crisis 1968, Vol. 18, Telegrams for Seoul, Tab 1 (1 of 2), box 35.

CHAPTER 13: HELL WEEK

236 "A bundle of feathers": Author interview with Charles Law.

238 "Penetration however slight": LBJ, NSF, National Security Files, *Pueblo* Crisis 1968, Vol. 8, Day to Day Documents, Part 17, box 30.

238 "Before this month is out": Lloyd M. Bucher and Mark Rascovich, *Bucher: My Story* (Doubleday & Co., Inc., Garden City, New York, 1970), 348.

239 "Very beautiful!": Ibid., 350.

239 Stuck his head in the animal's harmless maw: "My *Pueblo* Nightmare," *Boston Globe* series, May 24, 1969, episode 14.

240 "Get the hell out of my way": Bucher, op. cit., 352.

241 A welcome "he would long remember": Edward R. Murphy Jr. and Curt Gentry, *Second in Command* (Holt, Rinehart and Winston, New York, 1971), 282.

242 "Why we Koreans hate you Americans": F. Carl Schumacher Jr. and George C. Wilson, *Bridge of No Return: The Ordeal of the U.S.S.* Pueblo (Harcourt Brace Jovanovich, Inc., New York, 1971), 170.

242 "A terrible atrocity had taken place": Bruce Cumings, *The Korean War: A History* (Modern Library, New York, 2010), 198.

243 "How ghastly!": Bucher, op. cit., 351.

243 The dark spots looked like mold: Ed Brandt, *The Last Voyage of USS* Pueblo (W. W. Norton & Co., New York, 1969), 193.

244 Nothing but icy disdain: Murphy, op. cit., 296.

246 Convinced he didn't have much time left to live: Bucher, op. cit., 357.

246 "Just couldn't hold out any longer": Ibid., 356.

247 "You CIA man!": Brandt, op. cit., 215.

248 "He went to college and uses big words": Ibid., 216.

248 A five-foot-long rod: Law interview, op. cit.

250 "My ribs felt cracked": Bucher, op. cit., 358.

250 "Something we can all be proud of!": Ibid., 359.

251 "Who made you try to fool us?": "One Hellish Experience," online essay by Harry Iredale, http://www.usspueblo.org/Prisoners/One_Hellish_Experience.html.

251 "I got stubborn": Author interview with Harry Iredale.

252 "Damn scared": CA, Vol. III, 1006–95.

252 Didn't touch him again: Ibid., 1006–97.

CHAPTER 14: BRIDGE OF NO RETURN

254 "Understandable!": LBJ, NSF, National Security Council Histories, *Pueblo* Crisis 1968, Vol. 18, Telegrams from Seoul, Tab 1 (2 of 2), box 35.

255 "Not sufficiently engaged": LBJ, NSF, Country File—Asia and the Pacific (Korea), container #256.

255 50 guerrillas came ashore: LBJ, NSF, Country File—Korea, folder: memos and cables, Vol. VI, 4/68–12/68.

256 "This might have [a] salutary effect": NA, RG 59, General Records of the Department of State, Central Foreign Policy Files, 1967–1969, Political and Defense, Pol 33-6, Kor N.–U.S., 7/1/68 to 7/1/68, box 2271, folder: 7/1/68.

256 A little rumor-mongering: Ibid., 10/15/86 to 12/1/68, box 2274, folder: 12/1/68.

256 "It was a bluff": Author interview with Nicholas Katzenbach.

257 "An average American as I am": NA, RG 59, op. cit.

257 "He evidently had no real conception": LBJ, NSF, Country File—Asia and the Pacific, box 262, folder: Korea *Pueblo* Incident, Seoul Cables, Vol. II, 2/11/68–3/68.

257 "No genuine interest": *St. Louis Post-Dispatch*, Jan. 13, 1969.

258 He blithely offered to pay $50 million: NA, RG 59, op. cit.

258 Naive, "very high-strung," and "unstable": Ibid.

259 "They respect us for this eccentricity": LBJ, NSF, National Security Council Histories, *Pueblo* Crisis 1968, Vol. 8, Day by Day Documents, Part 17, box 30.

260 "What sort of people we are privileged to serve": NA, RG 59, op. cit.

260 "This may sound nutty to you": Katzenbach interview, op. cit.

261 "We are agreeable": LBJ, NSF, National Security Council Histories, *Pueblo* Crisis 1968, Vol. 18, Telegrams from Seoul, Tab 1 (2 of 2), box 35.

262 "We are . . . perturbed": NA, Records Group 218, Records of Gen. Earle Wheeler, chairman of the Joint Chiefs of Staff, box 29.

263 Pump troops into the area: LBJ, NSF, op. cit.

263 "Not entirely medical in character": Lloyd M. Bucher and Mark Rascovich, *Bucher: My Story* (Doubleday & Co., Inc., Garden City, New York, 1970), 361.

263 "The warmongering United States on its knees": Bucher, op. cit., 362.

264 Bucher stood up, expressed his thanks: F. Carl Schumacher Jr. and George C. Wilson, *Bridge of No Return: The Ordeal of the U.S.S.* Pueblo (Harcourt Brace Jovanovich, Inc., New York, 1971), 215.

265 "You don't get medals for this": Ed Brandt, *The Last Voyage of USS* Pueblo (W. W. Norton & Co., New York, 1969), 231.

265 Americans were sure to be killed: "My *Pueblo* Nightmare," *Boston Globe* series, May 1969, episode 15.

266 "Shameful aggressive history": LBJ, NSF, National Security Histories, *Pueblo* Crisis 1968, Vol. 21, Telegrams from Canada and Europe, Tabs 1-2a, box 37.

267 Grief and revulsion: Bucher, op. cit., 362.

268 Tears dampening his cheeks: Author interview with Charles Law.

269 The soldiers did nothing: "My *Pueblo* Nightmare," op. cit.

CHAPTER 15: A CHRISTMAS PRESENT FOR THE NATION

271 "Known to be voluble": Admiral William J. Crowe Jr., with David Chanoff, *The Line of Fire: From Washington to the Gulf, the Politics and Battles of the New Military* (Simon & Schuster, New York, 1993), 69.

271 "I'm relieved to hear it from you": Lloyd M. Bucher and Mark Rascovich, *Bucher: My Story* (Doubleday & Co., Inc., Garden City, New York, 1970), 368.

272 "A study in agony and suspense": "Bucher Tells the Story," *Washington Post*, Dec. 24, 1968.

275 "Freedom is worth more than anyone's life": *Patriot Ledger* (Quincy, Mass.), Dec. 24, 1968.

275 "He is an unusual individual": LBJ, NSF, Memos to the President—Walt Rostow, Vol. III, Dec. 18–25, 1968, container 43.

276 "You guys are gonna get a lot of questions": Author interview with Lloyd M. Bucher.

277 "This was the nation's Christmas present": "Christmas Starts on an Airfield," *San Diego Union*, Dec. 25, 1968.

278 "Captain, I'm so glad you got back": "Incident Reports," an online book by Bucher's friend and former shipmate Allen Hemphill, who tape-recorded portions of the Miramar homecoming. http://www.allenhemphill.com/day_of_return.htm.

279 **His first really good laugh:** Bucher, *Bucher: My Story*, op. cit., 376.

279 **"You should all wave to them!":** Eleanor Van Buskirk Harris, *The Ship That Never Returned* (Christopher Publishing House, North Quincy, Mass., 1974), 257.

279 **"Crying into thin, gnarled hands":** Ibid.

280 **"Handshakes . . . nearly broke my hand":** Bucher, *Bucher: My Story*, op. cit., 377.

280 **"An *admiral* just fetched me a cup of coffee":** Edward R. Murphy Jr. and Curt Gentry, *Second in Command* (Holt, Rinehart and Winston, New York, 1971), 36. Emphasis in original.

280 **"When we sang 'Joy to the World'":** *Newsweek*, Jan. 6, 1969.

280 **"Never . . . have I been so burstingly proud":** *San Diego Union*, undated.

281 **"Restraint and patience have paid off":** LBJ, White House Central Files, Judicial, JL3/CO, container 37.

281 **"What can one believe?":** "*Pueblo* Case Perfidy," *St. Louis Globe-Democrat*, Dec. 24, 1968.

282 **"We sank you!":** *San Diego Union*, Dec. 26, 1968.

283 **Schumacher and Hammond's medical conditions:** NHHC, Records of the Immediate Office of the Chief of Naval Operations, *Pueblo* Incident, Court of Inquiry, box 116, "Medical Annex to a Report of a Court of Inquiry."

283 **"Consciously and carefully controlled":** LBJ, Papers of Clark Clifford, box 23, folder: *Pueblo*—March 1, 1968–Jan. 20, 1969.

284 **"'Brainwashing' techniques were unsuccessful":** Ford, Charles V., and Raymond C. Spaulding, "The *Pueblo* Incident: Psychological Reactions to the Stresses of Imprisonment and Repatriation," *American Journal of Psychiatry*, July 1972.

284 **"Exceptionally strong and an inspiration":** Spaulding, ibid. Spaulding's article cites only "a 25-year-old junior officer," but certain details and the context make it obvious he is discussing Schumacher.

285 **Triumphed . . . by simply surviving:** Author interview with C. W. "Bill" Erwin.

285 **A bit tipsy:** NSA, Oral History Interview, Eugene Sheck, NSA-OH-26-82.

285 **A written guarantee:** Murphy, op. cit., 327.

285 **"Relaxed atmosphere" and a "sympathetic relationship":** NA, RG 526, Records of the Naval Criminal Investigative Service, box 13, folder: US6500, USS *Pueblo*, Feb 1–7, 1968.

286 **"The kids became pretty free":** Sheck oral history, op. cit.

287 **"Several Hollywood starlets":** "*Pueblo* Men Entertained at Party," *San Diego Evening Tribune*, Jan. 13, 1969.

288 **"You don't just give up the ship":** *Los Angeles Times*, Jan. 24, 1968.

288 **"I haven't heard of anyone who is sympathetic":** *U.S. News & World Report*, Feb. 10, 1969.

CHAPTER 16: BUCHER'S GETHSEMANE

289 **Newsome worried that he wasn't up to:** Author interview with William R. Newsome.

290 ***Like they just saw Lindbergh*:** Ibid.

291 **"Emotions just leaked out of me":** Author interview with Lloyd M. Bucher.

292 **"Horrible chore":** U.S. Naval Institute, Reminiscences of Admiral John J. Hyland Jr., U.S. Navy (Ret.), Volume II, 1989, 460.

294 **Strict limits:** Memorandum of Understanding, Subj: *Pueblo* Matters, Department of the Navy, Sept. 26, 1968, copy provided to the author by William R. Newsome.

294 **"I didn't know what a court of inquiry was":** Author interview with E. Miles Harvey.

295 **"Come on board with Bucher":** Ibid.

296 **"Don't make him John the Baptist":** Newsome interview, op. cit.

297 **"No question in my mind":** RP, Vol. 1, 60.

298 **"A complete slaughter":** Ibid., 119.

298 **"No particular action took place":** Ibid., 136.

299 **Completely off guard:** Harvey interview, op. cit.

300 **His hands trembled:** Bucher's pauses and gestures are described in *The National Observer*, Jan. 27, 1969, and Trevor Armbrister, *A Matter of Accountability: The True Story of the Pueblo Affair* (Coward-McCann Inc., New York, 1970), 366.

301 **"An aura of unreality":** Armbrister, ibid., 367.

303 **"Appalling demonstration":** *Christian Science Monitor*, Jan. 25, 1969.

303 Bag after bag of angry mail: The letters are quoted in Armbrister, op. cit., 368, and Edward R. Murphy Jr. and Curt Gentry, *Second in Command* (Holt, Rinehart and Winston, New York, 1971), 362.

303 "Admiral Moorer is a horse's ass": NHHC, Records of the Immediate Office of the CNO, *Pueblo* Incident Files, box 127, folder: "Citizen mail."

303 "What do they expect": Ibid.

304 "A circus midget trying to slug Cassius Clay": *Miami Herald*, Jan. 27, 1969.

304 "A nuclear Sarajevo": *New York Post*, Jan. 30, 1969.

304 "If those five admirals think": *Boston Sunday Globe*, Jan. 26, 1969.

305 "Don't let Navy make a fool of itself": Richard Reeves, *President Nixon: Alone in the White House* (Simon & Schuster, New York, 2001), 30.

305 "Harvey was running the court": Admiral William J. Crowe Jr., with David Chanoff, *The Line of Fire: From Washington to the Gulf, the Politics and Battles of the New Military* (Simon & Schuster, New York, 1993), 72.

305 "Standing up against authority": Author interview with Bernard Weinraub.

306 "The public thronged": Murphy, op. cit., 363.

308 "If you were a betting man": RP, Vol. 1, 220.

309 353 southern fishermen aboard 50 boats: Inq, 683.

309 "Determined countermeasures": *New York Times*, Jan. 27, 1968.

310 An uncontrollable clash: AMHI, Bonesteel interview, Senior Officers Oral History Program, 1973, Vol. 1, 342.

310 Bonesteel wouldn't let the South Koreans help their *own*: CA, Vol. 1, 198-54.

310 "A diplomatic uproar": Ibid., 198–99.

310 "There was no means and no procedures": Ibid.

311 Bucher was specifically instructed: Ibid.

312 "Ill-concealed disgust": Murphy, op. cit., 376.

313 Johnson's cheeks reddened: Johnson's and Bucher's facial expressions are described in "Admiral Says He Lacked Forces to Rescue," *New York Times*, Jan. 30, 1969, 8.

CHAPTER 17: EVERYONE'S WORST NIGHTMARE

313 "A dent or some scratched paint": RP, Vol. 2, 421.

313 Didn't even know where the bags were stored: CA, Vol. 2, 626–48.

314 Prescribed a certain sequence: NA, RG 218, Records of the U.S. Joint Chiefs of Staff, Records of Chairman (Gen.) Earle G. Wheeler, 1964–1970, box 29, folder: 091 Korea (re: *Pueblo* Incident, Jan. 68).

314 "It seemed like no one was": CA, Vol. 4, 1846–49.

315 "Pale and skinny": *Time*, Feb. 21, 1969.

315 "An immense amount of junk": CA, Vol. 1, 114.

315 "Virtually to powder": RP, Vol. 2, 354.

317 "Everyone's worst nightmare": Thomas R. Johnson, "American Cryptology During the Cold War, 1945–1989, Book II: Centralization Wins, 1960–1972," National Security Agency, United States Cryptologic History, 1995, 439.

317 "I didn't pay any attention": Robert E. Newton, "The Capture of the USS *Pueblo* and Its Effect on SIGINT Operations," National Security Agency, United States Cryptologic History, Special Series, Crisis Collection, Vol. 7, 1992, 67. This 245-page study was declassified, at the author's request, under mandatory declassification review in 2007.

317 "A major intelligence coup": Johnson, op. cit., 446.

318 Soviet military intelligence inspected: Newton, op. cit., 173.

319 Impede U.S. intelligence-collection: "Damage Assessment of the Compromise of Operational Intelligence Broadcast Messages on Board USS *Pueblo* (AGER-2)," March 17, 1969, III-B-5. This 50-page report was prepared jointly by the CIA, Defense Intelligence Agency, Navy, Air Force and Army. It was declassified, at the author's request, under mandatory declassification review in 2007.

319 "Great danger": Newton, op. cit., 150.

319 "Could not be deceived"; "more talkative and cooperative"; and "terrified condition": Ibid., 129.

321 "We knew everything!": "Interview with the Spy Master," *Washington Post Magazine*, April 23, 1995, W18.

322 More than one million: Robert Hunter, *Spy Hunter: Inside the FBI Investigation of the Walker Espionage Case* (Naval Institute Press, Annapolis, Maryland, 1999), 202.

322 "If there had been a war": *Washington Post*, Jan. 22, 1989, D1.

322 Vehemently denied: Pete Early, *Family of Spies* (Bantam Books, New York, 1988), 72.

323 "We innocent peons": Langenberg's Feb. 2, 1969, letter to his mother, copy in author's possession.

325 Men still enjoyed strong public support: The poll is cited in "*Pueblo*'s Captain and Crew Given Support," *Los Angeles Times*, Feb. 10, 1969, 26.

325 "A 24-hour-a-day job": Author interview with Edward Grimm.

326 "Bail her out": Author interview with E. Miles Harvey.

326 "Welcome home, Captain": *Washington Post*, March 9, 1969.

328 The only lukewarm assessment: RP, Vol. 3, 714.

329 "My faith in God and my country": RP, Vol. 6, 1287.

330 He spoke evenly: *New York Times*, March 12, 1969.

330 "Just didn't occur to me": RP, Vol. 8, 1817.

331 "I never did actually surrender": Ibid., 1831.

331 "Abnormally concerned": Ibid., 1752.

333 "He still loves the Navy": *New York Times*, May 7, 1969.

335 "His greatest reward": RP, Vol. 8, 1863.

CHAPTER 18: BALM OF MERCY

338 "This is my home": *Omaha World-Herald*, April 24, 1969.

339 "The verdict has already been returned": *Congressional Record*, Senate, Vol. 115, No. 71, May 1, 1969.

340 "A single shot": *Time* magazine, April 25, 1969.

340 Near Cape Town: Record of a Telephone Conversation Between President Nixon and the President's Assistant for National Security Affairs (Kissinger), April 15, 1969, 10 p.m., http://history.state.gov/historicaldocuments/frus1969-76v19p1/d9.

341 "Strongly influenced": CIA Intelligence Memorandum, "Communist Reactions to Certain US Actions," April 17, 1969, http://history.state.gov/historicaldocuments/frus1969-76v19p1/d14.

342 800 other . . . reconnaissance sorties: Memorandum for Director of Central Intelligence, "JRC Monthly Reconnaissance Schedule for January 1968," Jan. 2, 1968, http://www.foia.cia.gov/sites/default/files/document_conversions/89801/DOC_0001458144.pdf.

343 "Cursory and perfunctory": Inq, 728.

343 "North Korean Air Force has been extremely sensitive": F. Carl Schumacher Jr. and George C. Wilson, *Bridge of No Return: The Ordeal of the U.S.S.* Pueblo (Harcourt Brace Jovanovich, Inc., New York, 1971), 64.

344 "Complete blithering idiots": NSA, Eugene Sheck, Oral History Interview, NSA-OH-26-82, 5.

344 "Saving our ass": Ibid., 7.

344 "A deliberate effort to bury": Report of the Special Subcommittee on the U.S.S. *Pueblo* of the Committee on Armed Services, House of Representatives, 91st Congress, First Session, Government Printing Office, Washington, 1969, 1656.

345 "No overt action": Ibid., 1672.

346 "I was lukewarm": Inq, 860.

346 "Are you in any way implying": Report of the Special Subcommittee, op. cit., 805.

347 "Not to contact the South Korean air force": Ibid., 877.

347 "It was kind of nice": Ibid., 881.

348 "He just didn't try": Findings of Fact, Opinions, and Recommendations of a Court of Inquiry Convened by Order of Commander in Chief, United States Pacific Fleet, to Inquire into the Circumstances Relating to the Seizure of USS *Pueblo* (AGER 2), 88. The Navy released a copy of the report to the author under the Freedom of Information Act.

348 "Completely failed": Ibid., 172.

350 "They would have hung Bucher": Author interview with William Newsome.

351 Hyland was appalled: "The *Pueblo* Incident," *Naval History*, Fall 1988, Vol. 2, No. 4, 55.

351 "Grumbling and dragging his heels": Oral History of Admiral William J. Crowe, Jr., U.S. Navy (Retired), Naval Historical Foundation, Washington, D.C., 2009, 631.

352 "A very poor fourth": NHHC, "Memorandum for Admiral Thomas H. Moorer," Records of the Immediate Office of the CNO, *Pueblo* Incident Files, Correspondence, box 123.

353 "Must in fairness be borne": *New York Times*, May 7, 1969.

354 "Dashed to pieces": Lloyd M. Bucher and Mark Rascovich, *Bucher: My Story* (Doubleday & Co., Inc., Garden City, New York, 1970), 395.

CHAPTER 19: A DAY IN THE SUN

357 **"With respect to stopping the ship":** RP, Vol. 8, 1814.

358 **"My most experienced officer . . . had robbed me":** Lloyd M. Bucher and Mark Rascovich, *Bucher: My Story* (Doubleday & Co., Inc., Garden City, New York, 1970), 192.

358 **The lie-detector test:** HI, Papers of Lloyd M. Bucher, box 17.

358 **"I regret having done it":** Author interview with Lloyd M. Bucher.

359 **"I am lost all the time":** HI, Bucher Papers, op. cit.

359 **"A tremendous amount of stupidity":** *Washington Post*, June 10, 1970.

359 **"In any capacity":** Bucher interview, op. cit.

360 **"It was like I had the plague":** Ibid.

361 **"What ships did I surrender today":** Ibid.

364 **"We could not have it both ways":** "Commander Bucher Replies," *Naval History*, Winter 1989, 49.

365 **"One hell of a sight better":** Ibid., 50.

367 **"Just easing the pain":** *New York Times*, May 29, 1988.

367 **"Rifle butts and boot kickings":** *Los Angeles Times*, Jan. 17, 1988, 34.

369 **"One hell of a lot of conflict":** Bucher letter to Rep. Montgomery, copy in author's possession.

370 **"The thing that really gnawed at me":** Author interview with Nicholas J. Mavroules.

370 **"They have earned it":** Statement of Vice Admiral Jeremy M. Boorda before the Subcommittee on Investigations, Armed Services Committee, U.S. House of Representatives, June 23, 1989, copy in author's possession.

372 **"I apologize for all the citizens of this nation":** United Press International, May 5, 1990.

EPILOGUE

373 **Disguised it as a freighter:** *The New York Times*, July 19, 2005.

377 **"My ankles were raw":** Author interview with William T. Massie.

379 **"We've not been successful":** Author interview with Daniel T. Gilbert.

BIBLIOGRAPHY

BOOKS

Acheson, Dean, *The Korean War*, W. W. Norton & Co., New York, 1969.

Andrew, Christopher, *For the President's Eyes Only: Secret Intelligence and the American Presidency from Washington to Bush*, HarperCollins Publishers, Inc., New York, 1996.

Armbrister, Trevor, *A Matter of Accountability: The True Story of the* Pueblo *Affair*, Coward-McCann Inc., New York, 1970.

Ball, George W., *The Past Has Another Pattern: Memoirs*, W. W. Norton & Co., New York, 1982.

Bamford, James, *Body of Secrets: Anatomy of the Ultra-Secret National Security Agency from the Cold War Through the Dawn of a New Century*, Doubleday & Co., New York, 2001.

Barron, John, *Breaking the Ring: The Rise and Fall of the Walker Family Spy Network*, Avon Books, New York, 1987.

Bermudez, Joseph S., *North Korean Special Forces*, Naval Institute Press, Annapolis, Maryland, 1998.

Bradshaw, Thomas I., and Marsha L. Clark, *Carrier Down: The Story of the Sinking of the U.S.S.* Princeton, Eakin Press, Austin, Texas, 1990.

Brandt, Ed, *The Last Voyage of USS* Pueblo, W. W. Norton & Co., New York, 1969.

Bucher, Lloyd M., and Mark Rascovich, *Bucher: My Story*, Doubleday & Co., Garden City, New York, 1970.

Burrows, William E., *By Any Means Necessary: America's Heroes, Flying Secret Missions in a Hostile World*, Plume, New York, 2002.

Busby, Horace, *The Thirty-First of March: An Intimate Portrait of Lyndon Johnson's Final Days in Office*, Farrar, Straus and Giroux, New York, 2005.

Buzo, Adrian, *The Guerrilla Dynasty: Politics and Leadership in North Korea*, I. B. Tauris and Co., London, 1999.

Califano, Joseph A., *The Triumph & Tragedy of Lyndon Johnson: The White House Years*, Simon & Schuster, New York, 1991.

Clifford, Clark, with Richard Holbrooke, *Counsel to the President: A Memoir*, Random House, New York, 1991.

Cowger, Thomas W., and Sherwin J. Markman, *Lyndon Johnson Remembered: An Intimate Portrait of a Presidency*, Rowman and Littlefield Publishers, Lanham, Maryland, 2003.

Craven, John Pina, *The Silent War: The Cold War Battle Beneath the Sea*, Simon & Schuster, New York, 2001.

Crawford, Don, Pueblo *Intrigue*, Tyndale House Publishers, Wheaton, Illinois, 1969.

Crickmore, Paul F., *Lockheed SR-71: The Secret Missions Exposed*, Osprey Aerospace, London, 1993.

Cristol, A. Jay, *The* Liberty *Incident: The 1967 Attack on the U.S. Navy Spy Ship*, Brassey's, Dulles, Virginia, 2002.

Crowe, William J., with David Chanoff, *The Line of Fire: From Washington to the Gulf, the Politics and Battles of the New Military*, Simon & Schuster, New York, 1993.

Cumings, Bruce, *The Korean War: A History*, Modern Library, New York, 2010.

Dallek, Robert, *Flawed Giant: Lyndon Johnson and His Times, 1961–1973*, Oxford University Press, New York and Oxford, England, 1998.

Dobrynin, Anatoly, *In Confidence: Moscow's Ambassador to America's Six Cold War Presidents*, Times Books, New York, 1995.

Downs, Chuck, *Over the Line: North Korea's Negotiating Strategy*, American Enterprise Institute, Washington, D.C., 1999.

Doyle, William, *An American Insurrection: James Meredith and the Battle of Oxford, Mississippi, 1962*, Anchor Books, New York, 2003.

Early, Pete, *Family of Spies: Inside the John Walker Spy Ring*, Bantam Books, New York, 1988.

Eckert, Carter J., et al., *Korea Old and New. A History*, Ilchokak, Publishers, Seoul, South Korea, 1990.

Ennes, James M. Jr., *Assault on the* Liberty: *The True Story of the Israeli Attack on an American Intelligence Ship*, Random House, New York, 1979.

Gallery, Daniel V., *The* Pueblo *Incident*, Doubleday & Co., Garden City, New York, 1970.

Goulding, Phil G., *Confirm or Deny: Informing the People on National Security*, Harper & Row, New York, 1970.

Halberstam, David, *The Best and the Brightest*, Modern Library, New York, 2001.

Harris, Eleanor Van Buskirk, *The Ship That Never Returned*, The Christopher Publishing House, North Quincy, Massachusetts, 1974.

Harris, Stephen R., and James C. Hefley, *My Anchor Held*, Fleming H. Revell Co., Old Tappan, New Jersey, 1970.

Helms, Richard, *A Look over My Shoulder: A Life in the Central Intelligence Agency*, Random House, New York, 2003.

Hendrickson, Paul, *The Living and the Dead: Robert McNamara and Five Lives of a Lost War*, Vintage Books, New York, 1996.

Herring, George C., *LBJ and Vietnam: A Different Kind of War*, University of Texas Press, Austin, Texas, 1994.

Hersh, Seymour M., *"The Target Is Destroyed": What Really Happened to Flight 007 and What America Knew About It*, Random House, New York, 1986.

Hooper, Edwin B., Vice Admiral, USN (Ret.), *Mobility, Support, Endurance: A Story of Naval Operational Logistics in the Vietnam War, 1965–1968*, Naval History Division, Department of the Navy, Washington, D.C., 1972.

Hunter, Edward, *Brainwashing: The True and Terrible Story of the Men Who Endured and Defied the Most Diabolical Red Torture*, Pyramid Books, New York, 1956.

Hunter, Robert W., *Spy Hunter: Inside the FBI Investigation of the Walker Espionage Case*, Naval Institute Press, Annapolis, Maryland, 1999.

Ignatius, Paul R., *On Board: My Life in the Navy, Government, and Business*, Naval Institute Press, Annapolis, Maryland, 2006.

Johnson, Lady Bird, *A White House Diary*, Holt, Rinehart and Winston, New York, 1970.

Johnson, Lyndon B., *The Vantage Point: Perspectives on the Presidency, 1963–1969*, Holt, Rinehart and Winston, New York, 1971.

Johnson, Sam Houston, *My Brother Lyndon*, Cowles Book Co., New York, 1969.

Kaiser, Charles, *1968 in America: Music, Politics, Chaos, Counterculture, and the Shaping of a Generation*, Weidenfeld & Nicolson, New York, 1988.

Kalugin, Oleg, with Fen Montaigne, *The First Directorate: My 32 Years in Intelligence and Espionage Against the West*, St. Martin's Press, New York, 1994.

Katzenbach, Nicholas deB., *Some of It Was Fun: Working With RFK and JFK*, W. W. Norton & Co, New York, 2008.

Kearns, Doris, *Lyndon Johnson and the American Dream*, Harper & Row, New York, 1976.

Kim, Chong-shin, *Seven Years with Korea's Park Chung-hee*, Hollym Corp., Seoul, South Korea, 1967.

Kinkead, Eugene, *In Every War But One*, W. W. Norton & Co., New York, 1959.

Kirkbride, Wayne A., *Panmunjom: Facts About the Korean DMZ*, Hollym Corp., Seoul, South Korea, 1985.

Koh, Byung Chul, *The Foreign Policy of North Korea*, Praeger, New York, 1969.

Lech, Raymond B., *Broken Soldiers*, University of Illinois Press, Urbana, Illinois, 2000.

Lerner, Mitchell B., *The* Pueblo *Incident: A Spy Ship and the Failure of American Foreign Policy*, University Press of Kansas, Lawrence, Kansas, 2002.

Li Yuk-sa, *Juche!: The Speeches and Writing of Kim Il Sung*, Grossman Publishers, New York, 1972.

Liston, Robert A., *The* Pueblo *Surrender: A Covert Action by the National Security Agency*, M. Evans and Co., New York, 1988.

Mann, Robert, *The Walls of Jericho: Lyndon Johnson, Hubert Humphrey, Richard Russell, and the Struggle for Civil Rights*, Harcourt Brace & Co., New York, 1996.

McGarvey, Patrick J., *CIA: The Myth and the Madness*, Penguin Books, Baltimore, Maryland, 1973.

McLellan, David S., *Cyrus Vance*, Rowman & Allanheld, Totowa, N.J., 1985.

McNamara, Robert S., *The Essence of Security: Reflections in Office*, Harper & Row, New York, 1968.

———, *In Retrospect: The Tragedy and Lessons of Vietnam*, Vintage, New York, 1996.

McPherson, Harry, *A Political Education: A Journal of Life with Senators, Generals, Cabinet Members, and Presidents*, Little, Brown and Co., Boston, 1972.

McWhorter, Diane, *Carry Me Home: Birmingham, Alabama, the Climactic Battle of the Civil Rights Revolution*, Touchstone/Simon & Schuster, New York, 2001.

Moorer, Thomas H., *Speeches and Statements by Admiral Thomas H. Moorer, USN, Chief of Naval Operations, United States Navy, 1 August 1967–1 July 1970*, no publisher or date given.

Morison, Samuel Eliot, *John Paul Jones: A Sailor's Biography*, Atlantic-Little, Brown & Co., Boston, 1959.

Murphy, Edward R., and Curt Gentry, *Second in Command*, Holt, Rinehart and Winston, New York, 1971.

Nitze, Paul H. (with Ann M. Smith and Steven L. Rearden), *From Hiroshima to Glasnost: At the Center of Decision—A Memoir*, Grove Weidenfeld, New York, 1989.

Oberdorfer, *Don Tet!*, Avon Books, New York, 1971.

———, *The Two Koreas: A Contemporary History*, Basic Books, New York, 1997.

Offley, Ed, *Scorpion Down: Sunk by the Soviets, Buried by the Pentagon: The Untold Story of the USS* Scorpion, Basic Books, New York, 2007.

Park Chung Hee, *The Country, the Revolution and I*, Hollym Corp., Seoul, South Korea, 1962.

Party History Institute of the Central Committee of the Workers' Party of Korea, *Brief History of the Revolutionary Activities of Comrade Kim Il Sung*, Foreign Languages Publishing House, Pyongyang, 1969.

Pasley, Virginia, *22 Stayed: The Story of the 21 American GIs and One Briton Who Chose Communist China—Who They Were and the Reason for Their Choice*, W. H. Allen, London, 1965.

Plumb, Charlie, *I'm No Hero: A POW Story as Told to Glen Dewerff*, Independence Press, Santa Barbara, California, 1973.

Reeves, Richard, *President Nixon: Alone in the White House*, Simon & Schuster, New York, 2001.

Richelson, Jeffrey T., *The U.S. Intelligence Community, Third Edition*, Westview Press, Boulder, Colorado, 1995.

Rostow, W. W., *The Diffusion of Power*, The Macmillan Co., New York, 1972.

Rusk, Dean, and Richard Rusk, *As I Saw It*, Penguin Books, New York, 1991.

Schumacher, F. Carl, and George C. Wilson, *Bridge of No Return: The Ordeal of the U.S.S.* Pueblo, Harcourt Brace Jovanovich, Inc., New York, 1971.

Shesol, Jeff, *Mutual Contempt: Lyndon Johnson, Robert Kennedy, and the Feud That Defined a Decade*, W. W. Norton & Co., 1997.

Sontag, Sherry, Christopher Drew, and Annette Lawrence Drew, *Blind Man's Bluff*, PublicAffairs, New York, 1998.

Spiller, Harry, ed., *American POWs in Korea: Sixteen Personal Accounts*, McFarland & Co., Jefferson, North Carolina, 1998.

Stebenne, David L., *Arthur J. Goldberg*, Oxford University Press, New York, 1996.

Stone, I. F., *In a Time of Torment*, Random House, New York, 1967.

Suedfeld, Peter, ed., *Psychology and Torture*, Hemisphere Publishing Corp., New York, 1990.

Suh, Dae-Sook, *Kim Il Sung: The North Korean Leader*, Columbia University Press, New York, 1988.

Tart, Larry, and Robert Keefe, *The Price of Vigilance: Attacks on American Surveillance Flights*, Ballantine Books, New York, 2001.

Tennant, Roger, *A History of Korea*, Kegan Paul International, London, 1996.

Tucker, Spencer, and Frank Reuter, *Injured Honor: The* Chesapeake-Leopard *Affair, June 22, 1807*, Naval Institute Press, Annapolis, Maryland, 1996.

Vance, Cyrus, *Hard Choices: Critical Years in America's Foreign Policy*, Simon & Schuster, New York, 1983.

White, W. L., *The Captives of Korea: Their Treatment of Our Prisoners Versus Our Treatment of Theirs, An Unofficial White Paper*, Scribner's, New York, 1957.

Witcover, Jules, *The Year the Dream Died: Revisiting 1968 in America*, Warner Books, New York, 1997.

ARCHIVES

National Archives at College Park (Archives II), College Park, Maryland

Lyndon Baines Johnson Library & Museum, Austin, Texas

Gerald R. Ford Presidential Library & Museum, Ann Arbor, Michigan

U.S. Naval History & Heritage Command, Washington, D.C.

Vanderbilt University Television News Archive, Nashville, Tennessee
U.S. Army Military History Institute, Carlisle Barracks, Pennsylvania
Hoover Institution, Stanford, California

ORAL HISTORIES

Bonesteel, Charles H., III, Senior Officers Oral History Program, 1973, by U.S. Army Lieutenant Colonel Robert St. Louis, U.S. Army Military History Institute, Carlisle Barracks, Pennsylvania.

Crowe, William J., Oral History of Admiral William J. Crowe, Jr., U.S. Navy (Retired), Naval Historical Foundation, Washington, D.C., 2009.

Hyland, John, Reminiscences of Admiral John J. Hyland Jr., U.S. Navy (Retired), Volume II, 1989, U.S. Naval Institute, Annapolis, Maryland.

Katzenbach, Nicholas deB., Oral History Interview III, 11 December 1968, by Paige E. Mulhollan, Internet Copy, Lyndon Baines Johnson Library & Museum, Austin, Texas.

Lee, Kent L., Reminiscences of Vice Admiral Kent L. Lee, U.S. Navy (Retired), Volume II, 1990, U.S. Naval Institute, Annapolis, Maryland.

Sheck, Eugene, Oral History Interview, 1982, NSA OH-26-82, National Security Agency, Ft. George Meade, Maryland.

Smith, John Victor, Reminiscences of Vice Admiral J. Victor Smith, U.S. Navy (Retired), 1977, U.S. Naval Institute, Annapolis, Maryland.

GOVERNMENT STUDIES AND PUBLICATIONS

Bolger, Daniel P., "Scenes from an Unfinished War: Low-Intensity Conflict in Korea, 1966–1969," *Leavenworth Papers* No. 19, Combat Studies Institute, U.S. Army Command and General Staff College, Ft. Leavenworth, Kansas, 1991.

Congressional Record, U.S. Government Printing Office, Washington, D.C.

Executive Sessions of the Senate Foreign Relations Committee (Historical Series), Volume XX, Ninetieth Congress, Second Session, 1968, made public in 2010.

Foreign Relations of the United States, 1961–1963, Volume XXII, Northeast Asia, U.S. Government Printing Office, Washington, D.C., 1996.

Foreign Relations of the United States, 1964–1968, Volume XXIX, Part 1, Korea, U.S. Government Printing Office, Washington, D.C., 2000.

Smith, Robert W., and J. Ashley Roach, *Limits in the Seas: United States Responses to Excessive National Maritime Claims*, U.S. State Department, Washington, D.C., 1992.

Strauch, Ralph E., *The Operational Assessment of Risk: A Case Study of the* Pueblo *Mission*, a report prepared for the United States Air Force Project Rand, Rand Corp., Santa Monica, California, 1971.

Van Nederveen, Giles (Captain, U.S. Air Force), *Sparks over Vietnam: The EB-66 and the Early Struggle of Tactical Electronic Warfare*, Airpower Research Institute, Air University, Maxwell-Gunter Air Force Base, Montgomery, Alabama, undated.

PROFESSIONAL JOURNALS AND ACADEMIC PAPERS

Armbruster, William A., "The *Pueblo* Crisis and Public Opinion," *Naval War College Review*, Vol. XXXIII, No. 7, March 1971.

Finer, Joel Jay, "The Second Ordeal of the *Pueblo* Crew," *American Bar Association Journal*, November 1969, pp. 1029–33.

Ford, Charles V., and Raymond C. Spaulding, "The *Pueblo* Incident: A Comparison of Factors Related to Coping with Extreme Stress," *Archives of General Psychiatry*, Vol. 29, September 1973.

———, "The *Pueblo* Incident: Psychological Reactions to the Stresses of Imprisonment and Repatriation," *American Journal of Psychiatry*, 129:1, July 1972.

Fubini, Eugene G., "First Person Singular: Recollections of Radar Development," *Journal of Electronic Defense*, Dec. 1, 2001, No. 12, Vol. 24, p. 74.

Harvey, E. Miles and William R. Newsome, "Rebuttals to 'The Second Ordeal of the *Pueblo* Crew,'" *American Bar Association Journal*, February 1970, pp. 148–51.

Humphrey, David C., "Tuesday Lunch at the Johnson White House: A

Preliminary Assessment," *Diplomatic History*, Vol. 8, No. 1, Winter 1984, pp. 81–101.

Kim, Joo Hong, et al., "History of Korean Politics: The Park Chung Hee Era," jointly published by the Institute for Peace Studies, Korea University, and the Asia Center, Harvard University, 2000.

Lissitzyn, Oliver J., "Electronic Reconnaissance from the High Seas and International Law," *Naval War College Review*, February 1970, pp. 26–34.

Mobley, Richard, "*Pueblo*: A Retrospective," *Naval War College Review*, Spring 2001.

Radchenko, Sergey S., "The Soviet Union and the North Korean Seizure of the USS *Pueblo*: Evidence from Russian Archives," Cold War International History Project, Working Paper #47, Woodrow Wilson International Center for Scholars, Washington, D.C., undated.

Spaulding, Raymond C., "The *Pueblo* Incident: A Follow-up Survey Conducted Eight Years After the Release of the USS *Pueblo* Crew from North Korea," Naval Health Research Center, San Diego, California, Report No. 78-37, 1978.

———, "The *Pueblo* Incident: Medical Problems Reported During Captivity and Physical Findings at the Time of the Crew's Release," *Military Medicine*, Vol. 141, No. 9, September 1977.

———, "Some Experiences Reported by the Crew of the USS *Pueblo* and American Prisoners of War from Vietnam," Naval Health Research Center, San Diego, California, Report No. 75-28, 1975.

NEWSPAPERS

Boston Globe

Boston Herald Traveler

Boston Record American

Boys Town (Neb.) *Times*

Buffalo Evening News

Chicago Daily News

Chicago Sun-Times

Chicago Tribune

Christian Science Monitor

Daily Advance (Lynchburg, Virginia)

Electronic News

Escondido (Calif.) *Times-Advocate*

Florida Times-Union

Ft. Lauderdale News

Independence (Kan.) *Sunday Reporter*

Indianapolis News

Korea Herald

Korea Times

Los Angeles Times

Louisville (Ky.) *Courier Journal*

Lynchburg (Va.) *Daily Advance*

Miami Herald

Miami News

National Observer

New York Daily News

New York Post

The New York Times

Omaha World-Herald

Petoskey (Mich.) *News-Review*

Philadelphia Bulletin

Philadelphia Inquirer

Phoenix Gazette

Pittsburgh Press

Quincy (Mass.) *Patriot Ledger*

Rochester (N.Y.) *Democrat & Chronicle*

San Diego Evening Tribune

San Diego Union

San Francisco Chronicle

Santa Monica (Calif.) *Evening Outlook*

Southern Start, United States Forces Korea

St. Louis Globe-Democrat

St. Louis Post-Dispatch

Washington Daily News
Washington Post
Washington Star
Watsonville (Calif.) *Register-Pajaronian*
White Plains (N.Y.) *Reporter Dispatch*

NEWSMAGAZINES

Life
Newsweek
Time
U.S. News & World Report

ACADEMIC THESES

Heath, Laura J., "An Analysis of the Systematic Security Weaknesses of the U.S. Navy Fleet Broadcasting System, 1967–1974, As Exploited by CWO John Walker," master's thesis, U.S. Army Command and General Staff College, Ft. Leavenworth, Kansas, 2005.

Koebke, Kent Donald, "The U.S.S. *Pueblo* Incident: Warning Cycle," master's thesis, Defense Intelligence College, Washington, D.C., 1984.

Lerner, Mitchell B., "The Lonely Bull: The *Pueblo* Incident and American Foreign Policy," PhD thesis, University of Texas, Austin, Texas, May 1999.

INDEX

Photo by Kathtleen Matz

★ ★ ★

Jack Cheevers is a former political reporter for the *Los Angeles Times*. He and his wife, Kathleen Matz, live in Oakland, California.

CONNECT ONLINE

jackcheevers.net